Glenn Killinger,
All-American

Glenn Killinger, All-American

Penn State's World War I Era Sports Hero

TODD M. MEALY

Foreword by HOWARD W. BEDELL

McFarland & Company, Inc., Publishers
Jefferson, North Carolina

LIBRARY OF CONGRESS CATALOGUING-IN-PUBLICATION DATA

Names: Mealy, Todd, author.
Title: Glenn Killinger, all-American : Penn State's World War I era sports hero / Todd M. Mealy.
Description: Jefferson, North Carolina : McFarland & Company, Inc., Publishers, 2018. | Includes bibliographical references and index.
Identifiers: LCCN 2018011879 | ISBN 9781476670515 (softcover : acid free paper) ∞
Subjects: LCSH: Killinger, Glenn, 1898–1988. | Athletes—United States—Biography. | Football players—United States—Biography. | Pennsylvania State University—Sports—History.
Classification: LCC GV697.K74 M43 2018 | DDC 796.092 [B] —dc23
LC record available at https://lccn.loc.gov/2018011879

BRITISH LIBRARY CATALOGUING DATA ARE AVAILABLE

ISBN (print) 978-1-4766-7051-5
ISBN (ebook) 978-1-4766-3152-3

© 2018 Todd M. Mealy. All rights reserved

No part of this book may be reproduced or transmitted in any form or by any means, electronic or mechanical, including photocopying or recording, or by any information storage and retrieval system, without permission in writing from the publisher.

Front cover: Quarterback Glenn Killinger (Penn State University Libraries)

Printed in the United States of America

McFarland & Company, Inc., Publishers
  Box 611, Jefferson, North Carolina 28640
  www.mcfarlandpub.com

For Adeline, Carter, and Melissa.
My team of All-Americans.

Table of Contents

Acknowledgments — viii
Foreword by Howard W. Bedell — 1
Preface — 4

Part One: First Quarter

1. Beginnings — 13
2. Evolution of an Athlete — 27
3. Dreams and Diversity in an American City — 38

Part Two: Second Quarter

4. Wartime Football Adventure — 57
5. War Season — 68
6. Massed Athletics Experiment — 82

Part Three: Third Quarter

7. The Veterans — 107
8. War, Sport and Brotherhood — 120
9. Harold Lamb Moments — 130

Part Four: Fourth Quarter

10. Class of 1921 — 155
11. A Crafty Field General — 164
12. All-American Hero — 189

Epilogue: Post Game	203
Chapter Notes	229
Bibliography	252
Index	261

Acknowledgments

My first and greatest appreciation goes to Jessica Killinger. Jessica, the granddaughter of Glenn Killinger, has been a wonderful supporter and liaison between her father and me during the writing of this book. Her father, Bill, who passed away only weeks after I completed the first draft, was gracious enough to welcome me into his home at Maris Grove Senior Living Community in Glen Mills, where, on several occasions, we spoke about his father. We logged nine hours of interviews. I'm so happy that he was able to learn about his father's life before his own death.

This book draws slightly on interviews with Glenn Killinger's football and baseball protégés, all in their 60s and 70s, from West Chester University, which was, of course, West Chester State Teachers' College until 1960. I want to thank, in particular, Howie Bedell, John Furlow, Ken Campbell, Gump May, Paul Chenger, and everyone involved in the Leisey Lunch Bunch for allowing me to disrupt their lives. I offer a special token of gratitude to the late Dick Yoder, who was one of the first people I spoke with at the onset of this project. Fortunately, Yoder had the chance to read an early draft of this book before he passed in May 2016.

The people at Penn State University Harrisburg, particularly Charles Kupfer, who advised me throughout the process of writing this book, were a great help. Meredith Weber and Jacqueline Esposito, two archivists at the University Park campus, were very kind. I received help from people at many other colleges, including Don Sailer at Dickinson College, Carolyn Weigel at Ursinus College, Tammy Gobert at Rensselaer Polytechnic Institute, Jennifer Coggins and Tyler Gilmore at the University of North Carolina at Chapel Hill, Kim Demyan at Moravian College, and Tara Wink at West Chester University. Kent Stephens, the historian and curator of the College Football Hall of Fame, was very helpful. Cathy Horner at the Centre County Historical Society was an important resource for finding documents concerning Penn State during the First World War. I am also grateful to the advice given to me by Kyle Weaver, editor of *Pennsylvania Heritage*.

As always, I have benefited from the counsel of my family. My parents, Thomas and Maurene, provided sage advice from start to finish. I could not have written this book without the love and support of my wife, Melissa, and our son, Carter, and daughter, Adeline. As I worked late into the night either researching or writing, Melissa held down the fort. She was also my go-to for editing advice, while Carter and Adeline offered many enjoyable distractions.

Foreword
by Howard W. Bedell

This book is not just about William Glenn Killinger, or athletics at Penn State some one hundred years ago. Todd M. Mealy does a remarkable job of combining the biography of this Nittany Lion icon with the history of the Great War to explain how heroes are made through an unwavering competitive belief in performing "better than your best." Killinger, of course, was the gifted three-sport athlete that measured up to some of the most celebrated names of the Golden Age of Sports—Thorpe, Grange, and Gipp were just a few that measure among the talent of that special era. When Killinger strapped on his leather helmet between 1918 and 1921—and "strapped" is a peculiar verb, considering that rules did not yet require that helmets be worn—he was described by one newspaper as "the greatest running back in the history of the game." Brains and braun he certainly had. But it is his resolve that, even a century later, as he was written off as a serious intercollegiate athlete, lingers in the souls of Penn State students, faculty, and fans alike.

Killy, as he was known in State College, died in 1988 having been fortunate to showcase his talents in three intercollegiate sports at Penn State. Walter Camp, known ostensibly as the Father of Football, named Killy the best player in college football after the 1921 season. His feats have been tamed now by time and history in a way that has expunged his career's unrivaled talent—faded away, sadly, as not so much a great football player as a great Penn State football player, and, at that, a relic of a time that the history books call The Roaring Twenties. What a heartening thing it is, then, to think of Killinger's image reappearing to us now in what we tend to think of as a more exciting era, and that it does so in conjunction with the reemergence of Penn State athletics across so many fields and courts of play. One feels guilty for not knowing more about this incontrovertible superstar, and yet we should be grateful to follow in the footsteps of such trailblazers that endured during two world wars while investing blood, sweat, and tears into everything that has made The Pennsylvania State University an institute of envy across the country.

As a pinch hitter for the Philadelphia Phillies, I was blessed to become the one to break Don Drysdale's string of 58 consecutive scoreless innings on June 8, 1968 when I hit a sacrifice fly to deep center field, driving in a run. My thirteen years in professional baseball afforded me the opportunity to play alongside many greats, including Hall of Famer Hank Aaron as well as my good friend Dick Allen. After retirement, I received three World Series rings while working in the front office of the Philadelphia Phillies (1980), Kansas City Royals (1985), and the Cincinnati Reds (1990). Those opportunities would have never been if it were not for Glenn Killinger, my baseball coach at West Chester State Teachers College (now West Chester University) in 1955–56. I am now in my eighth decade on earth, but not a day goes by that I don't think of the man who was able to bring out the best in me. Though in high school I received more than 60 scholarship offers, I decided to pay full tuition at West Chester because of my relationship with Dr. Killinger. Many years later when my baseball career ended, Killinger was the first person to reach out to me. As the Dean of Men at West Chester at the time, he demanded that I return to college to obtain a degree in education. Dr. Killinger never left my life. He was there for me until the day he died.

It is a privilege to write the foreword to a book that combines sports, war, and Penn State as to prove how overlooked, marginalized, and underestimated people can become heroes too. This, I believe, is Happy Valley's story. Penn State is one of the few schools in the country that now offers both a world-class academic experience and big time athletics. Today, 75,000 people attend its spring football game every year. More than 107,000 fans attend every home game. Happy Valley is a very special place. To that end, Mealy has helped retrace the history of how Penn State obtained this singular position.

Through an impressive review of hidden documents, Mealy is able to reconstruct the home front atmosphere of State College, the faculty and students, and their circumstances with powerful precision. Mealy's take on all of this goes beyond sports. Too often in reliving stories of the glory days we focus most on statistics and overall records. Of course these are valued sketches about one of the most successful eras in Penn State athletics. But to see these sports tales as nothing more than the stories that decorate Beaver Stadium and the walls at the Penn Stater Hotel and Conference Center is to misunderstand Killinger's generation.

Mealy sees another, more virtuous, meaning that defies such sports trivialities. It is that in a time of war—or during a challenging period of hardship within a university community—there is something said for being part of a team that trusts, loves, and respects one another that enables an average team to become a championship team. In describing the life of William Glenn Killinger, Mealy also shows us how an individual with a great work ethic, the wherewithal to give better than his best, and the willingness to make sacrifices can become heroes in their community. *Glenn Killinger, All American* turns out to be an overdue vindication for a man who made Penn State an exceptional institution.

Howard W. Bedell played baseball at West Chester State Teachers' College for Glenn Killinger during the 1950s. With Killinger's mentorship and guidance, Bedell enjoyed a long career in Major League Baseball as a player, coach, and front office management member. As a pinch-hitter for the Philadelphia Phillies on June 8, 1968, it was Bedell's sacrifice fly that drove in a runner that snapped Don Drysdale's string of 58⅔ scoreless innings.

Preface

The October air was frigid, as it always is in the remote college town burrowed in the mountains of Central Pennsylvania, with the smell of manure and pounding sounds coming from one of the many mineral factories at the foot of Mount Nittany. It was the autumn of 1921. There they were, Killy and Bez, the dynamic player-coach tandem, leaning up against a Model T Ford. Both were future College Football Hall of Famers: Hugo Bezdek was already an All-American. W. Glenn Killinger was about to become one. The two men, dressed in Chesterfield coats and flat caps, sat there on the car's front bumper, posing for a picture to promote Penn State's upcoming game against the Naval Academy. When the photograph was developed and later published under the headline "Ready for Bumps," the United Press article referred to the slim chance that Bezdek's overachieving gridiron unit, which had already attained an unimaginable 6-0-1 record, had against the undefeated and seemingly infallible Midshipmen football team. The game, which ended in a 13-7 upset victory for Penn State, turned out to be just a speed bump when compared to the world war that first brought Killinger and Bezdek together.

When the conflict that enveloped Europe, and ultimately much of the world, erupted during the summer of 1914, Glenn Killinger had little understanding of its relevance to the United States. He was just about to enter his junior year of high school when the guns of August ushered in the world's first great war. Killinger, who grew up within the multicultural Allison Hill district of Harrisburg, Pennsylvania, was more concerned about running the streets and playing sports. He was happy—and proficient—playing any sport. As long as there was a ball or stick in his hands, Killy was in his happy place.

Sports were first and foremost in his life. This likely would not have been an option a generation earlier, when Americans worked on farms, plowed along the frontier, or were besieged as part of the urban working class. But as the 20th century dawned, and as the country modernized and grew more industrial, people of the Killingers' working-class stature found themselves with more leisure time to shop, go bathing, play sports, and spend money.[1] By the time Killinger entered high school in 1912, sports had become an essential part of American culture, designed to help develop boys into tough and responsible young men. Commander of the Rough Riders in the Spanish American War and later President of the United States, Theodore Roosevelt, who said a leader "can't be efficient unless he is manly," espoused that message.[2] To achieve in sports was presented as a metaphor for the American dream, one in which lower- and middle-class men of any pedigree could move up the social ladder. Although social status did not matter much to Killinger in his adolescent and teenage years, something fundamental about toughness made his desire to achieve in sports so important.

Glenn Killinger became a First Team Walter Camp All-American in 1921. He walked on to Penn State's football team at the peak of World War I (Penn State University Libraries).

Despite his diminutive size growing up—he stood 5'1" and weighed 110 pounds when he entered high school and had grown just five inches and added 30 more pounds by his senior year—his best sport as a teenager was basketball. He seemed to excel as an infielder in the city's most competitive baseball league. Football was his favorite sport to play, but he just did not fit in; and quite frankly, he was just terrible. Tagged with the nickname "Shrimp" by his high school classmates, Killinger was always undersized and failed to make the team until his senior year. Even then, he lasted just two quarters in the only game he started and saw very limited action in the remaining contests. "I was the worst player on the worst team Harrisburg Tech ever had," he divulged to sportswriters later in his life.³ But he never gave up on his dream. When other kids tried to bully him, he fought back. Instead of sitting at home or in his father's hardware store, there were many nights that he dragged his older brother, Earl, a popular sports referee in the city, to the park to practice skills that would make him a better player.

Then the United States declared war on Germany on April 6, 1917. Unduly influenced by the volume of propaganda distributed by the Committee of Public Information, Killinger hungered to answer the call to duty. But he was too young for the draft, and his parents forbade him from volunteering. Consequently, five months later, he enrolled in The Pennsylvania State College as a metallurgical engineering major, the most popular field in academia due of war demands. Thinking that he would give college football a shot, Killinger arrived late to practice on the first day of fall camp and watched from the sidelines. Seeing that he weighed much less than the smallest person on the team, he walked away feeling that football at Penn State would be as much of a waste of his time as it was in high school.

In the meantime, the game of football changed for good in 1917. This is due to the level of attention military training brought to the sport. Before Killinger arrived at Penn State, and before the intercollegiate football season got underway that autumn, the United States War Department took measures to make service sports an integral part of combat training. Every military encampment from Boston to Seattle offered intercollegiate athletics to thousands of cadets. Led by Commission on Training Camp Activities director Raymond Fosdick, tens of thousands of soldiers chose one sport from football, boxing, wrestling, baseball, track, and basketball to occupy down time during combat training. Football was the sport of choice for most servicemen. The game received an unmatched level of attention from the media. Parades usually preceded intercompany clashes. The annual rivalry game between Army and Navy held at the Polo Grounds yielded $120,000 for military training necessities. Benefit games to raise money for the Red Cross were often scheduled between a team from an army or navy installation and a varsity 11 from the intercollegiate association. Sports historian Steven W. Pope called the 1917 season "an unexpected success." Writing in *Patriotic Games: Sporting Traditions and the American Imagination, 1876–1926* (1997), he provides insights into how service football manufactured an intense sense of passion for the gridiron sport, resulting in the new national pastime in the decade that followed the world war. "For those athletically inclined," Pope says, "service football was more accessible than the select collegiate game. And the nonplaying soldiers experienced the music, color, drama, and spirit of the game, previously limited to the collegiate crowd."⁴ In spite of war clouds hanging overhead, the 1917 college football season did more "in the way of the spread of the spirit of the game" than any effort before or since.

The season in 1917 was the country's first wartime football experience. The sport had not been interrupted 19 years earlier during the Spanish-American War, which began in the spring and ended in August 1898. Therefore, not everyone knew how to respond. College football's trendsetters—Harvard, Yale, and Princeton—announced the cancelation of their football seasons shortly after the declaration of war. Athletic departments at other colleges followed suit. Citing "patriotism" and difficulty fielding rosters, each Ivy League school held out until November before playing a game that fall. For instance, out of 412 male students who were supposed to enroll at Yale in 1917, just 100 showed up to class on the first day of the semester. The rest were already in the service. Only one player from the 1916 team showed up at the start of camp. By October, Yale had 17 players in uniform. It was enough to schedule three games that fall, against Loomis Institute, Hampshire Naval Base, and Trinity College. The issue of player unavailability was ubiquitous. In 1917, Penn State returned just three of 18 varsity lettermen and nine of 16 members of the previous season's freshman team.[5] The Blue and White added a 13th player before the end of the season and finished that autumn with a respectable 5–4 record.

One year into the war, nonetheless, Penn State's football team was drained further by military enlistment. Every starter and coach was taken by the War Department and sent off either to the Western Front or to one of the officer training camps along the eastern seaboard or Midwest. The campus was placed under military occupation and was made host to a new division of the War Department called the Student Army Training Corps, a newly formed cooperative with some 540 colleges that gave students the opportunity to be trained as officers in the Army while earning credits toward a bachelor's degree. Almost 2,000 student-soldiers at Penn State, including Glenn Killinger, enrolled in the training program.

In the summer of 1918, when the "Big Three" Ivy League schools again threatened to terminate their football seasons, the pre-eminent football authority, Walter Camp, known in football circles as the Father of American Football who had recently been assigned as athletic commissioner for the U.S. Department of the Navy, assembled a conference of college coaches to reassure them that the Wilson Administration was wholly behind college sports. Indeed, earlier that summer the federal government launched the "Keep The Boys In College!" campaign. Cautious of losing skilled workers and future army and navy captains, the government actually discouraged citizens from volunteering for military service. As an inducement, the War Department established the Student Army Training Corps to force undrafted college students into a daily routine of military drills and competitive sports. For one hour a day, every college student was mandated to participate in either an intramural sport or varsity intercollegiate sport, in addition to completing all mandatory war aims courses. As you will read in the pages that follow, military training was predicated on getting college-age men acclimated to playing sports. Football, wrestling, boxing, swimming, baseball, and basketball were just some of the sports used to get idle and privileged young men into physical and mental shape for combat. Sports historian Michael Bohn observed in *Heroes and Ballyhoo* that "when 30 percent of recruits failed draft physicals, alarmed military officers turned to sports to improve the soldiers' fitness."[6] Thereafter, it became characteristic to see doughboys return home with a desire to play sports like football, or to watch others play athletics as they waxed nostalgic about the good old days of military training.

The sports world, in other words, aided the president's call for a return to normality after the war. As sports both helped distract and calm families that had sons and fathers in France or Italy during the war, sports were instrumental in restoring a daily routine of work and play after the war. With greater disposable income and cars to navigate on newly paved roads, Americans became regular sports fans. Almost annually new professional teams were formed in urban centers. Colleges went on to what historian Benjamin G. Rader called a "stadium-building binge" as new stadiums were constructed or renovated to outfit growing crowds after World War I. For instance, for its first homecoming game in 1920, Penn State's Beaver Field was renovated with a slightly taller and wider set of bleachers to accommodate 10,000 fans and a parking lot with 5,000 new parking spots. A number of newly constructed stadiums were dedicated to veterans of the First World War: among them are Memorial Stadium (1923) in Champaign and Soldier Field (1924) in Chicago, Illinois, the Los Angeles Memorial Coliseum (1923), California Memorial Stadium (1923), also known as the Berkeley Bowl, Gaylord Family Oklahoma Memorial Stadium (1923) in Norman, Oklahoma, and Darrell K. Royal–Texas Memorial Stadium (1924) in Austin, Texas. Other athletic behemoths were constructed during the decade following the war, including Ohio State's "Horseshoe" (1923) and Michigan's "Big House" (1927) of the Big Ten. Louisiana State's Tiger Stadium (1924), Georgia's Sanford Stadium (1929) and Alabama's Denny Stadium (1929) made up the Southern Intercollegiate Athletic Association (present-day Southeastern Conference) schools with new stadiums; and the Pasadena Tournament of Roses Association built the Rose Bowl in 1922 in the shape of a horseshoe. The completion of the southern stands six years later gave it its bowl shape.[7] In 1920, only one college stadium could seat 70,000 fans; ten years later, there were seven. Penn State and other eastern colleges moved popular sporting contests to larger, neutral venues in big cities like Philadelphia's Franklin Field or New York City's Polo Grounds. Bohn said, "the combination of youth, money, and spare time spawned a demand for entertainment" after the war.[8]

Thanks to new mass media paradigms of the golden age, such as daily newspapers with separate sports sections, radios, and movies, sports attained a different level of attention. Bohn calls it the era of "the ballyhoo." Newspapers were devoting "at least 15 percent of [their] reporting to sports" after World War I, Bohn writes, adding that it was "up from less than 1 percent in 1880."[9] As the public demanded more, newspapers assigned beat reporters to cover specific teams year-round because local audiences wanted to read more about their favorite players. "Sportlight" columnist Grantland Rice of the *New York Tribune* and Robert "Tiny" Maxwell of the *Philadelphia Public Ledger* were two lionized sportswriters of the period who spoke favorably of Glenn Killinger's accomplishments. At the conclusion of his senior football season at Penn State in 1921, newspapers ranging from the *New York Herald* to the *Seattle Star* printed half-page artwork featuring Killinger as the college sports icon of the year.

Furthermore, and very importantly, Killinger's final autumn at Penn State was covered at times by radio broadcasts: the cutting edge media medium of the era that made its debut in 1920. Granted, the technology that inaugural year came in the form of wireless telegraphy, a version of Morse code, or dots and dashes, transmitted by electromagnetic waves. Within a year, however, both commercial and non-profit radio stations were carrying audio broadcasts into the homes of thousands of people. Penn State was always a frontrunner in radio technology. As early as 1903, the college integrated special classes in wireless telegraphy. During World War I, the War Department selected the college as its center of training for the U.S. Army Signal Corps. After the military ban on civilian radio stations was lifted in October 1920, the newly inaugurated president, Dr. John M. Thomas, allowed students and faculty in the Electrical Engineering Department to use the Army Signal Corps' station as an experimental radio station called 8XE. Operating lawfully with an experimental license issued by the U.S. Department of Commerce, 8XE's first wireless broadcast covered the presidential election in November of that year as it picked up dots and dashes from Westinghouse Electrical Company's station under the call sign 8ZZ, later KDKA, which reported the election of Warren G. Harding as the next president of the United States.

The following year, Penn State began construction on a new broadcasting station that could transmit audio point-to-point. For Killinger's final football game of his career, a thriller played in Seattle against the University of Washington, the student body in State College received play-by-play details of Penn State's 21–7 victory.[10] By 1922, Killinger's professional football and baseball exploits were covered by radio stations that now had the capacity to cast a broader net of voice broadcasts. Radio would become a fixture in American homes by the end of the decade. College football deserves much of the credit, as spellbound audiences were provided another conduit to teach young men teamwork and toughness, in addition to delivering entertainment to an eager audience.

The wartime environment paved the way for Killinger to become one of the most formidable quarterbacks ever to play the game at the college level. After having started only one game as a high school player, he would go on to earn the starting quarterback position at Penn State in the third game of the 1918 season. In the three years after the First World War, Killinger emerged as the most popular athlete at this point in Penn State's history. How good was he? Well, two coaching legends, Glenn Scobey "Pop" Warner and John Heisman, each rated Killinger alongside Jim Thorpe as America's greatest multi-sport athlete. Another legend from the golden age, sportswriter Grantland Rice, who coined the nicknames of Notre Dame's famed Four Horsemen and Harold "Red" Grange as the "Galloping Ghost," called Killinger "one of the greatest running quarter-backs that football has ever seen."[11] He could run, pass, punt, and kick just about better than anyone in the country except for George Gipp. The *Philadelphia Evening Public Ledger* called him "the greatest running back in the history of the game."[12]

While Killinger's accomplishments at Penn State occurred during a tumultuous period in American history, his athletic exploits along with the important role that intercollegiate sports played in keeping the home front as normal as possible are absent from almost all works of history. There are a few social historians who covered home front aspects of the Great War. Among them are Mark Sullivan's daunting volume titled *Our Times: The United States 1900–1925* (1995) and David Kennedy's *Over Here: The First World War and American Society* (2004). Both works, however, fall short of describing the country's important service sports programs of 1917 and 1918. Three brief yet concise scholarly articles introduce the topic of service sports as a home front imperative. In 1973, Guy Lewis first wrote "World War I and the Emergence of Sports for the Masses," about sports training programs, for the *Maryland Historian*. Almost a decade later, Timothy P. O'Hanlon wrote "School Sports as Social Training: The Case of Athletics and the Crisis of World War I." And in 1983, James Mennell revived the topic in an article for *Journal of Sport History* titled "The Service Football Program of World War I: Its Impact on the Popularity of the Game."[13]

All of the aforementioned studies of football's cultural legacy provide important views into intercollegiate athletics in the years surrounding World War I. Yet while those historians effectively undertook the topic of America's first football season played under war clouds, no attention at all was given to the Student Army Training Corps, a student-soldier program launched in autumn 1918 as a complete overhaul of physical education requirements, intramural sports, intercollegiate competition, and massed athletics at civilian colleges. For this reason, *Glenn Killinger* offers a lens into the interplay between the U.S. War Department and intercollegiate sports between the fall of 1917 and winter of 1918. In doing so, this biography of W. Glenn Killinger falls within the conversation of sports-war culture by stating firmly that service sports was the reason why the 1920s became the Golden Age of Sports and why the sports-oriented method of training soldiers for war ultimately resulted in the public's craze for American heroes. This golden age was shaped by the war, forcing the heroism of the battlefield to give way to the rise of popular celebrities and sports icons of the 1920s. Consider that many of the sports figures of The Roaring Twenties aided in the war effort in some capacity, whether it be service on the Western Front or as cadets in the Student Army Training Corps. Sports heroes became icons for the nationalistic ideas and patriotic feelings associated with winning a global war. In the end, they became symbols of American greatness.

I came across the name William Glenn Killinger in 2014 when I was working on a book about the history of Harrisburg. *Glenn Killinger* is the offspring of that project. In October 2015, Killinger's unpublished memoir surfaced when his granddaughter, Jessica, who, after bravely handling the death of her own father—and Killinger's only child—unearthed the dossier in a pile of boxes at the retirement home where her dad had lived. The memoir was a boon to the narrative I was trying to compose as it corroborated much of the research I had previously completed. It was, up to that moment, a study based on media coverage of Killinger's athletic feats and interviews that I conducted with people close to Killinger, including his son, Bill, before he passed away. As it turned out, I became fascinated with Killinger's experience as a student-athlete at Penn State during the Great War. Though mostly forgotten in the 21st century, I soon learned that Killinger was one of the most popular athletes in the country—including Jim Thorpe and Babe Ruth—during the first five years after World War I. He was first considered a college phenom and later became a venerated intercollegiate coach.

This book attempts to address several questions: How did college sports enhance patriotism during World War I? Why and how did the government use college sports to prepare soldiers for the realities of combat? How did a booming sporting culture make the 1920s the so-called "Decade of the American Hero?" And how was Glenn Killinger part of that cultural trend? I make an effort to answer all of these questions in a way that may appear untraditional. This book is part biography and part cultural history. It is divided into four quarters. Quarters one and two, or Chapters 1 through 6, are spent discussing intellectual sporting theories and home front culture in order to explain why The Roaring Twenties was primed for heroes who were athletes and other celebrities instead of returning doughboys. The book's second half, quarters three and four, or Chapters 7 through 12, illuminates Killinger's career as a three-sport athlete at Penn State. I have included an Epilogue in the Post Game section of the book. The Epilogue is extensive, as my aim is to engage an ongoing investigation into the remainder of Killinger's life as well as draw comparisons to the federal government's method of using college sports to train soldiers during World War I and World War II. In this vein, Killinger's life fundamentally serves as an archetype for how someone at the start of the 1920s came to be hailed as an American hero.

PART ONE: FIRST QUARTER

1

Beginnings

At the age of 89, Glenn Killinger had become a ghost of his former self. He grew blind due to age-related macular degeneration, a disease that was unforgiving, soon to be followed by an exterior that looked frail and weak. His appearance near the end of his life was nothing like the man that so many had come to know: All-American, Hall of Famer, fabled athlete with mythical tales of triumph, legendary coach, university administrator, war veteran, faithful husband of 65 years, firm father, and doting grandfather. As delicate as his body had become, his mind was still strong. Upon request, he would talk about his days at Penn State, Chapel Hill, and West Chester. Most of all, he spoke about his family: a wife, son, and two grandchildren.

Macular degeneration, a genetic disorder caused by the loss of cells in the retina, had caused great strain on the Killinger family. Both Glenn and his wife, Wilda, suffered long with vision degeneration. Their son, Bill, praised Wilda for her will to cope with the disorder better than Glenn. "She was the best cook in spite of her condition," he said lovingly. On the contrary, Glenn, always the staid and unyielding fighter, had little fight in him near the end.

This obstinacy may have been the result of his constant struggle to deal with appearing weak in front of others. Glenn was once a hero on and off the gridiron, the baseball diamond, and the hardwood. Many admired him for his talents. He was always strict, maintained discipline, and held those standards to those under his supervision.

Glenn Killinger was an individual with an improbable story. And he knew it. As a young boy, he always believed he could become great. Despite improbable odds, he did. His future was inconceivable as a teenager. He stood 5'6" and weighed a little more than 140 pounds when he graduated from high school. He was cut from his high school's varsity football and basketball teams every year except his senior year. He played baseball for community teams, but as a teenager he was not a respected athlete.

Superstardom came after he enrolled at the Pennsylvania State College, when he grew four inches, added 40 pounds, and World War I helped to open every varsity football position as Uncle Sam conscripted the original starters. He seized the moment. The remainder of his college career was nothing short of stunning. He shined as an all-star in the three major sports at Penn State—football, basketball, and baseball. How did he accomplish this? He was strict on himself by balancing disciplined habits with a perpetual effort to learn the rules of each game. This approach positioned him ahead of his teammates and, ultimately, his opponents.

But now, unlike his wife, he waited to die. His tired body had shrunk two inches. He kept losing weight. "He talked about dying," his son remembered somberly, clearly regretful of his father's defeated attitude. "We stayed positive around my dad," said Bill.[1]

In retirement, Glenn and Wilda moved into the Churchman Village Homes in Newark, Delaware, to be close to their grandchildren, Mark and Jessica. Glenn tried hard to dig deep, suck it up, and remain strong like the best athletes and coaches do when faced with difficult circumstances. "When we visited him he behaved like he was all right," said Bill, "although he wasn't, of course, and we all knew he wasn't."[2]

Glenn was always on the shorter side—under six feet, strong-boned, gracefully structured—but now, needing family and friends to guide him around, he was becoming smaller. One might think of delicacy found in a museum, nervous to touch yet possessing a surfeit of admiration. Often crabby, sometimes exhausted, intermittingly contrite about what could have been, he was surprisingly self-effacing. There had always been intensity about him. It showed in his signature glare, puffed chest, focused eyes, squeezed eyebrows, big nose, commanding thrust of the fist, and gritty voice right before he made a point, and a commanding one he had been when making points.

"He didn't really have to say much," explained John Furlow, a former player and assistant coach with Killinger at West Chester State Teacher's College in the '50s. "He could just look at you," he recalled, "and you knew damn well that you had to pick it up or you'd be taken out."[3]

"He told people how it was," a former student, Bob "Gump" May, said briskly. "He told us what he thought of us, and he didn't put it politely."[4]

Perhaps he sometimes was too blunt, but it was a product of his upbringing. Glenn was part of the GI Generation. He endured two world wars, the Great Depression, and the conflicts in Korea and Vietnam. In the 1910s, he witnessed the rebirth of the Ku Klux Klan and bombing attacks on politicians' homes by foreign anarchists. He cheered when women got the right to vote and when Charles Lindbergh flew across the Atlantic. He regretted the disappearance of Amelia Earhart and admired 20-year-old Gertrude Ederle's swim across the English Channel. He struggled to make sense of the debate between evolutionists and creationists in Tennessee as he listened to the

Scopes Trial on the radio. He pondered the Soviet launch of Sputnik as much as the development of Hollywood as the epicenter for cinema. He tried to serve in the First World War, only to find relative opportunity in the Second. Perhaps most of all, he worked hard to identify with the activists of the '50s, '60s, and '70s.[5] He remained virtually apolitical, yet as an employee on a college campus in Chester County, Pennsylvania, for 33 years, there was no escaping civil rights rallies or Vietnam War demonstrations.

In his day, he did and said a lot of things that cannot be done or said to people in the 21st century. He did so because he had jumped hurdles. He accomplished feats that no one thought he could. He absorbed criticisms that were difficult to hear. He suffered setbacks that were not customary. The difficulties helped him become a living institution in West Chester before his death.

Glenn Killinger was a formidable man. Determined to speak his mind. Determined to have his way, determined to shape others into his mold. In that time, Glenn Killinger had hurled himself at life with clenched fists, focused eyes, and an energy that made him perform better than anyone ever expected.

"Better than your best!" was Killinger's mantra. He heard it first from his college coach, Hugo Bezdek. During halftime of a close game in 1918, Bezdek was giving his team an ear-beating; Killinger remembered it as a "skull session." The coach called out one of his players about his knowledge of the game. The player made a feeble attempt at drawing blocking assignments on the blackboard.

"What's the matter with you?" Bezdek probed.

"Coach, that's the best I can do," the player countered.

"Your best isn't good enough," the coach thundered back. "You've got to do better than your best!"[6]

The message, like the moment, was defining for Killinger. It reverberated throughout his lifetime. He used the mantra during World War II when he was stationed at several Naval Air bases and the Pre-Flight School in Chapel Hill, North Carolina, assigned to use sports to prepare cadets for battle. He still used it as his modus operandi when he coached football and baseball until 1970 at West Chester State Teachers' College. "He made you better," said Dick Yoder, Glenn's quarterback at West Chester from 1955 to 1958. "If you came in as a star, he made you [even] better."[7]

But now the fight for greatness was near the end.

Just as the sight in both eyes faded, he struggled to accept the inevitable. His impulse was to fight the disease harder. But once he lost complete vision, he lost his will to keep on living.

Now, three decades later, Glenn Killinger has become someone new, someone almost forgotten. So has his legend. Although the house where he grew up in Harrisburg still stands, it now operates as a church. There is nothing else visible that indicates that he once lived there. Few outside of the Penn State or West Chester communities could tell you about Glenn Killinger. The disappearance of his contributions to the sports arena, like his death, has become a depressing reality.

The fame that Glenn Killinger received during the decades between the two great wars was much different from the fame he received after World War II. Killinger was made into a sports god, who, in some circles, floated in the same clouds as Babe Ruth and Jim Thorpe. He was a living legend who made people want to spend big bucks to watch him call out formations and plays on the football field, both as a player and coach. He was a projected all-star who many thought would become the next Ty Cobb. The accomplished athlete was famous during a time when American heroes symbolized the virtues of the good old days. Dueling sportswriters of the Golden Age wrote about his athletic feats. They revered his talent, along with his intellectual capacity to understand each game. And this was an age when sportswriters were as famous as the athletes they were covering. It was a golden time.

For William Glenn Killinger, this time began in Harrisburg, Pennsylvania. Its name, Harrisburg, dates from its 18th-century co-founders—John Harris, Sr., and John Harris, Jr. By the time Glenn came along, the city spanned seven square miles, including 290 streets and over 40 alleys.[8] At least 25 miles of roads had been paved. Motor traffic was not the only source of transportation. A trolley system had already been established between Harrisburg and Hummelstown. With a population of 80,000, everybody but the "old fogies" in town met the trolley with great optimism.

Glenn Killinger was always proud of his upbringing. He was proud of his father, a former police officer who owned a successful hardware store in one of the most racially mixed neighborhoods in the city. He was proud of his mother, the ubiquitous caregiver who watched over every family member with unwavering love. He was proud of his older brother—a baseball-bat-toting local icon always looking to help out a member of the community—who never grew to resent Glenn's fame and success. He was most proud of his older sister, the Red Cross devotee and fixture of Progressive Era Harrisburg who often seemed wrapped up in making moves as a trendsetter. This sense of pride manifested itself in his eagerness to talk about his parents and siblings with outsiders, his friends, and especially his son, Bill.

If there was one thing that was clearly noticeable about the Killinger family, it was their German heritage. It is an interesting part of Glenn's background that was never addressed by sportswriters of his lifetime.

The Killingers' roots in the United States extend back three generations. Dauphin County genealogist Luther Reily Kelker identified the first Killinger to arrive in the area as Glenn's great-great-grandfather, Michael Killinger.[9]

Michael arrived in Dauphin County around the first decade of the 19th century. He purchased a large tract of land near present-day Hummelstown and lived there as a farmer. The name of his wife is unknown in genealogical records. He did have three sons: John, Michael, and David. Although they dabbled in a myriad of trades, the first two Killinger generations were farmers.

Michael's son, David, was a shoemaker by trade, but he spent much of his life managing farms in Lebanon and Dauphin Counties. He raised his family—wife Catherine Rotz and nine children—on a farm in Fishing Creek Valley, north of Harrisburg, in Dauphin County.

John Killinger, the second son of David and Catherine, grew up on his parents' farm in Fishing Creek Valley. When he was old enough, he was apprenticed to a millwright in Grandville, also in Dauphin County. John worked as a tradesman for 11 years. He enlisted into Company D, 48th Regiment, Pennsylvania State militia, on July 1, 1863. He was honorably discharged on August 26 of the same year. He moved around for the next three decades while trying to establish himself as a millwright. In 1894, he returned to Central Pennsylvania, finally settling in Harrisburg, where he opened a wheelwright's shop. John and his wife, Louise Stoudt, worshipped at the Lutheran Church in the city and had four children: Emma, born 1861, Jemima Margarita, born 1864, William Henry, born 1869, and Sherman Brooke, born 1880.

William Henry Killinger, or "Billy," was the third child and eldest son born to John and Louise. He was born in Jonestown, Lebanon County, on June 6, 1869. The family moved to Linglestown when he was one. It was there that Billy attained a public school education. Growing up on the outskirts of northern Harrisburg in the late nineteenth century, public schools in the area were segregated. That is, until June 1881, when a statute was passed by the legislature forcing racial integration throughout schools in the Commonwealth. The law had little impact on Billy's schools, as Linglestown contained almost no African American residents. Yet, in the city, there was a substantial African American population that expanded south into Steelton and east toward Penbrook. Knowledge about the desegregation law was pervasive, nonetheless, as African Americans in Harrisburg were elected to political offices, hired as policemen, and worked as educators. Racial integration became apparent to Billy in 1885 when John Barth & Son Grocers hired him. The grocery store was located at 1025 N. Seventh Street. The exposure to different clientele developed some racial sensitivity against what he perceived as the usual prejudice of the day. Yet, no matter what racial viewpoint Billy maintained, he never turned away a customer. In 1891, he and his father opened up their own merchandise store—Killinger & Son—at 110 Market Street, located in an ideal part of center city.[10] Billy took a respite from the retail business to work as a brakeman for Philadelphia, Harrisburg, and Pittsburgh branch of the Reading Company, also known as the P. H. & P. Railroad Company, for three years and as a city police officer for four years. In 1899, he purchased a hardware store at 27 South Thirteenth Street, in the heart of the Allison Hill District of the city of Harrisburg.

A contemporary of the Killingers,' Luther Reily Kelker, described Billy as "a man of progressive ideas and much force of character."[11] Many in the capital city shared the sentiment, as his resume reveals how in touch he was with the community. Billy was a member of the original Sons of Veterans Drum Corps and was involved in the Free and Accepted Masons; Zembo Temple; Harrisburg Sovereign Consistory; the Knights of Malta; the Cincinnatus Commandery, No. 96; the Phoenix Lodge, No. 59; the Knights of Pythias; and the John Harris Commandery, Jr., No. 174. He was an active member of the United Order of American Mechanics. Billy's wide acquaintance in Harrisburg knew him as an ardent sportsman, one who enjoyed all sports, loved to fish and went out each year during the hunting season.[12] He took his family to the Lutheran Church. And he was a proud Republican.

Glenn Killinger's parents—Billy and Florence—were married on December 25, 1890.[13] Glenn's mother, Florence, was an impressive woman, deriving from a valiant military family. Her father, Henry Harrison Wilson, was a printer by trade but enlisted in Company F, 16th Pennsylvania Cavalry, 106th Regiment at the onset of the Civil War. He rose to the rank of captain of the company before war's end. After the war, Henry Harrison spent the remainder of his days working as a mail carrier between Harrisburg and Pittsburgh. Florence had two industrious siblings, older brother Ira Homer, editor of Mifflin County's *Newton Herald*, and younger brother Edwin, who worked for the Pennsylvania Railroad Company.

The couple first took up residence on Green Street between the city's Uptown and State Capitol. The house was located two miles from the Killinger Hardware Store in Allison Hill, but the location was convenient for Billy's participation in various independent orders. The Zembo Shrine Center and the Harrisburg Consistory Scottish Rite building were both located a few blocks from Green Street. So was the Lutheran Church. It was in the Green Street home where Billy and Florence's four children were born.

Their first child, according to an interview in 1966 with Glenn, was a girl, born in 1891, who died shortly after birth.[14]

The first survivor of Billy and Florence's brood, born August 1893, was Earl Wilson. A teller at the East End Bank in Harrisburg, Earl was a promising player and manager of the Allison Hill League's Rosewood Athletic Club baseball team. He balanced his work at the bank and his involvement in the Rosewood Athletic Club with course work at the Harrisburg branch of the University of Pennsylvania's Wharton Business School. He earned extra money by officiating high school basketball games and umpiring twilight baseball in the area. Earl was married on November 24, 1915, to Marian Elizabeth Mumma in a quiet ceremony held at the Centenary United Brethren Church. The newlyweds settled at 1831 Zarker Street, located half a mile north of the family's hardware store. They had their only child, a daughter, whom they named Jane Mumma, on February 1, 1917.

Earl was the Killinger family member who had the greatest influence on Glenn's athletic development. The brothers frequently tested their physical mettle against one another. Earl was better at tennis, ice hockey, and basketball, while Glenn bested his older brother at sprinting and handball. Even at the peak of Glenn's college career, Earl performed as an equal on the baseball diamond of the Allison Hill League. He could do it all; pitch, field, catch, hit and steal bases. Though there are no records, Earl, who towered over his younger brother during their teenage years, may never have gotten the better of Glenn at football. The two were inseparable; Glenn would gravitate to his older brother and pester him to play anything. Earl, who Glenn called his "guiding light" and "guardian angel," often acquiesced; not surprisingly, he refused to hold anything back. Earl would turn a game of catch into tough-love competitions.[15] The streets in Allison Hill were narrow, sloped, and consumed by dirt. The steep gradients never discouraged the boys from trying to outdo one another in sprints home from an afternoon at the park, no matter the age difference.

Earl, five years older, would taunt young Glenn. He would speed pitches by his younger brother with ease. He bullied Glenn in sibling basketball contests. Florence thought Earl was too harsh. Glenn, meanwhile, hated to lose, but allowed the setbacks to teach him to search for advantages against his older brother. In sandlot games, Glenn focused on becoming a better fielder. On the basketball court, he worked to develop a smoother set shot. And he spent many mornings sprinting up the steep roads of Allison Hill to build mental strength.

Glenn's sister, Elizabeth, was born next, in 1895, though there is confusion about the exact year she was born. Most people knew her as "Biz." Biz was a socialite. The local newspaper often covered her afternoons of tea. She occasionally attained acting roles in the local theater. She hosted masquerade parties for her peers at the YWCA Business Girls' Class. For many years, Biz was a member of the Young Women's Christian Association and the Reservoir Tennis Club. At the tennis club, she worked as recording secretary of the house committee. Her boss was the local political authority, city councilman, and Superintendent of Parks and Public Property, Maris Harvey Taylor.[16] He assigned Biz the job of supervising the clubhouse and distributing lockers to club members. When it was appropriate, she played in the club's doubles tennis tournaments with her brother, Earl. Glenn's sister was dignified and voluptuous, with dark hair cut short. She stood no taller than 5'4". Pale in complexion, she possessed an enchanting smile with alluring charm that made her quite the catch among single women in Harrisburg, and her smile reeled in one of the most accomplished bachelors in the city.

If Glenn looked up to Biz for any reason, it was more for whom she married. In December 1918, she was engaged to business magnate and Penn State track and field star Earl Lyter Kunkle. With a lean build, broad shoulders, chiseled jaw, pointed chin, straight nose, and parted hair, "Kunk" drew many whispers when he walked by crowds. He impressed with his third-place pentathlon finish in the 1914 national track and field championships. He fancied doting women for his confident appearance, coupled with his family's affluence. But it was Biz, five years his junior, who captured his heart. Kunkle and Elizabeth were married by 1920. They moved into a house on Brisban Road in the Paxtang district of greater Harrisburg.[17]

Glenn looked up to his brother-in-law because he was an accomplished, strong-minded sort who had a resume like no other. A 1914 graduate of Penn State, "Kunk" was a young man with immeasurable energy and intelligence. Like he did on the track, he fared adequately as a Mechanical Engineering major. His mantra throughout college was: "To secure high efficiency." This he did accomplish. Upon graduation, his peers described him as one who "will work on the football field three hours a day and still be able to climb four floors of 'Old Main.'" Kunk used his degree to attain a job at the Harrisburg Auto Transportation Company as an engineer and manager. He also used his collegiate track success to attain the head coaching position of Harrisburg Central High School's track team in 1917.[18] Kunkle selflessly enlisted in the army at the outbreak of World War I. By 1918, he received the rank of lieutenant in the Ordnance Department of the Army, receiving his commission at Camp Raritan in New Jersey.

With Earl, Biz, and Kunk, Glenn was blessed to have so many positive influences in his life. All three family members displayed a balanced approach to life that came to define Glenn's future as a college student and in the professional ranks.

Glenn was the youngest child born into the Killinger family. He entered the world on September 13, 1898. His first name, William, was that of his father, but he went by his middle name, Glenn, the name of his great-grandfather on his mother's side of the family. The family name, however, was spelled with only one "n."[19] When Glenn was four, the Killinger clan moved into an apartment above the family hardware store at 27 South Thirteenth Street in Allison Hill, later renumbered 37 South Thirteenth Street, valued at $19,000. Along with Earl, Biz, Glenn, and their two parents, a domestic servant, Stella Runkle, a German immigrant with a heavy accent, resided in their home.

The new Killinger home, including the shop, was a three-story, gray stucco attached building. In those days the uppermost floor presented a splendid view to the northwest of the capitol rotunda, which sat one mile away. The trolley line ran along Thirteenth Street, diverging north toward Reservoir Park and south down either Market or State Streets, toward center city and the capitol building, respectively. The trolley existed as a fascination to young Glenn. He often stood at the stop to watch passengers get on and off. But when he needed to get to a destination, Car Four, with red and white lights, costing a nickel, took him into center city.

Named for its founder, William Allison, the area in the southern end of Harrisburg encompassed three distinct sections—North, Central, and South

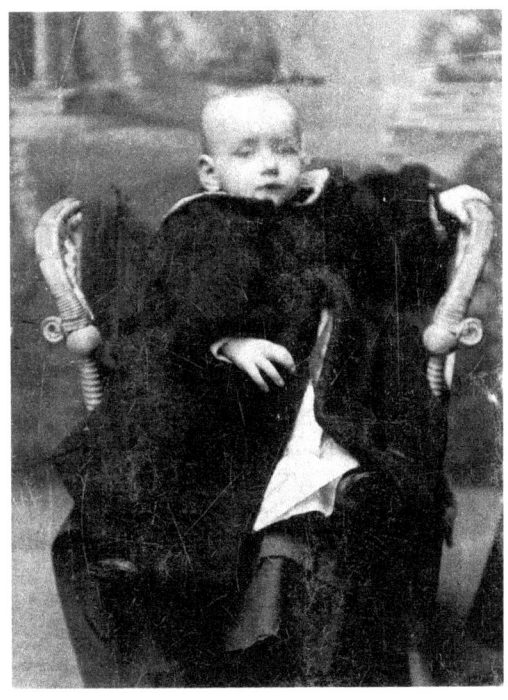

William Glenn Killinger was born September 13, 1898, in Harrisburg, Pennsylvania. This is the first photograph of Killinger in 1899 (Jessica Killinger).

Allison Hill. "The Hill," as many called it, contained three-story family homes, stone churches, a synagogue, a recreation center, a doctor's office, and small, family-owned businesses like the Killinger Hardware Store. Most of the architecture was Italianate or Victorian. The roads were narrow, and they all sloped in and out of the city. So any exit out of Allison Hill meant a trek uphill, the only way back into the district. German-Americans mixed with Jews and African American residents throughout the district. It was—and still is—one of the most racially mixed areas of Pennsylvania's capital city. The Hill, and the varied experiences therein, was the center of Glenn's universe for the first 19 years of his life.

Sports were always a part of the environment at the Killinger house, with friends of the three children coming and going. Glenn and his siblings were raised with tenderness but taught to possess an industrious approach to life. Their father pushed their athletic pursuits, while Florence kept a close eye on their approach to academics. Each would report back to the other. If a serious problem arose, Papa Killinger handled the discipline. In 1961, Earl said their father was "a genial, good-natured, lovable man with a sense of humor, and a great love for athletics." He described his mother as, "energetic, decided in thought and deed, never idle, and considered by her children as the salt of the earth."[20] The kids were allowed to cavort around the neighborhood with friends as long as Billy and Florence knew where they were playing.

They were proud parents, but it was especially difficult keeping track of Glenn's active life. Jay W. Clark, a childhood friend, explained Glenn's assiduous approach to sports as "insatiable." As a youngster, watching sports was as important for his development as playing them. "I never missed an opportunity to watch the local sandlot and high school teams play," he wrote wistfully in his memoir at age 87. Recalling the Harrisburg Senators of the New York–Pennsylvania minor league, which played its games on Island Park, present-day City Island, he said he attended games regularly "when I could beg twelve cents from my Dad." In those common occasions when he was too afraid to ask for money, he admitted, "I would sneak into the games with some of my pals." The island-based field near his Harrisburg home was "wide open with no fences." He gloated vivaciously, "It was easy to outrun the policeman at the main entrance."[21]

Though Glenn usually obeyed the rules as a juvenile, he did have many ethical lapses. He had mentors in his life who steered him away from serious trouble. And yet, on occasion, adolescent impulses unlocked moral counterforces, especially when he spent time with his gang of friends. Pulitzer Prize–winning historian Oscar Handlin wrote of a "consciousness of belonging" that second- and third-generation immigrants like Glenn Killinger clung to as urban youths. Killinger joined an ethnic gang as a way to establish an identity in the peculiar Allison Hill environment. "[E]ach individual had a role [in the gang] which reflected his own capabilities and qualities," explained Handlin in his seminal book *The Uprooted: The Epic Story of the Great Migrations that Made the American People* (1951).[22] Most of Glenn's peers were as obsessive about athletics as he was, but some were on the lookout for trouble. All craved a sense of fitting in that was tied to the neighborhood. Racial divisions normally caused the scuffles. Glenn's friends, mostly of Jewish and German heritage, who inhabited much of South Thirteenth Street bumped shoulders with African American kids throughout the neighborhood. "Every other night they would fight," Glenn's son Bill remembered about his father. "They'd meet and fight."[23] Glenn was a small kid, skinny, just a tad over 100 pounds when he entered high school, Bill described. He may have been scrawny, with more of an erudite appearance, but his squirrel-like agility made him never shy away from scrapes around Allison Hill. The skirmishes were far from momentous. None of the local newspapers reported racial incidents among adolescents and teenagers taking place in The Hill. Killinger's fractional ramblings among the troublemakers in the city taught him some street skills of survival. Even better, this element of rebellion absent the parental dictates of Billy and Florence helped to shape a competitive attitude on the playing fields.

The spots for young Glenn then were the two municipal parks in Allison Hill—the Twelfth Street Playground and Reservoir Park. Both refuges were a respectable distance from the Killinger home. Each was a bit more than a mile away, and for seven years, when he was between the ages of 12 and 19, Glenn spent nearly every day at one of these parks. The park on Twelfth Street was designed especially for the amusement of children. It encompassed swings, slides, and a space to play catch. Reservoir Park was much bigger and offered more for the high school and college ages. Easily accessible by trolley, the park, 88 acres in entirety, was complete with the city's reservoir, park houses, tennis courts, volleyball nets, golf links, pavilions, a foot-powered merry-go-round, stages for concerts, swings, an ice-hockey rink, and fields for soccer, football, baseball, and the like. The parks helped provide a break from the structure in Glenn's life, given the discipline imposed by his parents.

Allison Hill was far from a delight, but it was, perhaps, ideal to prepare Glenn for life in the 20th century. Apart from its racial quarrels, it had chronic trash problems. The fire department was understaffed. The local newspaper often reported about mischief in the area, but never announced the names of culprits, hinting that the police usually never solved the crimes. While Glenn's brother and father were away at work, and before his sister's marriage, he spent many summer days at home with the Killinger women. Not old enough to understand how society expected women to behave, the two women modeled 19th century femininity for Glenn. "She taught me many social graces," he said of his sister.[24] At times, Biz possessed tendencies to break that perception when she took to the tennis court. Glenn often tagged along with his big sister to the tennis club. On the way, he would notice waves of Germans, Irish, Italians, African Americans, and Jews. None were rich. The Killingers lived comfortably when compared to others in The Hill.

Beginning in 1905, Glenn enrolled in public schools in Harrisburg. For grades one through five, he attended Webster Grammar School on the corner of Thirteenth and Kittatinny Streets. For sixth grade, his parents transferred him to the Forney Grammar School, located at Eighteenth and Chestnut Streets. The Killingers never went on record about the transfer, but the local media made Forney out to be a top-notch athletic school for middle school–aged students. Glenn's focus on academics was not a secondary thought. On the contrary, he performed so well that he was able to complete his seventh and eighth grade work in one year at Forney. Long hours of watching his older siblings coast through school left him with an acute sense of the importance of a quality education.

After graduating from Forney in 1912, Glenn enrolled in the city's industrial training school, or Harrisburg Technical High School as it was officially called. Opened in 1905, the Harrisburg Tech school building had one of the most distinguished appearances in the city. Located on the corner of Walnut and Aberdeen Streets, a sizable distance from the Killinger home, the building in 1982 was added to the National Register of Historic Places. The school was a four-story, concrete Collegiate Gothic building that sat on a brownstone foundation.

Harrisburg Technical High School operated as an alternative to Harrisburg Central High School. Most students attended the liberal arts high school, but Tech grew in popularity every year leading up to the time Glenn enrolled. Many saw it as a solution for the nascent problems of attendance, tardiness, and poor conduct. Still, the school lacked diversity. Harrisburg Tech was an all-boys school and was racially segregated.

The program Glenn entered at Harrisburg Tech was designed to prepare students for higher technical colleges, professional schools, entrepreneurship, advanced apprenticeships, or simple mechanical and engineering work. There was little classical education, but by graduation he was expected to have mastered composition, literature, German or French, history, and civics. Mathematics, science, drawing, and different forms of practical shop work were heavily emphasized.[25] His mathematics course load included arithmetic, algebra, plane and solid geometry, logarithms, and plane trigonometry. His science courses were physical geography, physics, electricity, chemistry, and steam engineering. Drawing courses included free-hand, mechanical and architectural drawing, shop drawing, blue printing, and tracing. A double period existed daily to give students shop experience. Accordingly, Glenn took wood working, sheet metal work, wood turning, pattern-making, molding, ornamental iron work, machine tool practice, and steam engineering.[26]

The school years at Harrisburg Tech were divided into three equal semesters—Fall, Winter, and Spring—with the goal of seeing students graduate within three years. The workload was demanding, but school officials found time to take students on field trips to places like the Pennsylvania Steel Company in Steelton. The school established a credible relationship with various colleges and universities. Many of Tech's students were admitted into Cornell University, the University of Pennsylvania, Penn State College, and Dickinson College.

This was a world that seemed to resemble the rough and tumble of Allison Hill, where Glenn could have had his nose broken out on the playground. The school was located about ten minutes away by trolley from South Thirteenth Street. Sometimes, Glenn and his buddies footed it to school, which took under 20 minutes with haste. The school was situated in eyesight of the imposing State Capitol, three blocks from the Susquehanna River.

His classmates came from all sections of the city. Most, Glenn realized early on, were just as formidable at learning as he was. When it came to sports, many were better at the grind.

At the three public schools he attended—Webster Grammar, Forney Grammar, and Harrisburg Tech—Glenn had his classmates fooled. His peers at Tech described him as both a "pool shark" and "card shark." Among those his age, Glenn was considered a master at pocket billiards. He monopolized pool tables at Leonard's Billiards and Bowling, the local hangout at 321 Market Street. He was even more impressive in games of pinochle, which is likely what gave those his age the impression that he was a shrewd tactician. He was never an imposing figure in high school. The most laughable nickname under his high school yearbook picture was "Shrimp." Boyishly handsome, he parted his hair to the left, appeared as if he hardly ate, and possessed a trace of haughtiness. He was clever, but concealed it by singing and whistling in the hallway. Ernest R. Ball's "Love Me and the World is Mine" was his favorite song. The yearbook mentioned that "the only work he does is work his jaws."[27]

In the streets, his appearance was unkempt. He dressed for sport and wore his rough edges on his sleeve. Being a Killinger, there was no surprise that he would end up as a competent engineering student. After all, as much as his peers teased him, most people at Tech liked and respected him. He had little time for girlfriends, choosing instead to work hard at sports, hoping someone would give him a chance. He even held his own against the best athletes in the school, but everyone knew he was undersized and sure to be cut from the team.

To his father and mother and siblings, sports must have seemed like a pastime. They nat-

Killinger's senior portrait at the Harrisburg Technical High School in 1916. He was cut from the varsity basketball and football teams until his senior seasons (Historical Society of Dauphin County and Harrisburg School District).

urally assumed that giving Glenn a ball was giving him nothing more than a toy to occupy his time. His appreciation for carrying around a football or baseball bat grew into a lifetime love. Those toys were actually devices that would soon come to pave the road for an enduring career.

Glenn's young and healthy eyes were focused on the path ahead.

2

Evolution of an Athlete

Writing in his cultural study of American athletics, *Sports and Freedom*, historian Ronald A. Smith sees athletics as a foundational institution for cultural development throughout American history. College sports, he emphasizes, offers the means to hone American success skills. "The physical nature of the individual and of American society appeared to be a desired quality in the age of Darwin," he writes. "Athletic victories gave an image of virility to institutions of higher learning." Through success, athletics has the potential to both enhance visibility and generate revenue for a school, city, or locale. It can produce the same level of popularity and affluence for the individuals who play them. A sport, Smith argues, has the potential of paving a path to social mobility. Moreover, athletes become unencumbered from all such dictates of parents and institutional authority figures. "In a like manner," the noted historian says, "athletics spoke for freedom of the body."[1] That sense of "manly independence," and the prestige that came with it, was pervasive throughout the more than 16,000,000 young athletes at the turn of the century.

Glenn Killinger was just like many teenage boys in those days who sought the fame and fortune of America's professional athletes. "As soon as I was able to read the newspapers," Glenn said reflecting on his childhood, "I became an avid reader of the sports pages." He studied the sports columns in the Harrisburg and Philadelphia newsprints. He was "intrigued" by the "great football and baseball athletic heroes." As an unabashed youth in Harrisburg, he consequently played every sport in the style that "these great athletes" performed. "One day I would imagine I was Christy Mathewson of the New York Giants, the next as Walter Johnson of the Washington Senators, the next day as Ty Cobb of the Detroit Tigers." He said wistfully, "I worshiped the deeds of Jim Thorpe of the Carlisle Indians." Little did he realize as a boy that one day he would compete against some of his childhood heroes.[2]

As a beneficiary of a middle-class German and Scots-Irish family, with a father who managed a popular hardware store and two impressive older siblings, Glenn virtually never faced social obstacles when it came to participation in sports. Highbrow or lowbrow, it never mattered to the aspiring boy who seemingly fit right in games played by upper and lower classes. He played most of them—football, baseball, basketball, tennis, golf, swimming, ice hockey, wrestling, and handball. He participated in the most popular sports in organized settings, while often tagging along with brother, Earl, and sister, Biz, for the others. There was a mythos of the golden age of sports that was prevailing in Glenn Killinger's day: sporting trends imposed many unseen racial and economic divisions among America's athletes. Writing for the *American Quarterly* in 1977, historian Benjamin G. Rader argued that recreational sports "could be easily transformed into a multifaceted social agency" while also existing as "an instrument for social exclusion."[3] Glenn slipped through those socioeconomic cracks. Still, the divisions were inescapable in early 20th century Harrisburg.

His sister, Biz, loved tennis. At the time, both in and out of Harrisburg, the game existed for the privileged and was predominantly an all-white sport. The fact that she came from a middle-class household did not deter her from playing. This was mainly due to her job at the Reservoir Park Tennis Club, which gave her access to the courts. She played with her friends whenever possible.

Rader's *American Quarterly* article, "The Quest for Subcommunities and the Rise of Sport," addresses the exclusivity of private clubs in the Progressive Era. Particularly noteworthy is Rader's assertion that socially exclusive clubs were formed at the turn of the century to maintain social status within an urban-industrial society flooded with European immigrants. He notes that private sports clubs promoted a specific style of life that "would exclude outsiders." Foremost among the lifestyles were a proper manner of dress and speech, education at the best schools, and a host of in-group behavioral nuances. Such traits brought harmony among highborn society members, Rader writes, by providing "an intricate web of primary group milieu which [gave] ... form and structure to an otherwise impersonal urban society composed of secondary groups."[4] While the wealthy class resided within the northern end of Harrisburg, where many ball fields and recreational parks were placed, the southern end, where the Killingers lived, was a hubbub of immigrant life. In a way, the teenager drifted between the two societies as he traded one sport for the next.

While identifying with half the characteristics expected within upper-class barometers of early 20th-century status, Glenn took an interest in tennis because of his older sister. He often played, with nominal success, singles and doubles matches in summer tournaments held at Reservoir Park. Comically, he once finished in last place at the 1913 city championship. He went home with the "Booby Prize," which was a pair of tennis shoes.[5] He even tried out for the Harrisburg Technical School's tennis team in the spring of his senior year, only to quit after a few weeks to play interscholastic baseball against rival schools.

Like tennis, golf was and has remained a sport for the country club crowd. Glenn grew to love golf in the 1920s after he left Harrisburg. He even became a West Chester Golf and Country Club champion several times in the years following World War II. However, he had little interest in the game when he lived in Harrisburg. Few people spoke about it in his hometown, and the media seldom covered the sport.

Then there were the middle-class sports. A look through the local newspapers reveals bowling as a sport most city residents enjoyed playing, as did much of the country during the first six decades of the 20th century. The media also covered wrestling, but few in Harrisburg paid much attention to the sport at any level.

Not surprisingly, football was Killinger's favorite to play. Although it gave him the most hardships in his athletic pursuits, it ultimately made him one of the most accomplished college athletes of his era. Admittedly, Killinger unequivocally embraced the violent nature of the gladiator sport. Ever since the Americanization of football as a byproduct of British rugby, each year the sport had grown in popularity: college football conferences emerged, as did annual rules committees; the media coverage became obsessive, making it apparent that football really was becoming a national fixation. According to Smith, the growth in football's popularity was due in large part to Walter Camp's relentless efforts to promote the sport through his publications in various media outlets, *Outing, Harper's Weekly,* and *Collier's,* in addition to his columns in newspapers across the country.[6] Camp's message to his readers was that football is a manufacturer of manhood; its violence (in place of combat experience) gives American boys the skills to become, in his words, "virile and effective leaders of the modern age." Camp's doctrine of masculinity, discussed so articulately in Julie Des Jardins's *Walter Camp: Football and the Modern Man* (2015), was convincing to young Killinger, who agreed that the game was transformative.[7] This outlook was only buttressed by Camp's journalist colleague Grantland Rice, who wrote of football in 1954: "courage, mental and physical condition, spirit and its terrific body contact which tends to sort the men from the boys." Football, Rice continued, "remains one of the great games of all time."[8] Whereas many people had already died from injuries sustained while playing the sport, the undersized Killinger was never deterred from the game's savagery. In an age before mouthpieces, the fearless footballer would have six teeth replaced before his career came to an end.

While the public craved college football during the teens and '20s, professional football was hardly recognized as a sporting phenomenon. The difference was the extent of school pride, rivalries between student bodies and faculties, and the degree of media coverage that made the college game a cultural spectacle. Beginning with rowing competitions between Ivy League schools along the East Coast, and through the subsequent growth in popularity of baseball as an intercollegiate sport at the turn of the century, football rapidly became America's fall pastime at the start of the Progressive Era, claims Benjamin Rader, as students returned to college after an extended summer break by bonding "diverse groups into larger college communities" and helping "to unite students behind a common cause."[9] Moreover, print media and later, radio, helped elevate intercollegiate football rivalries from campus to campus. Ronald A. Smith says football brought "students of various colleges together in displays of excellence and competition that faculty saw only rarely in the classroom."[10]

College football appealed to the high as much as the low. During Killinger's era, teams from the Ivy League and military academies were among the nation's best football programs; yet every year, independent colleges and universities held their own against the traditional powers. This was important for college presidents and faculties that quickly recognized football's power over public relations. Owing to football's popularity, it grew easier for America's colleges to attract students who would have otherwise attended an Ivy League school. Rader says, "Administrators soon discovered that football was far more effective in attracting public attention than an institution's reputation for scholarship, religiosity, or inspired teaching."[11] Administrative reluctance combined with inevitable buy-in to football fostered the masculine image espoused by Camp in the years before the world war. Football, Rader affirms, projected the male collegiate as "rugged and fearless" with the capacity to "hold his own in the world outside the walls of academia."[12]

It was a simple era, but the sport's violence generated intense waves of attack on two occasions during Killinger's childhood. Football's early form was played in a rudimentary fashion with players on both teams packed closely to the line of scrimmage. Instead of the flash and finesse that modern football offers, offensive linemen could go in motion before the snap and they usually formed a wedge so ball carriers could plunge forward for a few yards. In 1905, after 25 players died and 168 received serious injuries ranging from dislocated ankles to concussions, fractured ribs, broken arms and legs, cracked collarbones, and torn ligaments at all levels of football, which included high school, college, professional, and athletic club teams, college presidents and many from the public called for the abolition of the sport unless "the moral and physical evils" were expunged from the game. The President of the United States, Theodore Roosevelt, encouraged rule changes, but not before telling football aficionado Walter Camp, "I would a hundred fold rather keep the game as it is now, with the brutality, than give it up." The uproar from the public, however, was too vociferous. Modifications were needed. In December, the Intercollegiate Rules Committee, made up of head coaches and college faculty, and headed by Camp, with an unprecedented level of intervention by the United States President, created new benchmark rules that placed an emphasis on stricter measures of fair play, academic eligibility, ten yards for a first down, the neutral zone, and forward passing.[13] The game was saved for the moment at least.

In 1909, a second crusade against football developed as a result of an upsurge of player deaths, including ten fatalities at the college level and 30 on all levels. Sports historian John Sayle Watterson notes in an article for the *Journal of Sports History* that it was not the spike in the number of fatalities that "shattered this brief calm," but rather where and when the deaths occurred that enlivened the debate over safety regulations. On October 17, Earl Wilson, the quarterback for the Naval Academy, was paralyzed from the neck down after breaking his spine in a game against Villanova.[14] Two weeks later, three players died in a single day from concussions sustained in football games: Michael Burke of Medico-Chirurgical College in Philadelphia; Roy Spybuck of the Haskell Indian School in Haskell, Oklahoma; and Eugene A. Byrne of West Point. The death of Byrne, left tackle and team captain at West Point, received the most attention namely because the injury occurred against Harvard in a game played near New York City, the nation's media capital.

One scathing *New York Evening Post* editorial that was reprinted in newspapers throughout the country after Byrne's death attacked the brutality of the sport: "Football is not merely a sport now; it is a contrivance for injuring and maiming."[15] Then, on November 14, 18-year-old Archer Christian,

Table I: Deaths and Serious Injuries, 1905–1916

	DEATHS		SERIOUS INJURIES	
	All Levels	College	All Levels	College
1905	24	3	159	88
1906	11	3	104	54
1907	11	2	98	51
1908	13	6	84	33
1909	30	10	69	38
1910	14	5	40	17
1911	14	3	56	36
1912	10	0	26	17
1913	14	3	56	36
1914	12	2	na	na
1915	15	na	na	na
1916	16	3	na	na

Figures from New York Times, Chicago Tribune *and* Harrisburg Telegraph.[17]

Table II: Newspaper Reports on Causes of Death in College Football

	1905	1906	1907	1908	1909	Total	
Body blows	4	3	3	3	5	18	22.5%
Spinal injuries	4	0	2	3	5	14	17.5%
Concussions	6	3	2	3	6	20	25.0%
Blood Poisoning	2	2	0	1	2	7	8.8%
Other	2	3	5	3	8	21	26.2%
Total	18	11	12	13	26	80	

Figures from New York Times *and* Chicago Tribune[18]

halfback at the University of Virginia, died after sustaining a concussion in a contest against Georgetown University. As a result, Watterson notes, high schools in Washington, D.C., St. Louis, and New York suspended football. West Point and the universities of Georgetown, Virginia, and North Carolina abruptly ended their seasons.[16]

Most fans of the game wanted to save football, but several university officials became vocal in their opposition. Cornell's prominent anatomist, Burt Green Wilder, attacked the game as "a relic of barbarism." David Starr Jordan, president of Stanford University, said the injuries would lessen the popularity of American football and "may pave the way for the introduction of Rugby into the eastern colleges." And Syracuse University Chancellor James Day decried that his college could not "afford to have their men killed and maimed in a game that serves only an exceedingly small proportion of college men."[19] But in spite of the reputable voices calling for an end of football, Watterson has a theory that the outcry was not so much over player safety than it was a reform crusade in line with efforts common to the Progressive Era. The period was famous for "self-criticism and political unrest," writes Watterson, highlighted by congressional measures that cracked down on the meat packing industry and factories employing adolescent children as cheap labor.

Muckraking journalists, such as Ida Tarbell, Lincoln Steffens, Upton Sinclair, Jacob Riis, and Ray Stannard Baker, wrote critiques that generated social change during the period. Like the social reform efforts that led to the Children's Bureau and the Pure Food and Drug Act, the *Chicago Tribune's* John McCutcheon and *New York World* publisher Joseph Pulitzer produced cartoons showing young men carried off the field in various stages of death. The sensationalized images created a frenzy that nearly led to the demise of football, but instead secured modified rules pertaining to diving tackles, onside kicks, and other mass plays.[20]

Although the attacks drove a scare into players, coaches, and sportswriters who invested their livelihoods in the game, the rule changes between 1905 and 1910 actually made the sport more appealing for spectators. By early

20th century standards, however, that was not saying a lot. Playing fields were eyesores. The gridiron was a hundred yards long, but it had no special logos or hash marks. It was possible to snap the ball to begin a play at any location on the playing field. Not until the 1940s did the ball get moved back to the center of the field for the start of a play. Before 1927, the goal posts were positioned at the goal line, making it dangerous for the players. Each team had anywhere from 16 to 25 players on its roster. Both teams typically wore dark jerseys without numbers. It was nearly impossible for fans to distinguish one team from the other, let alone try to identify their favorite player. Some players wore the traditional leather helmet, which seemed to serve as the emblem of the golden age. Others chose not to wear one. No rule required a helmet to be worn until 1943. While some players fashioned their own nose and ear guards out of leather, facemasks and protective mouthpieces were still things of the future. Rules notwithstanding, the forward pass, trick plays, and an evolving offensive system made the game more alluring for onlookers.

It was a player-centered era that was strictly dependent upon the intellectual competency of the team's quarterback. A coach's ability to instruct during a game was limited. It was against the rules for coaches to bark directions or make schematic adjustments at all during regulation. Coaches were forbidden to send play calls or new alignments in with substitutes. So the burden of signal calling fell upon the shoulders of the quarterback, who hardly functioned the same way a quarterback operates in the 21st century. The quarterback was a glorified lineman, a blocking back, who rarely touched the ball. He was a field general with the all-important job of calling the play first, then assuming the role of lead blocker. Teams seldom huddled. Therefore, between every snap, the quarterback had to check out the defensive alignment, get his teammates into the proper formation, and make the play call. He called the plays, but in the single wing and double wing systems, it was possible for any one of the four backfield players to get the snap from center. The person fielding the snap would then spin 180 degrees to either hand the ball off, fake an exchange and plunge into the middle of the interior, throw a forward pass, or punt.[21]

The best players performed like iron-men. The 11 starters never came off the field unless due to injury. That meant that all 22 players who were on the field for the opening kickoff had to remain on the field the entire game. The rules stated that if a player had to come out of the game for any reason, he was prohibited from re-entering until the change of a quarter. Stamina was important to survive the game, though many players mastered the tactic of faking an injury, especially in moments of the second half when fresh legs were needed.[22]

Even at a young age, Killinger thrived on that amount of pressure. He worshipped everything about the game. He loved the fact that football was grungy. He always appreciated football's primal, yet cerebral precision.[23] In his book, *Football*, published in 1938, Killinger explained that he was most impressed with the game's sophistication, the amount of brainpower and mental toughness needed to perform well.[24]

Out on the sandlots, he learned the many skills that it took to have success as a football player. Dropkicking and punting had been pivotal aspects of the game since its inception. Passing, which had its limitations because the oblong ball, at 27 inches in circumference, resembled more the size and weight of a rugby ball, came of age in the mid-1910s. In 1906, the forward pass became legal, but the rule stated that the thrower had to be standing at least five yards behind the line of scrimmage. All passes, whether caught or dropped, were live balls, and must be thrown behind the line of scrimmage. When Killinger entered high school in 1912, the size of the ball was reduced to 23 inches and the forward passing rule was amended to allow passes down the field, but teams were penalized for incompletions. The rule was changed once again in 1914, stating that if a pass was dropped by a wide receiver and the ball rolled out of bounds, possession was given to the opposing team. Possession was also given to the opponent if an incomplete pass was thrown in the end zone. The rules treated that result like a touchback, giving the ball to the opponent at the 20-yard line.[25] When Killinger was playing at Penn State, the rule was changed again to nullify the penalty for incomplete passes and to allow passes to go beyond 20 yards.

It was very rare for a team to possess a dual-threat quarterback. In that day, dual-threat meant a quarterback was exceptional at play calling, running, passing, dropkicking, and punting. Glenn Killinger eventually became the pioneer for contemporary dual-threat quarterbacks.

Dropkicking was used to kick both extra points and field goals. Early in football, dropkicks had a higher point value than touchdowns. A rule in 1909 reduced the value of a field goal to three points—down from five points—and later, in 1912, a touchdown was increased to six points, up from two points.[26]

Punting was a big part of strategy. This aspect of the game was a key to Killinger's gridiron success. "The way to victory was not to possess the ball," wrote Chris Willis, "but to give it to your opponent deep in their territory and let him make a mistake."[27] As the signal caller at Penn State, Killinger called punts on first and second down to play for field position. A look at the box scores during his playing career shows a multitude of games ending in shutout scores, or one-score victories.

Killinger's attention was also drawn mostly to America's summer pastime, baseball. It was a sport that signified the Killingers' middle-class values above all else. By the 1910s, the sport had long been established as America's pastime. It was especially popular in Harrisburg. There were three amateur league baseball clubs in the area, with the Allison Hill Twilight League existing as the city's prevailing league, perhaps because it offered the most playing opportunities for locals. Local competitions attracted huge crowds; in many cases, media coverage for the Allison Hill League was as prevalent as that for the professional game. Postgame festivities and talks with brooding sportswriters usually followed games at Reservoir Park and other public parks. In unison with what was taking place across the United States at the turn of the century, baseball had quickly become Harrisburg's pastime, which meant that the role of the spectators became as important for the game as the role of the players.

Sports historian Steven W. Pope wrote that baseball brought together men of similar class backgrounds "to fraternize and play together."[28] Harrisburg was no exception to this interpretation. Baseball possessed a steep history in the capital city. More than any other sport, baseball came to reveal general aspects characterized in the socioeconomic disposition of the city. People in Harrisburg more easily identified with their neighborhood, or city district, when they attended ballgames at the various parks. The sport provided a tangible comparison between lower-middle-class life in Allison Hill to upper-class Uptown and the posh Midtown. Residents of The Hill were especially eager to show that their athletes were able to one-up those born with a silver spoon. This was especially evident on Killinger's team—the Rosewood Athletic Club, which dominated the Allison Hill League between 1916 and 1920.[29]

Baseball, like many other sports, was an integrated game that became segregated by Glenn Killinger's day. Before the disreputable *Plessy v. Ferguson* decision in 1896, which upheld the constitutionality of segregation and thus hardened Jim Crow's hold on America's public institutions, ballgames between whites and blacks were played at the city's Island Park as early as 1870. The ruling effectively led to the segregation of the nation's sports. The city was destined to acquire the Harrisburg Lincoln Giants of the Negro Baseball Eastern Colored League. Many of the Harrisburg Giants' players lived at the foot of Allison Hill, in an area called Shipoke.

Harrisburg's first semi-professional baseball club was formed in 1901. The same year that Glenn Killinger entered high school in 1912, Harrisburg won the New York–New Jersey–Pennsylvania Association championship. They won it again in 1914. And the Washington Senators' minor league team was brought to Harrisburg in 1924. Killinger actually served as player-manager of the Senators that first year and helped the club win back-to-back New York–Pennsylvania League pennants in 1927 and 1928.

Near the end of his junior year in 1915, Killinger's high school incorporated baseball into its athletic budget. Exhibitions were scheduled against Lebanon Valley College and the Harrisburg Academy, but high school baseball never quite became something the community rallied around, especially when compared to the excitement and passion that was shown for one's school in either football or basketball. Baseball at area high schools was half-hearted, and Harrisburg Tech did little for Killinger's development as a player.[30] Rather, it was in the city's extremely competitive Allison Hill Twilight League where he honed both his skills and passion for the game. Indeed, community baseball was the way he achieved his respectable reputation for athletic prowess and how he had gained a sense of belonging among his peers.

In time, boxing managed to catch fire in Harrisburg. It was, remarkably, the most popular sport of the first three decades of the 20th century. Perhaps more than football, world heavyweight boxing champions were considered, in the words of American cultural critic Gerald Early, the "Emperor of Masculinity."[31] No sport during the era brought greater gate proceeds than prizefighting. In the few years before World War I, gate receipts reached up to $300,000. While the sport was overwhelmingly popular in the 19-aughts and 1910s, due in part by the deeds of John L. Sullivan and James Corbett, and after them, boxers like Jack Johnson and Jess Willard, during the war, boxing was utilized for combat training to prepare soldiers for potential hand-to-hand clashes that might occur on the battlefield. After the war, prizefighting reached new heights. In the 1920s, boxing promoter Tex Rickard proclaimed that at least five bouts exceeded million-dollar gates.[32]

Since the combat sport engaged underprivileged competitors against one another, most boxers were in the sport to make money. Like football, pugilism allowed status seekers to climb up the nation's social hierarchy.[33] Additionally, boxing mirrored late-19th and early-20th century cultural conflicts. Rader states, "native workers saw in foreigners scapegoats for their plight." English and German Protestants in urban America lost autonomy in their work to Irish Catholic and Jewish immigrants. Prizefighters, therefore, found ethnocentric and religious redemption in boxing matches. "Competition for jobs and political power further kindled ethnic hostilities," Rader says, adding, "Prize fights dramatized these rivalries."[34] The sports historian also suggests that boxing "manifestly mocked Victorian values, especially the cardinal virtue of self-restraint." While the middle-class Victorian culture of controlling impulsive behavior had some influence on would-be athletes, the steady influx of immigrants left Americans to continue to adhere to their traditional ways. Fighting became the means for settling disputes and maintaining status among juveniles. Rader observes, "survival in the slums for a boy could depend as much on his skills in using his fists as on his intelligence."[35]

Though Glenn Killinger was involved in his share of scraps on the streets of Allison Hill, it was seemingly the only organized sport he chose not to attempt. His upbringing was responsible for that. Glenn's mother, Florence, was an unwavering dove who had difficultly even letting her youngest boy play football. She always had a difficult time watching Glenn box his older brother in the living room. "Earl would get down on his knees and we would box," Glenn said. The bouts usually began with Earl holding out his left fist, poking short jabs at Glenn's face. "I would become infuriated and rush him, swinging both arms wildly," he recalled. Occasionally, he would "land a good blow" on his brother's jaw. Most of the time, however, he was on the receiving end of a good beating. The scraps "made me fearless," he admitted years later.[36]

This was a revelatory insight coming from a man who valued team sports. Boxing and football did share one parallel: both sports, like military combat, were in the business of developing tough-willed men. Rader suggests, "[They] offered opportunities for male comradery [sic], shared excitement, and a refuge from femininity, domesticity, and the demanding routines of the new economy."[37]

Boxing was always under legislative debate. Some states allowed it, others had it banned. Harrisburg's city council once passed an ordinance barring boxing matches for a time that spanned nearly the length of Killinger's high school tenure.[38] When boxing returned to Harrisburg in 1916, he did enjoy watching matches with Earl at the Chestnut Street Auditorium and the Orpheum Theater.[39] Fighters demonstrated wind and speed stamina. They exuded self-confidence. Their physical and mental toughness was steadfast. Both Killinger boys were entertained by the sheer savagery of the sport. Glenn and Earl were drawn to the ring at any opportunity to witness the sport turn boys, many of whom were once wayward youngsters, into accomplished men. Glenn knew there were lessons about life to be learned from boxing even if he had to discover those as an observer.

Since his mother refused to let him box, Glenn spent his winters playing one of America's newest indoor sports, basketball. Americans may not have been enthusiastic about basketball until the '50s, but the public in Harrisburg adored the new sport. Every city-district athletic club, public school, and Young Men's Christian Association had a team. To accommodate each team, every available auditorium and theater in the city was utilized to host games. One local newspaper cartoonist even joked that rooftops had to be cleared of snow, baskets placed at each corner, and on the water tower if necessary, so that games could be played.[40]

Trading one sport for another every season, Glenn Killinger grew accustomed to the array of games early in his high school career. He did the best that he could to become a factor in Harrisburg Tech's athletic programs; but at his size, the odds were stacked against him.

3

Dreams and Diversity in an American City

Glenn Killinger entered high school in 1912 as a short and puny 110-pound freshman, especially when compared to the boys his own age.[1] He showed little promise as an athlete, especially in his most treasured game, football. It did not help that he battled hay fever attacks annually as football tryouts approached. The bouts of eye irritation and constant sneezing were as difficult to overcome as absorbing the hits of players much bigger than he. When he tried out for football as a freshman, Tech's treasured coach, D. Forest Dunkel, who felt the boy was too incompetent a player to make any of the three teams offered at the school—the varsity, the scrub team, and the Tech juniors—cut him. After he got over the disappointment of not making his school's roster, he joined an independent team made up of middle school-aged kids called the "Hill All-Stars." The Hill All-Stars played in a community league made up of city grammar schools.[2] Killinger quarterbacked the mediocre All-Stars in games against other primary and secondary schools. "Killinger had the hardest time imaginable getting his high school coach to even let him don a football suit," wrote Glenn's hometown newspaper, the *Harrisburg Evening News*, in 1921, "he was regarded as far too light for likely football timber."[3]

If the Killinger men were known for meeting challenges head-on, Glenn, at the age of 14, apparently struggled to live up to the family's expectation. The pressure nearly drove him to quit school sports in 1912. The thought was repressed quickly when he heard about an improbable feat accomplished by his boyhood hero, Jim Thorpe.

Glenn Killinger first witnessed the talent of Thorpe in a football game played between the Carlisle Indian School and Villanova University at Island Park in Harrisburg on Wednesday, October 2, 1912. After school, he and his friends walked a few blocks to Island Park, situated on an island in the Susquehanna River connected to the city by a walking bridge, and watched Thorpe score three touchdowns and dropkick seven goals after touchdown in an easy

65–0 victory.[4] A month later, he opened the sports page in the local newspaper and read that Thorpe had led the Indians to an unexpected yet convincing 27–6 victory over Dwight Eisenhower's West Point Cadets. Killinger was left sputtering as Thorpe became his sports hero. The Carlisle Indian School was located just 20 miles away from Harrisburg. It was accordingly easy for him to follow his new hero's career.

Thorpe was being tallied as the greatest athlete of all time. "He is the greatest halfback of all American football history and perhaps the greatest gridiron warrior of all time," said the *El Paso Herald*. Thorpe had won two gold medals in the 1912 Olympics earlier that summer in Stockholm, Sweden. In addition to football and track and field, he was praised as the best baseball, basketball, soccer, hockey, and handball player in the country. Many were trying to get him to take up boxing. "He'd be a champion in that sport as well," said the *Harrisburg Evening Times*. At six feet tall, stout, and able to take a beating, "There isn't a man in the ring better built for boxing than Jim Thorpe."[5]

Considering that the Carlisle Indian School played many games in Harrisburg, Thorpe's 15-year professional reign at the top of football and baseball had actually begun adjacent to Killinger's hometown. To Killinger, he was the defining sports figure of the decade, especially with Babe Ruth two years away from entering major league baseball. Thorpe's accomplishments and popularity were yet to be rivaled in the sports world.

Glenn Killinger wanted to be just like him. He knew he would never grow to the size of his hero. So instead, he set out to refine other skills, particularly his speed and his mind.

It was a difficult road for the middling athlete. Even among his peers at Harrisburg Tech, he was a jokester and nearly invisible on the playing fields. His friends later described him as an ineffectual competitor who tried hard, but struggled to live up to the tradition already established by the local legends who scrapped on the gridiron and hit the hardwood. Among those legends who wore the maroon and gray was Eugene "Shorty" Miller, Tech class of 1909. Miller, who grew up, according to Killinger, "only a few blocks from my home," was presently in his senior year quarterbacking the Penn State Blue and White to an undefeated season and an imminent College Football Hall of Fame career.[6]

Killinger dealt with one setback after another for virtually his entire career at Tech. In the fall of 1913, he was cut again from the varsity football team. There was a need, however, for a quarterback on Tech's third football squad, called the "Tech Juniors." Since he loved the sport so much, he apathetically accepted the role.

Because of his size, Killinger, a high school sophomore, weighing under 130 pounds, was eligible to play in the junior league. He was never named a captain—his behavior in school always prevented him from the honor. Nevertheless, his team was better than average, and he was a major contributor.

The Tech Juniors competed against local grammar schools and other junior teams. On November 27, he threw a touchdown pass for the game's only score, which gave the Maroon and Gray a 6–0 victory over Sycamore Juniors for the Junior City championship.[7]

In the winter of 1913–1914, Killinger tried out for Harrisburg Tech's basketball squad. The coach cut him before the start of the season. He ended up playing in a community basketball league as a forward for St. Andrew's of the local Young Men's Christian Association.

It was near the end of his sophomore year when Killinger reached out to his older brother for help. For the next several months, Glenn and Earl spent much of their time discussing the rules of various sports. Earl, a trusted high school football official, basketball referee, and baseball umpire at the time, offered to discuss the rulebooks for each game with Glenn.

The brothers focused most on making Glenn better at football. The two would discuss one rule a day. They would meet in the solitude of their parents' home, then head to the football field at Island Park to practice. Ira Stone, a lifelong friend of Earl and Glenn who witnessed some of the sessions, once described the brothers' workouts: "They passed and punted and ran and fell on the ball. Through the winter and on into the spring this practice went steadily on."[8]

The sessions were hardly flawless. Glenn was brash and would at times frustrate his older brother. However, when he suffered a setback, he was back at the park with his brother. "In the good old summertime Killinger still dallied with that football and made the island his rendezvous," recalled Stone. "He was an amateur Captain Kidd and this was his Treasure Island."[9]

As the youngest in a family known for self-made success, Glenn Killinger could never stop trying. He was surprisingly light of foot but he hardly looked the part. He had the body of a lightweight wrestler, a tad too big to be a jockey and too small to become a contender in any of the major sports. Everyone called him "Too light," Stone explained to a reporter in 1921 after Walter Camp announced Killinger part of his All-American team. Closer to Earl's age, Stone often took Glenn with him to the annual University of Pennsylvania–Penn State games at fabled Franklin Field in Philadelphia. "Watching this game from the stands one day," Stone recalled, Killinger said "he was going to play on the Penn State team some day on historic Franklin Field." Stone admitted that he laughed at him. He said, "[I] repeated those fatal words, 'too light.'"[10]

None of the detractors meant much to Glenn Killinger. He simply loved sports. That summer, he registered for the annual 13-to-16-year-old junior tennis tournament at Reservoir Park. He played in singles and doubles matches. He won some and he lost some. He never made a deal about it either way. His family loved the sport, but there was no future for him in tennis.

When his junior year started, he was hardly bigger or stronger. He was, however, smarter. He hoped that would be enough. Yet when over 40 boys showed up for practice on the first day of football tryouts in September 1914, Glenn was certain to be cut from the varsity roster again. He thought maybe the gradual popularity of forward passing would give him a slight advantage since he and Earl studied the rules so vigorously. He also showed off his ability to dropkick from various distances. He hustled from one drill to the next. Even then, it was not enough for Coach Dunkel, who considered him too small and too fragile to survive the beating of varsity football. He was again waived from the varsity team.[11]

Killinger was placed on the Tech Juniors for a second consecutive season. He quarterbacked the team to victories over the Camp Hill Juniors twice and the All-Grammar School All-Star team of Allison Hill. His team went down in defeat only once, a disconcerting 34–0 loss to the Harrisburg Academy's third team.[12]

As maligned as he was, Killinger played well enough on the Tech Juniors to catch Coach Dunkel's eye. On October 12, he was promoted to Harrisburg Tech's scrub team, the 21st century's equivalent of junior varsity football. Tech's scrub team was filled with sophomores and a few mediocre juniors. There, Killinger ultimately stood out. In his first game, he played as a substitute quarterback against local rival Steelton High School. Tech started slowly, but when he entered the game, the offense began to click. He was Tech's major contributor in a convincing 52–0 victory.[13] His performance that day won him the starting quarterback position on Tech's scrub team for the remainder of the season.

A week later on October 19, he guided Tech's Scrubs to a victory over Camp Hill. He dropkicked four points after touchdowns to help the Scrubs win, 40–0. He started again a few days later in a rematch against Steelton's scrubs. He threw one touchdown pass and made one dropkick for a point after touchdown, but his team fell, 12–7. He struggled thereafter in his lead role. His offensive production progressively waned in the scrubs' final three games. Tech earned a 34–0 victory over Enhaut Athletic Club, but then went down in defeat to the Highspire Athletic Club, 6–3, and tied their city rival, the Harrisburg Central Scrubs, 0–0.[14]

Killinger's experience playing basketball during his junior year was much like that of his football season. In December, he tried out for the varsity team, but was given a spot on the scrub unit. As a forward on the junior varsity, he was one of his team's leading scorers. Yet he did not manage pressure well at this stage of his life. While selected by his coach to be the team's designated foul shooter, he sometimes ended up being more of a liability, especially in big games. In their biggest game of the year against the Harrisburg Central High scrubs, a game in which he scored half of his team's points, he shot just eight-for-20 from the foul line. Tech lost the game, 33–28 in overtime.[15]

He kept his grades respectable during his junior year. Just before the completion of the school year, he received the news that he had earned second honors on Tech's Academic Honor Roll. The accomplishment was reported in a column of the local *Telegraph*.[16] It was the only time in his four years at Tech that he received an academic honor.

After weathering a difficult beginning of high school, Killinger started to come into his own as an athlete by the beginning of his senior year. When he entered Tech for his final year, he was 5'6" tall and weighed 137 pounds.[17] In reality, he was still too small to play on the varsity football team. Needless to say, an auspicious opportunity presented itself at the start of the football season.

Before the season began, Coach Dunkel resigned so he could practice law in West Palm Beach, Florida.[18] Athletic Director Percy L. Grubb commenced a hasty search for someone to fill the head football coaching position. The Tech students and many of the faculty wanted Eugene "Shorty" Miller, the former Tech legend and quarterback who set the Penn State career rushing record and was named by Walter Camp to the third-team All-American list in 1912. Miller played professional football for the Massillon Tigers in Ohio on Sundays while working at the Pennsylvania Steel Company during the week. His busy schedule prevented him from accepting the position. So the former football and basketball standout from Yale and Lehigh Colleges, Fred "Red" Green, was hired to head the Tech 11.

On Killinger's 17th birthday, 76 students tried out for the team when practice began on Monday, September 13, 1915. Coach Green had a tall order in front of him. The 1915 team was hardly a solid unit. "Tech has the hardest schedule in its history," announced the *Telegraph*, "and with the cream of last year's team graduated, the Maroon and Gray will have a difficult time winning the Central Pennsylvania honors." According to newspaper articles in the *Telegraph* and *Star Independent*, Tech returned just six players from the 1914 roster. So the bulk of the 1915 varsity squad would be made up of reservists and scrub team members like Glenn Killinger.[19]

There was no practice field on the Walnut Street campus. So the Harrisburg Tech boys had to try out on Island Park field, where most of their games were played. Back for another try at his favorite sport, Killinger put on his equipment at school and jogged across the Walnut Street Bridge, crossing part of the Susquehanna River, and onto an island where the football field was situated. Members of the team were supposed to treat the hike as their warm-up before the start of practice.

At first sight, Coach Green was not impressed with the budding yet feeble backfield player. He thought Killinger was too small, bow-legged, and undisciplined. All of it was true. Killinger was still undersized, even for a quarterback or halfback in the 1910s. Coach Green liked to throw forward passes, which was an uncommon aspect of the game during the era. Hardly tall enough to be a passer, Killinger struggled to see beyond his offensive linemen.[20] He had impressive speed, but he lacked the ability to break tackles. He also had a reputation for being cheeky in school, a trait that made Green circumspect.

Would Glenn Killinger be too much of a nuisance for the team? There was just something about the kid that made Green consider making him one of his 20 varsity players. Was it because Green needed more than one quarterback? Or was it because Killinger had a fair reputation as a quarterback on the third team and scrub team the previous year? Or could it have been his dogged attitude about playing varsity football? No matter the reason, he finally did it. He finally made the varsity football roster.

The euphoria of being selected to play varsity football lasted just a short time. By the first game, he was beaten out for the starting position by a sophomore, Reese Lloyd. On September 25, Reese shined in Tech's 20–0 victory over Pottsville in the season opener. Killinger did not play in the game.

Not only was Killinger absent from the opener, he missed the first six games. Sources are unclear, but he was either hurt or ineligible. According to the *Telegraph*, a significant number of Tech players missed the first half of the season because of injuries and poor grades. The local newspaper did not report the reason why Killinger sat out, but both are realistic possibilities.[21] Before he returned to the lineup, the Tech Maroon and Grays compiled a record of three wins and three losses.

His first appearance in a game was on November 6 against Steelton High School. It was a game Tech was picked to win. Just two weeks earlier, Tech had handed Steelton an 18–6 defeat. Coach Green made the decision to start Killinger at quarterback in place of Lloyd. It was the young coach's first significant mistake. While the game presented itself as his first taste of varsity football, it was also his first varsity start. As one would expect, it was a disappointing debut. He played terribly and was pulled from the game at halftime. Tech lost, 13–0.

Eight days later, on November 14, the Tech football team and roughly 60 fans boarded a train to Lancaster to play the Red Roses of Lancaster High School. Killinger replaced Lloyd at quarterback after the latter threw two interceptions.[22] The adjustment in the backfield did not change the outcome. Tech lost, 13–6.

Killinger's customary broad grin had quickly faded as the season progressed. With two games remaining on the schedule, he hoped to make some contribution that would change the downward spiral of the season. A fleeting glimmer of hope appeared on November 20 when Tech defeated Allentown, 13–0. He did not start, but he substituted in and scored the game's first touchdown—his first and only varsity touchdown.

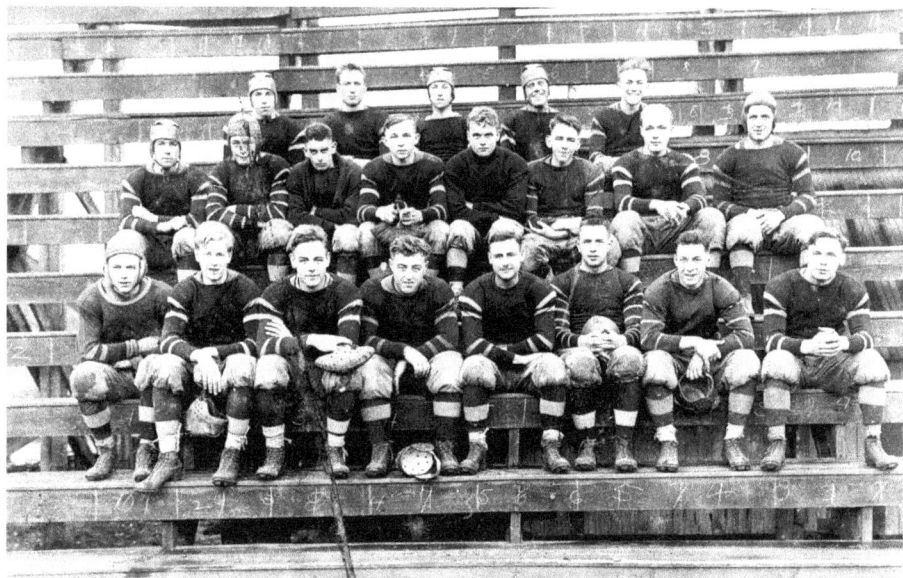

The Harrisburg Tech Maroon and Grays had the dominant high school program in Pennsylvania during the 1910s. The worst team of the decade was Killinger's in 1915. Killinger is pictured second row, sixth from the left (Jessica Killinger).

Tech's biggest contest every year was the Thanksgiving Day city championship played on Island Park against arch-rival Harrisburg Central High School, a school located half a mile away on the corner of Forster and Capital Streets and considered Pennsylvania's finest secondary school between Philadelphia and Pittsburgh. Thanksgiving Day football contests had become the premier athletic event in many cities and towns across the United States by the mid–1910s. The custom dated back to November 30, 1876, when Yale defeated Princeton in the first Turkey Day game.[23] Since that long forgotten moment in football glory, colleges, high schools, and professional football teams have made Thanksgiving Day the day of choice to play annual rivalry games. Ronald A. Smith, writing about the tradition in *Sports and Freedom* (1988), said the holiday spectacle spread across the nation in part because many realized its profitability. Speaking more specifically of college football, Smith wrote that as schools looked for money, "it was only logical that Thanksgiving Day became a commercial day [for high schools and colleges]." By the mid–1890s, he claimed, approximately "5,000 football games, involving 120,000 athletes, were played on Thanksgiving Day."[24] That number would grow exponentially over the next 20 years as high schools jumped on the holiday game bandwagon.

As popular as football is in the Commonwealth of Pennsylvania in the

21st century, few high school football rivalries have ever compared to the turn-of-the-century City of Harrisburg championship game played between Harrisburg Tech and Harrisburg Central High School (a game that would evolve into a showdown between John Harris High School and William Penn High School, and later Bishop McDevitt and Harrisburg High Schools). While still a rivalry in its infancy—the series began in 1905—Thanksgiving Day gave the 64,186 residents of Harrisburg and scholastic football fans within a 50-mile radius something to look forward to each year. The student bodies of both schools traditionally marched in unison to the island as almost a quarter of the city's population squeezed into Island Park's football stadium, the largest in Central Pennsylvania, to cheer on their respective teams.[25] Despite the fact that Central High dominated the series, the proximity of the two schools, buttressed by neighborhood quarrels, socioeconomic jealousies, and student body as well as professorial rivalries, year in and year out, the game was the talk of the state. Heading into the 1915 game, Tech's all-time record against Central was one win and 11 losses. Tech had been shut out in

The Harrisburg Technical High School All Sports Parade in 1916. Killinger is pictured standing in the back (Jessica Killinger).

every game against Central except the only match it won, a 19–12 triumph in 1914.[26]

For the Tech-Central showdown of 1915, 8,500 people filed into Island Park stadium—a favorable turnout for the city championship game, especially considering Tech's lack of talent and mediocre season. Every available seat was filled, described the *Harrisburg Telegraph,* and a line of "several hundred automobiles" surrounded the field. People stood between the cars and the rope, "four lines deep" it was reported. While the scene of thousands of fans huddled around one another at the island field must have been a beautiful sight from above, the game itself was an unsightly display of football. The game was ugly from the opening kickoff. "One point in yesterday's game the spectators just couldn't understand was Tech's high tackling," complained the *Telegraph*. Harrisburg Central's skill players were too big and too fast for Tech's defenders. Hoping to get his team on the scoreboard, Coach Green sent Killinger in at right halfback while Lloyd remained at quarterback. Green thought having two experienced field generals on the field at once would help Tech advance the ball against Central's "stonewall" defense. Disappointingly, the scheme was just as ineffective. Tech failed to score. Meanwhile, Central scored at will. The contest ended 34–0, and Harrisburg Central walked away with the P. G. Diener silver football cup, the traditional trophy named on behalf of Harrisburg's wealthy jewelry mogul who sponsored the game.[27]

At season's end, Tech had defeated four teams, but lost six games in convincing fashion. The Maroons earned only one victory in four tries after Killinger returned to the lineup.[28] At a quirky ceremony held at the high school on December 23, Killinger received his first and only varsity football "T" and letterman cardigan. A member of the faculty dressed as Santa Claus gave the letters to Killinger and 18 others. The honor would become something he often joked about. Years later, he conceded to his closest friends, "I was the worst player on the worst team Harrisburg Tech ever had."[29]

• • •

There were certainly better classes that passed through Harrisburg Tech before and after Killinger's graduating class. However, the period within the decade that they walked the halls was unlike any other. The Tech student body was racially segregated during its early years. High school-aged African American students either attended Harrisburg Central or went right into the work force. None was interested in attending the technical school. Killinger was German-American, the dominant ethnicity in Harrisburg. He was never kicked off the playground. He was never told to leave the theater. He had gone to school each day never having to think about the struggles of coming from a marginalized family. He never had to deal with prejudice in any form. That is, until his senior year.

3. Dreams and Diversity in an American City 47

The Great War, which began in the summer 1914, was escalating in Europe. Anti-Germany headlines appeared more and more frequently on the front pages of local newspapers. The United States was years away from entering the war, but Germany was making a steady habit of sinking ships in the Atlantic Ocean that were carrying American citizens. War preparedness advocates doubled down on their stance after each incident. As a result, racial hostilities between those of German heritage and non–German heritage in Harrisburg were mounting. The local food administration, believing the German name resulted in "patriotic persons refusing to partake" in the business of local restaurants, reported the *Harrisburg Telegraph*, changed the name of sauerkraut to "pickled cabbage." Vigilantes in town forced German-American residents to salute and kiss the American flag lest they be lynched. Harrisburg Technical School pondered discontinuing German language classes. Before school administrators made a final decision, most of the students made the choice themselves to transfer into French class. For those who remained in German class, school administrators told the *Telegraph*, "all German books in use had been censored carefully."[30]

The war's impact on onlookers in Harrisburg helped Killinger notice the sting of racism. It is true: he had his share of run-ins with other racial groups in his neighborhood while growing up. For so long, he proved guilty of lacking sensitivities to prejudice even while living in the most racially inclusive neighborhood in Harrisburg. The war introduced something new, and dangerous, about race and ethnicity in the United States. Meanwhile, Killinger, in his teenage years, was slowly becoming aware of how the various ethnic issues sweeping the country were impacting daily occurrences in his hometown.

As Killinger's football team took on its archrival on Thanksgiving Day, a 35-year-old Spanish-American War veteran named William Simmons climbed to the top of Stone Mountain in Georgia with a group of friends and inaugurated the new Ku Klux Klan in a cross-burning ceremony. For 40 years, the Klan had remained dormant before Simmons' ceremony. Reacting to profound nativist influences against Eastern European immigrants and the steady fight for equality among America's black population, the new Klan was set on opposing anybody who was not a native-born Anglo-Saxon. Stories about the Klan's rebirth spread among ruffians in Allison Hill, which already had their share of run-ins with Catholics, Jews, and African Americans in the neighborhood.[31]

Simmons's Klan was formed soon after the release of the silent epic drama *The Birth of a Nation*, which hit theaters in February 1915. Based on the novel *The Clansman*, the movie's producer, D. W. Griffith, who started production on July 4, 1914, just days after the heir to the Austro-Hungarian empire was assassinated by a Serbian nationalist, which eventually led to the start of World War I, created the film to show life in the South after the close of the Civil War. Starting early in the history of the South at the time of the arrival of slaves, the film quickly arrives at the outbreak of the Civil War. In rapid fashion, the movie covers the call for volunteers, several big battles, General Sherman's march to the sea, the Appomattox surrender, and the assassination of President Lincoln. Griffith's epic climaxes with a series of Ku Klux Klan rides that aimed to restore civility among newly oppressed white Southerners, particularly abducted and molested white women kept under duress by belligerent and monstrous African American men who had recently been set free from bondage.[32]

Griffith said that he produced the movie "to tell the truth" about the Civil War. "It hasn't been told accurately in history books," Griffith asserted in an interview after the film's release, arguing further that "the winning side" distorted the facts behind the war. The film's thesis danced around emancipation and black suffrage, claiming that both had been a terrible mistake. Author Dick Lehr writes in his 2014 book by the same title as the haunting 1915 motion picture that Griffith's theories were predisposed by the school of thought espoused by Columbia University professor William A. Dunning. The xenophobic revisionist history on Reconstruction, in which he called the "Tragic Era," presumed "Negroes as inferior, ignorant, and incapable of the honest exercise of political rights and power." Griffith was also influenced by the anatomical studies conducted by University of Michigan professor Robert Bennett Bean, who theorized in 1909 that African American brains weighed less and were smaller, thus were genetically inferior to those of their white counterparts.[33] The message in Griffith's film and the theories of the Dunning School permeated white America as the so-called Jim Crow laws and lynching amplified fear among black Southerners and racial divisions increased as thousands of African Americans migrants arrived in Northern cities in search of jobs. "The birth of the nation began with the Ku Klux Klans [sic]," the Kentucky-born director said after the release of his moving picture, "and we have shown that." Griffith would say in a later interview, "The Klan at that time was needed. It served a purpose."[34]

Marketed in the press as the "Eighth Wonder of the World," the silent film's arrival in Harrisburg was delayed until the winter of 1916, just three months after Killinger's senior football season concluded. Evaluating the film's impact on American society in later years, Lehr maintains that the movie has endured the test of time because it was a cinematic masterpiece, albeit an ugly milestone in American race relations. He writes, "the complete legacy of D. W. Griffith's *The Birth of a Nation*—a masterpiece that, due to its bigoted slant, became a dramatic flash point in 1915 for a changing America in mass media and marketing, civil rights, and civil liberties."[35] The content of the movie created a stir among racial groups throughout the country, which fostered ambivalence among the populace in Harrisburg that the teenage

Killinger could not ignore. A Klan chapter existed in the capital city, where reports of "Tar and feather" parties, beatings, and maltreatment of non–White Anglo Saxon Protestants were rampant by the end of the decade.[36] There were two popular movie-houses in town at the time: the Victoria Theater on Market Street and the Orpheum Theater on Poplar Street. The Victoria was already undergoing a legal battle over allegations of discrimination after an African American movie-goer was refused a ticket to the theater's lower floor; whereas the Orpheum faced no such accusations.[37] So on February 16, 1916, complete with a symphonic orchestra, *The Birth of a Nation* was shown for the first time in Harrisburg.

As Killinger grew up in The Hill, running from park to park seeking adventure, it was easy to get caught up in unruliness among those who emanated from unhinged and less tolerant households. Acclaim about *The Birth of a Nation* and the Klan's regeneration undoubtedly caught fire among some of his peers. With him, however, there was little of that. Playing organized sports helped him mature as a young man. There was an amalgamation of Christians and Jews, wealthy and poor, on his football and basketball teams that bonded together in a way that those who lived in Allison Hill failed to do.

In the winter of his senior year, the hardwood offered a distraction from the outside world. Killinger made the varsity roster and won one of the starting guard positions in spite of being the shortest and frailest person on the team. In the first game of the season against York High, he was held scoreless. Shortly thereafter, he found his way, finishing the season as the team's second-leading scorer, averaging 9.2 points per game.[38] Given the nickname "Shrimp" during the season, he set a Central Pennsylvania Scholastic Basketball League record on January 10, 1916, for making the most shots from the field in a single game when he made 11 baskets in a victory over Lancaster High School. It was a remarkable feat considering there was no rush to score points, and in this era of basketball every shot taken from the floor was either a one-hand lay-up or a two-handed set shot (the jump shot was not introduced until 1931 by University of Missouri guard John Miller Cooper, but this is still under debate). Killinger's record stood until March 1918.[39]

The Tech tossers started the season on fire, winning seven of their first ten contests. When league play began, unfortunately so did a streak of 11 consecutive defeats. Lackluster shooting and careless play came to define the season. Harrisburg Tech finished last in the newly created Central Pennsylvania League, with two wins and ten losses, and an overall record of nine victories and 20 defeats.[40]

In the waning days of his senior year, Glenn Killinger thought about playing tennis at Harrisburg Tech, but after one week on the team he decided to join the school's on-again-off-again baseball club. Earlier in 1913, Tech had dissolved the baseball program, claiming "a lack of competition with scholastic teams." After a two-year hiatus, the students lobbied school officials to bring baseball back.[41] The administration agreed and a team was formed in 1915, Killinger's junior year. During the winter months of 1916, the students and administration resumed talks about the future of baseball at Harrisburg Tech. When the administration decided to continue with baseball in 1916, Killinger quit tennis so he could try out for the squad.[42] He made the team and started at second base. The season, however, featured only a best-of-five series against the Harrisburg Academy.[43]

With the pressure of scholastic athletics behind him, Killinger coasted into his high school graduation. Merely an average student throughout high school, usually bringing home Bs and Cs on his report card, he received no honors at the commencement ceremony on June 15. Fifty students graduated from Tech in 1916. The *Telegraph* reported that the majority of Harrisburg Tech's students "will continue their studies in higher institutions of learning with the opening of colleges in the Fall."[44] Killinger, however, was not one of them.

He had no plans after graduation beyond working for his father in the family hardware shop. Truthfully, he wanted to go to The Pennsylvania State College that his hometown hero and former Walter Camp 3rd team quarterback Eugene "Shorty" Miller attended college. Only he was afraid to ask his father to pay for it. He wrote years later in his memoir, "My father pleaded poverty because his hardware store was not doing very well financially." There was, honestly, a hue of teenage laziness in young Glenn Killinger. He had just received a degree in Industrial Careers, but he was in no way motivated to take on adult responsibilities. He specifically frustrated the Killinger men: his father, Billy, and brother, Earl. His father was a popular entrepreneur, a self-made success story who often cavorted with the city's former mayor, John D. Patterson. His older brother was in the early stages of balancing a long career as a teller in the East End Bank of Carlisle and a wartime job as a consultant in the Constructing Quartermaster's Department in Washington, D.C.[45] Meanwhile, Glenn had no plans other than playing sports.

For the first year after graduation, his world of work and play was confined to the borders of Allison Hill. He was given a job making three dollars a week in the Killinger Hardware Store. He told people that he took the job out of loyalty to his family, but later admitted, "I probably played more sports, like baseball, tennis, and went swimming in the Susquehanna River more than I worked."[46] Much of his leisure time was spent at the Rosewood Athletic Club, located in the Hess Building two blocks west of his house, on the corner of Thirteenth and Market Streets.

In the summer after high school, he played twilight baseball for Rosewood, which competed in the extremely popular and competitive Allison

Hill League. Listed as a shortstop, he displayed some toughness after he bruised several ribs attempting to steal second base in a game played on July 24. His speed was frightening for opposing catchers in the Allison Hill League that summer. This time, to no avail, he slid awkwardly feet-first into second base, lifting his right leg in an attempt to gash the shortstop trying to tag him out. His opponent fell on top of him, resulting in the injury. Killinger struggled to trot off the field after he was thrown out. The pain was too much, and he could not finish the game.

The rib injury occurred with a month left in the season as his team was nearing the Allison Hill League championship. Here is where he displayed the mental toughness that ultimately came to define him as a competitor. The opportunity to win a pennant in a community baseball league was the pinnacle for Glenn Killinger in 1916. So he gutted it out in spite of the pain. Rosewood defeated a team called the Galahads, 1–0, for the Allison Hill League pennant on August 24. He went hitless in the title game, but he was hit by a pitch, stole a base, and made no fielding mistakes in the shutout victory.[47]

The Rosewood Athletic Club championship baseball team of 1916. Killlinger is seated first row, third from the left. His brother, Earl, is seated first row, first on the left (Jessica Killinger).

The experience should have been honorable for the brash high school graduate. His team's performance that summer exemplified unselfishness and polished fundamentals. "Not a member of the championship Rosewood team hit above the .300 mark," the *Telegraph* reported. Their pennant run was attributed "largely to good fielding and excellent twirling."[48] Killinger, somewhat expectedly at this stage of his life, instead looked like a haughty teenager with his cap tipped to the side in the team picture that appeared on the *Telegraph's* sports page applauding the championship.

His play unquestionably gave him a boost of overconfidence. He executed all 77 of his opportunities in the infield without making an error. He finished the summer league ranked tenth in batting average, second in the number of games played, second in runs scored, and second in hits. He tied for first in the league in doubles.[49]

In November, he tried out for the Rosewood Athletic Club's basketball squad, a team managed by his brother, Earl. Rosewood competed in the Harrisburg City Amateur Basketball League.[50] At 18 years old, Glenn was the youngest to make the roster, which was predominantly made up of 20-somethings.

The Killinger brothers warmed up for the season by playing in the annual Alumni versus Harrisburg Technical High School basketball game on December 8, 1916. Glenn scored a game-high 22 points in the alumni's 60–10 victory over the high school squad.[51]

The Rosewood Athletic Club basketball team had success similar to that of the baseball team earlier that spring, except for a bad stretch in February when Earl Killinger and his wife, Marion, gave birth to their only child, a daughter that they named Jane Mumma, on February 1. Earl missed two games after the birth of Jane, which left the team without its coach. In the end, Rosewood coasted through the season on their way to clinching the City Amateur League championship by the end of March 1917.

Due to their dominance in the city league, a game was scheduled against the Pennsylvania Motive Power Athletic Association two and a half weeks later for the Independent Championship of Harrisburg. Rosewood was outplayed in a 48–33 loss.[52] Though important for Killinger, the defeat was overshadowed by something much greater.

The United States declared war on Germany on April 6, 1917. America's entry into the war might put an end to Killinger's carefree athletic pursuits.

Immediately a patriotic fervor swept across Harrisburg. Just three days after war was declared, a local citizen climbed to the top of Kittatinny Mountain, which overlooked the city from the north, "in the midst of the flurries of snowflakes," the *Harrisburg Telegraph* reported, and hoisted the American flag on the top of the mountain. Liberty bond drives brought more than $4,000,000 in Harrisburg and vicinity within two months.[53] T. O. Lapp, the

The Rosewood Athletic Club championship basketball team of 1916–1917. Killinger is kneeling second row on the right. His brother, Earl, is seated first row on the right (Jessica Killinger).

owner of a Newberry restaurant, displayed a sign stating that hamburgers sold at his establishment would thereafter be called "Harrisburgers." American flags decorating homes and windows of big stores throughout the city added to the patriotic spirit. The governor of Pennsylvania, Martin Grove Brumbaugh, called for the creation of "food growing groups" among students so they could plant "in available schoolyards and upon their home soil all forms of food plants to the end that these children, too young to enter the army or navy, may perform an important patriotic duty."[54] Door-to-door canvasses were launched to enroll every woman in Harrisburg into the nationwide food conservation plan. Complicit to social pressure, Killinger's mother signed a pledge of affiliation with the food administration, agreeing to "carry out the advice and instruction of the food administration as far as her circumstances permit."[55]

President Woodrow Wilson's war machine wasted no time getting people excited about the war. The Committee of Public Information, sometimes derided as the censorship bureau, with George Creel, the revered writer for the nationally syndicated magazine *The Century*, as chairman, dutifully disseminated among the populace strong anti–German silent films, pamphlets, and speakers. Immediately following Wilson's declaration of war, the censorship bureau got started writing curriculum centered on the president's war measures, including footnote references and notations for detailed study in schools. Professors in the field of history, most notably University of Minnesota scholar Guy Stanton Ford, and the National Board for Historical Service were responsible for editing the manuscript. Within the space of two months, the bureau authorized the "Four Minute Men," which presented arguments to the public that were "strictly limited, confined and restricted to four minutes" and limited exclusively to topics related to the war. The CPI presented the subjects of the speeches each week and mailed the data, including a sample 500- to 700-word speech, to every Four-Minute Man throughout the country. Speeches were usually made in front of an audience at a picture house after a silent film. The censorship bureau further undertook the publication of a brochure titled "Why We Are Fighting for Many," which was disseminated nationally in many languages. Its purpose, Creel noted, was "to answer completely and effectively questions concerning our participation in the great war."[56] For confused citizens like Glenn Killinger's parents, the publication of the brochure provided a detailed report about the reasons for entering the conflict against the German aggressors who "had made the attack upon us" which forced America's hand.[57]

Additionally, the Treasury Department's effort to fund the war by selling Liberty Bonds to the public bolstered an aggressive patriotic zeal in support of the war. On Saturday, April 21, more than 14,000 marchers arrived in Harrisburg to take part in the "Everybody's Patriotic Parade." Thousands more gathered to cheer and applaud the "marching patriots" in what the *Harrisburg Telegraph* reported to be the "largest demonstration in the city's history." Flags were draped over the fronts of stores and houses. People cheered, whistled, shouted. A large float representing America's Allies led the procession. Forty-eight schoolgirls, dressed in white, each representing a state of the Union, carried a huge American flag. Much to the amusement of the parade-goers, a submarine built around a three-wheeled electric truck rolled down Front Street, shifting to starboard, then backward, before swinging hard to port "in bewildering succession," said the *Telegraph*.[58]

The month following the declaration of war was exhilarating, and it did much to influence Killinger's attitude about wanting to defend his country against the German savages. But then came the announcement on May 10 that draft registration was limited to men ages 21 through 31. He was too young to register with the Selective Service. He received no additional help from his parents. Both objected to his volunteering for the expeditionary force. His mother Florence was especially adamant about forbidding Glenn from enlisting. He admitted that his mother was a pacifist, which was puzzling considering her father—Glenn's grandfather—was a Civil War veteran. Raised to appreciate the valor of his antecedent, Glenn was never shy in blaming his mother for his absence from combat on the Western Front. He said in 1966, thinking back on his wartime experience, that she "hated war and refused to sign the papers" which would have allowed his enlistment.[59]

But Glenn Killinger was far from giving up. The United States had just joined the fight. So in his estimation, the war would go on for several more years. He trusted one day he would have his opportunity to prove his manhood.

Part Two: Second Quarter

4

Wartime Football Adventure

Glenn Killinger was three months away from his 16th birthday when the Archduke Francis Ferdinand, inspector general of the Austro-Hungarian Empire, died at the hands of Gavrilo Princip, who was part of a conspiracy concocted by a Serbian nationalist group called the Black Hand, hell-bent on unifying Serbia and Bosnia. A month later, on July 28, 1914, Austria-Hungary declared war on Serbia. Killinger was entering his junior year at Harrisburg Technical High School with goals of making the football team. However, the war became real to him during the first week of August when Germany declared war on Russia and France. The Killinger household was a little different that week as mild disputes between his parents transpired over whom to side with, the Central Powers or the Allies.

Killinger never really understood why the war was being fought; nationalistic dogma was above his intellectual capacity during the early stages of the war. His interests centered on competitions at the playground, music, and silent films. Then, when the United States entered the war in 1917, he started to think more about the lofty vision of a democratic world government promoted so vigorously by the Committee of Public Information. Still, he cared most about the news of submarine attacks resulting in the death of his countrymen, threats of domestic sabotage in the blowing up of buildings and destroying factories in various areas of the country, and that for three years the Germans waged a barbarous war against civilization. He wanted to fight.

So the fact that Killinger found himself enrolling at The Pennsylvania State College in 1917 instead of the Army was perplexing. Earlier in the spring, after he conceded to his parents, who prevented him from enlisting in the service, he recruited Earl and Biz to help convince their father to give him a shot at college. He revealed in his unpublished memoir, "My older brother and sister were on my side and continually needled my father to send me to Penn State."[1] When his father finally capitulated, he remembered, "Before the words were hardly out of [his] mouth, I was on my way to talk to Dr. [Charles B.] Fager," the principal at Harrisburg Tech, who agreed to advise him through the application process as long as he majored in metallurgy, an art of preparing metals for use, which was the focus of Killinger's academic career while at Tech. He was to become the first in his family to go to college.

The road to Penn State was not easy. Getting accepted was one thing. But having no one in his family to counsel him on how to prepare for college or what to expect upon arrival was just the start of his problems. It must have been a frightening experience for the impetuous youth, particularly since mustering up money to pay for all expenses was a major complication. While tuition for attending an instate college was free, Killinger needed to raise almost $150 a year, which included $10 per week for room and board and contingent fees that amounted to $50 per semester. The three dollars a week earned at his family's hardware store would hardly make a dent in the cost. He needed a better job. Killinger found war-related work at the Harrisburg Pipe and Pipe Bending Works Company, a newly converted factory that produced shrapnel cases and air cylinders to fulfill government demands for war production. It is likely that Dr. Fager helped Killinger obtain the job by reaching out to the general manager, William T. Hildrup. In any event, he spent the summer operating a steel lathe used to make products that would be used for submarine construction and to fill munitions orders from the Allies.[2]

Killinger was also clever in the way he managed to find a place to live on campus. He had friends already at Penn State who were metallurgical engineering students and members of Alpha Chi Sigma, a professional chemistry fraternity founded at the University of Wisconsin in 1902, with a chapter established at State College in April 1911. Since Killinger was enrolling as a major in the chemistry field, he was eligible to pledge the fraternity. His friends helped arrange a room for him at the Alpha Chi Sigma house, but he had to survive pledge week to establish it as his permanent residence.

In subsequent years, doting hometown sportswriters applauded Killinger for his ability to pay for college on his own. "Killinger did not have things so rosy," observed the *Harrisburg Evening News* in December 1921. "It is understood that it was necessary for him to borrow some [money], but this is virtually all paid back." Killinger never revealed who lent him money to offset remaining college expenses. "This is also to his credit," wrote the local newspaper.[3]

Before heading off to college, Killinger spent his evenings playing twilight baseball for the Rosewood Athletic Club. On June 22, he hit a home run in the final inning of a game against Galahad in front of 750 spectators, a considerable crowd for any twilight baseball game.[4]

He was still a firebrand, and the summer baseball league was interrupted on August 26 when Killinger punched out an opposing player near the end of a game against the West End Athletic Club. Rosewood had given up four runs in the first inning and another in the third. His team found themselves in a 5–0 hole heading into the sixth inning, when they scored once. They scored three more runs to mount a rally in the seventh inning. In the bottom of the eighth, down 5–4, Killinger was on first base as the tying run. He was tagged out in a rundown during which he was accused of trying to spike West End's first baseman. Overcome by anger and noticeably embarrassed, Killinger gave him "one hard punch," reported the *Harrisburg Telegraph*.[5]

The fight evidenced one of many routine controversies for Killinger at that point. The episode took place in front of a large crowd, including women and children gathered there to celebrate the West End Carnival and to send off soldiers of Company I to the Western Front. The newspaper refused to give the teenage scalawag a pass. His scrap was the lead in the *Telegraph's* article about the game.

Stories like this fixed Killinger as an enigma. He admired both of his parents and always credited his father for getting him interested in sports, but the household of stern discipline made him a mischief-maker on the streets and playgrounds. Going to college, which coincided with the United States' entry into the war, his family hoped, would help him mature.

• • •

Penn State was founded in 1855, located in Centre County, 90 miles west of Harrisburg, in the exact center of the state. Within seven years, the United States Congress ratified the Morrill Land-Grant Act, and Penn State became Pennsylvania's first land-grant institution. The student body was divided among the schools of agriculture, engineering, liberal arts, natural science, mining, and home economics. Since its inception, the institution was co-educational, with over 200 female enrollees.[6]

Enthusiasm over military enlistment deeply sank enrollment at Penn State after Congress voted to declare war on Germany. Total attendance when the college opened in September 1917 was 2,276, about 400 students short of the registration in 1916. Glenn Killinger was one of 700 freshmen, approximately 60 fewer than the previous year. Despite reduced enrollment, his field of choice, metallurgical engineering, showed "a healthy gain," suggested the *Pittsburgh Gazette Times*, a fact attributed to the wartime demand for technically trained men as the conflict carried on.[7]

Penn State's metallurgical program—officially called the Department of Industrial and Manufacturing Engineering—was the first of its kind in the United States. Many considered it the most rigorous degree that a student could attain in college. Killinger worked hard and enjoyed the tutelage of Robert Lemuel Sackett, one of the most distinguished members of the faculty. Writing years later to a friend, he admitted that no Killinger is destined to ever bring home remarkable grades. No one can ever take away the fact that he enrolled in one of the most respected and rigorous majors academia had to offer. "He took up one of the most difficult courses at the institution, that of metallurgy," wrote the sports editor of the *Harrisburg Telegraph*. "And in his studies his marks have been high."[8]

Despite the accolade bestowed on him by his doting hometown newspaper, Killinger had grades that were actually nothing to write home about. His final transcript was full of Cs and Ds. Of the 72 courses he enrolled in during his four and a half years at Penn State—many of which were one-credit workshops, research laboratories, and wartime required courses—he earned only one A and 19 Bs.[9] Still, the ability to juggle three intercollegiate sports and a myriad of college courses was quite a feat.

Killinger's first official day at Penn State was September 10, 1917, three days before his 19th birthday. "When I first stepped on the Penn State campus, I imagined I was in Heaven. The first and greatest event had succesfuly [sic] taken place in my life," he wrote nostalgically in his memoir.[10] He spent most of his time the first few weeks pledging Alpha Chi Sigma. "We were subjected to all kinds of hazing," he noted. Killinger and the pledges were forced to perform menial jobs around the frat house, including shoveling soft coal into the furnace late hours into the night. One evening, pledges were pelted in the face with eggs and rotten fruit as they marched single file out of the frat house and were led to the center of town, where they were told to storm into the movie theater without purchasing tickets. "The few policemen were helpless and wisely offered no resistance," he recounted.[11] While generally hot-tempered and brazen, Killinger remained obedient as he was forced one night to go on coal walks over a series of bonfires while being paddled by the frat brothers.

The hazing lasted just three weeks. And as time wore on, Killinger's frat brothers accepted him into Alpha Chi Sigma. He ended up bunking with James Porter Harris, a longtime friend of Killinger's older brother from Harrisburg and a senior agricultural chemistry major.[12]

In reality, Killinger was most excited about trying out for Penn State's football team. There was so much about the game he loved. The hard hits. The element of savagery. He was not quite ready to let the game go just because he was in college. All first year student-athletes at Penn State were forced to adhere to the "one-year rule" which prevented freshmen from playing varsity sports. This rule was not enforced at every college in the country—and would not be for another ten years. But at Penn State in 1906, the athletic department had voted to prohibit its freshman from playing varsity sports. So on September 11, about two weeks later than usual because of the new regulations produced by the nation's wartime environment, Killinger set out for freshmen football tryouts.

Penn State's football team was coached by Richard C. "Dick" Harlow, an alumnus who shined as an offensive tackle in 1911 and 1912, and in addition received varsity letters in baseball and track and field. A boxer from Philadelphia, Harlow became Penn State's football coach in 1915, replacing William M. Hollenback. As the Penn State program floundered under Hollenback in 1913, finishing with two wins and six losses, Harlow joined the staff as the line coach in 1914. His contribution is credited for Penn State's respectable 5–3 finish that year. "Much of the credit for last year's success belongs to him, for it was through his coaching that the line, which was State's strong point, was developed," said the *Harrisburg Star-Independent*.[13]

Upon receiving the Penn State job, Harlow, a sturdy 27-year-old with an already balding head, broad shoulders with no visible neck, implemented an entirely new system—a system that Killinger would make special note of decades later when he was coaching at West Chester State Teachers' College. Harlow adhered to the college's one-year residency rule for freshmen and transfers, and a full-year player supervision program in which he would have full charge of all football players' activities during the school year.[14]

Harlow hired two powerful assistants. His backfield coach on the varsity was Lawrence A. "Bud" Whitney, a former captain of Dartmouth's football team who excelled on the Ivy League school's basketball and track teams. He was also a member of the 1912 Olympic team, which presented him the chance to compete alongside Killinger's hero Jim Thorpe in Stockholm, Sweden. Harlow's freshman coach was Burke "Dutch" Hermann, who doubled as the head varsity basketball coach.

Both the varsity and freshman teams were highly successful during Harlow's tenure. The Blue and White varsity had finished 7–2 and 8–2 in 1915 and 1916, respectively. The freshman teams led by Hermann finished 6–0–1 and 7–0 during that span. The outlook for each team in 1917, however, was in question. The football team was heavily hit by the departure of many players to the service. Just three of 18 varsity lettermen and nine of 16 freshmen from the 1916 teams tried out for Harlow's new wartime unit. An additional setback came when backfield coach Whitney and freshman boss Hermann both left to enter the service two weeks before the start of the season. The 1917 Penn State Blue and White looked totally depleted from the outside. At the start of the season, the *New York Tribune* called the team "scant, light and inexperienced." Harlow and his squad embraced the assessment by dubbing the 1917 season the "war-time football adventure."[15]

The call for troops had hit every other American college devastatingly hard too. A combination of patriotic fervor and voluntary enlistment compelled Harvard, Yale, and Princeton, college football's leading exponents in addition to West Point and Annapolis, to announce the cancelation of all sports that autumn.[16] Though each university and military academy would eventually bring back football in the 11th hour, most colleges and universities had equal trouble trying to field a team. And yet, individual collegians who answered the call found new opportunities to fulfill their athletic interests at military installations throughout the United States. In the summer before the start of the 1917 fall sports season, the United States War Department took measures to offer organized football, in addition to boxing, wrestling, and baseball, to drafted and enlisted soldiers stationed at a plethora of the country's army and navy camps. In short, the intercollegiate football season would continue as scheduled, but with several modifications to suit wartime necessities. While big and small colleges across the country had rosters cut and game schedules shortened, the War Department oversaw actions to established service sports at each base which offered its servicemen a much-desired leisure activity, while instilling a necessary must-win spirit within soldiers who would soon see the battlefield on the Western Front.

According to sports historian James Mennell, service football programs "can be traced to a military sex scandal during 1916." After Pancho Villa's deadly attacks on civilian populations in towns along the Mexican border, National Guardsmen were ordered to Fort Sam Houston in Texas to help defend the border. With nothing to do during free time, the young Guardsmen promenaded into town, Mennell writes, "to look for fun, but found venereal disease and cheap alcohol instead."[17] As the rate of servicemen who had contracted some form of sexually transmitted infection increased, Secretary of War Newton D. Baker appointed former New York police chief Raymond Fosdick to serve as chairman of the Commission on Training Camp Activities, a role that compelled him to investigate the living conditions at every American army and navy installation. After studying several camp towns in the United States and the Canadian and British army training systems, Fosdick urged the War Department to arrange "clean entertainments and amusements" to maintain the health and well-being of the soldiers.[18]

Before the autumn sports seasons began, Fosdick's committee announced that service sports teams would be implemented at each military installation. Grantland Rice wrote a column that ran in newspapers throughout the country supporting the measure: "The soldier in fine physical condition, used to long walks or hard exercise, may not have a soft and dapple time of it in war, but compared to the citizen who has never trained the athlete's way is replete with roses and velvet."[19] Soldiers shook the countryside with hurrahs to celebrate this call to sports. The necessary appropriations for service teams in football, boxing, baseball, hockey, wrestling, track, and basketball were made through the Army and Navy Departments to cover the cost of equipment for each sport. Fosdick appointed Joseph Raycroft, a Princeton University physical education professor, Athletic Director for the Army, and Walter Camp, former Yale standout and coach turned pre-eminent football authority, Athletic Director for the Navy. The two men were tasked with appointing athletic directors at every army and navy encampment and to craft game schedules.

In 1917, military teams generally scheduled intercompany clashes—similar to a branch campus playing a game against the team from the original university or college, or one branch campus would going toe to toe with another. In other words, Army would play Army, Navy would play Navy, or Army would play Navy.[20] Fifteen cantonments for the national army and navy established service football teams in 1917 and 1918, including the New England National Guard camp in Massachusetts; Camp Wheeler in Macon, Georgia; Camp Hancock of Augusta, Georgia; Camp Upton in Yaphank, Long Island; Camp Pike in Little Rock, Arkansas; Camp Sherman in Hamilton, Ohio; Camp Meade in Maryland; Camp Dix of Wrightstown, New Jersey; Camp Funston in Fort Riley, Kansas; Camp Wadsworth of Spartanburg, South Carolina; Camp Shelby at Hattiesburg, Mississippi; Wissahickon Naval Barracks in Cape May, New Jersey; Great Lakes Naval Station near Chicago, Illinois; Bremerton Navy Station outside of Seattle, Washington; and Camp Lee of Petersburg, Virginia.[21] Some camp teams were lucky to schedule Red Cross benefit games against opponents from the intercollegiate football association. For instance, Princeton, once reluctant to field a team, elected to schedule just two games that fall against Army's Fort Dix and Navy's Wissahickon Barracks, the two military installations in New Jersey. Penn State, meanwhile, opened its season in 1917 with a 10–0 decision over the Army Ambulance Corps of Allentown, Pennsylvania, a team that featured two former Penn State players, Ben Cubbage and Clarence Beck, while the University of Pittsburgh ended its national championship run that year with a 30–0 victory over the service team from Camp Lee.[22] A year later it would become easier for army and navy service teams to schedule games against regular varsity opponents. And those games would be played for more than just charity.

Fosdick was excited about his service sports programs. He said, "there will be more real and widespread athletic activity in this country during the next twelve months than ever before in our lifetime."[23] He explained that each cantonment consisted of anywhere between 15,000 and 40,000 troops. The training camps, Fosdick said, "will be sizeable cities in themselves, and the need for social and relaxational [sic] facilities is going to tax the efforts of all those of us who are interested in providing a sane, well rounded life for the men in the camps."[24]

Each sport was designed to train soldiers in battlefield survival skills. Historian Steven W. Pope described Fosdick's service sports program as superlative for preparing recruits for frontline combat. Baseball throwing fundamentals were good for grenade tossing. Wrestling maneuvers helped with hand-to-hand combat. Gymnastic skills like scaling, balancing, jumping, and vaulting helped out in the trenches. "The greatest attention," Pope described, "was given to boxing as a training for bayonet fighting."[25] An added emphasis was placed on pugilism since the sport was illegal in most places in the country, and most soldiers were being taught the basics of close-range combat for the first time.

Joseph Raycroft's public statement in defense of service sports reaffirmed Fosdick's initiative. While speaking directly about boxing, the Army Athletic Director said any criticisms of boxing as a method to teach bayonet fighting "are based upon ignorance of both bayonet fighting and military boxing." Raycroft told Fosdick the conscripts lacked "self-reliance," "courage," "quick thinking," and "quick decisions under fire" since they had "little or no experience in physical contact games" prior to entering the service. An influx of white middle-class soldiers, many of them privileged youths, had never been in a fight in their lives. Bayonet training, in other words, was needed for "speed, endurance and skill in handling the weapon." The problem, Raycroft illustrated, was that "in the nature of things there can be no practice contests with the bayonets." Boxing, Raycroft concluded, "furnishes a means of training men to keep their heads and to carry out an effective plan of attack." Qualities needed in a bayonet fighter could be developed by means of boxing "to an extent and with a rapidity that is impossible in any other plan of training thus for tried."[26]

Football was deemed the most popular service sport to play by both army and navy cadets. However, owing to the considerable expenses needed for outfitting football players with equipment, Fosdick initially doubted that the game could be implemented as a service sport until the YMCA, Knights of Columbus, and the Red Cross provided generous financial donations specifically so military installations could carry football teams.[27] Citing courage, pluck, strength, speed, agility, and the ability to think quickly under pressure, Walter Camp claimed, "No sport is quite so closely allied to modern warfare as football."[28] From his own experiences playing and coaching football, and with his new perspective as the commissioner of service sports at navy camps throughout the country, Camp understood the importance of using football to give American soldiers an advantage overlooked by other warring nations. "If anyone were to ask a commander what qualities he wished in the body of men he was about to train for war," he explicated, "he would repeat, in a great measure, the above football requirements."[29]

Once established, the trouble with service football was that the resulting military teams would lack the skill and proficiency of traditional intercollegiate teams. Camp resisted all entreaties against service football: he claimed that since all service teams would have veterans "from former college gridirons, if properly coached, will have been shaped into formidable organizations." He observed that thousands of current and former college football players were already in the service. Wherever a cantonment has "a fair nucleus" of star athletes, Camp said, "it will be possible to build up with the other material and by coaching develop a strong aggregation."[30] That is exactly what occurred. The service football team gathered at Camp Sherman in Ohio had six former Walter Camp All-Americans on its roster.[31] The Army Ambulance Corps featured the University of Pennsylvania's star fullback and intercollegiate decathlon champion, Joe Berry. The result was something unparalleled in American sports culture.

Never before did so many Americans play and pay attention to football, noted *Outlook* magazine. "In every army cantonment," the magazine's editor explained, "footballs were as thick as pumpkins in an autumn cornfield."[32] Mennell suggests that service football in 1917 helped the sport become the foremost game played and watched by American citizens in the decade following World War I. "Not only was service football winning new civilian fans for football," he writes, "but it also had a significant impact on thousands of soldiers and sailors." For one thing, service football teams were actually star-studded, owing to transfers and training deployments. He added: "This quality of play had not been expected when the season began."[33]

While the combination of dominant performances by large college teams and the pageantry of all-star service teams put the public's interest in the gridiron game at fever pitch, some might argue that new rules passed between 1906 and 1917, many of which were discussed in Chapter 2, made football more enjoying for spectators. Rule changes after the player safety crises of 1905 and 1909 banned mass and momentum plays, designed to make the game safer. Allowing the modern form of snapping between the legs (rather than rolling the ball to the quarterback with a foot), forward passes, and gimmicks opened offensive systems up for more exciting and crowd-pleasing action. Additional rules designed to improve the game were passed just before America's entry into the war; they included a touchback on kickoffs, two points for a safety, and penalties for pass interference and roughing the kicker.[34] This was a radical paradigm shift in football, which previously featured middle wedges, something that 21st century coaches describe as "three yards and a cloud of dust" plays that usually left fans bored. One year after the forward-pass rule was implemented, Illinois threw 30 completions against Northwestern and the University of Chicago connected on 21 passes against Purdue. That same year, the Pop Warner–like Carlisle Indians upset the University of Minnesota, 12–10, after connecting on two touchdown passes. The Oklahoma Sooners, led by one-armed coach Bennie Owen, averaged 35 forward passes a game in 1913. Historian David M. Nelson calls Owen "the founding father of the forward-pass tradition in the Southwest." In the early 1910s, Notre Dame obtained national prominence for its exciting forward-passing offense. Nelson writes in *The Anatomy of a Game*, "The 1913 Army–Notre Dame game provided the forward pass the biggest one-game promotion ever recorded before or since." The historic contest featured Irish quarterback Gus Dorais completing 14 of 17 pass attempts, connecting most of the time with chemistry major Knute Rockne, in Notre Dame's dominant 35–13 victory. For all the attention the introduction of the forward pass has received for its benefits to offensive play, it was just as rewarding to the defensive unit in these early years. For every touchdown pass completed in 1913, Nelson explains, "two forward passes were intercepted for touchdowns." A notable addition to the football rulebook came in 1916 when the rules committee, led by Walter Camp and Amos Alonzo Stagg, co-authored "The Football Code." The code aimed to make football a "distinctively academic game—the game of the schools and the colleges." The code, Nelson writes, "maintained high standards of sportsmanship." Also in 1916, placekicking replaced the dropkick as the method of kicking a point after touchdown or a field goal.[35]

Sports revisionists agree that football's popularity cannot be credited to the rule changes, but to the war. Their assertions are substantiated by a *New York Times* editorial that claimed, "football owes more to the war in the way of the spread of the spirit of the game than it does ten or twenty years of development in the period before the war."[36] Walter Camp corroborated the *Times* editorial when he said, "A great deal has been said about the football season of 1917 being like the play of Hamlet with the omission of Hamlet. But as matters progress, it is very evident that this fall will see more football played probably than any other year for a long time."[37]

Amidst all of these wartime transitions that warned him of a looming hell on earth, Glenn Killinger arrived on campus that fall inspired by the prospect of making the freshman team. Practice began as scheduled on September 11. Killinger, now about 5'7" and weighing 140 pounds, was eager to prove himself. "I reported to the Old Track House where the two squads dressed," he recalled years later. "Just as I arrived, Dick Rauch, a Harrisburg native on the varsity squad, came out of the dressing quarters and I hailed him." After being asked how to obtain a uniform, Rauch looked over Killinger "with disapproving eyes" and told him to find the team manager.[38]

Bill Martin was the man Killinger was looking for. Martin was an intransigent Penn Stater known for his scrupulous management of the football program. He was spotted resting under the shade of a tree waiting for practice to begin. Killinger moved close to Martin and asked about being fitted for equipment. Martin steadied his gaze straight ahead, watching a few of the players who had gathered early on the practice field. Sitting idly, he responded, "wait until practice is over."[39]

Milling about nervously and clearly self-conscious, Killinger paced, arms crossed, sizing up each player as the team filed out of the locker room. "Most of the squads were big and burly," he recalled, "all but a few needing a shave." His pacing settled. Killinger now stood there petrified, wondering why he believed that he could actually become one of those pseudo-gladiators. He conceded, "my ambition to play football diminished rapidly." Not long into practice, Coach Harlow divided players into two teams for a physical 20-minute intra-squad scrimmage.[40] After a few minutes, Killinger decided that he no longer wanted any part of playing football at Penn State. He confessed, "I walked away from the field and had no further desire to obtain a uniform that year."[41] He spent the fall as a supporter.

Harlow's varsity 11 eventually finished with five wins and four losses. It was a respectable record considering that it was the first year that intercollegiate football was played during wartime. Penn State proved to have one of the nation's most potent offensive units. It racked up high-scoring victories of 80–0 over Gettysburg College, 99–0 over St. Bonaventure, and 57–0 against Maryland State College.[42] Meanwhile, the Blue and White freshman 11 dominated its opponents by finishing the fall with a 7–0–1 record. The yearlings' season was highlighted by an overall scoring margin of 291 points to three. It was clear that Killinger would not have made a difference on the season. Self-consciously, he admitted, "[I] hid from the manager for the rest of that year for fear of being asked why I did not remain to pick up a uniform."[43]

5

War Season

In 1925, comedian Harold Lloyd's silent film, *The Freshman*, offered a rare combination of football and college lore as the actor played an imprudent and obnoxious college freshman named Harold Lamb, who tries to make his way onto the varsity football team at fictitious Tate University. The film begins with Lamb in his bedroom, gazing longingly at a poster of a made-up movie titled "The College Hero" pinned on his wall. While eager to leave home, Lamb is the first in his family to go to college. Accordingly, he endures fits of anxiety about what may come of his future. No one in his family could tell him what the college experience will be like. He deals with the uneasiness by mimicking the personality of the movie's protagonist, Lester Laurel, down to the varsity letter cardigan, moxie, and playful jig he performs when meeting peers on campus. The character Lamb even gives himself Laurel's nickname, "Speedy." The movie's second part dramatizes student life on a college campus, where Lamb naively becomes a laughingstock among his peers.

Harold Lloyd biographer Annette D'Agostino Lloyd (no relation) called *The Freshman* unique in "personifying the comedy of embarrassment like, perhaps, no film has ever." While explicitly subjective—her passion for the subject is apparent—her point about Lloyd's comedic originality could be argued. Throughout the film, Harold "Speedy" Lamb is humiliated and hazed "at the hands of both fellow students and faculty," she writes, adding, "It is hard not to cringe when you see all the things that happen to Speedy in his quest for the golden ring of popularity."[1] In the film, he is often teased, shoved to the ground, and conspired against. In the middle of *The Freshman*, Lamb is mocked for trying out for the football team. When he breaks the tackling equipment used during tryouts for the varsity football team, Lamb is forced to stand in as the tackle dummy. He becomes the laughingstock of the entire college when the team captain convinces the coach to make him water boy while letting him think he has earned a spot on the roster. Lamb never realizes he is being ridiculed.[2]

The theme of the film would be that of a can-do spirit, which, like Glenn

Killinger's life, embodies the great American Horatio Alger promise. "The idea was simply that the Boy had an obsession," Harold Lloyd wrote years later, "to go to college and be the most popular boy there." Lamb's problem was that he had no idea that the way he was behaving to become popular was all wrong, "so it got him in trouble," explained Lloyd.³ That view can be seen in Lloyd's other films. Movie historian Steven Winer writes of Lloyd's anthology: "In *Safety Last* (1923), he wants to succeed in the city. In *Girl Shy* (1924), he wants to succeed as a writer/lover. In the sound film *Movie Crazy* (1932), his dream is to become a movie star." In all of these films, Winer says, "by a combination of will and determination, he achieves these goals."⁴

The fact that this movie debuted in the mid-'20s does not remove suspicion that Lloyd's character, Harold Lamb, strikingly resembles the life and college experience of Glenn Killinger, an undersized and middling footballer who was cut from his high school's varsity team, but, with a mound of good fortune, became the Nittany Lions' All-American quarterback four years before the release of *The Freshman*. Both the fictional character Lamb and real-life Killinger were the first in their respective families to go to college. Moreover, they both understood that going to college during this era was not so much about enhancing intellectual skills at all. According to sports historian Benjamin G. Rader, attending college during the first quarter of the 20th century was a means of "achieving a [higher] social position." A degree from an institute of higher learning was "a passport to high society."⁵ It was just the thing that unsophisticated and credulous tenderfoots like Lamb and Killinger needed in order to become part of the national upper class. Down to the lifelong dream of becoming the star football player and most popular man on campus, Killinger and Lamb share this unique, albeit comedic bond during a time the nation craved heroes.

The Freshman draws another conspicuous comparison to the fledging Penn State footballer. In the movie's final scene—the big rivalry game filmed on November 22, 1924, at the Berkeley Bowl at the University of California–Berkeley in front of an actual crowd of about 90,000 spectators gathered to watch a real game between Stanford and California—Lamb becomes the star, thus the college's hero, when his coach is forced to give him a uniform and insert him into the game because too many of Tate's players had sustained game-ending injuries and the bungling coach ran out of substitutes.⁶ Lamb's performance during the game is mediocre, at best. He is knocked unconscious several times. He misses blocking assignments and fails to bring down opposing ball carriers. However, on the last play of the game, Lamb, sporting Lloyd's signature shell-rimmed goggles, knocks the football loose from an opposing ball carrier, picks up the fumble and weaves his way down the field for the winning touchdown. In the end, Lamb becomes the college's hero and wins over the affection of the much sought after darling, played by Jobyna Ralston, an actress who co-starred as Lloyd's love interest in six movies, including *Why Worry?* (1923) and *Girl Shy*. He is carried away on the shoulders of adoring fans and hailed as the savior of Tate University.[7]

Not only has the film been hailed for generating enthusiasm for movies based on sophomoric pranks; it is, in some ways, reflective of Killinger's first and last years at Penn State crammed into Harold Lamb's freshman year. In fact, Lamb's mental and physical transformation at the hands of upperclassmen bullies gives him incentive to persevere through the hard hits that knocked him out cold more than once during the final scene of the film. But what *The Freshman* does best for the narrative of Killinger is embrace the spirit of the American Dream while suggesting that sports is a mechanism that can create social mobility. Silent film historian Donald McCaffrey suggests that Harold Lamb's rise to social acceptance "seems to be centered on the achievement of success through an unusual way (which is thus comic in nature)—through luck and determination and not through any particular skill." *The Freshman*, McCaffrey continues, is the "embodiment of the social forces that keep Harold Lamb an outcast." A line might be drawn here between the attitude of the college students who mock Lamb throughout the film and the troubles of middle-class Americans laboring in a capitalist society that does not guarantee rewards of a better life one day. The thing that keeps Lamb striving for popularity comes from his obsession with his love interest, Peggy. This notion is no different from a middle-class American powered by the possibility that a better life could be created for one's children.[8] From this synopsis, it can be argued that the chase for a combination of social acceptance while in pursuit of the material are inherited characteristics of real life '20s-era athletes like Glenn Killinger, who would soon find his chance to play varsity sports as the United States of America engaged with Germany in World War I. To understand each theme presented in *The Freshman*—issues related to the Horatio Alger myth, anxiety, ridicule, acceptance, attaining popularity through athletic feats—it is necessary to know and appreciate the life of Glenn Killinger, who is, arguably, the best example of an ambitious yet disadvantaged athlete that reached the apex of intercollegiate sports and the summit of fame in American sports culture.

Just like the young chap in *The Freshman*, Killinger's body began to mature by the winter of his freshman year. "I had grown almost two inches in height and gained about 15 lbs," he later noted. And fortunately, his class schedule, which ended by three o'clock every day was, in his words, "rather light." A young man with a lot of time on his hands, little interest in studying, and an urge to fulfill his competitive desires, he often went to the Armory, where the gymnasium was located, to play pick-up basketball or to wrestle. It wasn't quite wrestling season yet, but Killinger found himself surrounded by members of the team working out. "The wrestlers needed bodies to practice their skills," he explained. Penn State's 125-pound champion, Dave Detar, invited Killinger to wrestle with him. "I bashfully refused," he confessed. Detar hardly cared. He grabbed Killinger's arm and jerked him to the mat. Much like Tate University's football players using Harold Lamb as their tackle dummy, Killinger was used as Detar's sparring partner. "He gave me a thorough going-over," Killinger recalled nostalgically. He continued his sessions with Deter almost daily in 1917 and 1918. He said, "I credit wrestling with helping me get mentally tough and lose all fear of physical contact."[9]

Killinger's new physique and toughness was on display that winter as one of seven members of Penn State's freshman basketball squad. Still, as one of the unlikeliest members of the team, he had to prove himself. His action was limited in pre-season play as the freshman team often scrimmaged against the varsity. Killinger persisted and found himself starting at left guard by the first game of the season. "I learned about rough basketball as the varsity [often] gave us a good going-over, especially under the baskets," he said. "I learned to protect myself and return the rough tactics of the varsity."[10]

With Killinger as a contributing force at guard, the first-year men coasted to one of the most successful freshman seasons in years at the college. Much of their success was due to scheduling limitations placed upon the nation's colleges by the wartime modifications. Most of Penn State's freshman games were scheduled against area preparatory and high schools. When the season ended in March with a victory over Lafayette High School, Killinger had become a primary scorer on the team.[11]

His performance did not go unnoticed. During one of the final scrimmages of the season between the varsity and freshman teams, Coach Harlow stood in the corner of the gym, impressed by Killinger's refusal to back down from the bigger varsity players. "Harlow talked with me after practice and invited me to come out for spring football practice," he recalled. Of course the young acolyte said yes.

It was on Penn State's basketball court that Killinger gained the confidence he needed to compete on a college level. In this environment, he was removed from both the traditional Allison Hill setting, where people expected from him a certain behavior, and from the playing fields of his old high school, where opponents from rival schools held little respect for him. At Penn State, no one knew who he was. His durability was less of a factor in being selected for a team. He displayed poise and passion for team victories rather than the self-absorbed reputation that once characterized him.

He took his new attitude with him to the gridiron in March to participate in Coach Harlow's spring football practices. There was considerable opportunity for Killinger to prove himself at spring camp because Penn State's roster was still bleeding for reasons of enlistment. A number of expected returnees to Harlow's lineup had chosen to take an active hand in the war. Among those who turned up in the spring were four returning lettermen, the 15 who made up the previous season's freshman team, and non-scholarship walk-ons like Killinger.

Killinger, of course, could play better and run faster than most. He just needed an opportunity to be taken seriously, and this was the perfect time. With a depleted roster, he seized the moment. For two weeks, he ran around the football field perfecting offensive and defensive drills, participating in inter-squad scrimmages, and learning Harlow's system. "I also learned that I could take the rough tackles with ease," he wrote in his memoir, "I actually enjoyed the physical contact."[12] He spent most of his time at halfback that spring, responsible for taking or faking handoffs from youth sensation Charlie Way, a swift-footed athlete who turned out to be Penn State's most pleasant surprise of the previous season.

Way, a sophomore electro-chemical engineering major from Coatesville, Pennsylvania, was able to earn the starting job at quarterback at the midway point of the 1917 season. Despite his small build—he stood 5'7", 140 pounds—he became a consistent force for the Blue and White when, in the last 30 seconds of the West Virginia–Wesleyan game, he picked up a punt and ran 45 yards through the opponent's coverage for a touchdown. The miraculous play resulted in a one-point, 8–7 victory. When the 1917 season ended, the school yearbook illuminated how people in State College were excited about "the uncovering of a sensation in the form of diminutive Charlie Way."[13] There was no way of knowing at that point, but Way and Killinger were on the verge of establishing an enduring bond in the form of dual All-American honors and a lifelong friendship.

Killinger's moment on the gridiron that spring was fleeting. But it was for good reason. He wanted to prove to Coach Harlow that he was serious about playing football, but he also possessed a deep desire to play baseball, the sport that he excelled at more than any other, and it was quite possible that he could make the freshman nine. So earlier that spring he cut a deal with Harlow, who was once a multi-sport athlete at Penn State and would clearly understand. Killinger vowed that he would do as much as he could at spring football practices, but once baseball season commenced in April, he would turn in his equipment. At that point, Coach Harlow would let him know if he would be needed for the football team in the fall.

As planned, in April, Killinger departed from the football team to report to Coach Dick Harley's baseball training camp. This brief time spent with the football squad made the right impression on the Penn State coach. Killinger later recalled that Harlow told him to "report early in September, 1918, for fall football practice."[14]

• • •

5. War Season

While Killinger was reinventing himself, the overall atmosphere at Penn State was overwhelmingly hawkish. The war hit student life pretty hard. There were 1,513 former and current Penn State students training in the various military camps across the East Coast and amid the throes of combat by the end of the school term.[15] This fact came to occupy more and more of Killinger's attention, especially as the fighting in Europe continued to escalate. On the eve of spring training, the Germans mounted the first of five major offensives on the western front. The world was just weeks away from witnessing American troops face off against the Germans at Chateau-Thierry.

Within weeks of the deadly battle, colleges and universities across the country were taking measures more suitable for the wartime demands. Penn State joined 21 other Pennsylvania colleges in shortening the spring semester. Instead of the traditional five-month term ending with commencement in June, Penn State had moved up the end of the semester to April 23.[16] Baseball at Penn State, like all of the other spring sports, accordingly suffered because of the accommodations.

The athletic department at State College chose not to abandon the spring sports season altogether, but instead devised abridged schedules. The track and field season was abbreviated, albeit with a lot of success. Penn State squeezed in one of the best wrestling seasons in the school's history before the semester ended. The athletic department was able to maintain only one game for the baseball team. So in April, the baseball coach proceeded with spring training in preparation for Penn State's lone game against Carnegie Tech, scheduled for April 24, the day after the term was to expire.

There would be no freshman baseball club in 1918. As far as the rules were concerned, the one-year rule barring freshmen from varsity competition applied to baseball as it did every other sport at Penn State. So when Killinger showed up for baseball tryouts, he did so to impress the coach, while also hoping to earn a seat in the dugout for the varsity game against Carnegie Tech.

It is unclear how difficult it was for Killinger to make the ball club. Evidence suggests the baseball roster was as depleted as any other sport at State College. The turnout likely did not matter; baseball was the sport that he was most comfortable playing. He had proven himself among the best in Harrisburg's considerably competitive Allison Hill League, which featured many collegiate baseball players. That confidence helped him prove his mettle in front of Coach Harley. The week before Penn State's one and only game, he was told to play second base on the practice squad.[17]

Killinger enjoyed his view from the dugout as he watched Penn State defeat Carnegie Tech. The headline of the *Philadelphia Evening Public Ledger* announced, "Penn State Plays Season in Single Day." It reported, "Penn State opened and closed its baseball season here yesterday with a victory over the Carnegie Tech nine by the score of 6 to 3."[18]

After the game, Killinger and his teammates were forced to return to their homes without certainty about the future. The college was closed until September 25.

• • •

Understandably, everything about the spring, summer, and fall in 1918 was overshadowed by the war. Voluntary enlistment seemed to be ubiquitous, especially among those in close proximity to Killinger. "Many of the students enlisted in the armed forces at the conclusion of the school year," he explained.[19] His friends in Harrisburg also took up arms. He was not persuaded by the departure of his friends. He remained respectful of his mother's wishes by choosing not to volunteer.

The only benefit Killinger could see from the abrupt end to his freshman year was the chance to return home in time for the start of the city's amateur baseball season. He spent his summer days in one of two locations, the factory of the Harrisburg Pipe and Pipe Bending Works Company, where he retained his defense job, and the baseball diamond on the corner of Seventeenth and Chestnut Streets, where he played baseball in the Allison Hill League. He returned to play for the Rosewood Athletic Club, which his brother Earl was serving as player-manager. "Some of the best athletes in the city have been picked to represent the Rosewoods," one local newspaper reported. Rosewood, however, "received a severe blow" when two of Killinger's friends, "Snowball" Winters and, arguably the team's best player, Warren Lyme, took up arms to serve.[20]

Rosewood opened the season with an 8–6 victory over Hick-A-Thrift, a club carrying Carl Beck, a schoolboy god considered by many as the most popular sports figure in the city of Harrisburg. Beck came from a family of successful athletic boys who all attended Killinger's alma mater, the Harrisburg Technical High School. Beck was already called "a second 'Jim' Thrope [sic]" by the local media for his prowess in football, baseball, and track and field.[21] In the Allison Hill League season opener, Beck's two hits and one run in the box score looked slightly better than Killinger's one hit, one run, and stolen base. But Killinger got the last word when Rosewood secured the win. The victory was the first of many, as Rosewood fought for the 1918 Allison Hill League pennant.

Along with Earl, Glenn Killinger made a notable impression on the fans during the summer. "When it comes to knocking out the ball," wrote one local sportswriter with enthusiasm, "those brothers Glenn and Earl are surely killing'er." The brothers provided the twilight league with more fans than ever at the Allison Hill grounds. A clear distraction from the events taking place in Europe, crowds between 700 and 1,500 packed onto the empty grass for each game. Rosewood's games were especially crammed with supporters. The

Harrisburg Telegraph said of the Killingers' following: "No team in the league shows more 'pep' than the *Killinger crowd*."[22]

The absence of two starters from Rosewood's lineup because of military demands forced Earl and Glenn to play several positions throughout the summer. Especially early on, it was important to find the right rotation as Rosewood fought to keep pace with Reading for the division lead. While usually a second baseman, Glenn also played shortstop, first base, and catcher. Earl was typically the team's catcher, but he sometimes pitched. Both brothers hit well all season and were notorious base runners. At the season's midpoint, Earl maintained the league-leading batting average at .526. Killinger held steady at 12th, with a .388 average.[23] At nine wins and seven losses, Rosewood found themselves in second place, four games behind Reading. That was when Killinger and his Rosewood teammates really caught fire. In a game against Reading on July 18, he hit a three-run home run in the sixth inning to lead Rosewood to a 10–4 victory, which helped to move his team within a game of first place.[24] When the season closed on July 26, Rosewood and Reading were tied for first place with identical 15–9 records.

A best-of-three game series was arranged by the Allison Hill board of directors to decide the pennant. A media circus surrounded the game. Pictures of each team appeared in the *Telegraph* on July 30. Announcements were made throughout the city informing fans that a Red Cross benefit was planned for the game. And stat sheets about the lineups for each club were published in the newspaper.

The newspaper reported that "no less than 2,500 people" came to watch the post-season series. With help from Earl, who threw out two base runners attempting to steal second base in game one and batted .275 for the series, Rosewood was able to sweep Reading by scores of 2–1 and 2–0. Rosewood's two pitchers—"Lefty" Landis of West Virginia University and John Jones of Villanova University—received most of the credit for the victories. But it was Glenn Killinger's performance that turned out to be the main course to his productivity throughout the summer. By batting .750 for the series, and without committing any errors, Killinger became the difference for Rosewood in the title games. Especially in game two, with the scored tied 0–0, Killinger hit a triple to center field in the top of the sixth to drive in the game's only two runs.[25]

This time around, as Rosewood team members and their fans took to celebrating the city championship, Killinger looked like somebody who genuinely cared about his team. When the August 7 edition of the *Telegraph* printed a picture of the Rosewood pennant club, Killinger was found standing in the back row, arms crossed, hat on straight, shoulders back, and eclipsed by the 6'3" Villanova slab artist-phenom, John Jones.[26]

Killinger had moved beyond his boyhood dream of playing in the professional leagues. He learned that to get the most out of football, basketball, and baseball, he had to play for the love of each game. His early tests at Penn State, combined with his observations of what the war was doing to the community at large, was central to his emerging view of organized sports. He came to look at football, basketball, and baseball as competitions between two teams instead of individual tests of will. There were moments in the course of a game when Killinger knew he had to face off in a one-on-one battle; there would be situations on a football field when he had to call a play to give himself the ball, and times on a court that he would have to dribble around the opponent guarding him to score a bucket, and tests in baseball when he would narrow his focus to a head-to-head showdown between himself and the pitcher. He came to believe, after those moments of individualism, that the single way to be great was to help his teammates become better players, which would consequentially make the team great. Decades later, in the midst of his Hall of Fame coaching career at West Chester State Teachers' College, he often said the key to the team's success was for each player to "play hard, play fair, and above all, want to play."[27] It was a creed he developed early in the throes of war clouds.

• • •

When America's war in Europe entered its 16th month in August 1918, the United States War Department announced the establishment of a new division of the Army to consist of college undergraduates: the Student Army Training Corps. There had previously been two methods by which a man could enter the Armed Forces. He might enlist as a volunteer in the Army or the Navy, or he might carry on in civilian life until chosen by the draft after the age of 21. At that moment, Glenn Killinger only had one option if he wanted to serve, which was to enlist voluntarily. Yet he was forced to submit to the demands of his dovish parents. He was still too young for the draft, so he watched many of his friends from Harrisburg and State College enter the national services earlier that winter and spring.

An overwhelming number of colleges and universities across the country had depleted enrollment numbers. "Uncle Sam was hard put to supply man power for the final drive to win the war," Killinger would later remember of his wartime experience.[28] By fall, no one could guess when the war would end. The volume of college-age enlistees multiplying during the 1918–1919 school terms was inevitable. Fittingly, the War Department feared that if students continued to leave college before graduating, it would lead to a disaster both overseas and on the home front; the Army was without skilled personnel or capable officers. The *Washington Post* suggested these men would be of "far greater value" to the army if persuaded "to complete their college courses and qualify for work as engineers, chemists, physicians, or other services."[29]

Additionally, the War Department acknowledged the need for educated men with "college training" to fill vital roles in the work force once the war came to an end.

In an effort to undercut the bleeding, the War Department created the Student Army Training Corps to offer a third option for entering the service. By 20th-century standards, this military training program was unprecedented, an untested experiment in preventing students from exiting college too early by offering a fast track to Officer Training School, money for college, and a stipend. Cooperative colleges had campuses commandeered by the military; classrooms, playing fields, dormitories, Greek houses, gymnasiums, and dining halls were seized for the Army's and Navy's use. The War Department even took control of the college curriculum. This did not make previous majors of study obsolete. Rather, course material was altered to meet the demands of the government's war machine, which combined an aggressive anti–German curriculum with strict military standards like punctuality, proper demeanor, and appropriate dress code. Penn State's 1,375 student-soldiers were integrated with approximately 1,000 civilian students on campus for 42 out of 53 hours of class per week.[30] In a circular letter from Secretary of War Newton Baker addressed to the colleges of the United States on August 28, 1918, it was made clear that the primary purpose of the army training program was to "utilize the executive and teaching personnel and the physical equipment of the colleges to assist in the training of our new armies."[31]

This was an experiment in military and civil relations with the onus on the academic institutions. The War Department expected colleges to "devote the whole energy and educational power" in assisting the government to prepare the minds and bodies of prospective soldiers.[32] Faculty members were expected to set aside research interests and daily lessons to lecture on war aims. Many professors, especially historians, were subjected to breaking objectivity ethics to misrepresent the history of German-American relations and to publish anti–German propaganda.[33] In addition to pedagogy, intercollegiate athletics were eventually placed under the watchful eye of the War Department. Animosity would mount at several S.A.T.C. colleges as faculty scoffed at what they saw as "military arrogance." There was a sense of confusion among faculties about the status of their universities. "We were not sure whether we were a University or a training camp," wrote David Kinley, vice president at the University of Illinois, adding, "It was not clear 'whether the Commandant or the President was boss.'"[34]

Male students between the ages of 18 and 21 were encouraged to enlist. By enlisting in the Student Army Training Corps, a student-soldier instantly became a private on active-duty status in the United States Army, obligated to wear a uniform of a soldier including a service hat, olive-drab cord, and collar insignia of a bronze disk bearing the letters "U.S."[35] Members were given military drill instruction under officers in the United States Army. Each private was paid $30 a month and given free tuition. After a certain period, the student-soldiers were tested to determine qualifications as officer candidates and technical experts such as engineers, chemists, and doctors. Most privates in the program expected to attain the rank of 2nd lieutenant after one semester and be sent to officer training school at Plattsburgh in New York.

There were two organized cadet sections of the Student Army Training Corps: the Collegiate Section and Vocational Section. The Collegiate Section was composed of student-soldiers who met the admission requirements of the college. Each college capped enrollment into the Collegiate Section at 1,375 student-soldiers, including 1,150 men reserved for the Army and 225 men for the Navy. (If the war had continued into the winter, these men would have graduated to officer training camp in January 1919.) These cadets were placed under ten hours of military instruction a week: six focused on rifle practice and outdoor training, while four hours were spent on academic work for which military credit was earned, such as mathematics, chemistry, engineering, economics, geology, and hygiene.

The Vocational Section was composed mostly of men not meeting educational requirements for admission into college. Others were college graduates preparing for military vocations such as motor truck driving, trench digging, and trench telephoning.[36] Each college accepted 500 vocational cadets into the Student Army Training Corps.

Every private in the training program was required to take a course called "War Aims," which possessed a curriculum designed to enhance morale by providing cadets with a clear picture of the war's causes and explanations for why the United States had declared war on Germany.[37] The course addressed a list of 100 questions, with an accompanying reading list. Prize-winning historian David M. Kennedy writes in his classic, *Over Here: The First World War and American Society* (2004), that the War Aims course "varied considerably" from one college to next, but that the curriculum examined 19th- and 20th-century European history designed to "fix blame for its outbreak squarely on Germany."[38] An integral part of the class was to indoctrinate students with cultural stereotypes and anti–German propaganda.

The War Department's training program offered an attractive alternative to early enlistment. Support for the Corps was prevalent throughout academia. "Keep the boys in college!" became part of the refrain that arose from the rate at which students dropped out of college after the war declaration. It was estimated that 40,000 students had already left American colleges during the previous school year to enter active service in the Army.[39] Thousands of others dropped out to take up jobs in defense industries where the war had created labor shortages; the possibility of earning a high wage was difficult to forgo.

Perhaps no college administration was more vocal about keeping its students than Penn State's, who had lost more than half its male enrollment to the military. The college's officials joined in on the campaign: "Keep the boys in college!" was the message the school promoted in the weeks leading up to the start of the new semester.

To keep the boys at Penn State, in particular, administrators had to maneuver quickly. The Pennsylvania press kept a close watch on servicemen who were either previously enrolled at Penn State or were recent graduates. In August, the *Harrisburg Telegraph* praised former Blue and White football players Lt. Richard S. Davis, W. C. "Whitey" Thomas, Levi Lamb, and B. C. "Casey" Jones for their valor on the battlefield. Story after story added to the nationalistic fervor that compelled Penn Staters to enlist. The *New York Tribune* confirmed "a dozen or more" varsity lettermen were already in France. It reported: "A few are with the fleet, others are in ambulance service, some are with the expeditionary forces, but the majority are in the aviation service."[40] The college yearbook, *La Vie*, verified the *Tribune*'s report at the end of the school year when it stated that all of the fraternities were nearly "depopulated" and the senior class was "greatly reduced" at the start of the 1918 fall term.[41]

Of the 540 colleges that ultimately became hosts for the Student Army Training Corps, Penn State became one of the first schools in the East to welcome the trainee program on campus that fall.[42] A Penn State alumnus, Major James Baylies, retired, class of 1913, was detailed to Penn State as a professor of military science and tactics and made commandant of the college's Student Army Training Corps regiment, which was expecting over 1,500 cadets to arrive when the college was schedule to reopen on September 25.[43] Induction for trainees into the Corps was scheduled for October 1. When the Pennsylvania State Draft Headquarters tallied S.A.T.C. figures at war's end, Penn State's 1,477 Army infantrymen and 75 seamen inducted into the program rated first among schools in Pennsylvania, surpassing the University of Pennsylvania at 1,090 and Pittsburgh University's 964.[44]

Glenn Killinger was at his parents' home the July morning that Penn State announced it was aligning with the War Department's initiative. He vacillated about wanting to enter the officer trainee program. It made him part of the Army, gave him a uniform, and offered the prospect of being deployed overseas like many of his friends already had. And while he looked forward to digging and holding trenches during training, he held reservations about the course work. For all intents and purposes, Killinger was not enthusiastic about the curriculum that trainees were obligated to take. He did not go to Penn State to take geology or hygiene. He was even apprehensive about economics, though it would come in handy years later when he obtained ownership of his family's hardware store.

Killinger's military burden was eased when the Corps offered assurances that intercollegiate athletics would continue with significant interference from the military. At its inception, the War Department declared that it would invest heavily in intercollegiate and intramural athletics, particularly boxing, wrestling, baseball, and football—the four sports that were vital for the 1917 service sports drive by Raymond Fosdick and his Commission on Training Camp Activities; and those were the four sports considered best to prepare student-soldiers for improvised decision-making and hand-to-hand combat. It was made clear that a wartime change to college curriculum required that every enrolled student take courses in physical training.

Certainly, the opportunity to play football in the fall was favorable for Killinger. However, intercollegiate football at Penn State was hardly a guarantee for the coming season. Despite President Woodrow Wilson's public statements encouraging athletics of all forms in American colleges, there was a very real possibility that intercollegiate football would be suspended until the end of the war. In July, a panic developed among coaches, players, and fans after Harvard, Yale, and Princeton—college football's trendsetters—announced for the second consecutive year that they were likely going to cancel their 1918 football seasons. The head coaches of several major college football programs, including Dick Harlow of Penn State, met in Philadelphia to express unanimously their sentiment toward going forward with football in the fall no matter what the big three decided.[45] The paramount leader of the college football ranks, Walter Camp, working then as the commissioner of the athletic division of the U.S. Department of the Navy, presided over the meeting. He reminded the coaches that the War Department was facing a serious health disaster. The selective service figures in the summer of 1918 showed that one-third of the young men drafted were rejected for being physically unfit. "What a pity!" Camp told the coaches. "Exercise develops your engine, makes you supple, quick and active."[46] The nation was in need of physical regeneration, therefore Camp assured the coaches that intercollegiate sports were necessary.

Camp was paramount in ensuring a 1918 college football season. A *New York Times* article vouched for Camp's physical-fitness program: "Uncle Sam's army of stay-at-homes is behind the army of gone-to-war and has organized a system of athletics which is far better systematized than the athletics of the leading eastern universities since the date of the war's beginning." Earlier that summer, Camp had begun circulating his "daily dozen" exercise routine encouraging all Americans to keep physically fit. Now, near the end of summer, Camp ensured a nervous group of coaches that the football season would be played simply because of its importance for raising the physical efficiency of future troops. "The men who had gone into the opposing football line when their signal came went 'over the top' with the same abandon," Camp said as he assessed the effects of the previous year's service sports program. Those footballers "who had made a stand on the last 5-yard line in the grim determination of the gridiron field faced the scrimmage of war with the same do-or-die fortitude."[47]

Camp's reassurances had some effect on the coaches. While Yale eventually annulled its season in 1918, Harvard and Princeton maintained a reduced schedule of just three games. Discussions among various athletic directors, university presidents, sportswriters, and officials from the War Department were held in the final month of the summer, but the decision to carry on with the season was ultimately left in the hands of individual colleges. Some institutions were cautioned about the kind of image that having a football season might give the college while so many of its students were off at war. Other colleges were concerned about having enough players to fill teams. But more than anything, the reason for cancelling a football season was over fear that intercollegiate sports would interfere with the Student Army Training Corps' drilling.[48]

Earlier that summer, Columbia University became the first school that offered a solution when it waived the "bothersome freshman rule," which had prevented first-year students from playing varsity football.[49] Nebraska and West Virginia were next to suspend the freshman rule. Soon Notre Dame, Pittsburgh, and most of the Ivy League colleges jumped on board.

Penn State did not make a decision to waive the one-year residency rule until September 25, several weeks after pre-season football camp commenced; but the college only did so after ordered to by the War Department.[50] Before the fall semester began, officials at Penn State announced that the college intended to proceed with the football season as planned, but changes to the season's schedule were likely to ensue after all of their opponents were contacted to confirm if games could actually be played.

The announcement that football would carry on with obvious modifications to game schedules was accompanied by a crippling blow to the Penn State program, and in particular, Killinger's hope of making the team. On the morning of August 6, about a month before football camp was to begin, Coach Harlow announced his resignation as the head football coach of the Blue and White so that he could enlist in the Army. In fact, several East Coast newspapers reported that most of Penn State's athletic coaches were enrolling in a month-long Officer Training Camp at the Plattsburgh military base in New York, which was established as early as August 1915 as a volunteer pre-enlistment training program designed to prepare prospective Army officers.[51]

Killinger never went on record about how he viewed Harlow's departure. The loss undoubtedly caused reasonable distress since Harlow had offered him a shot at making the football team. An interesting fall was coming. Killinger now had no idea what would come of his future in football.

6

Massed Athletics Experiment

By August 1918, the tide of the war had turned in the Allies' favor following a push against the German line in the Battle of Amiens. Led by French Field Marshal Ferdinand Foch and British General Douglas Haig, the Allies abandoned the trenches to raid German forces north of the Somme in Normandy with a total of 19 British divisions, 12 French divisions, one American division, approximately 2,000 aircraft and more than 500 tanks. The offensive allowed the Allies to dictate the tempo of combat during the remainder of the war. Notwithstanding German General Erich von Ludendorff's insistence that it was time for Kaiser Wilhelm to seek a peace settlement after the Allied victory, the war carried on through the fall.[1]

At Penn State, the most dominant story was whether or not the Blue and White would field a football team after all of the changes that had taken place on the home front. Despite the loss of Coach Harlow and most of its returning players, and facing the "stiffest list of games ever planned for a State College gridiron eleven," the *New Castle News* remarked, the athletic committee announced on August 26 that the school would "do its best" to field a team.[2]

Once the announcement to resume intercollegiate football was made, Penn State's president, Dr. Edwin E. Sparks, took only 24 hours before broadcasting Harlow's replacement. On August 27, Hugo Bezdek, who was hired away from the University of Oregon, agreed to assume the daunting duties of head football coach, director of the physical education department, and director of mass athletics at Penn State.

A Czech by birth, Hugo Francis Bezdek was born in 1884 in Prague, a northern city in the Bohemian region of the Austro-Hungarian Empire (typically known as Austria). His upbringing was so compelling, his life story reads like a Horatio Alger tale. Bezdek's family arrived in the United States when he was six years old, choosing to settle in Chicago. He attended Lake High School (present-day Tilden Technical High School) where he was among the best at football and baseball. Barrel-chested and agile, the youngster was additionally known for his prowess in the boxing ring. Bezdek nearly lost his college eligibility for being a prizefighter under the name of "Young Hugo" when he was 16.[3] He wanted nothing more than to attend the University of Chicago and play for one of the greatest innovators the game of football has known, Amos Alonzo Stagg.

A former Walter Camp All-American, Coach Stagg, who began his coaching career at the YMCA in Springfield, Massachusetts, in 1889 with James Naismith, who invented basketball, as his team's captain, is credited with creating the direct snap from center, tackle dummies, lateral passes, uniform numbers, sending a man in motion, the unbalanced line, the dropkick, and the tradition of issuing varsity letters to deserving players.[4] Bezdek must have been in awe at the way Stagg continued to reinvent the game. Chicago was among the first teams to use the huddle on offense and linebackers on defense.

In 1903, Bezdek enrolled as a chemistry major at Chicago. Though there is doubt in contemporary scholarly circles, he proclaimed to have attained medical and linguistic degrees. His academic interests aside, he was always interested in the competitive disposition of American sports. "I have been interested in athletics since I came to

Hugo "Bez" Bezdek is shown at Penn State about 1921. Bezdek coached at the University of Chicago, Arkansas, and Oregon before arriving at Penn State in 1918. He is the only person to have coached in both the National Football League (Cleveland Rams) and Major League Baseball (Pittsburgh Pirates) (Eberly Family Special Collections Library, Penn State University Libraries).

America," he said in 1917 when he was coaching three sports and serving as director of athletics at the University of Oregon, "and I am more interested in them now than when I was a boy or a young man. It is in me.... I would die if I pursued a sedentary occupation." He admitted, "it is in self-defense that I stick to athletics and keep away from the chemist's retort and the physician's chair."[5]

Playing for Coach Stagg, Bezdek was able to establish an immeasurable reputation as a football player. Harvard All-American Charles Brickley said, "Hugo was as clean as a hound's tooth, a hard-worknig [sic], sterling athlete, commanding the respect of Coach Stagg and every sportsman."[6] Heavier, stronger, and rougher than most of his competitors, Bezdek was the bowling-ball fullback who guided Chicago to the national championship as a senior in 1905. Stagg gave Bezdek the nickname "The Human Shell" for the way he plunged into opposing defensive lines. During Bezdek's freshman year, Stagg doubted the youngster's ability to tackle. "If you'd only cuss me out, I'd be better," Bezdek told his coach.[7] Shortly thereafter, his tackling ability improved noticeably.

In a year considered the deadliest in the history of college football, when three deaths occurred from injuries sustained during games, sportswriters still glorified Bezdek as "the best line plunger the West has ever seen." Once, two broken ribs were hardly an excuse for him to come out of a game. At halftime, he took a steel plate off a wash boiler in the locker room and stuck it under his uniform. "This was before the rules prohibited metallic guards," said one witness. Bezdek played the entire game "with the tin shield to protect his body."[8] It was precisely this visceral toughness that earned him a selection to Walter Camp's All-American third team as a fullback.

Interestingly, he excelled in baseball at the University of Chicago also under the tutelage of Coach Stagg. Writing for the *Philadelphia Daily Journal*, Robert "Tiny" Maxwell suggested that Bezdek was "one of the best second basemen in the college ranks." Before the start of his senior baseball season, he accepted a semiprofessional contract for the Logan Squares of the Springfield Central League, choosing instead to waive his last semester of intercollegiate baseball.[9]

In the summer of 1906, at the age of 22, Bezdek was announced as the athletic director at the University of Oregon. His duties put him in charge of the physical education department as well as made him the head coach of the football and baseball teams.[10] At the time, he became Stagg's sixth player to attain a collegiate head coaching position.[11] He guided the Webfoots 11 to a 5–0–1 record in his inaugural season.

Bezdek returned for one year as an assistant to Coach Stagg at Chicago, then moved to Fayetteville, Arkansas, to serve as the head football and baseball coach at the University of Arkansas. Between 1908 and 1912, Bezdek achieved a 29–13–1 record, including Arkansas' first undefeated football season in 1909. While there, Bezdek was able to give Arkansas a new identity. At the end of the 7–0 campaign in 1909, Bezdek said his team "fought like a band of wild razorback hogs."[12] The moniker stuck, and Arkansas was hereafter known as the Razorbacks. His baseball teams at Arkansas had relative success by accumulating 81 wins and 37 losses. When he left Arkansas, his teams were among the best in the South.

Bezdek returned to the Pacific Northwest in the spring of 1913 after he signed a contract to work as the West Coast scout for major league baseball's Pittsburgh Pirates. The duty for the Pirates helped him retain his coaching jobs at Oregon. Between 1913 and 1917, the Webfoots acquired a 30–10–4 record, including an undefeated 7–0–1 record and a victory over the University of Pennsylvania in the East-West Football Game (known presently as the Rose Bowl) in 1916. In the days leading up to the game, Oregon held closed practices, while Penn's coach, Bob Folwell, opened his to the public, including Bezdek. Penn's quarterback, Bert Bell, who later became the first commissioner of the National Football League, remembered Bezdek asking Folwell to show him Penn's famous reverse-pass play. "Folwell told me to run it, and I did," Bell recollected many years later. "Imagine our chagrin when Oregon scored its first touchdown against us with our very own play."[13] The victory over the East Coast's perennial power put intercollegiate football in the West on the map. Football historian Maxwell Stiles claims it was "the first significant victory of a Pacific Coast team over a big-time team admitted to be truly representative of eastern football at its best."[14]

Bezdek tried something new at Oregon during that five-year period. He dissolved the "one captainship" to avoid rifts of jealousy among his players. At Oregon, he noticed "more or less rivalry for the position." So he named each captain "a few minutes before the contest" began.[15]

Bezdek's ability to make Oregon's footballers into one of the most cohesive units witnessed in the country stretched way beyond the gridiron. Before the start of the 1917 season, his entire Oregon championship team enlisted in the same ambulance unit for service in France. Not one player from the 1916 team was among his first string. "Coach Hugo Bezdek will have to build an entirely new team next fall," wrote the *El Paso Herald*.[16] Bezdek's inexperienced team eventually finished 4–3.

Perhaps earlier that year, Bezdek's imminent Hall of Fame adroitness was put on display when he was injected into the position of manager of the Pittsburgh Pirates, the worst team in major league baseball. Pittsburgh's original manager, Jim Callahan, was fired in July. Callahan's replacement, Honus "Hans" Wagner, lasted just two days. The owner of the Pirates then went with Bezdek, who was recognized as "more or less of an experiment" by the nation's sportswriters.[17] Bezdek never played major or minor league baseball. His coaching experience was limited to Arkansas and Oregon. So for a big league owner to hire a team manager "from among the ranks of college coaches," wrote the *New York Tribune*, "is something unprecedented."[18]

The hiring of Bezdek was what Western sportswriter J. B. Sheridan called "the theory of the superman, that a man who can do one thing well can do all things well." The balance, persuasion, and rigidity displayed by Bezdek were the ingredients that brought out the best in every player who was tutored in his programs. There was no secret that he knew little about professional baseball. He was a chemist, a boxer, a wrestler, and a football player; he was "everything but a baseball player," wrote Sheridan with hyperbole.[19] It took just one year to show results. In late summer 1918, the Pirates were in the middle of a first division run. The *Philadelphia Evening Star* called the rapid rise of Pittsburgh as a National League contender one of the great "surprises" of 1918, "considering that this experimental team, under an experimental manager, was universally consigned to last place before the season opened." Bezdek utilized scientific base running and expert bunting. "With a mediocre pitching staff and an ordinary batting team," Bezdek won acclaim by utilizing clever "base running and bunting tactics" to make below-average players perform better than anyone anticipated. One Pennsylvania newspaper editorialized that Bezdek "has shown results in developing team work and infusing the right spirit in his men."[20]

The approaching season would be no easy task for Glenn Killinger. As war clouds hung overhead and a deadly influenza outbreak perpetrated fear throughout the nation, Coach Bezdek seemingly underscored the strength that held Killinger and his peers at Penn State together during that trying time. Years later, when Killinger was establishing himself as a distinguished college football and baseball coach, he often thought about Hugo Bezdek. The bold Bohemian's coaching style and competence across many playing fields were features that made up Killinger's dynamo and eventually landed him in the several halls of fame. "I think that athletic sports are essential to the vitality of a nation," Bezdek said just days after he arrived at Penn State. That attitude was reflective of what the United States War Department was looking for in 1918.

• • •

Recognized nationally for his ability to make something out of nothing, notably for the jobs he had done at Arkansas and with the Pittsburgh Pirates, Hugo Bezdek was to become director of Penn State's new wartime massed athletics physical education program. As department director, the new professor in State College was expected to collaborate with the Student Army Training Corps (henceforth S.A.T.C.) to design a curriculum that incorporated competitive sports into the physical training of all S.A.T.C. student-soldiers.

To make Penn State's physical education curriculum the vanguard for the nation's colleges was clearly on Bezdek's mind when he accepted the job that August. After meeting with Dr. Sparks and representatives within the War Department, he went ahead and designed a massed athletics program that required every student on campus to "participate in some form of outdoor sport" for one hour a day.

The consensus was that sports made American doughboys better soldiers than the Germans. "Athletics surely are putting muscle and 'pep' into the young men who must handle the rifles, artillery, grenades, spades and other implements of warfare," observed the *Brooklyn Daily Eagle*. Bezdek wholeheartedly believed that mass athletics could make resilient warriors out of privileged and out-of-shape young men. His new physical education program, which cooperated with S.A.T.C. authorities, was designed to increase strength and physical fitness, as well as better students' competitive disposition that ultimately produced a courageous fighting spirit needed for combat. Students not involved in intercollegiate athletics were offered a choice among ten elective sports, of which football proved to be the favorite form of athletics at Penn State. In October, the S.A.T.C. released a report that showed that 354 students elected football, 243 chose basketball, 169 selected tennis, 125 preferred wrestling, 121 cross-country, 100 soccer, 71 boxing, 36 baseball, 15 volleyball, and ten signed up for quickening exercises.[21]

All S.A.T.C. cadets were divided into intramural companies, or teams, requiring them to participate in daily games against one another. The companies competed for points in each sport. The winning company was the one with the most points at the end of the week. Eventually, the sight of games played concurrently all over Beaver Field while boxing and wrestling matches were held inside the college's Armory "produced a sight never before seen," remarked one *Harrisburg Telegraph* editorial.

Student-soldiers who harbored a desire to play a particular sport on an intercollegiate level, like football, tried out for varsity roster spots on Penn State's teams. The approach meant that the success of Penn State's football team, for instance, was secondary to the overall development of the cadets. Nonetheless, Penn State's S.A.T.C. program was the nation's "Mass Athletics" frontrunner. Soon, other colleges and universities were to adopt similar systems that looked toward dual facility control over both physical education courses and intercollegiate athletics.[22]

Bezdek said the American soldier had something that the Germans lack — "the git up and git," he emphasized.

> I think that had the Germans tuned themselves up on athletic games, instead of laboring twelve hours a day or dawn to dark, they would have put up a much more lively, dashing fight than they have put up. I think that athletic sports are essential to the vitality of a nation. The Germans are enduring and they are strong, but they lack the life, the vivre, the elan, the "git up and git" of the Americans.[23]

I do not mean that you can make men strong or a nation great on athletics alone. Hard work gives a power that no athletics can impart. Too much hard work slows men up. Then comes athletics to enliven them, to give them dash, go. The athlete will derive fun from fighting.

Remarks like that persuaded Dr. Sparks to bring Bezdek to State College. Sparks gave Bezdek the freedom to enforce a complete overhaul of the physical education department at Penn State.

Before his arrival, physical education at Penn State was casually operated. Consisting of calisthenics and random exercises given to 100 to 200 students at a time, Bezdek alleged, it was "treated more or less as a necessary evil."[24] The transformation began with a budget request of $525,000 to construct a gymnasium and an 80-acre outdoor field. The gymnasium, according to Bezdek, would be used five of the nine months during an academic year and would "practically be the center of activities" for the students during the winter months, complete with staff offices, adequate dressing and shower space, lecture halls, a general gym floor for boxing, basketball, volleyball, wrestling, handball, and squash, and an indoor track. The building, when finally constructed ten years after the war, also contained a swimming pool and a bowling alley. In contrast, Bezdek's outdoor field was his "playground," a space large enough for nine holes of golf, a track, a dozen football fields, five baseball diamonds, courts for basketball, tennis, and volleyball, and multiple fields for soccer and lacrosse.[25]

In addition, he requested $30,300 for staff salaries. Prior to Bezdek's program, athletic coaches monitored the students' physical activity. Their salaries were based on revenue taken from gate receipts at intercollegiate contests, guarantees received by host teams during away games, and the $10 athletic fee that each Penn State student was obligated to pay. Bezdek's request assured yearly salaries for a head of the department, a director of intramural sports, a women's athletic director, six instructors, a stenographer, a field maintenance crew, and custodians.[26]

Bezdek was charged with overseeing the facilities and staff while also writing a new curriculum designed to prepare men and women seeking degrees to become physical education teachers. To attain a physical education degree, students after 1918 had to take courses in hygiene and health, pass health efficiency tests, fulfill required course work for seven semesters, and learn the rules for most of the sports played in the United States.[27]

• • •

In addition to acting as the physical education director, Bezdek officially became the replacement for Dick Harlow as the new football coach. Perhaps Glenn Killinger's reaction to the hiring of Bezdek is indicative of how most Penn Staters reacted in the early fall 1918. "When I read about Bedek's [sic] appointment, I was greatly enthused," wrote Killinger in his memoir. Well aware of Bezdek's playing and coaching acumen, Killinger said, "Here was my opportunity to learn football and baseball, providing I could play well enough to be chosen as a member of the varsity squads.... Bezdek was always a winner."[28]

Killinger's anticipation over the impending season finally ended in early September when a letter arrived from Penn State announcing that the preseason camp would start as scheduled on September 12, two whole weeks before classes were to begin. In the letter, Bezdek notified aspiring football players to report "in order to get into condition for the opening game," which, at the time, was scheduled for September 29 with Muhlenberg College. Even Killinger understood that the turnout would be on the low side, but he had no idea how many veteran players were not coming back for the 1918 season.[29]

The first day on the practice field was discouraging for Coach Bezdek, as Charlie Way was the only returning letterman from the previous season's team. All of Way's teammates were already called to arms. In addition to Way, just two candidates for the team reported to camp that first day. Notwithstanding the low numbers, Bezdek ran the three through drills.[30] There was now the real possibility that Penn State would not have enough to field a team.

Killinger was not one of the three at tryouts that first day. His arrival was delayed because he was called to appear in front of the draft board in Harrisburg. The United States War Department had designated September 12 as the nation's draft registration day. Just a day away from turning 20, Killinger proceeded to register for conscription into the military under the terms of the amended Selective Service Act, which, for the first time, lowered the draft age to 18, making him an eligible draftee. The revised law required him to report to the local selective service board located at the Horace McFarland Company building on Crescent and Mulberry Streets to sign up. He drew card A1720, which now meant that he could be called into service at any moment from his Dauphin County district. He put pen to paper: "William Glenn Killinger, 37 S. 13th St.," he began to write. He abbreviated Harrisburg—"Hbg"—and Dauphin County—"Daup." He then incorrectly wrote "18" for his age. In a sudden rush to fix the mistake, he took his pen and darkened the "8" into a "9" to indicate his proper age. Killinger marked that he was "white" and "native born." Under Present Occupation, he checked "student." As for Description of Registrant, he identified himself as having blue eyes and brown hair. He check-marked "Slender" and "Tall."[31]

He was growing taller with each passing season. Just days away from his 20th birthday, Killinger had grown to 5'8½" and weighed 155 pounds.[32] He still looked thin, but firmly built with broad shoulders and powerful-looking biceps. His face seemed more mature, too, with a strong jawline and a Brilliantine-coated part down the center of his hair. Fleet footed with deer-like speed and the same cocky assurance he once possessed as an adolescent running the streets of Allison Hill, off he went to State College to try out for the varsity football team.

Killinger's first day on the gridiron was Friday, September 13.[33] He arrived with one of his teammates from the freshman basketball team, Gene Farley, whom he described as "a striking blonde about 6'5" tall and over 200 lbs." Coach Bezdek averted his attention toward Farley as the two brooding young men approached the registration table. "Obviously I made a mistake reporting with Farley," Killinger regretfully said of his first encounter with the man who would eventually become a father figure. Bezdek showed "great interest" in Farley, he admitted. The coach's cold shoulder angered him. It was something he would use as motivation as he tried out for the team.[34]

At the moment, there were two weeks before the opening game. With depleted numbers, common wisdom held that in spite of his fragile physique, Killinger would likely obtain a spot on the roster. "When the 1918 squad reported for the first practice session," he wrote in his unpublished memoir, "I examined the backfield candidates critically and was very excited [about making the roster]." Charlie Way was a lock. "There was a third string fullback and several other backs I recognized from spring practice," he remembered.[35] However, he was still a long way from proving that he was good enough to play on a national stage against some of the best teams in the country. Right away, he plunged himself into drills with the aspiring backfield, led by Way, the unanimous decision for team captain and a peer Killinger called "my hero ... [with] All-American potential."[36] Killinger spent each workout following Way around as they practiced long punts, dropkicks and field goals, catching shotgun snaps from the center, and various deceptive pivots to either hand the ball off or fake an exchange.

Coach Bezdek ran the men through practice in military fashion. Harry Wilson, one of Killinger's backfield mates who would become an All-American in 1922, noted that Bezdek's strength was his drive. "He was always demanding," Wilson once said.[37] The ball players moved from one drill to the next at the sound of a whistle. Players were drilled on blocking and tackling, and tested on mental toughness throughout each session. Bezdek coached non-stop with "vim" and "enthusiasm." If Bezdek's players failed to share his passion, practice would come to an abrupt stop, and the discipline was handled on the spot. "The more you put out for something near to your heart the more you love and respect it," Wilson understood. "So I believe that as tough as Bez was he was responsible for a lot of our affection for Penn State."[38] By fostering his players' love for their school, all of those who played for Bezdek were willing to sacrifice life and limb on game day.

Bezdek's stern coaching style was different from what Killinger was accustomed to. Each practice was a well-ordered regimen. For the benefit of the players, Bezdek's routine was predictable. Each practice began with a half-mile jog followed by five repetitions apiece at interference (blocking) and tackling. The team was then run through stance-and-starts, emphasizing perfect form. Kicking drills followed, including punt and kickoff placement. The remaining hour of practice was spent installing and drilling audible signals, forward passes, having every backfield player take snaps from center, and hard-hitting inter-squad scrimmages.[39]

As challenging as practices were, Killinger grew to appreciate (and later mimic) Bezdek's methods. The incessant coach took time before practice to meet with Killinger about the day's plan, explaining in detail how certain plays should work. On the practice field, Killinger's performance was held to a high standard. Every subtle movement was critiqued. "He insists upon and gets results," Killinger and his teammates often conveyed to reporters. When Killinger made a mistake, there was little delay before he heard Bezdek's voice correcting him. When Bezdek reproached Killinger, he did so in a way that was both demanding and respectful. Bezdek "doesn't cuss and fume on the field," Killinger said of his coach. "He tells the men when he is disgusted with their work." It was Bezdek's subtle remarks of affirmation that kept Killinger loyal; "he doesn't forget to tell them when he is pleased," Killinger added.[40]

The constant back-and-forth between criticism and approbation was Bezdek's way of establishing a player-coach relationship based on respect and trust. To outsiders, Bezdek's behavior could be taken less tolerably. Once when Killinger was walking across campus reading a book written by Princeton's coach, Bill Roper, *How to Play Football*, Bezdek sneaked alongside, eyed the book, snatched it away, and tossed it 25 feet across the courtyard. "I never got the book back," Killinger remembered. "Bez said he'd teach me how to play football."[41]

Most coaches of the era preferred to watch practice from a raised tower so they could see all over the field. Bezdek loathed the custom. He once told Bill Roper that he "would never be satisfied to be confined to any one place for a single minute, and that he liked to be all over the field on every play."[42]

Killinger was drawn to Bezdek's philosophy of scoring points. Bezdek often said, "A good offense is the best defense."[43] He taught a variation of the single-wing offense that was complicated for novice players to learn, but once mastered by the right kind of athletes, had the potential of rivaling even the most high-octane spread systems of the 21st century.

Killinger must have wondered why anyone would not want to play for a coach who, while drilling players under constant pressure, took the time to teach the game. To his satisfaction, people gradually started showing up on the practice field. By the end of the second week of camp, 13 players were in uniform.

Penn State's fans perceived their players as they perceived themselves: eager, willing to learn, unpretentious, but inexperienced and needy. The lack of football knowledge and demeanor, standing around at practice until commanded to a drill, and undisciplined execution were surprising to nobody. It was far from being a source of embarrassment and instead became a matter of pride, for they simply confirmed the effect that the war had on the home front. The war had thrust them into a situation that they all wanted.

The roster was large enough to play the opening game, that is, if Muhlenberg College had not cancelled. On the morning of September 18, Neil Fleming, graduate manager of athletics at Penn State, informed his boss that authorities at Muhlenberg had suddenly cancelled its football season.[44] Bezdek was saddened but not surprised. He just hoped that the termination of Muhlenberg's program wasn't going to become contagious.

The cancellation of the game offered Bezdek more time to find the right lineup among his ragtag personnel. The next game was planned for October 5 against Gettysburg College. The arrival of students in a week also meant the prospects of more talent.

Eighteen hundred students arrived at State College on Wednesday, September 25. At their orientation meeting that first day, students were told that "some form of outdoor sport" was required by orders of the S.A.T.C. All students were allowed to select their favorite sport "for daily exercise."[45]

Suddenly, there were about a hundred players dressed in football uniforms. To someone of Bezdek's stature, they were in despairing shape. With some help from just two assistant coaches, he had to manage each practice with a hundred inexperienced players who had to learn some of the most basic elements of the game. The *New York Tribune* called the new candidates "light and inexperienced." One critic noted, "the prospects have assumed a more roseate hue."[46]

It was never a secret that Bezdek rebuffed the idea of allowing freshmen to play varsity sports. Because of his position, Penn State was one of the last colleges to concede. On September 28, the *Washington Times* published an article detailing the S.A.T.C. order forcing Penn State to "waive [the] freshmen rule," making all 1,100 first-year students eligible for the school's intercollegiate varsity teams.[47]

The eligibility of new talent convinced Bezdek to arrange an inter-squad scrimmage in the last days of September to pick his first string. Killinger would have to perform flawlessly to make the cut. He was up against six others vying for the position of halfback; two would be selected for first string, while two more would be carried as substitutes.

On September 29, the Penn State football team was divided into two squads for a 90-minute scrimmage. Killinger was picked for the first team but was told to wait on the sideline to be substituted in. He stood there watching three other halfbacks—Henry Crum, Frank Unger, and George Snell—each score touchdowns. When suddenly Crum went down with a sprained ankle, Bezdek inserted Killinger into the lineup. Near the end of the scrimmage, Killinger, now running with the starters, weaved through the defense on an outside sweep to score an impressive touchdown.

Two weeks later, Bezdek announced the first string. No surprise to anyone, Charlie Way was named quarterback, while George Snell and Henry Crum were appointed halfbacks, assuming the latter's ankle would heal in time for the first game. Bill Gehring was made fullback. Killinger's performance, though limited and not measuring up that of his competitors, had earned him a spot on the 20-man varsity roster as a backup to Snell and Crum. He was given jersey number 2 to wear.

• • •

In October, issues within and outside of the United States compelled the War Department to further regulate the intercollegiate football season. The military demanded that every college adjust football schedules to conform to S.A.T.C. weekend obligations. Typically, students enrolled in the Corps were barred from missing any drill instruction. But after significant deliberation with several colleges, the War Department authorized no more than two away contests per school; that way privates in the officer training program would miss just two weekends' worth of drills instead of four or five as previously scheduled. Because S.A.T.C. induction day—October 7—was the same among the nation's colleges, to assure a smooth start to the student-soldier program, the War Department trusted colleges to decide on a schedule that would not interrupt military drilling for at least two weeks after the training program commenced at the respective schools.

Adhering to the wartime measures, Penn State officials pushed the football season back to October 19, the date of its home game against Bucknell College. Since October 7 was the date of S.A.T.C. induction and the contest against Bucknell was a home game, college and military officials agreed that there was a long enough window of time between the start of the training program and Penn State's first away game.

Meanwhile, Coach Bezdek worked on finalizing the new schedule. He first confirmed games with Bucknell and Rutgers, who were both previously scheduled to visit State College. He added the newly formed service football team from the Wissahickon Barracks Naval Station in Cape May, New Jersey, to be Penn State's first game in November. Contests against Gettysburg, Carnegie Tech, and Washington and Jefferson colleges were cancelled. That just left overnight trips to Lehigh and Pittsburgh to finish out the season.[48]

Shortly after Penn State's new five-game schedule was arranged, the team suffered a "rude jolt," reported the *New York Tribune*, when Charlie Way, Bill

Induction of the Student Army Training Corps at Penn State, October 1, 1918 (Eberly Family Special Collections Library, Penn State University Libraries).

Gehring, George Snell, Henry Crum, and five other starters were called to machine gun school at Camp Hancock in Georgia.[49] The *Pittsburgh Gazette Times*, the chief newspaper covering sports for the University of Pittsburgh, Penn State's biggest rival, ran the story immediately, gloating "the college eleven faces wreckage."[50]

The news was definitely troublesome, but as pragmatic coaches normally do, Bezdek acted quickly. He moved Ronald "Buck" Williams into the starting quarterback position. Glenn Killinger was exuberant when he learned he had been promoted to one of the starting halfback positions to replace Snell.

On the morning of October 19, Bucknell arrived at Beaver Field, eager to avenge an embarrassing 50–7 setback to Penn State when they last met two years earlier. To the uninitiated Killinger, well-drilled and eager to play his first college game, the arrival of game day was met only by another unfortunate setback.

For weeks, health services reports had whipped the public into a frenzy as word of a deadly outbreak of the flu made an appearance in all facets of American society. The so-called Spanish influenza, an H1N1 virus originating at American military installations earlier that spring, wreaked havoc throughout the country in the months leading up to the Penn State–Bucknell game. The first wave of the pandemic arose in March. The virus had grown deadlier as it mutated during the summer and fall of 1918, "resulting in significantly enhanced virulence," writes Jeffery K. Taubenberger, chairman of the Department of Molecular Pathology at the Armed Forces Institute of Pathology. Media reports in every local and national news outlet terrified the public about the likelihood that the flu would sweep through every military encampment, college and town in the United States.

Reports were horrifying: those sick with the flu suffered headaches, muscle pains, sore throat, coughing fits, nosebleeds, and debilitating bouts of hallucination. Fevers typically ranged from 100 to 104 degrees.[51] The stricken slowly suffocated—gasping for air to the consternation of those around them—as blood and other fluids suppressed oxygen in their lungs.[52] By mid–October, 26 states already reported cases of the flu. Almost 30,000 incidents were reported within the military. Among that number, already 530 soldiers had died nationwide in the first three weeks of the month. The Board of Health reported 4,597 civilian deaths from the flu in Philadelphia alone between October 12 and 19.[53] More than 11,000 people fell victim to the flu and other respiratory diseases by the end of the month. Within a year, 675,000 civilians, including 43,000 servicemen, and approximately 40,000,000 worldwide would die of the pandemic. Some who died had succumbed to pulmonary hemorrhage or pulmonary edema. Most, however, were strapping young men between the ages 21 and 29 whose demise, Taubenberger points out, was brought about by secondary bacterial pneumonia and respiratory failure "since no antibiotics were available in 1918."[54]

The lethality of the Spanish influenza took its toll on intercollegiate sports. The *Washington Times* was among the first to report that the flu was likely going to cause "quarantines to be placed around the players reporting for daily drills." Two weeks before the scheduled game against Bucknell, drastic measures were already underway to inhibit the transmission of the flu. Schools, churches, local sporting events, theaters, and all other public places were ordered closed by the Board of Health.[55] The flu had already brought all athletics to a halt at the Great Lakes Naval Station and imposed quarantines at many universities along the Eastern seaboard.

Both teams had already gone through pregame warm-ups and were settled in their respective locker rooms when state officials called the coaches together to explain that the U.S. Health Authority demanded the cancellation of every game played in Pennsylvania. Bezdek and Bucknell coach Edgar Wingard were both prepared to play the game in defiance of the public health order until state officials threatened to arrest the coaches and players if the game was played.[56]

Killinger, who was named the starting left halfback, was the most distraught by the news. "I believe I was the most disappointed player on the squad," he lamented, looking back. "In my early dreams as a youngster, I had imagined I was the great football star on a Penn State football team."[57] Yet with one setback after another, the start of the season was not a guarantee. Bucknell, which had another game against the University of Pennsylvania cancelled because of the influenza, ended up coasting to a 6–0 record against a rather weak schedule. Killinger and his teammates at Penn State, meanwhile, held their breath. He must have pondered: what else could disrupt the season?

If that was the question he asked himself, it was not long until he got an answer. On October 27, one week before the Wissahickon game, the War Department ordered Hugo Bezdek to report to Princeton to attend a two-week training camp in the Aerocraft Commission. Bezdek was told to share his experiences at Penn State to teach S.A.T.C. colleges and army campuses how to implement similar mass physical education programs. The appointment was a credit to the job Bezdek performed at Penn State. It took a special person to supervise more than 1,800 students as they participated in a myriad of outdoor competitive sports.[58] He was praised by one California newspaper: "Bezdek was famous as a football coach before he became a baseball team manager, and the government's call to him is a striking testimonial of his success as a handler of men."[59]

College president Sparks immediately began negotiations with the War Department aimed at keeping Bezdek at State College. A simple deal was struck. Neil M. Fleming, Bezdek's deputy in the athletic department, was sent to Princeton instead. The threat of losing Bezdek was over within 48 hours.

With his coach behind him, Killinger was ever so positive. He received an additional boost from his hometown newspaper on October 28. "If State College ever gets going," the *Harrisburg Telegraph* wrote, "coach Hugh Bezdek counts on our old friend, W. G. Killinger, the Harrisburg Tech radiant, to do wonders for his team." The headline was accompanied by a picture of Killinger standing proudly in his Penn State football uniform and headgear. "Killinger is in prime shape and probably the best backfield performer that Bezdek has. He knows how to gain ground, is a sure catch and works with brain and brawn. With the season wide open Killinger is bound to help keep the Capital City on the map."[60]

Without further delay, Glenn Killinger's debut as a big college varsity football player with Penn State arrived on November 2 in the game against the Wissahickon Barracks Midshipmen. To Killinger and his inexperienced teammates, Beaver Field looked larger than normal, and the speed and intensity of the game were unfamiliar. It took a quarter to get his bearings together. From his right halfback spot on offense and secondary position on defense, he made some early mistakes in a scoreless first half.

In the third quarter, Penn State's quarterback Buck Williams "displayed excellent field generalship," noted the *New York Tribune*, including a bold risk to call a trick play that led to a touchdown.⁶¹ He unfortunately missed the extra point.

Penn State's defense played flawlessly until the game's final minute, when Wissahickon completed its only forward pass of the contest, resulting in a game-tying touchdown. Somehow, the Midshipmen kicker shanked the point after, low and to the right of the upright. The game ended in a 6–6 stalemate.

Despite the heartbreaking final minutes, the *New York Tribune* reported that Penn State fans left "elated over the splendid performance of the Blue and White eleven." Wissahickon carried a weight advantage of "fifteen pounds to the man," but the first-time varsity players were able to battle to a draw. Most were impressed with Penn State's stout defense, which gave up just two first downs. As one would imagine with the inexperience on the field and the sudden loss of Charlie Way, the offense still needed time to develop.

Though he had a big heart, Killinger's fragility showed as he was forced to leave the game in the second half when Wissahickon's Duke Osborne, who would transfer to Penn State after the war, cracked three of his ribs during a scrum. The injury was unfortunate because the contest against the sailors exploited Penn State's drawbacks in the kicking department. Although it was only natural to have the quarterback operate as the team's punter, anyone could kick extra points and field goals. After the game, Coach Bezdek told the ailing Killinger that he would have an opportunity to earn the kicking duties once he was healthy.⁶²

Penn State limped into the approaching game against Rutgers, which featured eventual All-American, singer, actor and pioneer for racial justice, Paul Robeson. The game doubled as Pennsylvania Day at State College. Campus officials expected a multitude of outsiders there to watch the S.A.T.C.'s intramural competitions in the morning followed by the Penn State–Rutgers game in the afternoon. Even Killinger's parents, Billy and Florence, arrived with a small contingent from Harrisburg.⁶³ Penn State was considered a huge underdog against Rutgers, which previously defeated Ursinus, Pelham Bay Navy, Lehigh, and Hoboken Navy. As fate had it that morning, in addition to Killinger, two other backfield mates were injured so badly that they couldn't dress for the Pennsylvania Day game. Only the quarterback, Buck Williams, was healthy enough to suit up against Rutgers.

Killinger's team marched down the field on the opening possession and converted a dropkick for three points. Everything after that was hard luck for the Blue and White. One sportswriter called Penn State's ineffective offense "a futile plaything." Rutgers' defensive unit was just too powerful for Penn State's fledgling offensive line. "The Scarlet's line charged into State's play and regularly downed the runners before they got under way," reported the *New York Sun*.⁶⁴ Rutgers imposed its will on both sides of the ball throughout

The Penn State S.A.T.C. Football Team in 1918. Killinger is pictured sitting legs crossed, front row, on the left (Eberly Family Special Collections Library, Penn State University Libraries).

the first half, running up a score of 20–3 at intermission. The star of the half was Rutgers' imposing end, Paul Robeson. The *Pittsburgh Daily Post* described the performance of the future actor and civil rights activist as "masterful."[65] The situation grew dire in the second half when Rutgers scored once more and Penn State's quarterback suffered a knee strain as Robeson and his teammates on the defensive interior continued to penetrate the line of scrimmage at will. Williams finished the game, but was kept out of the next contest against Lehigh.

Penn State's record stood at an acceptable 0–1–1 with two games left.

• • •

On November 11, at the 11th minute of the 11th hour, the armistice ending World War I went into effect. While terms would be finalized later, the treaty established a 30-day truce, allowing Germany time to withdraw from the western European countries that it currently occupied. Germany was additionally forced to hand over to the Allies valuable military equipment, including machine guns, submarines, and airplanes.

That night, President Woodrow Wilson issued a jubilant statement on the war's demise. He said, "The armistice was signed this morning. Everything for which America fought has been accomplished." All draft calls in the United States were abruptly halted. However elated Killinger was about the war's end, he and thousands of others were told to remain in the S.A.T.C.

until December 21, at which time every student-soldier would receive an honorable discharge. For the next six weeks, Killinger continued on with military drilling.[66] He would continue to collect his rate of one dollar per day. And he would finish the semester free of tuition fees.

Whatever Killinger's opinion about the S.A.T.C., it was clear that football, at least, was the closest thing to war in American culture. Folklorist Simon Bronner has interpreted the meaning of football in its abundance of military metaphors and the American frontier experience. The football season in 1918 demonstrated that the sport was more than an inconsequential game. Although Killinger and other privates in the S.A.T.C. did not join the fight on the Western Front, they found resolve and tenacity in their engagement in combat training. And football was a meaningful part of that training. Writing in *Explaining Traditions: Folk Behavior in Modern Culture* (2011), Bronner observes that football has always been linked to the battlefield. He writes of the connection between football and war: "the scrimmage line as warfare in the trenches, quarterbacks (also called field generals) throwing bombs, teams marching down the field, and running backs accelerating as if shot out of a cannon." With a new wartime image of the game, the military rhetoric of "blitz," "formations on the front line," and linemen battling it out "in the trenches" came of age after World War I. A generation later, as war clouds gathered again over Europe, additional catchy metaphors became part of the game, Bronner notes, with "quarterbacks throwing missiles, receivers catching long bombs downfield, and coaches strategizing an aerial attack."[67] Bronner's view of football's existence as a metaphor for the hawkish tenets of America was certainly apparent in Killinger's participation in the home front's military culture.

In an example of football imitating war, folklorist Alan Dundes conjures up an allegory analogous to Bronner's point of view. In "Traditional Male Combat," an article subtitled "From Game to War," Dundes claims that sport and war revolve around one theme: "an all-male preserve in which one male demonstrates his virility, his masculinity, at the expense of a male opponent." Dundes observes, "games, sports, and war form a common continuum, with games at one end and war at the other." It is not a coincidence that those in the military refer to "war games" when practicing warfare, or that sport metaphors—particularly in college football—often refer to an "arms race" when dueling teams try to woo a quarterback prospect one way or the other. While Dundes wrote mostly about sport and war reaffirming masculine hegemony on a feminized opponent—"the victory entails some kind of penetration"—he shares the idea that if boys could not fully participate in actual combat, their manhood could otherwise be forged on a playing field.[68]

Nationally syndicated "Sportlight" columnist Grantland Rice, who spent the final months of the war in France and Belgium, would affirm the notion that sport and war are closely bonded together. "I found war to be a quick distillation of life's tribulations, all wrapped up in a red, raw bundle," Rice wrote in his memoir, *The Tumult and the Shouting*. He added, "In war, however, the good in a fellow surfaces—or sinks—much quicker than in civilian life. In many ways, the same applies to sport."[69]

Most in the sports world were convinced. "Football is, in a sense, something like a game of war," said Walter Camp in an interview with a correspondent of *The American Boy*. "The gridiron is the battlefield. The two teams are the opposing armies. The captain and the coaches and the players are the brains that plan the attack and prepare the defense."[70] He elaborated further:

> Moreover, there is a rapidity approaching similarity between the theory of modern war and the theory of football. In old time war, the privates and humbler officers were there only to obey. In modern warfare, individual initiative is becoming more important—yet, obedience and united action are imperative. So in football, the humblest players may plan a play that may rout his team's dearest enemy—yet instance obedience and discipline must govern the team's movements.[71]

Though no soldier liked the experience of living in a rat-infested trench or ducking from machine gun fire, not quite the same as enduring the horrors of modern war, the S.A.T.C. gave Killinger and his fellow cadets and teammates something close to combat. The burden of preparing for the beatings that occur on the gridiron against major college opponents in conjunction with a level of psychological pressure levied during daily military training allowed Killinger to make sense of the whole experience. The fervor of war made those in Killinger's position gain a sense of teamwork, self-sacrifice, resilience, and tradition. As he began to look ahead at a life in the post-war world, his path teemed with new insights and readiness. In his wake were two remaining football games against intrastate foes, Lehigh College and the University of Pittsburgh.

Penn State and Lehigh, a sister S.A.T.C. college located in Bethlehem, shared one common opponent that season—Rutgers. Both were badly beaten by the Scarlet 11. Like Penn State, Lehigh had arranged a five-game wartime schedule. They had already played three contests and accumulated a 2-1 record by November 16, when they lined up against Penn State.[72]

The game featured the return of Penn State's backfield, minus Buck Williams, who sat out due to a badly sprained knee. Lehigh was a slight favorite because of Penn State's paltry offensive production after two games. There was one report that acknowledged Penn State will be "fifty per cent stronger [with] Killinger, Unger and Brown recovered from their injuries and back in the lineup." After the departure of Charlie Way, and now Williams out of the lineup, what was Bezdek to do about the quarterback position?

Three practices before the Lehigh game were spent teaching Killinger how to quarterback the offense. The position change was, Killinger said, because Bezdek "told me later that he wanted to see how well I handled the team."[73] In all honesty, the problem at Penn State was hardly the backfield. Even though they were all first-year varsity players, Killinger, Unger, and Williams were as good as they get at their positions. They were elusive and speedy ball carriers with excellent football minds. Penn State took beatings on account of its offensive line, which was proven to be too small and inexperienced to achieve at the highest level of intercollegiate football. The Blue and White had a stout defense, and Coach Bezdek believed that as long as his team could limit Lehigh's scoring opportunities, they would have a chance to win no matter who was quarterbacking his club.

With a week of drills behind them and a shot of post-war adrenaline, Penn State was primed for the challenge. Excitement aside, both teams played the game sluggishly. Killinger's efforts in the first half yielded little productivity for Penn State's offense as they struggled to gain inches on the ground. Killinger did complete several forward passes that gave his team opportunities to punt for better field position. This strategy ultimately proved advantageous.

Penn State gave up a score to the host within the first five minutes. Fortunately, the extra point was missed. Then, Lehigh's quarterback and captain, Vincent Wysocki, suffered a fractured right arm. The injury to Wysocki greatly weakened Lehigh's offensive firepower. Before the end of the first half, Penn State lineman Ralph Henry blocked a Lehigh punt. The ball rolled to 5-yard line where, Henry recovered the loose ball and ran it in for a touchdown. Entrusted with the role as kicker, Killinger dropkicked the decisive extra point.

Penn State endured several scoring threats in the second half when Lehigh attempted but missed three field goals. Killinger threw two interceptions in the second half that gave Lehigh scoring opportunities. Despite the turnovers, Killinger was the star for Penn State. In addition to the dropkick he converted in the first half, he called plays, threw forward passes, kicked punts, returned punts and kicks, and ran off-tackle enough times to control the clock. He also captained the secondary, which thwarted every instant a Lehigh runner broke through the Blue and White defensive line. The game ended in Penn State's favor, 7–6.[74]

This appeared to be the beginning of a Harold Lamb moment as Killinger emerged as the student body's hero at Penn State—in fact, there would be plenty of them to follow. Just as Lamb's sudden ascent to hero status in *The Freshman*, the once frightened and self-conscious freshman who had tiptoed away from football tryouts now emerged as the big shot on campus. Killinger's hometown newspaper delighted, "The local lad then made history by booting the oval squarely between the posts for the one point that meant victory."[75] Killinger and his teammates felt a deep sense of accomplishment that day. No matter how ugly they played, or how many breaks went in their favor, the green and battered group from State College had defeated a better team. Killinger privately experienced a new emotion: he was over the moon, in fact. Even to an outsider, it was easy to see that Killinger and his young teammates could end up doing something special by the time they graduated.

• • •

Yet Glenn Killinger and his teammates were years away from proving how special they were to become. While eager to play their final game of the season, the annual Thanksgiving Day game was scheduled against archrival Pittsburgh at Forbes Field, the ballpark used by the Pittsburgh Pirates. The Panthers had not lost or tied 31 consecutive games, a streak that spanned four years. Their last defeat came to Washington and Jefferson College, 13–10, on November 7, 1914. Future Hall of Fame inductee Glenn Scobey "Pop" Warner coached Pittsburgh, recruited in 1915 from the Carlisle Indian Industrial School to bring winning ways to the gridiron in the Steel City. His savvy was much respected for mentoring the likes of Jim Thorpe. As a boy, Killinger spent occasional Saturdays watching Pop Warner and Jim Thorpe on Harrisburg's Island Park. All three of Warner's teams at Pittsburgh had won East Coast championships. During that stretch, two mythical national titles were bestowed on Warner's teams by a consensus of sportswriters in 1915 and 1916. What could have been a third title in 1917 was given to John Heisman's Georgia Tech contingent, which had piled up 491 points against just 17 points and a 9–0 record (Pittsburgh had amassed a 10–0 record in 1917 but dodged an offer to play a post-season title game against Tech).[76] Warner's 1918 team had yet to yield a point, having already defeated Washington and Jefferson, 34–0, Pennsylvania, 37–0, and the nation's top-ranked team, Heisman-led Georgia Tech, 32–0.

The epic rivalry between the two colleges began on November 6, 1893, when Penn State triumphed over Pittsburgh, 32–0. That first game was played at State College, as three of the first five meetings were played in the remote locale of Central Pennsylvania. Penn State won the first six showdowns by an aggregate margin of 167–4. After the sixth meeting in 1903—a 59–0 victory for the scholars from Mount Nittany—authorities at the University of Pittsburgh refused to travel into the farming valley of State College, a place so geographically isolated that football games lacked the pluck and enthusiasm of their urban college town in Western Pennsylvania. Penn State officials agreed. The next 28 games were played in the Steel City and added interest by scheduling the game on Thanksgiving Day—a popular tradition in intercollegiate competition dating back to the 1876 holiday showdown between Princeton and Yale.[77] For the level of pageantry that accompanied the game each year, the two teams did not play for a traditional trophy, which presented a great contrast with the showdowns played between Stanford and California, who competed for the Axe; Purdue and Indiana, which vied for the Old Oaken Bucket; and Michigan and Minnesota for possession of the Little Brown Jug.[78] Trophy or no trophy, the Thanksgiving Day game between Penn State and Pittsburgh became the premier football event in Pennsylvania by the late 1910s. It remained as such for much of the century. The move to Pittsburgh was about adding breath to the clash between Pennsylvania's big college football teams.[79] And it worked, especially for the Panthers, who won nine of 15 games in the lead-up to the 1918 S.A.T.C. showdown.

Since this particular intrastate clash was scheduled for Thanksgiving Day, November 28, it gave Penn State extra time to prepare to defend Pittsburgh's two All-American running backs: freshman Tom Davies and senior George McLaren. It also gave Bezdek's walking wounded time to heal. Killinger, who was still nursing an injury sustained nearly a month earlier, sat out three practices.[80]

On the eve of the game, Bezdek's team boarded a train bound for Pittsburgh. A large contingent of S.A.T.C. privates accompanied the team on the journey. On the train ride west, Killinger found a copy of the *Daily Post*, a Pittsburgh newspaper, and began to read. The paper devoted a good deal of attention to the Thanksgiving Day rivalry game. The sportswriter identified him as one of Penn State's stars, placing him among the opponents' players to watch list. A picture of Killinger appeared on the sports page.

Nobody expected Penn State to win; that was clear by the headlines in the newspapers Killinger read. He learned, instead, that fans only wanted Penn State to score. If Penn State could find the end zone against Pitt, it would be a testament to the job Bezdek did holding together a team in such dire wartime conditions. The *Daily Post* admitted, "If this is done it will be quite an accomplishment." The local paper added, "there is every reason to believe that a chance exists for the Mt. Nittany aggregation to cross Pitt's goal line."[81]

The players were lodged at the Fort Pitt Hotel and sent to bed early to focus on the contest. Bezdek, meanwhile, had no problem glad-handing with the local press. "Perhaps we will show Pittsburghers more football than they expect from us," he said, grinning to reporters in the hotel lobby, adding, "We do not intend to allow Glenn Warner's great team to run all over us without resistance, that is certain."[82]

But the next afternoon, as a comparatively small holiday crowd of 6,000 had anticipated, a war-ready Pittsburgh team imposed its will against Penn State, winning by a convincing 28–6 margin in cold and foul weather at Forbes Field. It was an odd game that featured both teams punting often on first down to gain field position.

Playing in the sloppiest of conditions helped Penn State jump out to an early lead. In the first quarter, Pitt's star halfback, Tom Davies, a freshman from Kiski allowed to play due to the wartime abolition of the one-year freshman residency rule, uncharacteristically fumbled the ball over to Penn State on Pittsburgh's side of the field. After Penn State's Buck Williams pooch-punted out of bounds, Pitt had the ball on their own 9-yard line. Pitt wisely chose to punt on second down, but the kicker's foot got stuck in the mud, and the ball traveled a short distance to the 18-yard line. On the first play, Williams ran right for eight yards.[83] Penn State was stuffed for a one-yard gain on second down. Killinger then ran left off tackle on third down, but missed picking up a first down by an inch. Instead of attempting a dropkick in the muddy conditions, Bezdek's team chose to go for it on fourth down. They handed off to Frank Unger, who picked up several yards, finally tackled on the 4-yard line.

Penn State had first and goal from the four. It took all four downs to get in the end zone. The first three attempts were all runs, which failed. On fourth down, Williams handed to Unger, the 5'11", 175-pound sturdy fullback, who followed Killinger off tackle right for the touchdown.

They were the first points scored against Pitt in almost two full seasons. Fans who were well aware of the handicaps placed upon Bezdek's team throughout the season considered the score "a moral victory," wrote the *Daily Post*.[84] There was another dimension to the touchdown. The points meant that Penn State completed a record of having scored in every one of its games. The milestone, as insignificant as it appears, was a bright light in an otherwise cloudy season. It was a feat that no other football team enduring the same disruptions over the course of the 1918 season had accomplished.

It was a short-lived celebration. The host dominated the remainder of the game. After Penn State's point after touchdown failed, Pitt scored four unanswered touchdowns; three were made by McLaren while only one was credited to Davies, who had several long runs that set up McLaren's scoring opportunities. Davies also threw a touchdown pass and kicked all four extra points. Witnesses believed the outcome would have been worse, but Pop Warner inserted his second string into the game at the start of the fourth quarter.

The still ailing Killinger was—and would be for the next three years—Davies' counterpart. The Penn Stater had a difficult time producing anything for his offense. The empathetic Pittsburgh press lauded Killinger, saying he played "a great game" despite the loss. But in fact, it was quite the opposite. Killinger, who played through pain in his chest, thwarted any chance Penn State had to keep the game close by fumbling twice in the second half.[85]

Penn State finished the year 1–2–1, with both losses coming to top-20 teams. They were one missed extra point against Wissahickon away from a .500 record.

The crushing setback to Pittsburgh left Killinger in a strange state, sore and sour because of the loss, but strangely confident about the future. What amazed him was how a nondescript raw collection of young men could have showed glimpses of talent against much more hardened teams that fall.

In all, Penn State overcame the loss of every original starter and every coach to the war. Killinger knew Bezdek was more than the savior of the football program: he was the glue that held the entire campus together as it adjusted to a military takeover and the change to a wartime curriculum. And his football team proved to be a pleasant distraction from the war that beckoned from across the Atlantic Ocean. For a time in September, it looked as if the school's intercollegiate athletic schedules were going to be cancelled for the semester. The threat was compounded when the flu epidemic caused more panic. Bezdek remained the poised leader through it all. Not just the football players, but also all of the students considered Bezdek the face of Penn State. "State made a ten strike when it signed him for the position of football coach and physical director for an indefinite term," the *Daily Post* said of him.

The 1918 football season placed Bezdek among the "few really great coaches in the country." The *Post* admitted Bezdek was a special find for Penn State.

> Not once, nor twice, but several times, he selected a first team from among the candidates, and, after having them work together for several days, had his combination ripped to pieces by drafts of players for officers' training camps and other service units. Never did he give up, though. Each team he put his shoulder to the wheel and started his task all over again.[86]

On November 29, the day after the Pittsburgh game, Killinger made his way back to State College with his team, then off to his home in Harrisburg for a small break from sports and S.A.T.C. drilling. Shortly before that happened, he took one final look at his coach and thought, "My coach was a god at Penn State."[87] It made him think over the season one last time. He criticized his own performance, blaming himself for not doing enough to help the team. He knew he had more to give.

Success in football is determined primarily by two factors: the bodily wherewithal to last without sustaining an injury that would sideline a player for much of the season and a cerebral capacity to comprehend the coach's style of play as well as week to week tendencies of each opponent. If a player has the physical durability to last the vicious pounding of each game but lacks the mind to understand how the game should be played, then the player is rendered useless on game day. Whereas if a player understands how the game should be played and can predict the opponent's next move based on down and distance or ball placement on the field but is prone to injury, then the coach tends to give practice reps to more robust and resilient players. But of course, a football player who has the combination of durability on one hand and acumen on the other can obtain the pinnacle of intercollegiate sports. Frankly, Killinger and his teammates proved to have the mind and skill to play big-time college football, but in the 1918 season they rated deficient in the category of physical durability. But what Killinger noticed that season, as he and his callow teammates competed at a high level, gave him every reason to believe that under Hugo Bezdek's direction, they could pull off a championship before they graduated.

Killinger vowed never to forget that season.

Part Three: Third Quarter

7

The Veterans

After a reasonable delay following the armistice, Glenn Killinger and approximately 1,500 cadets at Penn State (about 158,000 on campuses nationwide) were honorably mustered out of the Student Army Training Corps on December 21, 1918.[1]

As it developed, demobilization of the Corps meant a lot of things to the bemused cadet. For one, the allowance of $48 paid to him by the War Department (another $60 paid to him in April 1919 under Act of Congress), equivalent to a dollar per day while he was enlisted in the student-soldier program, was not what he anticipated when he signed up for the Corps.[2] The small sum did little to curtail college expenses. He was told, earlier that summer, that enlistment in the S.A.T.C. would guarantee a full year's college tuition free of charge.[3] Now that the War Department recanted that pledge, Killinger and thousands of cadets were left on their own to deal with the financial pressures of remaining in college. Killinger, of course, was assured of returning to Penn State in the spring by continuing to live in the Alpha Chi Sigma house while accepting loans from family friends to compensate for additional college expenses.

The departure of the War Department's program meant that Penn State's sports were handed over to the college's athletic authorities. That meant all athletic branches were now under the sole management of Hugo Bezdek.

Apart from his older brother Earl, perhaps no person was more important for Glenn Killinger's development than Bezdek. The bond was forged at the apex of the war, a difficult time in the life of an impressionable teenager trying to find himself. Throughout his lifetime, Bezdek spoke a lot on record about Killinger's athletic talents. Sadly, there is no recorded thought that illustrates his feelings about Killinger off the playing field, although it is quite clear he treasured his protégé.

The two often had moments of affection that seemed more kindred than sports-driven. "Killy" was the nickname Bezdek used for Killinger. His friends in Harrisburg first gave him the name. Although there was not any particular trait that it reflected, "Killy" seemed to stick at Penn State as his teammates echoed the coach's moniker. Conversely, Killinger began to call his coach "Bez."

When Bez first got to know Killy, he found that the youngster possessed skills as a runner. He was clearly undersized and on the slender side, but there was something different that set Killinger apart from every other player he had encountered at Arkansas and Oregon. Bezdek said Killinger had "football brains."[4] At length Bezdek came to see Killinger as an extension of himself, someone he could eventually trust whenever the circumstance called for him to delegate authority. The player-coach bond grew tighter in the winter of 1919.

The Alpha Chi Sigma fraternity house where Killinger lived on South Pugh Street was located a few blocks north from Bezdek's home on Allen Street. Reflecting back years later, Killinger admitted that most nights after team meetings and training table, "Bezdek would walk to my fraternity with me." Along the way, "He would tell me about the great football and basketball players of the past and present and why they were great." As a result, "I learned about what made them great and tried to emulate them." Like many who met Killinger, Bezdek developed a fondness for the boy. He was happy and spirited and always joked around. Better yet, he had such potential as an athlete. Due to the almost daily walks home together, Killinger recalled with affection, "there was no doubt in my mind the observations of many others [was] that I was 'Bezdek's baby.'"[5]

Killinger may have never been more proud of himself than on January 11, 1919, when he received his varsity "S" for his contribution to the football team. He had come a long way since the two full quarters of playing time he saw during his senior year of high school. His ego was in harness, tamed during his war-laden freshman year, but not entirely eliminated. There must have been a sense of assurance as Coach Bez and Killy stood on the banquet stage with one another.[6] Far from the danger of war, there existed a shared, if naïve, belief that they each helped one another through the trying time. Killinger's ability to be coached without challenging him offered Bezdek a diversion from the frustrations of his job; on the contrary, Bezdek showed Killinger a way to attain greatness. They were able to build upon that rapport even further at the onset of the basketball season.

Penn State was supposed to return one of the most seasoned teams in the East. The war, nevertheless, took two lettermen and the head coach, Burke "Dutch" Hermann, who was laid up in a hospital in Toul, France, site of America's primary Air Service Army base, suffering from a "severe case of shell shock," reported the *Scranton Republican*. In a letter written to friends in State College, Hermann explained that he was leading two platoons "in an attack on a hill after crossing a field swept by German machine gun fire"

Glenn Killinger's varsity football letter for the 1918 season (Jessica Killinger).

when "a big Hun shell" landed near him. Hermann's charge was part of the final Allied assault along the Western Front known as the Meuse-Argonne Offensive, the bloodiest battle that involved American doughboys. While reorganizing his men in the dense woods, German artillery opened four barrages of fire. During the final bombardment, a high explosive fell close to him and threw him 15 feet in the air. Although Hermann became conscious 24 hours later, he was left incapable of speaking for three more days. His injury, occurring on the same day the armistice was signed, forced him to spend the next month in a hospital east of Paris.[7]

Bezdek named himself the basketball team's interim coach while Hermann recovered. To alleviate some of his workload while on the road for extended periods of time with the basketball team, Bezdek hired Dick Harlow back to Penn State to work as his assistant director of physical education. After completing officer training school the previous summer, Harlow was sent by the War Department to supervise the Student Army Training Corps at Virginia Polytechnic Institute (known today as Virginia Tech). He spent the fall as an assistant football coach for the 7–0 Hokies. Now asked to return to Penn State, Harlow was put in charge of the school's intercollegiate boxing team and assisted with the intramural sports program that Bezdek developed. Bezdek additionally named Harlow his line coach for the football team.[8]

When basketball tryouts started in mid-January, Bezdek kept a close eye on Killinger. The absence of the team's captain, Lloyd L. Wilson, who was still stationed at the Great Lakes Naval Station but scheduled to arrive back to State College in February, left a temporary void in the backcourt. Killinger could score, but Bezdek especially liked the way he played defense and thought he should be given an opportunity to start on the varsity team. There was another guard on the team, George Ewing McMillan, a muscular Irish kid with some size and seniority, who Killinger realized had twice his own talent but none of his doggedness. They both started during the first part of the season, but when Wilson returned, Killinger earned the spot.

The Penn State basketball team won 11 of 13 games that year on its way to the college's best basketball season on record, defeating Pittsburgh twice, Western Pennsylvania basketball power Geneva twice, and earning a season-ending victory over Great Lakes Naval Station. Killinger, on the court for almost every minute of the season, performed well enough to impress sportswriters and rival coaches across the East. One Pittsburgh journalist touted him as "a star" with "uncommon ability" who was making "a wonderful record

The 1919–1920 varsity basketball team at Penn State. Killinger is standing in the back row, third from the left. Henry "Hinkey" Haines is standing to next to him, fourth from the left (Penn State University Libraries).

at Penn State" in his sophomore year.[9] He finished third on the team in scoring with a season total of 66 points, which was quite an accomplishment considering most of his energy was spent guarding the opponent's best offensive player each game.[10] The most telling moment of the season for Killinger came in the final minute of a victory over Lehigh, a rival school in the midst of an average year. The Lehigh College newspaper, the *Brown and White*, reported that he "took the joy out of life" when, down three points, he hit a shot with 30 seconds left to cut Lehigh's lead to 23–22. Killinger "dropped in a pretty shot from the center of the floor," then immediately stole the ball and passed to teammate Frank Wolfe, who hit a shot for the Penn State lead. Before the game ended, Wolfe made one more bucket, giving Penn State a 26–23 victory. Overcome with joy, a feeling that was becoming more common for him, Killinger knew he had stolen another game from Lehigh as memories of Penn State's one-point victory on the gridiron seeped into his mind.

It was another Harold Lamb moment.

• • •

Spring weather arrived unusually early in 1919. With it, Glenn Killinger had little time to get in shape for the baseball season. Pursuant to the advice of his football coaches, he chose to forgo spring football practice to put all of his focus and energy into playing baseball. His coaches agreed that he possessed value for the Penn State nine, and was projected to become a starter.

During the final weeks of the basketball season, Coach Bezdek, who would advise spring training before departing to Pittsburgh where he still managed the Pirates, held indoor baseball practices in the Armory, which functioned as the venue for basketball games and wrestling matches. Killinger worked out with the team as much as he could. Just two veterans from the previous season attended the workouts. Most had yet to return from war service. So Bezdek spent the few weeks working mostly with freshmen, who were still permissible in varsity competition. Since he was still contracted to manage the Pirates, Bezdek worked against a fast approaching deadline. Not only did he have a short window to groom a team, he had to find a manager by March 21, the date of his departure for Pittsburgh.

As he walked from one group of players performing a drill to the next, he was pleased with the effort and level of talent that he saw from every position except the pitchers. "The pitching outlook was especially dull," claimed the write-up about the baseball team in the college's yearbook.[11] Substandard pitching was a quandary Bezdek overcame in his first year managing the Pirates in 1917. At Pittsburgh, he was able to mitigate that problem by surrounding average pitchers with competent infielders. He hoped to pull off the same strategy at Penn State.

At training, Bezdek concentrated his energies on finding quality defenders while leaving much of the pitching duties to his assistant and subsequent replacement. Bezdek named George "Doc" Wheeling, a 22-year-old, recent graduate and former captain of the 1918 baseball squad, the team's manager. Bezdek fashioned a raw yet solid infield comprised of dual-sport athlete Nelson Korb at first, theater enthusiast Orville Baublitz at second, freshman Corwin Knapp at shortstop, and Killinger at third.[12] Meanwhile, Wheeling created a three-man rotation on the mound. Eugene Gramley was the only letterman with pitching experience. John Robert Hunter and Myles Thomas assisted him. With an unpredictable pitching staff, Bezdek found three dual-sport athletes to form the outfield—Bill Mullan in center field, Joseph Lightner in left field, and John Traphoner in right field. They were the strength of Penn State's defense. Each player, including Killinger, was interchangeable. Killinger was listed as a third baseman, but he occasionally played shortstop, second base, and catcher during the season.

With only a few days on the job, and no more than a four-year age difference from his players, Wheeling's first duty as boss found him standing in front of the team to inform them that his friend and the team's captain-elect, David Mingle, had died in a plane accident while instructing two other officers in a hydro-airplane at Pensacola, Florida.[13] For Killinger, the shock of his teammate's death was unsettling. Mingle and Killinger were never close friends, but they competed against one another many times. Regrettably, news like this reminded Killinger that, although the war was over, it was still a prevalent part of life. Even four months after the armistice, and with the world's leaders halfway into postwar peace talks, bad news still affected his life.

After having spent many practices inside, Penn State got in one good week of workouts on New Beaver Field before the opener against Maryland State College. After rain postponed the opener at College Park, on April 18 Killinger saw his first varsity baseball action of his college career at third base. Batting in the cleanup position, he performed admirably. He opened the second inning with a single through short and reached third on a throwing error. Three batters later, he was driven in by Baublitz for Penn State's first run of the 1919 season. Adversely, it was Penn State's only score of the game, having gone down in thrashing fashion, 7–1. To credit Killinger's unit, it was the fifth game that Maryland played that season. Killinger finished the game with two hits in four at-bats. He also threw out five batters from his third base position.[14]

The next day, Penn State traveled to Washington, D.C., to play Catholic University. Killinger turned in a modest performance. He still batted fourth in the lineup, but went hitless with two walks. He stole a base and scored twice, but also committed two errors. Despite being out-hit eight to four by the opponent, Penn State nudged out a 9–7 victory. One day later, Killinger batted one-for-three with a run scored, but he committed four crucial errors that helped Catholic rally back from a seven-run deficit to claim a 12–9 victory.[15] Penn State lost once more on April 22 to Washington and Lee College, 4–0. The setback was the last of the season as the Blue and White were poised to roll through the next eight opponents on their way to a 9–3 overall record. Supporters saw the season-opening Southern road trip through Virginia and the nation's capital as an opportunity to "season the team" and give head baseball coach Wheeling "an opportunity to get a line on the new men."[16]

Penn State's win streak began on its home field with narrow victories over Virginia Military Institute and West Virginia, 6–4 and 2–1, respectively. The Blue and White then pounded a strong West Point team, 7–2. With the contest tied 2–2, Penn State scored five runs in the eighth inning to blow the game wide open. Killinger went hitless in five at-bats but played exceptionally well in the field, finishing with four putouts and an assist.[17]

The season ended with victories over Lafayette, Lebanon Valley, Bucknell and Carnegie Tech twice. During the eight-game win streak, Wheeling moved Killinger to second base and down a spot to fifth in the lineup. He batted and ran the bases as well as any of his teammates. His performance in the field was superior. Penn State gave up just 14 runs during that stretch. *La Vie*, the Penn State yearbook, professed, "In Killinger on second and 'Red' Korb at short, the team had a combination that was hard to beat. Their fielding was like clock work and they were always full of the old-time 'pepper.'"[18]

The win streak created a sense of euphoria among those in State College. Only one player would be lost to graduation at season's end, and Penn State was soon to receive a transfer from Lebanon Valley College named Henry "Hinkey" Haines, a four-sport marvel destined for short careers with the New York Yankees and the New York football Giants. The prospect of Haines and Killinger playing together only forecasted greatness for Penn State athletics. (Before his career ended at Penn State, Killinger's baseball teams would finish with 50 wins and just nine defeats. They ran off the longest win streak in college baseball history—31 consecutive victories stretching from the last 11 games in 1920 through the first 20 contests in 1921.)[19]

There was more to come for Killinger. Shockingly, just around the corner was not triumph, but the bench.

• • •

As Glenn Killinger, Red Korb, Joe Lightner and the others who made up the Penn State nine concluded their unexpectedly fruitful nine-win season in the spring of 1919, millions of Americans concealed themselves in their homes and were extra cautious whenever a United Parcel Service package arrived at their front doors. On two occasions between April and June, packages containing dynamite were mailed to the homes of a cross-section of high-level politicians and businessmen. Industrial tycoons John Rockefeller and J. P. Morgan, Supreme Court Justice Oliver Wendell Holmes, and Pennsylvania Governor William C. Sproul were among the targets of the April 30 attack. Although every bomb was intended for a reputed public figure, every citizen from San Francisco to New York seemed concerned about a violent overthrow after Russia's new dictator Vladimir Ilyich Lenin openly encouraged communists worldwide to revolt. Most of the bombs were intercepted at post offices in New York, Atlanta, San Francisco and Seattle.[20] However, one bomb blew off the hands of Georgia Senator Thomas W. Hardwick's housekeeper when she opened a package that arrived at Hardwick's front door. The Senator was a target for co-sponsoring the Immigration Act of 1918, which made punishable by deportation membership in anarchist affiliations in the United States.

The country was stunned again on June 2 as a second wave of terror attacks resulted in explosions outside the homes of Attorney General A. Mitchell Palmer, Judge Charles C. Nott, and Massachusetts State Representative Leland W. Powers. Cleveland Mayor Harry L. Davis and Immigration Chief William W. Sibray were also targeted in the second attack. This time each package arrived with a flyer declaring war on American capitalists that read, "War, Class War, and you were the first to wage it under the cover of the powerful institutions you call to order, in the darkness of your laws. There will have to be bloodshed; we will not dodge; there will have to be murder: we will kill, because it is necessary; there will have to be destruction; we will destroy to rid the world of your tyrannical institutions."[21] Everything about the terror attacks was frightening, forcing the government to reshuffle the Justice Department in order to suppress radical labor organizations by creating the Bureau of Investigation and General Intelligence Division. Attorney General Palmer, now twice victimized by anarchist terror, named 24-year-old J. Edgar Hoover to direct the new departments.[22] As the spring baseball season came to an end, Palmer and Hoover were on the verge of launching a series of police raids, eventually dubbed the "Palmer raids," that would result in the detainment of 10,000 Eastern European immigrants living in over 12 cities of the United States. More than 550 foreigners would be deported under the Immigration Act of 1918.

The raids, detainment, and deportation actually fostered a new level of xenophobic racial profiling as paranoid, working-class, White Anglo-Saxon Protestants felt threatened by this fleeting period of criminality unleashed by an influx of foreigners from such countries as Italy and Russia. This inexplicable period following the First World War left many in America anxious about the changes that had come to their country. Even Killinger, one of the most apolitical students at Penn State, wondered what might come of this unprecedented upsurge of ethnic unrest and domestic terrorism.

There were, however, other reasons why it was not easy for Killinger to focus on his studies during his sophomore year at Penn State. Playing three sports meant a lot of time was spent on the road instead of in classrooms, and a mixed curriculum composed of military drill with metallurgical courses would have been agonizing for anyone. His college transcript shows him to be a proficient, yet unimpressive student. In his sophomore year alone, his marks were abysmal. Killinger failed two courses, chemistry and military drill (two courses that he was forced to retake during his extra semester of college in 1921). He finished the spring semester with a 62.47 average grade.[23]

His bad grades did not hurt his chances of being re-admitted to Penn State. Nor did the report make him ineligible to play football in the fall. Instead, he received a lot of ribbing from his teammates and coaches. Most of his teammates were serious undergraduates who were just as involved with campus activities as Killinger. Unlike Killinger's approach to academics, they operated under the assumption that their athletic career would culminate upon graduation. So they took their lives beyond sports very seriously. While it is true that Killinger was a daffy kid with flaws, but he was charming and had a lot of potential. So his friends put up with him.

In ways large and small, Killinger never quite buckled down to make academics his top priority. During his sophomore year, Killy behaved like a naughty teenager, often making scenes in the campus's quadrangle. Dick Yoder, Killinger's quarterback at West Chester State Teachers College in 1958 and 1959, grew up listening to stories about Killinger's antics from his father, Walter, who attended Penn State with Killinger. "Killy was a character in college," Yoder jested. His father suggested that Killy's inattention toward academics was not a perilous thing. Rather, he lacked "some maturity." That was especially evident years later when peers of Killinger admitted they often spotted him at frat parties late into the night on the evening before some of his baseball games. However, he was never out very late before football or basketball games. Yoder said, "Killinger liked to have fun, joke around. But nothing overtly obnoxious. I'm sure it had an effect on his grades."[24]

Killinger's issues could be dealt with. It was clear that he was not a worldly fellow. But he came from a family that expected hard work. While only a malleable sophomore, he was still developing character. And he possessed enough humility to keep him from being an upstart college punk who had little to offer beyond the athletic arena. Nevertheless, his popularity on campus grew exponentially near the end of his sophomore year, when he was elected by his peers to serve as a student council representative for the Class of 1921. Additionally, he was admitted into the Friars, an athletic fraternity promoting volunteerism within the community at State College.

• • •

Being home in Harrisburg for summer break had a calming affect. The Harrisburg Pipe and Pipe Bending Works Company cut jobs after the war, so Killinger found employment in the family hardware shop on South Thirteenth Street where he grew up. His nights, however, were filled with baseball, which added a few dollars to his summertime gains.

That summer of 1919, Killinger supplemented his college baseball season with an extensive sandlot schedule that served to showcase his game. He divided his time between two amateur teams, the Rosewood Athletic Club of the Allison Hill League and the Commonwealth Travelers of the West End–Harrisburg League, and one semiprofessional ball club that competed in the Pennsylvania Independent League called the Elizabethtown Klein Chocolate Company. Killy played with Rosewood only out of loyalty to his hometown teammates, which still included his brother, Earl, who occasionally caught for the ball club. In fact, he appeared in just three games with Rosewood. In his first game against Reading on May 29, Killinger pinch-hit in the bottom of the seventh inning when the team was down, 7–2. "The Penn State star responded by rapping out a double to right center," reported the *Telegraph*.[25] He was driven in for a score by his old hometown nemesis, Carl Beck, who was setting all kinds of football and track and field records at Harrisburg Tech, which had become one of the best high school football teams in the country. The scoring stopped there, and Rosewood went down in defeat, 7–4. Killinger went hitless in six attempts in his two other games with Rosewood.

Of the three teams, Killinger spent most of his evenings barnstorming the state with Klein Chocolate, whose owners, brothers William and Frederick Klein, earlier that spring failed in their attempt to buy the team into minor league baseball's International League. Klein Chocolate was comprised of college and former major league stars. This meant that Killinger was playing with and against ballplayers in their mid-20s or older who had experience playing at the highest level. The team's owners were former employees of Milton Hershey's Chocolate Company who had relocated to Elizabethtown in 1913 to open their own chocolate business. While they shared a passion for America's pastime, the entrepreneurs felt they needed to draw more attention to their young company. So they sponsored a baseball team in 1919 and actively recruited the best ballplayers available from the Mid-Atlantic. Benjamin G. Rader speaks about this practice in his book *American Sport: From the Age of Folk Games to the Age of Televised Sports* (1999). He writes that investors in joint-stock baseball clubs like the Klein brothers were usually less interested in financial profits than they were about gaining publicity, which required high-profile players and victories.[26] Accordingly, the Klein brothers were able to reserve most of their ballplayers by giving them employment at the chocolate factory in Elizabethtown, located about 20 miles south of Harrisburg and even closer to Hershey. All of their players were given a guaranteed sum per game plus travel expenses.[27] The team would journey by train to backwoods towns of Pennsylvania and major cities in the Mid-Atlantic and Midwest, challenging the best talent in those parts of the country. While showcasing the players' talent in front of semipro and professional competition, the barnstorming trips utilized the ballplayers as breathing billboards that advertised Klein Chocolate in areas of the country that otherwise would have never heard of the company. The Klein brothers asked Killinger to join the team, thinking that he might be the top draw in contests played in Pennsylvania. And Killinger agreed.

Two of the team's pitchers once played for the New York Giants. Others played for teams in both the International and New York–Pennsylvania minor leagues. The Klein brothers and the team's manager, Johnny "Jack" Brackenridge, set up a traveling schedule between May and October against instate semiprofessional teams from York, Lancaster, Ephrata, Hershey, Middletown, Hummelstown, Williamsport, Philadelphia, and Pittsburgh. The owners scheduled games against a team made up of African American war veterans from New York called the Harlem Hell Fighters and the Bacharach Giants of the Atlantic City Independent Negro League. Klein Company played exhibition games against the New York Giants, Philadelphia Athletics, Babe Ruth's Boston Red Sox, Brooklyn Dodgers, Cincinnati Reds, and an all-star select team with players from Detroit, Cleveland, and Chicago. At season's end, Klein Company finished 66–14–3. They dominated their Pennsylvania foes, scored unanticipated victories over the Dodgers, the Athletics, the Red Sox, and the major league all-star team. Seemingly, Klein's biggest struggles were against the aforementioned Negro leagues teams from New York and New Jersey.[28]

On May 30, one day after his pinch-hitting cameo with Rosewood, Killinger played shortstop and batted second in the lineup for Klein Chocolate on its opening day doubleheader against Harrisburg's West End League team, Motive Power. In the first game, he hit a home run and tripled while driving in two runs. In game two, he recorded two more hits, including another home run, which helped his team begin the season with two wins.[29] He failed to appear in games for Klein Company over the next two weeks. When he rejoined the team on June 14 against a ball club from Coatesville, his second at-bat went for a three-run home run. He also recorded five putouts and one assist. Each home run earned him the team's incentive-prize—boxes of almond bars from the Klein brothers.[30] He played six games in June, proving to be a batting sensation by scoring 11 runs and averaging almost two hits per game.

With July came a noticeable slump as Killinger's performance receded significantly. In the eight games he played that month, he recorded two hits and scored five runs. He was walked a bunch, but he struggled when pitchers gave him something to hit. His manager, Jack Brackenridge, dropped him from second in the batting order to seventh. In two games played on Sunday, July 13, Killinger was moved to right field in Klein's 6–4 victory over York Chain Works and left field in the second game, a 4–1 decision over Fulton Athletic Club.[31] Soon afterwards, Brackenridge may have dropped him entirely from the starting lineup, because Killinger appeared in only one more box score that summer for Klein Chocolate.

The reason for his abrupt departure is unclear. It is fair to assume he was benched and accordingly left the team. His lackluster performance at the bat was not measuring up to the former big-leaguers who surrounded him, and the fact that he could not lock down an infield or outfield position must have frustrated the youngster. That reason is feeble, however, as a more pressing matter arose in mid–July.

Earlier in the summer, manager Brackenridge had reached out to several major league baseball clubs for contests. Games against the Philadelphia Athletics and Boston Red Sox were on the horizon. With it would follow an unparalleled stream of media attention. Killinger, about to enter his third year at Penn State, had already arrived on a road of foul play as a member of the Klein ball club. In theory, if anyone would accuse him of having been paid to play a professional sport, there was certainly a month's worth of evidence that could be used to incriminate him in a case of professionalism. But if he could disappear from the roster before the big leaguers came to town, then no one would ever notice. For decades, college athletes got away with playing summer ball for money. *McClure's Magazine* journalist Henry Beach Needham wrote as early as 1905 that "there was no one to say they [collegiate athletes] should not take it [the money], or that, by so doing, they forfeited their eligibility to the college team."[32] Brackenridge, with an unobstructed track record of winning at all costs, was no exception to this form of exploitation. Since winning was the bottom line, professionalism was rarely, if ever, explained to amateur athletes by their coaches, thus the intercollegiate codes of amateurism were not clearly understood by collegians like Killinger. While violators knew that their eligibility was at risk by accepting money, coaches usually assured their amateur athletes that their subterfuge would go unnoticed. More often than not, college players participated in summer professional baseball under names other than their own. "The practice of playing under an assumed name is growing," Needham cautioned in 1905, "The act in itself makes a man a professional." Since legal proof "is very difficult to obtain," wrote the *McClure's* columnist, "players usually got away with it."[33] Moreover, there were cases of blatant maneuvering among college faculties, which had seized control of collegiate athletics from undergraduates beginning in 1903. In the few cases when collegians were caught violating codes of amateur athletics, it usually meant that a rival school unearthed a very large degree of empirical evidence against the violator.

For whatever the reason, Killinger played left field in his final game with the Klein Company on July 14, when he went hitless in a 2–1 victory over Hummelstown.[34] Killinger chose to ride out his final days of the summer on his brother's West End League team, the Commonwealth Travelers. He was a below-average hitter for Commonwealth, hitting .150 with three hits in 20 at-bats in seven games. His addition to the team did nothing to improve Commonwealth's league record.[35] They were .500 when he joined them, and remained .500 when he left for college.

Once confident that he performed among the best athletes his age in the state of Pennsylvania, it appeared as if Killinger had run out of luck. The war, a year ago, adversely offered him many opportunities on the baseball diamond, on the football field, and on the hardwood. But once soldiers arrived home, Killinger no longer stood out. He quickly became an average athlete. If he wasn't aware that his life in the sports world was already more difficult, he would soon learn it when he returned to Penn State that fall.

8

War, Sport and Brotherhood

They arrived at different times in 1919. In one perspective, there was a platoon of war veterans that made Penn State fans clamor for the approaching football season; on the other hand, it was a squad of bigger, faster, and stronger athletes, many with combat experience who posed a threat for Killinger to retain his starting position in the backfield.

But the reality was that this could be the year Penn State would triumph over Pop Warner's Pitt Panthers contingent. Hopes were never higher at State College than in 1919; could this be the year Penn State entered the realm of America's top football outfits? Sidney Sanes, a sports columnist for the *Pittsburgh Post Gazette*, predicted that Penn State would finish among the top teams in the country. Typically, a prediction like that was based on the number of returning lettermen. At Penn State, conversely, it was more than the number of lettermen expected to report to camp. More than 30 doughboys were expected at tryouts on September 2. Each war veteran was eligible to play after having missed either the 1917 or 1918 season, or both. Combined with the ten returning lettermen from 1918 and new faces of underclassmen on the squad, there was good reason to be optimistic about the approaching season. In the *Post Gazette*, Sanes wrote, "Penn State elevens are going to be as tough to down this fall as a pack of Jack Dempseys or [Stanislaus] Zbyskos."[1] In addition to the nearly three dozen war veterans who attended Penn State on scholarship, Hugo Bezdek retained coaches Dick Harlow and "Dutch" Hermann, both servicemen, to help manage the skilled squad. Harlow, former head coach of the Blue and White, was assigned to coach the line, while Hermann, who was also the head basketball coach, reclaimed his duties with the freshman team.

Leading the list of war veterans who returned to campus were four ex-captains: Bob Higgins, Larry Conover, Charlie Way, and Harry Robb.

Higgins was captain of the 1917 team during Killinger's freshman year. Choosing instead to volunteer for the American Expeditionary Force, Higgins attained the rank of lieutenant and served a brief time in France with the

79th Division. While serving in Europe, he played end on the 79th Division's football team and was unanimously selected for the All-American Expeditionary Force team. He was 24 years old, 5'10", and weighed over 180 pounds when he arrived in camp that fall. Higgins's replacement as captain in 1917 was Larry Conover, a 180-pound, 21-year-old center. Conover received his call to serve before the start of the 1917 season. He was assigned to Camp Hancock, where he captained the Ordnance football team in 1918.[2]

As Higgins' and Conover's size offered muscle to the Penn State line, the return of the famed diminutive quarterback and 1918 captain-elect, Charlie Way, provided a modicum of intelligence. When Way, now 21 years old, 5'7", was called to machine gunnery school in Georgia, his replacement as captain, Harry Robb, was soon after called to officer training camp in Plattsburgh, New York. Unlike Way, Robb, age 22, 5'10", 165 pounds, who owned the school's single-game touchdown record (six of them against Gettysburg in 1917—a record that still stands), ended up playing intercollegiate football in 1918. He was detailed to Columbia University to serve as a military instructor in the S.A.T.C. program after having won a Captain's commission in the Army. He was permitted to play football at Columbia, where his teammates voted him team captain. Robb "proved the sensation of the year," a New York sportswriter claimed. He made Walter Camp's All-American second team. The accolade of receiving a varsity letter from Columbia made him one of the few who received football letters from two colleges.[3]

The 1919 team was made up of 22 lettermen. Of that group, nine were backfield players, ten were linemen, and three played the end position. Fifty players were chosen for the roster, which was divided into 25 first-team players and 25 scrub team players. Taken together, the average age of the team was 21. The average size of the line was 5'10", 172 pounds. The backfield's average was 5'10½", 162 pounds.[4]

In addition to seeing war veterans fresh from officer training camps and the bloody battlefields of Europe, Killinger's hopes of attaining a backfield position grew more difficult with the arrival of Henry "Hinkey" Haines. A year earlier, Haines, of York County in Pennsylvania and son of six-term United States Congressman Harry L. Haines, had given up an auspicious start in athletics at Lebanon Valley College to enlist in the Army. After the armistice, he chose to transfer to Penn State instead of returning to Lebanon Valley. Haines, who attended Red Lion High School, which had no football team, had previously played tennis, baseball, and track and field at Lebanon Valley. He had a "wicked" serve on the tennis court, which made him the best tennis player on his college team as a freshman. As captain of the track team, he was untouchable in the pole vault and broad jump. Haines was touted as a future baseball megastar who was already under tentative agreement with the New York Giants.[5] However much in love he was with baseball, football may have become his favorite. In 1917, Haines got his first taste of football as a halfback on the Lebanon Valley scrub team. His first career offensive play was a 95-yard touchdown run against the Carlisle Indians. By the end of the season, his name decorated the headlines of Lebanon Valley's newspapers. "His end runs are usually rather long, numerous, and spectacular," said his friends at Lebanon Valley College. Standing 5'9" with a flair for bashing his body into opposing running backs, Haines was considered the toughest defender at his old school. After a few days of competing with him on the practice field, Killinger said Haines "was very fast and [was] a slashing type-runner with great courage and determination."[6] If there was a player at Penn State who possessed an erudite approach to the game while being one of the most elusive ball carriers like Killinger was, it was Hinkey Haines.

Complicating matters further for Killinger at the start of the season was the absence of Coach Bezdek, who was still managing the Pittsburgh Pirates. Bezdek was not scheduled to arrive back to Penn State until a week before the October 4 opening game against Gettysburg. Coach Dick Harlow, who scarcely knew of Killinger's abilities on the gridiron, acted as the interim head coach. Harlow had worked with Killinger during two short weeks of spring football in March 1918. That team was greatly depleted, however, and Killinger appeared as a beam of sunshine among a maladroit group. It was hardly a way to measure his talents among the best that Penn State had to offer. This was Harlow's first chance to see him in live action against Penn State's elite.

Killinger was surely giddy at the start of the season when Harlow asked him to explain the basics of Bezdek's fancy offensive system featuring unbalanced formations, backfield shifts, line shifts, straight bucks, cross-bucks off tackle, short passes, and deceptive downfield passes. "Bezdek had paid me a compliment when he suggested to Harlow that I was more knowledgeable in the Bezdek system than any other player on the squad," said Killinger as he remembered Harlow's doubtful eye during the exchange.[7] It took confirmation from George Brown, an end on the team, before Harlow took Killinger's report seriously.

The first two weeks of tryouts went well for Killinger. He was drilled to the bone at both halfback and quarterback. The entire team was worked almost nonstop from the time the whistle sounded to begin the day's first practice to the team's post-practice breakdown well after sundown. Killinger was part of an eight-man rotation in the first team's backfield, which included three imminent Walter Camp All-American selections, five future professionals, and four future professional and college head coaches. He felt entirely comfortable in his new surroundings, despite the level of competition. His self-assurance showed on the field. Killinger was doing "fine work of late," revealed Harlow's evaluation after two weeks of practice, and "he cannot be discounted in the final makeup of the backfield."[8]

The truth was that Killinger felt that he fit in on the team. Though a walk-on competing against a collection of scholarship players, he entered tryouts in fine shape. At 5'10", 156 pounds, Killinger was taller than ever, but was still considered rather fragile for the weekly poundings dished out at practices and games. The persona was certainly puzzling to Killinger, who watched tiny Charlie Way run circles around the scrub team every day without anyone questioning his durability. Killinger possessed an aura of self-righteousness; due to the circumstances, he felt that he had to act bigger and heavier than he actually was. Walking into that first meeting room filled with servicemen was reasonably daunting. So he set out to disprove that façade.

An intra-squad scrimmage was arranged for September 20. The best 22 players were divided into two teams. One onlooker described the scene: "the fact that there are so many veterans on the squad made the two teams nearly equal in strength."[9] Killinger impressed. "Killinger's appearance is deceiving, but there isn't a single sport in which he lacks unusual ability," Coach Harlow told a local correspondent after the scrimmage. "He is comparatively small, but powerful, and added to that he is a real fighter." Harlow predicted there is "a bright athletic career" ahead for Killinger.[10]

A week later, a second scrimmage was held. The eight backfield players were the feature that day. Buck Williams and Thomas Ritner were made dueling quarterbacks for the first string and scrub team, respectively. The first-team fullback was William Hess, while George Snell played the position for the scrubs. Halfbacks for the first team were Harry Robb and Charlie Way, while Killinger and Hinkey Haines were made the halfbacks on the scrub team. Behind the running and passing of Killinger and Haines, the scrubs defeated the first string, 3–0. The *Post Gazette* reported: "Sensational runs by Charlie Way gave the varsity several chances to score, but they failed to penetrate the scrub [defense]. Haines and Killinger starred for the scrubs."[11] A 20-yard dropkick by Thomas Ritner was the difference in the scrimmage.

Killinger remembered this scrimmage as a "dog-eat-dog" competition "in the fight for starting jobs." In his unpublished memoir, he wrote of the scrimmage in striking detail.

> The war veterans cared not for life nor limb, especially those of their opponents. Charley Way had lost none of his brilliant running ability and won the right halfback job. A truly great athlete emerged as the other halfback in the person of one of my closest friends, Hinky [sic] Haines, a walk-on transfer student from Lebanon Valley.[12]

Two superior athletes may have beaten him out, but if there was one thing that Killinger proved after surviving two violent scrimmages, it was that he was resilient. Four potential starters suffered injuries, none worse than Buck Williams, who broke a bone in his hand.

An extra surge of assurance consumed Killinger at the start of practice on Monday, September 29, five days before the opening game, when Hugo Bezdek returned from Pittsburgh. Bezdek's arrival at New Beaver Field was a staged exhibition highlighted by a pack of elated students, a military band, and the football team looking on suspiciously, since most of them had never seen him before. A special telegram in the *Pittsburgh Gazette Times* reported that "nearly the entire student body surrounded the field and cheered" as Bezdek ran out on the practice pitch still dressed in his Pirates uniform and his cap turned backward. He wasted no time in admonishing the players and coaches: "we are away [sic] behind and will have to work hard." Bezdek ordered an impromptu scrimmage between the first and second teams. The scrimmage lasted the duration of practice, and Bezdek refused to end the scrimmage until the starters scored four touchdowns against the scrubs.[13] "Evidently, he was not totally pleased with the team," Killinger recalled years later. "He made a few corrections in our plays and the manner in which they were executed." The most noticeable vexation, he remembered, was the philosophical quarrel between Bezdek and Harlow that first day. Having two larger-than-life head coaches with colliding egos was an early-season handicap the talented team struggled to overcome. "It was clearly evident that Bezdek and Harlow were not going to be bosom pals," Killinger described grudgingly.[14]

Bezdek ended the practice by lecturing his team. He stressed that every player had to "come through with not just his best, but also with more than his best!" While Killinger appreciated the reprimand, his veteran teammates did not. Dick Rauch, one of the oldest players on the team and who hailed from the same hometown as Killinger, let out a loud and insolent sigh. Ridge Riley, author of *The Football Letters* (1977), called Bezdek's dramatic return "poorly conceived for a squad dominated by older war veterans already well acquainted with martinet types."[15]

Killinger did everything that was asked of him during the weeks leading up to the opening game. He stunned Harlow with his aptitude of the game. He held his own against the much-acclaimed war veterans. To his chagrin, he was left out of the starting lineup when Penn State faced off against Gettysburg on October 4. Haines and Clarence Beck started at halfback. Robb got the start at quarterback over Way, who never truly recovered from a broken hand attained while playing baseball a few years earlier and consequently had difficulty handling the ball from that position. And Hess was named fullback.

Tied 0–0 at intermission in a day the *Pittsburgh Post Gazette* described as "too hot for football," Bezdek made halftime adjustments that resulted in 33 unanswered points. He substituted Way for Beck and inserted Killinger at quarterback for Robb.[16] The adjustments suddenly "speeded up the Penn State attack." After Bob Higgins scooped up a fumble and ran it 25 yards for a touchdown to put Penn State on the board in the third quarter, the elusive

Way ran for gains of 23 and 30 yards on the next possession, placing the ball at Gettysburg's 2-yard line. Hinkey Haines scored on a goal-line plunge. Haines scored again in the fourth quarter, as did Way and Higgins. Penn State won by a misleading margin, 33–0. Very late in the game, Haines was hurt.[17] The *Gazette* claimed he sustained "general bruises." The injury must have been severe; his play was very limited the remainder of the season.

The injury to Haines meant one of the halfback positions was open for the taking. Killinger worked hard during the week leading up to Penn State's next game. One sportswriter called him "the scrappiest man on the squad" after watching him race through drills that week. Bezdek rewarded him for his diligence by naming him the starter at right halfback against Bucknell. Way became the quarterback, while Robb played left halfback and Hess started at fullback.

The Blue and White came in as a slight favorite, but Bucknell played a clean game in an otherwise soggy environment that, as the *Pittsburgh Daily Post* illustrated, "was better fitted for water polo than for football." Penn State struck first in the second period when Larry Conover, an offensive tackled turned place kicker, nailed a field goal for the early lead. Later that quarter, Way broke a 50-yard run to Bucknell's 5-yard line.[18] Bucknell's defense held Penn State on downs, but then shanked a punt to the 12-yard line on their first play. Way scored three plays later. Penn State held a 9–0 lead at halftime after Conover missed the extra point.[19] Both teams were kept scoreless in the second half that, according to the *Daily Post*, featured a punting duel as a downpour turned New Beaver Field into a "sea of mud." The nine-point victory was hard-fought. Killinger was taken out of the game before he could do anything memorable, and his name did not appear in any of the postgame commentary.

One week later, sportswriters along the East Coast plugged Penn State's major showdown against Dartmouth as the nation's top contest. The game was hardly a disappointment to the 4,500 fans who showed up at Hanover ballpark. It featured an up-tempo pace by each team. Each of Penn State's touchdowns—both by Charlie Way—was scored in unusual fashion. Way, who was then called "Rabbit" or "Pie" by his teammates, scored the first on an 85-yard kickoff return, and the other was a fumble that he scooped up and took to paydirt. Penn State led in the first half before Dartmouth's best player, Jim Robertson, scored two touchdowns to tie the game at halftime. In the third quarter, the Green and White's Pat Holbrook scored the go-ahead touchdown. The final was 19–13 in Dartmouth's favor. Killinger saw some action when he was substituted in for Harry Robb.[20] There is no indication that he played any role in an unsuccessful Penn State rally.

The loss to Dartmouth exposed the copious level of dissension that permeated the team. Ever since Bezdek's first practice with the team, the older war veterans never got over their first unfavorable impression of their coach.[21] The veterans likewise loathed the younger players. Many of the war veterans were more loyal to Coach Harlow—their coach before the war—which made them less inclined to respond to the discipline of Bezdek's system. Some of the younger players, like Killinger, found themselves in backup roles and were accordingly frustrated about playing time. It was clear within the group that the quarreling seriously impeded the talent of Penn State's individuals, a revealing point made when considering they were shut out for a half by non-major college Gettysburg, defeated a mediocre Bucknell team by just nine points, and lost to Dartmouth. In an odd way, Bezdek and Harlow were representative of the team's contrasting demographic. Harlow, like all war veterans currently wearing the blue and white, had voluntarily given up his job to serve his country. The battle-hardened war veterans begrudged Bezdek and the others, who, in contrast, made fewer sacrifices as they remained on the home front during the final months of the war.

"Knowing Bezdek after a football and basketball season," Killinger said diagnostically of the fragmented team chemistry, "I could feel an explosion coming." At midweek in preparation for Ursinus, Bezdek called the varsity squad together before practice for a meeting. Killinger recalled that Bezdek "gave each member of the squad an opportunity to express his true feelings without fear of any retaliation." Bezdek said to the team:

> Now you fellows decide which eleven of you are to compose the team. It makes no difference to me how you choose them. If you want to have a free-for-all and the eleven survivors be the chosen ones, have a free-for-all. Now as to system. I understand that there is objection to my system of play. All I have to say is, choose your own system. It makes no difference to me which one you choose. I can coach any of them.[22]

Bezdek left the room to let the players have it out.

Team captain Bob Higgins insisted that two teams be created, one pro–Harlow and the other pro–Bezdek, not to choose a style of play, but to find a permanent starting lineup for the remainder of the season. In jest, Killinger referred to the two teams as "good guys" and "bad guys." He admitted, "The two teams played a hard-fought and vicious game with the bad guys winning by one T.D." When the scrap ended, a point had been made, and the mutiny was diverted. Each player agreed thereafter on doing things Bezdek's way. "It came forth as a body, united of purpose and pro–Bezdek to the core," reported the *Indianapolis Star*.[23]

The next time Penn State took the field, on October 25, they went on to roll over their opponent, Ursinus College, 48–7. Despite a comfortable lead from the start, Bezdek never inserted Killinger into the game. Bezdek used 33 players by substituting three different 11s. A frustrated Killinger just stood and watched.[24] Ursinus's only score came near the end of the game after a player scooped up a bad center snap that got past the third-string back and went 80 yards for a touchdown. To rub salt in the wound, the *Harrisburg Evening News* boasted about a season record accomplished by the "flashy halfback" Charlie Way, who returned a kickoff for a touchdown for the second consecutive week. "Way is a hero in the minds of the Penn State student body," the broadsheet expounded. "Way does not weigh more than 152 pounds, but is a speed marvel."[25]

On November 1, Bezdek took 20 players on the road trip to Philadelphia to face off against the University of Pennsylvania's football machine that had given up only one touchdown all season and had outscored its opponents, 237–7. Because of the loss to Dartmouth, the game against Penn, then considered the best team along the Eastern seaboard, was a must win for Penn State to stay in a position to claim the championship of the East. For Killinger, the opportunity to play on Penn's Franklin Field was important to him; it was a chance to fulfill his childhood dream. He went through the week with a better attitude and was included on the travel roster as a substitute. His work ethic that week must have been apparent because the day before the game Bezdek told reporters: "There's not a boy on my team who won't fight from the beginning to the end."[26]

Almost 20,000 fans sat in an incessant drizzle to watch Bezdek's unit shock Penn, 10–0. The conditions should have neutralized Penn State's speed while favoring the Quakers, who possessed a size advantage over the Blue and White. Yet one critical mistake gave the visitors the confidence they needed to hold on for a victory. In the second quarter, Penn's Bots Brunner fumbled the ball at his own 2-yard line. With short field position, Henry Robb was able to power his way in for a touchdown. A 25-yard field goal in the fourth quarter by Larry Conover iced the game for Penn State. When the final whistle blew, the visiting student body rushed Franklin Field like "wild men," reported the *Post Gazette*. Killinger, who substituted into the game to give Charlie Way a rest in the third period, was pleased to join in on the celebration.[27]

After the game, Lou Little, an offensive tackle for Penn, regretfully admitted, "We didn't think much of Penn State. We hadn't lost a game. We were conquering heroes." He added, "We thought all we had to do was blow up the football and go out and run over those birds. As a matter of fact, they had a whale of a team. So there we were, all swelled up like poisoned pups, fit to be killed—and they killed us."[28]

Penn State rolled over Lehigh and Cornell in the next two games with scores of 20–7 and 20–0, respectively. Killinger entered the Lehigh game in the first quarter for Hinkey Haines, who was carried off the field after having his bell rung, but did not see the field against Cornell.[29]

The win streak and upcoming annual clash at Forbes Field against Pop

Warner's undefeated Pittsburgh outfit had all of State College abuzz. Penn State had lost to Pitt in six successive Thanksgiving Day contests. But this year, Penn State turned out its best performance all season. While outgaining the host 372 yards to 81, Penn State held Pitt to just four first downs, and only one before the final period. Using fancy forward passes on offense while packing the run defense tight to the line of scrimmage to shut down Pitt's All-American Tom Davies, who had shredded Penn State's defense for over a hundred total yards and a score a year earlier, Bezdek's team shut out Warner's unit, 20–0. The game's highlight was a trick play in the first quarter when Penn State faked a punt out of its own end zone, which drew ten Pitt players up on the line to rush the punter, leaving space for team captain Bob Higgins to swing open in the center of the field to receive the forward pass from teammate William Hess. On the advice of assistant coach Dick Harlow, who was responsible for scouting Pitt during the preceding weeks, "The team practiced this play the entire week before the Pitt game," Killinger recalled years later, adding, "Hess was not a very accurate passer and had trouble throwing the ball to Higgins." But when Penn State stopped Pitt inside its own 5-yard line, quarterback Harry Robb signaled his unit into kick formation on an early down. The formation drew ten Pitt players up to the line of scrimmage with center Herb Stein, usually a safety on punt return plays, eager to rush the punt. After catching the snap in his end zone, Hess rolled a few steps to his right, then heaved the heavy, wet and muddy ball toward Higgins, who made the catch in stride. "Charley Way, because he was our fastest runner," Killinger described, "was selected to go downfield and block the Pitt safety." Higgins then motored the length of the field for a 95-yard touchdown.[30] The play, officially credited in *Spalding Guide of 1920*, has stood as Penn State's longest passing touchdown in its history.[31] Penn State later scored on a 3-yard plunge by Hess in the second period and a 47-yard run by Way in the third.

Despite the margin of victory, Killinger did not play in the game. He needed just one more quarter to qualify for a varsity letter. While stunned that his beloved coach denied him that opportunity, Killinger never expressed disappointment toward Bezdek.[32]

The season's success, especially victories over Penn and Pittsburgh, won Bezdek favor in the eyes of the trustees. At season's end, he was granted a new contract that included a three-year extension and an increased salary of $7,500 for coaching and $4,500 for his services as physical education director.[33]

Sportswriters were divided over how good Penn State was in 1919. Neither the Associated Press nor College Coaches Polls existed. Moreover, the only bowl game played at the time was the Rose Bowl. Consequently, there were no post-season opportunities for Penn State to prove itself among the best in the country against formidable competition. Usually sportswriters ranked teams geographically, then accordingly issued mythical titles. Much of the talk nationally was about Notre Dame, which had gone 9–0, and Illinois, which finished 6–1 in a difficult Midwest schedule. The loss to Dartmouth, a worthy opponent that finished the year 6–1–1 and ranked seventh in the country at the time they played, plus Penn State's inability to run up the score on its opponents presented problems for sportswriters to name them the nation's top-ranked team. Penn State's highest output that season was the 48 points scored against an overmatched Ursinus team. Against ranked opponents, Penn State scored no more than 20 points, which they did against both Pittsburgh and Cornell. Bezdek's offense scored 173 total points. In contrast to the offense, the Blue and White defense pitched five shutouts, while giving up a total of 33 points in eight games.

There was a consensus among Eastern sportswriters that Penn State did have the most difficult schedule among Eastern teams. Because of that, Penn State was named the hypothetical champion of the East ahead of Syracuse, Colgate, Dartmouth, Pittsburgh, West Virginia, Pennsylvania, and Harvard. Robert Maxwell of the *Philadelphia Evening Ledger* ranked Penn State first in the country, declaring that although it was beaten by Dartmouth early in the season, "the big green team would not now have a chance." Maxwell added that Penn State "looked to be the best at the end of the season." He remarked further, "I believe State could have beaten any team in the country." Jim Isaminger of the *Philadelphia North American* argued, "If Penn State has the championship of the Keystone State clinched, it also has a peep-in on the national title." The *Pittsburgh Gazette Times'* Harry Keck wrote, "The Pitt game was a triumph, indeed. It wiped out the stigma of a seemingly endless chain of setbacks at the hands of the Panthers and it carried with it the collegiate championship of the State of Pennsylvania and rounded out a record that compared favorably with, if it doesn't overshadow that of all other contenders for the Eastern championship."[34]

A week after the Pitt game, Coach Bezdek issued varsity letters to just 12 players. Killinger was not one of them. He recalled missing out on the letter (which by graduation would have earned him four varsity football letters and ten overall) "by not playing in two full quarters of that football season."[35] He did receive a miniature gold football as a minor award along with everybody on the roster. Bezdek explained why he was so selective in issuing varsity letters: "from the Penn game on, the coaches stood pat on their first team and only made changes in case of injuries."[36] Killinger, consequently, after the intra-squad skirmish following the Dartmouth loss, hardly saw the field during the second half of the season.

Killinger took it well, nonetheless. He was all too excited for the 1920 season. Why would he not be? Penn State was riding a five-game win streak, and just four lettermen would to be lost to graduation.

9

Harold Lamb Moments

The Armory at State College was an uninviting gymnasium saturated with the sweat of boxers, wrestlers, and basketball players. It was used as the indoor facility for baseball in the early spring. Students often gathered there to play intramural sports in the evenings. Sometimes Bezdek ordered his physical education professors to hold classes there.

Glenn Killinger was all too familiar with the Armory. Half of his spring semesters were spent there playing basketball and fitting in early baseball training.

It might be odd to think that basketball and baseball at Penn State were kinder to Killinger than football was. There is no denying that he made quite a name for himself in each sport by the end of his sophomore year.

Practices for the 1920 basketball season began immediately following the Thanksgiving Day football game against Pittsburgh. After a two-year absence, Coach Burke "Dutch" Hermann assumed his job as boss of the Penn State five. Over 70 candidates tried out. Of that number, just eight would be retained for the varsity.

All eight players were good enough to start for almost any team in the country. Some of them were returning lettermen, like Nathaniel Replogle at center; Bill Mullan, Frank Wolfe, and Lloyd Wilson split time at the forward positions; Glenn Killinger became the team's right guard. Henry "Hinkey" Haines made the team as the left guard. Two war veterans made the team, Francis Young and John Robert Hunter. Hermann watched his varsity unit run through drills and there was little to scrutinize. His first impression of his new team made his heart beat faster.

As Hermann got to know his players, he found he had something in common with them: diligence. Hermann bristled with fresh theories, and his players were open to the most extreme of them. Best of all, Hermann was pleased to discover that they were fast and observant learners. No sooner would he draw something on the blackboard than the players made his chalk marks come alive on the court. Penn State lore suggests that Hermann was the creator of the five-man-weave, an offensive system whereby the players passed the ball around and continuously cut through the center of the key. As Killinger once remembered his coach's pointers, "Short, snappy passes are the rule with every man moving at all times."[1] The scheme demanded that the man with the ball look for the teammate cutting under the basket first. Recognizing that Hermann's system was still in a primitive stage, which eventually allowed future generations to perfect the weave, Killinger admitted, "Had we really developed the weave, we would have blown the opposition right out of the Armory."[2]

The duo of Hinkey Haines and Killinger had much to do with the team's ability to grasps new plays and defensive adjustments. The two shared a brilliant understanding of the game, and combined with their speed on the defensive end, it was incredibly difficult for opponents to score from the backcourt.

After spending the past year recuperating from shellshock, Hermann felt at ease in his role as coach. He was known for enjoying a whisky every evening after practice. His talented 1920 team gave him fewer reasons to consume the spirits. Incidentally, the habit of drinking a glass of liquor was no longer an option for the weary coach. Something disenchanting materialized on the eve of Penn State's first game of the season. The Eighteenth Amendment, banning the manufacture, sale and transportation of intoxicating beverages, had gone into effect. Debated for decades as a measure to reduce crime, corruption, gambling, and to suppress immoral houses of debauchery while promoting wholesome recreation and sports, such as clean motion pictures, baseball and football, the elimination of saloons as the medium to consume alcohol picked up heavy steam during the war as the need for reserved supplies of grain for food production trumped traditional social behaviors. In February 1919, Pennsylvania became the 45th state to ratify the Eighteenth Amendment. One year later, at midnight on January 17, 1920, the Volstead Act, establishing prohibition as the official law of the land, overrode President Wilson's veto of the amendment. Suddenly, the United States became a dry country.

The reaction to prohibition was paradoxically satisfying and venomous. The earliest reports coming from prohibition law enforcement officials were upbeat and triumphant. On January 28, the Civil Service Commissioner in Chicago rejoiced in the fact that, for the first time in 20 years, because of prohibition the police trial board docket did not contain a single case.[3] In Philadelphia, a father and son were arrested for operating an illegal still that was manufacturing whisky and whisky-flavored cigars.[4] Near State College, one police officer was fired from the service when caught consuming the demon rum at a New Castle speakeasy while on duty. However, prohibition's opponents now went ardently to work, sketching out their views of the law in ways that insisted that the Eighteenth Amendment was a disgrace to traditional

American values. One cartoon appeared in the *Harrisburg Telegraph* presented the lifeless body of British folksong character John Barleycorn dragged through the marsh of the River Styx by ferryman Charon.⁵ The entire notion of eradicating alcohol from society was mocked in silent film as moviegoers were entertained by the re-release of the 1919 Mack Sennett comedy, *The Speakeasy*, about a hotel proprietor who tries to operate a speakeasy in the cellar of his boarding house.

Prohibition had little bearing on Hermann's ability to coach his team. Meanwhile, neither Glenn Killinger nor his teammates went on record about how the new constitutional measure impacted their lives at college. They were a focused bunch who devoured every drill that Hermann made them do. It must have worked. Penn State opened the season impressively with six straight victories; after one setback, they finished the season with six consecutive wins.

The Blue and White's high-scoring offense embarrassed its opponents, who did not take it well. Among the lopsided outcomes were victories over Juniata, 56–18, Dickinson, 62–18, Washington and Jefferson, 43–25, Lebanon Valley College (Hinkey Haines's old team), 69–10, and George Washington, 60–6.⁶ Penn State defeated Pittsburgh twice, Lafayette, an Alumni team that counted on the record, and Lehigh. They squeaked out victories over West Virginia by seven points and Swarthmore by two. In a playbook he kept after his senior season, Killinger explained Coach Hermann's philosophy of beating an opponent: "Go hard for [the] first 10 minutes and then take time out if necessary and then go hard for 5 minutes and then rest up a minute and go hard [the] rest of [the] half. Take everything out of the [opposing] team at [the] start!"⁷

That attitude helped Penn State achieve a 12–1 season, their only defeat coming to the best team in the country, the University of Pennsylvania, 23–16. Despite the loss, Killinger and Haines may have put forth their best defensive effort against the much bigger Quaker team led by the Ivy League's leading scorer, Lou Martin. The guards were forced to shoot from the middle of the floor all game. Killy and Hinkey made it impossible for Penn's guards to get close enough to take shots from under the basket.⁸

At season's end, the Blue and White scored 515 total points, an average of 40 points a game. They gave up just 232 points, an average of 18 points a game. Three times they scored more than 60 points, and once they held an opponent to single digits.⁹ Those were astonishing numbers for the era.

Penn State was rewarded with a number four national ranking and a second-place finish behind Pennsylvania among teams in the East. In addition, the team elected Killinger captain of the 1921 squad. The *Harrisburg Telegraph* announced: "W. Glenn Killinger, of this city, star guard for past two seasons, was yesterday elected captain of the Penn State basketball team for next year."

"He is an all around athlete," the hometown newspaper reminded readers.[10]

Penn State's victory over Lehigh on March 12 ended its basketball season. The following day, Killinger was back in the Armory, getting ready to play baseball as inclement weather prevented outdoor work. He was one of seven lettermen returning to the lineup, which was important because Athletic Director Hugo Bezdek manufactured "one of the hardest schedules ever arranged for a Penn State Nine," as he put it, which included extensive trips North, South, East, and West.[11]

To Killinger's surprise, Bezdek announced to the players that he had resigned his job managing the Pittsburgh Pirates so he could coach the Blue and White full-time.[12] Each day, Bezdek ordered bunting and base running drills, rundowns between first and second, and second and third. These drills were repeated daily. The drills and other activities of the team seemed to bore the players, but Bezdek was unrelenting in his approach. He had talent that he did not want to go to waste for lack of fundamentals.

Perhaps the most talented among the group was Bezdek's new left fielder, Hinkey Haines. Truth be told, many of the team members were all too familiar with Haines as a halfback on the football team and a guard on the basketball team. Haines was already a decorated right-handed hitter, and he continued to live up to the celebrity against the best baseball talent in the country. During a game against West Point, Haines climbed the fence, robbing a home run among the branches of a tree. He was a much better outfielder than hitter in 1920, but was kept fifth in the lineup all season and led the team in stolen bases.[13]

Killinger, meanwhile, ended up giving his best performance yet, making him into one of college baseball's pre-eminent infielders by season's end. Remarkably, he missed the season-opening road trip through the South. Instead, he joined his meteorology class on a weeklong field trip through Eastern Pennsylvania. During the time away, Penn State had games against Yale and Catholic Universities cancelled because of rain. The Blue and White lost to Navy, but defeated Delaware and Maryland. Killinger returned to third base on April 14 and contributed in a 14–5 victory over Michigan played in State College.[14]

In his second game, Killinger had three hits and scored two runs, including a home run that lifted Penn State over Swarthmore, 8–4. Two games later, he blasted a two-run home run to deep left in the eighth inning to help Penn State defeat Fordham in a contest played in New York City.[15]

Throughout his career, Killinger was known more as an infielder than a hitter. The *Pittsburgh Post Gazette* called him the "guardian of the Keystone" from his third base position.[16] Bezdek said he was an excellent third baseman but had the ability to "play anywhere, and play well." The coach considered his protégé "one of those natural freaks." And he hailed Killinger for his "particularly strong and accurate throwing arm."[17] As it turned out, Killinger was as remarkable a right-handed hitter as he was a fielder in 1920, batting .301 in 15 games. Bezdek once praised Killinger's ability to bat well under pressure: "He hits his best in the pinches and usually his pinch punches are long swats."[18]

Killinger and his team were nearly invincible in 1920, scoring 167 runs against just 67. "It was a team with a great attitude and team morale," Killinger noted in his memoir. Owing to Bezdek's professional style of managing, Killinger said, "we played like major leaguers."[19] The Blue and White finished 18–3, with signature wins over Yale, Princeton, Pitt, Syracuse, and Colgate. Included in the list of those who fell prey to Penn State was the University of California. Although no official rankings were kept for intercollegiate baseball during this era, sportswriters considered California, 22–9–1, the best team in the West, while Bezdek's Blue and White was called by many the best in the East. Bezdek used his West Coast connections to arrange the post-season coastal challenge considered by writers in the East as the national title game.

The contest was scheduled the same day as Penn State's commencement ceremony, which brought nearly 10,000 fans to State College for the game. Many of the spectators drove their cars onto the back end of New Beaver Field, just beyond the outfield fence, and ruined the grass. They watched as Penn State pulled out a 6–3 victory. Killinger managed to get a single and score a run. The most impressive moment of the game came from Killinger on the defensive side when he snagged a hard-hit ball that screamed down the third base line with his bare hand and threw a strike to first base to complete the putout.[20]

The victory capped an 11-game win streak for Penn State and awarded them the mythical national championship.

The combination of Killinger and Haines began to capture the public imagination as the dominant duo of their era. They were each 21 years of age, with another year together ahead. It was common back then, as it is in the early 21st century, to see two players on the same team dominate a sport, but Killy and Hinkey marveled on the same playing surfaces in three sports: football, basketball, and baseball. The sports seasons of 1920 would become their gateway to immortality. They seemed to be equal in each sport; hitting and fielding in baseball; passing and running in football; shooting and defending in basketball. Lively debates began in State College, Pittsburgh, and among East Coast sportswriters about who was a better leader, which man was more reliable in the clutch, about what sport each should concentrate on. Their bond grew so close that Killinger admitted that the two "became inseparable as friends."[21] That summer, he decided to spend a few evenings playing with Haines in a twilight baseball league in Haines's hometown in Red Lion, Pennsylvania.

9. Harold Lamb Moments

Baseball had become a vital part of Glenn Killinger's life in 1920. He made it his primary sport, vaulting the hardball ahead of football and basketball. He utilized another summer both developing his skills while exposing himself to major league scouts in the state of Pennsylvania. In addition to the three or four nights he played with Hinkey Haines in the Red Lion Twilight League, Killinger split time with the Rosewood Athletic Club and a new semiprofessional team from Newport, Pennsylvania, of the Dauphin County–Perry County League.[22]

When he arrived home for summer break in June, Killinger spent the month playing for Newport. His time with the semiprofessional team was hardly newsworthy, but his motives were centered on playing against the best that Pennsylvania had to offer. His heart was really with his hometown's Rosewood team. So in July, Killinger joined his friends in Harrisburg.

Rosewood was 11–7 and in second place of the Allison Hill League when Killinger entered the lineup on July 9. When the regular season finished in late August, Rosewood had improved to 19–10, which was good enough to clinch the Allison Hill League pennant. During that span, hitting is where Killinger made his mark. He showed explosive power, belting a grand slam in a game against Reading on July 13. He had more hits and runs in the 11 games he played in than any member of Rosewood.

A best of seven city championship series was arranged between Rosewood and the West End Athletic Club of the Harrisburg League. Games were to be played on Harrisburg's Island Park, the Allison Hill ballpark on Seventeenth and Chestnut Streets, and at West End's diamond on Fourth and Seneca Streets. The college star's clutch hitting and nearly flawless fielding helped his team win the title while building his reputation. Rosewood was able to take down West End in five games. In the first game, a 6–2 victory, Killinger went 2-for-2, scored once, made three putouts, and assisted eight times from his shortstop position. After losing game two, 9–2, Rosewood rebounded with three consecutive victories. Glenn Killinger, the local *Telegraph* reported, "was shooting them to first in great fashion."[23] Moreover, he emerged as Rosewood's most consistent batter, hitting two triples and scoring four times in the final three games.

Killinger's devotion to the various summer legion and semiprofessional teams was in good order. Major league scouts were busy tracking his abilities. Coach Bezdek had something to do with that, but it hardly served as an acceptable excuse for Killinger to miss the opening of the 1920 football season.[24]

• • •

Though Hugo Bezdek could be a sentimental sort, he was first and foremost an obsessive winner. He pushed his players hard to achieve something greater than their best effort. The returning war veterans seemingly ceased their rebellious ways as Bezdek unveiled a new seven-days-a-week training program that included long hikes on Mount Nittany and extra scrimmages on Sundays for those who hadn't played in varsity games. Loyalty was loyalty, but it only extended so far. As much as Bezdek planned to give Killinger all the opportunity in the world to earn a starting position in Penn State's backfield, the fact that the Harrisburg lad arrived a week late to training camp and missed the first inter-squad scrimmage spoiled that chance.

Equally detrimental to Killinger's opportunity to win a starting position was the unseasonable weather that intensified his hay fever symptoms, an affliction that had plagued him since childhood. "I was suffering from my usual pollen fever that caused me to sneeze repeatedly and my eyes to water profusely," Killinger said unapologetically. He felt so miserable, in fact, it was "the worst" case of hay fever he ever had, he recalled, "that I almost gave up football."[25] His practice habits accordingly worsened, and he suffered because of it. That's why, in late September 1920, he had to accept that Buck Williams had won the starting position at quarterback, and Hinkey Haines, Charlie Way, George Snell, Joe Lightner, and William Hess were already duking it out for the three remaining backfield positions.[26]

After regaining his full strength by the second week of pre-season camp, Killinger became as determined a player as most Penn Staters had ever seen. Much of his free time was spent at New Beaver Field getting in extra running until he could barely breathe. The team trainer Bill Martin put the whole team on a strict diet; "no more pie, candy or smokes" was the order.[27] Killinger deliberately spent extra time on the tackling dummy and kicking punts. He knew there would be no shot to get on the field if he failed at either task. At the end of camp, Killinger "has broken into the second team backfield," reported a correspondent for the *Harrisburg Telegraph*. It appeared that Bezdek planned to use him "as understudy to Buck Williams, at quarterback."[28]

By the time Penn State kicked off its 1920 season with a September 26 visit from Muhlenberg College, Killinger still found himself in standby. In the lead-up to the opener, his hard-to-please coach called him the team's "pinch hitter." He could effectively play any position in the backfield, Bezdek said. "He is a scrappy player," said the *Telegraph*. "Bezdek considers him especially valuable to send in in a pinch."[29] Despite the approbation, Killinger unhappily resumed his role of supporter from the sideline as he was forced to watch the petite sensation and the college's long jump record-holder, Charlie "Rabbit" Way, run rings around the visitors' defense. Way scored twice on runs of 72 yards and 20 yards. Meanwhile, Williams played a solid game at quarterback, and Hinkey Haines and Joe Lightner were suitable additions at each halfback position in Bezdek's single-wing offense. Bezdek inserted

Killinger into the game at quarterback in the second half, but the contest was virtually over and uncompetitive at that point.[30] Muhlenberg's only score came on a scooped fumble returned for a touchdown. Penn State won, 27–7.

Afterward, Bezdek told his team he was far from satisfied, claiming ineptitude on the offensive and defensive lines and a lack of team play. He told his team that he would "make several shifts in his varsity lineup" before the next game against Gettysburg.[31] A couple of days later at practice, Killinger was leading the first-string offense. One *New York Times* reporter who observed the workout said that Killinger looked particularly impressive running with the ball. "When he tucks the pigskin under his arm he is even superior to Buck Williams," said the nationally syndicated daily. Identifying one shortfall, the *Times* wrote, "he is far from being the field general that the Monessen boy [Williams] is."[32]

Strangely, Killinger did not see a second in the contest against Gettysburg, which was a game Penn State eked out with a feeble offensive performance, 13–0. With a major showdown against Dartmouth a week away, the team that had handed Penn State its only defeat in 1919, the narrow margin of victory caused reasonable concern among the Blue and White contingent.

Such was the draw of Glenn Killinger. The seesaw experience of playing for Bezdek was reaching its tipping point. For years he was given opportunities at practice, but seldom had those chances morphed into playing time. Years later, Killinger admitted that he always felt he was a better quarterback than Buck Williams. His performances, however, were not good enough for his ultra-demanding coach. When Killinger was coaching at West Chester State Teachers' College in the decades after World War II, he applauded the coaching tactic. Bezdek used insistent, tough-love methods to drain every iota of talent out of his already remarkable athletes. Killinger confessed that was what Bezdek did to him at Penn State. He later acknowledged his refusal to respond to the tactic until after that Gettysburg game in 1920. "Following that second game," Killy would say 46 years later, "I began to put forth more and more effort each day during practice."[33] From that day forward, Killinger vowed to invest every step and breath into his practice habits. His new attitude won him the starting position in Penn State's first big contest of the year.

The Penn State–Dartmouth matchup was portrayed as college football's most important game of the young season. Dartmouth arrived in State College with the edge. The Green and White returned most if its 1919 team, significantly outweighed Penn State's interior linemen and was rated among the top teams in the East. The *Pittsburgh Daily Post* called it "one of the greatest football tilts ever seen on new Beaver field."[34] In addition, it was Penn State's first-ever alumni homecoming celebration. Advance tickets sold at $1.50 for general admission, indicating that a record-breaking crowd was to be on hand for the game. New bleachers were rushed to completion to accommodate 10,000 fans, room was made available for several thousand more, and a parking lot for 5,000 automobiles was created.

To the enjoyment of the home crowd, one of the paramount attractions was the presence of Penn State's new mascot. Historian and former co-editor of the Sports and Society Series of the University of Illinois Press, Benjamin G. Rader, suggests, "Mascots and nicknames offered even more room for the imagination." For those schools that used a nickname rather than be labeled by school colors, the choices often evoked humor. In the last decade of the 19th century, Washington was known as the Shoo Flies and later Sun Dodgers; Nebraska was the Bugeaters before it became the Cornhuskers; Oregon was known as the Webfoots long before the Ducks; Yale's students named their teams "the Elis" after the institution's founder, Elihu Yale.[35]

The mascot-naming frenzy hit the student body at Penn State in a way similar to most colleges and universities across the country. It was sports-driven. Since 1904, students and alumni espoused the nickname "Nittany Lions" after a student-editor of a campus satirical magazine and infielder on the baseball team, Harrison Dennington "Joe" Mason Jr., led a campaign to adopt the mascot. Mason's mascot campaign permeated Penn State's campus. In 1907, students convinced the trustees to authorize a senior honor's fraternity called the Lion's Paw (of which Killinger eventually became a member). One year later, an unbinding vote of the student body reaffirmed the support for making the Nittany Lion the college's mascot. Penn State students called their sports teams by the nickname, and the lion started to appear in campus publications. A lion resembling an African breed—not a mountain lion—appeared in *La Vie*, the college's yearbook, for the first time in 1908. Yet for more than a decade thereafter, there was hardly a newspaper, rival school, or organization that acknowledged the nickname. While most in the media still called Penn State the "Blue and White," there were just a few newspapers that accepted the Nittany Lion as Penn State's handle. One of these was the *Pittsburgh Daily Post*, which in 1908 became the first newspaper to call Penn State the "Nittany Mountain Lions" in an article about the baseball team's visit to Pittsburgh.[36] The next media references to Penn State as some variation of the Nittany Lions appeared during the 1911 football season, once in the *Washington Times* and again in the *Pittsburgh Daily Post*, in October and November, respectively.[37] The two newspapers called Penn State the "Mt. Nittany Lions." At the start of the 1920 season, finally, the *Daily Post* and its sister publication, the *Pittsburgh Gazette Times*, embraced Penn State's new nickname. This was likely caused by the first-ever appearance of a student dressed in a lion costume at Penn State's football games.

In 1919, at Penn State's home opener against Gettysburg, a new fight song written by alumnus Jimmy Leyden, who had once set several half-mile

Coach Hugo Bezdek is shown with the first Nittany Lion mascot (an "African" Lion), circa 1920. Richard Holmes Hoffman was the first to wear the African lion mascot uniform. Pre–Nittany Lion mascots included a mule named "old Coaly" and local resident Andy Lytle (Penn State University Libraries).

records running track at the college, was a member of the glee club, and was a veteran of the Great War, titled "The Nittany Lion," was sung for the first time by the student body.[38] The song weighed Penn State's Nittany Lion against colleges with already established nicknames in this early period of intercollegiate student-body squabbling: there was Indiana's Hoosier, Ohio State's Buckeye, Michigan's Wolverine, Princeton's Tiger, and the biggest rival of them all, Pittsburgh's Panther.

Like most colleges in the 1920s, Penn State's cheer group normally consisted of one to five male cheerleaders. That changed when an Industrial Chemistry major and thespian from nearby Howard, Pennsylvania, named Richard Holmes Hoffman dressed up in a lion costume.[39] The annals of Penn State regrettably fail to provide the date of Hoffman's first game as the mascot, but a photograph of Coach Bezdek standing proudly with Hoffman, down on all fours, as the Nittany Lion—actually an African lion, not the American mountain lion that is now used by the University—during homecoming weekend is an indication that Penn State's new nickname was growing in popularity in 1920.[40] Moreover, during one of the practices leading up to the Dartmouth game, the team posed for a picture that was used as a promotion for the college's first-ever homecoming game. Bezdek and 14 of his players straddled a sideline bench and smiled. The image was later superimposed on the back of an African mountain lion and circulated in the days leading up to the game.

Though the atmosphere for Penn State's homecoming game was at fever pitch, the home crowd's enthusiasm over the festivities quickly developed into uncertainty as Dartmouth found the goal line first. In the opening quarter, after a Killinger pass was intercepted, the Big Green scored moments later on a play-action pass that fooled Killinger and his fellow safety Charlie Way, who charged the line thinking the ball was handed off to one of the halfbacks. Penn State struck back in the second quarter after a 20-yard punt return by Way, when off-tackle runs by Hinkey Haines and Killinger put the ball on Dartmouth's 40-yard line.[41] During the drive, Dartmouth's All-American tackle, Gus Sonnenberg, got chirpy at 145-pound Charlie Way, who said to his quarterback, "Come on, Killy, I don't want to run into that fellow."[42] Killinger confidently called Way's number anyway, and he scampered 20 yards around left end to put the ball inside the red zone. Killinger then completed

Hugo Bezdek and the 1920 Penn State football team. This picture was superimposed on an African lion for promotional purposes during the 1920 season. Killinger is sixth from the left (Jessica Killinger).

a pass to the 8-yard line, and runs by Killinger and Haines put the ball inches from the goal line before George Snell plunged through the interior for the score. Way added the extra point, tying the game at seven-all.

The game remained tied throughout the second half, when Penn State suffered a pivotal setback. Charlie Way was forced to leave the contest in the third period after injuring his hip. Joe Lightner, a two-year reservist who had grown up near Killinger in Harrisburg, replaced him. Fortunately for the home team, Dartmouth was dealing with its own set of injuries. The Big Green's captain, Jim Robertson, played only two quarters due to an ailing shoulder. Dartmouth's fullback, John Shelburne, the college's first African American football player, who would go on to play one year for the Hammond Pros of the American Professional Football League, left the game in the fourth quarter after hurting his knee.[43]

The injuries were likely caused by exhaustion. In 1987, looking back to his experience playing in the game, Killinger observed that by game time it was "above 90 degrees and the humidity about as high." Penn State wore wool jerseys, heavy canvas pants, high-top cleats, and substantially heavy helmets.

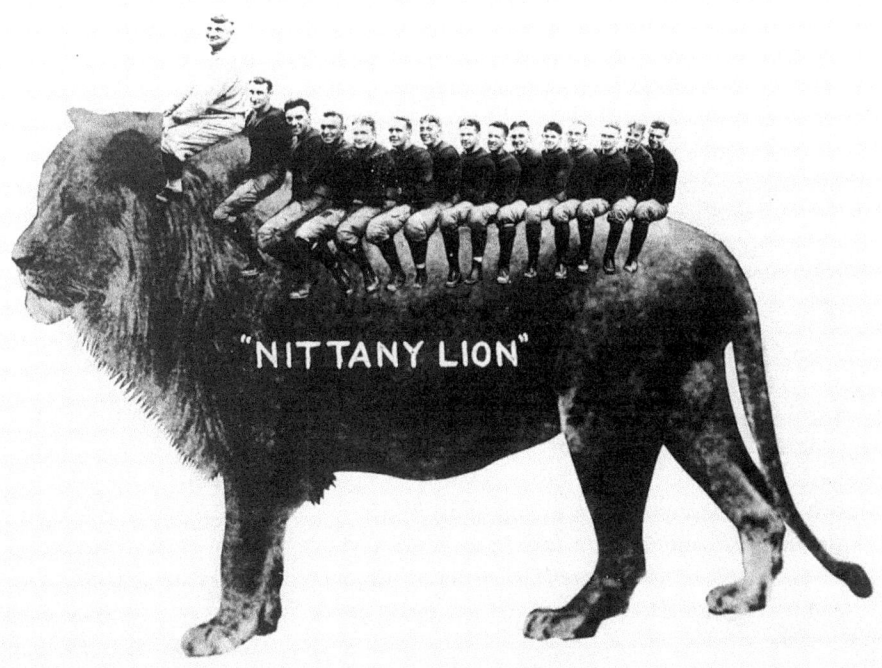

Hugo Bezdek and the 1920 Penn State team superimposed on an African lion. Killinger is tenth from the left (Penn State University Libraries).

He remembered that the game was great fun, but "about the end of the third quarter both teams were exhausted." He recalled, "I played the entire game and lost seven pounds. One of our tackles lost 13 pounds."[44]

Penn State was able to keep the game even due to its "considerable ability to penetrate the Dartmouth line," reported the *Pittsburgh Daily Post*. At no time in the second half did Dartmouth have the ball near Penn State's end zone. The visitors tried a 53-yard dropkick, but it fell well short. When it seemed like one of Dartmouth's ball carriers broke free through the front line, Killinger, from his safety position, "never failed to make his tackle," wrote the *Boston Post*. "We were using a seven-man line on defense with a two-two box defense in the backfield," Killinger remembered.[45]

Dartmouth tried to mount one final scoring threat before Glenn Killinger became the hero of the day. With two minutes to go and the ball at midfield, Dartmouth attempted a forward pass. Killinger stepped in front of the receiver and intercepted the ball. He weaved through Dartmouth's coverage before he was pushed out of bounds at the 2-yard line. On the ensuing play, Killinger called Lightner's number, and he plunged in for the score. Dick Rauch, another product of Harrisburg, kicked the point after touchdown. The game ended, 14–7, moments later.[46]

It surprised most people when Killinger credited an unexpected individual for the interception that set up the game-winning touchdown. "Dick Harlow had scouted Dartmouth and gave us a true account of their strengths and weaknesses," he told people after the game. "They used a forward pass to their right end running a 45 degree angle to his right. When we practiced defense, I told Harlow that I was going to intercept that pass and run for a TD," he said with self-assurance. Then, in the fourth quarter with the game on the line, Killinger, from his safety position, thought to himself, "[I] was hoping they would call that 45 degree pass to their right end. Fortunately they threw the pass I was anticipating. I maneuvered to the proper defensive position and easily intercepted the pass."[47]

Like Harold Lamb's winning score in *The Freshman*, the heroic performance against Dartmouth was a balm to Killinger, who had longed for this moment. No longer the shrimp, Killinger won his coach's respect for toughness and steadiness, and his performance against Dartmouth cemented his future in the Penn State lineup. The *Pittsburgh Daily Post* said, "Killinger showed rare judgment in calling his plays and his running of the team indicates that Bezdek's quarterback worries are over. This was his first start at calling the signals and he more than made good."[48]

• • •

With Killinger at quarterback, Penn State absolutely dominated its next two opponents. In a 41–0 win over North Carolina State, Killinger scored the game's first touchdown on a plunge through the left side of the line. Later in the game, he threw a "brilliant" 35-yard touchdown pass, the *Daily Post* reported after Penn State's shutout, to his tight end, Lloyd Jones, in the second quarter.[49]

Penn State then ran all over Lebanon Valley College by a whopping 109–7 score. Oddly, Lebanon Valley scored first when a forward pass was deflected by Hinkey Haines (a Lebanon Valley transfer) and fell into the arms of a Dutchman receiver standing in the end zone. Thereafter the slaughter ensued. Killinger scored Penn State's first touchdown, then Charlie Way scored on three long runs to build up a 27–7 lead at the end of the first period. Before the first quarter ended, Killinger suffered a serious injury to his left shoulder and was pulled from the game out of fear that he had broken his collarbone. As he watched from the sideline, Penn State scored 82 more points. In what is considered an amazing feat for an era characterized by frequent punting on early downs, Penn State was not forced to punt the ball over to Lebanon Valley during the entire game.[50]

Word about Killinger's injury spread across the country as quickly as the fact that Penn State had just scored a record-breaking 109 points in one game. His status was the talk of the nation, driven by the impending game

The Penn State starters in 1920. Back row (left to right): Charlie Way, Glenn Killinger, George Snell, Henry "Hinkey" Haines. Front row (left to right): "Squeaks" Hufford, Dick Rauch, Harold Hess, Newsh Benz, "Red" Griffith, Clarence Beck, and George Brown (Jessica Killinger).

against the University of Pennsylvania, which was being considered as one of the top East Coast matchups of the coming week. Reports on Killinger's health varied. The *Washington Post* reported that the injury "has not proved to be as serious as was at first believed, but it is still doubtful if he will be able to play against Penn on Saturday." On the Tuesday before the game, the *Harrisburg Telegraph* ran the headline, "Killinger's Injuries Slight, No Broken Bones as Yet." Two days later, the same newspaper reported, "Killinger Still Unable to Play."[51]

Killinger was given a thorough examination midweek to check the extent of the injury. The report revealed his shoulder to be "considerably bruised" with "badly strained" muscles. The Penn State student body was "overjoyed," wrote the *Philadelphia Evening Public Ledger*, when it learned that Killinger's injury was not season-ending. However, no assurances were given that he would suit up against Penn.[52] Perhaps Coach Bezdek wanted it this way. Not only was Penn State facing off against one of the premier football programs in the Ivy League, Bezdek was about to duel it out with Penn's new coach, John Heisman, who had just finished a highly successful 16-year tenure that included a national championship at Georgia Tech in 1917. The tactic is commonly used, even to this day, as one coach issues fabricated information to the media in an effort to mislead an opponent. Bezdek closed his practices that week to the public and said only unenthusiastic things to the band of sportswriters who hovered around State College.

With Killinger, Penn State would have been the favored ball club. Without him, the Quakers were the favorite. In his three games as a starter, Killinger had become the star of the team. By keeping his status a secret, Bezdek hoped it would throw off Heisman's preparations. Up against a coach who had a rich reputation for installing trick plays to be used against each opponent, it was a gimmick worth the effort.

When game day arrived, Killinger was dressed in his uniform and assigned to start at quarterback and safety. The opportunity to play through a serious injury sustained just seven days earlier allowed Killinger to demonstrate the level of masculinity that Walter Camp and Theodore Roosevelt expected to see in America's football players, especially those hardened by combat training. If he had any pain in his shoulder before the game, it disappeared during his coach's spirited pregame speech. "I pick men who can always do a little better than their best," Bezdek reaffirmed his life code. "A player says to me, 'Coach, I'm doing my best.' I say, 'No good. It's absolutely no good. I want something better than your best.'" Killinger and his teammates were sky-high for the encounter, not to mention inspired. They struck first in the opening quarter as Killinger didn't wait long to prove he was tough enough to play with a sore shoulder. Behind a determined offensive line, Killinger, Hinkey Haines, and Charlie Way, who was later injured and would miss the entire second half, put on a running display that appeared as if they were still practicing against the scrub team. With the ball inside the Penn 5-yard line, Killinger called his own number and scored the game's first touchdown. It was his third touchdown in as many games as a starter. Penn threatened to tie the contest late in the second quarter when it had the ball on the 1-yard line, but a fourth down pass broken up by Killinger in the end zone spoiled the opportunity. The score at intermission was still 7–0.[53]

But while this play would be the most enduring memory of the game, a few newspapers praised Heisman's men for the first half effort. "The Red and Blue team put up a game but vain fight," said the *Harrisburg Evening Star*.[54] The second half turned out to be a lopsided display dominated by Penn State, who turned up the heat on the opening kickoff. With Way dinged up, the team was confused as to who would return the kick. "Who gets the middle on the kickoff?" Hinkey Haines asked the coach.[55] Bezdek replied, "You do."

Haines fielded the kick at the 10-yard line and sliced through the center of the field all the way for the touchdown.

Glenn Killinger (middle) with his former teammates at his 50th class reunion. Left, Charlie Way; right, Hinkey Haines (Penn State University Libraries).

Just like that it was 14–0, but Penn State wasn't through. Killinger brilliantly guided his team to two more scores, extending the lead to 28–0 in the final period. Bezdek then decided to replace Killinger, who had his bell rung early in the game, with Buck Williams. Heisman's unit added a score by way of a fake punt after Killinger was taken out. The game ended 28–7.

Killinger's performance that day left an indelible impression on Heisman. Reflecting back years later, Heisman, who spent three substandard seasons at Penn before coaching at Washington and Jefferson College and Rice Institute and retiring after the 1927 season, claimed that Killinger was among the top 100 players ever to play college football. In a lengthy compilation he called "Heisman's Hundred in the Hall of Fame" that was reprinted in magazines and newspapers around the country in 1928, Heisman said Killinger "sparkled and scintillated." The coach's approbation of Killinger came with a touch of nuance: "he started fast, kept going faster, and then, when pressed, showed you just how much faster a man could go when he really had to."[56]

With Killinger as field general, Penn State was the real deal. The Nittany Lions were 6–0 at midseason. Its defense ranked among the best. Only Boston College and Princeton had given up fewer points. In addition, Penn State had the top scoring offense in the country; halfbacks Charlie Way and Joe Lightner ranked third and fourth in the nation in total points. By now, Killinger was gaining notoriety for his management of Coach Bezdek's com-

A scrum is shown from Penn State's 28–7 victory over John Heisman's Pennsylvania Quakers on October 30, 1920 (Jessica Killinger).

plicated system of misdirection runs, fake passes, fake kicks, and both intermediate and long forward passes. His favorite play to run was the cross-buck, a play designed for guards to pull while the quarterback faked to the fullback one way before handing off to the halfback, who followed his blockers in the opposite direction. In a 1923 op-ed in the *Ironwood Daily Globe*, Killinger described how he depended on the play.

> If I was to be pinned down to one certain play as a consistent ground gainer, I would have no hesitation in selecting the cross-buck or off-tackle run ... running off-tackle or a short end run, you have a chance to spread the opponent's line. Usually a hole opens up somewhere in the line where a good runner can slip through. Incidentally, the cross-buck offers a chance for deception. It is possible for the player with the ball to start wide and then cut back or start cutting in at the inception of the play and then switching to a wide end run, according to the manner in which the other team is playing. During my career at Penn State under Coach Bezdek, most of our scoring was done in the manner described despite the fact that opposing teams knew we used the cross-buck on a majority of our plays. By changing our pace in making the same play we kept the opposition from concentrating on any one point.[57]

Killinger's exploits on the field attracted the attention of Walter Camp, the world's eminent football mind, who claimed in a November column that his "eyes [are] glued on Killinger as a field general" and that in a year's time, he would be in consideration for an All American team.[58]

Penn State's schedule grew more difficult on November 6 when the big Nebraska Cornhuskers team, coming off a convincing 28–0 triumph over Rutgers at the Polo Grounds in New York City, visited State College. If they could win this one against a Western foe whose only setback was a 16–7 loss to Notre Dame, Penn State would cement itself in a reasonable position to be considered by sportswriters as the best team in the country. Only Knute Rockne's Notre Dame 11 was having a season similar to Penn State's.

Nevertheless, beating Nebraska would be a tall task. Killinger's shoulder and head injuries and Charlie Way's hip injury kept the duo out of practice all week. Bezdek's right tackle, Richard L. Schuster, was taken to the hospital with an infected leg, and right end Stan McCollum was limited at practice after suffering injuries in the Penn game.[59] Each injury was a serious concern to Bezdek, who considered his players undersized and was accordingly circumspect about his team's endurance during a physical 60-minute contest.

A loss to Nebraska would hurt Penn State's national standing, but it would hardly damage its chances of being named the top team in the East. Bezdek's group already proved it could defeat the best that the prominent Ivy League had to offer. He accordingly chose to start Buck Williams at quarterback in place of Killinger. The more-than-capable Joe Lightner was inserted into the starting lineup in place of Way at right halfback. Both Killinger and

Way were in uniform. Bezdek planned to insert them into the game if needed. Bezdek had developed a game plan fixated on throwing the ball and backfield shifts. He saw the pass game as an equalizer against a "fast, wide awake" and powerful team like Nebraska. Backfield shifts, he considered, could give his undersized players a mental advantage aimed at confusing the Cornhuskers' defensive secondary.

The teams appeared evenly matched in the first quarter and a half. Both teams had golden opportunities to score early when drives ended at the other's 2-yard line without putting points on the board. With five minutes left before halftime, and Penn State's offense unable to do anything productive, Bezdek inserted Killinger into the game. On his first offensive series, Killinger completed a 45-yard pass to Hinkey Haines down to Nebraska's 10-yard line. But he threw an errant pass on the ensuing play that was picked off by a Nebraska secondary player. A defensive play moments later put Penn State back in scoring position when Lightner stepped in front of a Nebraska receiver at the 50-yard line to intercept a forward pass. He carried the ball to the 32-yard line. Killinger shot a long pass to Ross "Squeak" Hufford, who was playing for the injured McCollum, for the game's first score. The Nittany Lions led 7–0 at halftime.

Hugo Bezdek's team clung for dear life to their one-score lead as much of the second half was controlled by Nebraska's ground game, including two opportunities from "within the very shadows of Penn State's goal twice," said the *Daily Nebraskan*. Fortunately for the home team, the Cornhuskers failed to penetrate the goal line.[60]

The entire time, the Penn State boss contemplated the best time to insert fresh-legged Charlie Way into the game. The substitution finally occurred at the change of the quarter. Nebraska's two guards, the Munn brothers, Monte and Wade, admonished Way as he ran onto the field toward Killinger. "So this is the famous Way," one of them bellowed. Decades later, Bezdek remained impressed—and mystified—by the sequence of plays that followed as an unruffled Killinger steered Penn State to a game-clinching drive as he ran Way's favorite play, "Old 42," at the Munn brothers. He recalled: "Penn State, greatly outweighed, was having a rough going against the giant 'Husker team, although leading 7–0 early in the second half." Bezdek's team had the ball close to the left sideline. Since the right halfback typically runs to the left, Killinger saw that he couldn't get the ball to Way in the open field from his normal position. "Killie [sic] sized up the situation in an instant," Bezdek explained, "and when Way had reported to the referee, Killinger placed him at the left half instead of at right. He called for a kick formation." Killinger's strategy was to deceive Nebraska with a punt formation on first down to play for field position—it was a tactic Killinger was known for. "I saw at once what was coming," said Bezdek. Nebraska did not know which halfback spot Way ordinarily played, "since he had just entered the game. Expecting a kick as the logical play deep in our territory, they were foiled, and Way broke off right tackle, where he had the whole field to run in." He picked up 52 yards. On the ensuing play, "Killinger's brain was working, for this time he placed Way at his regular position, right half, and on the next play sent him whirling around the left end for the remainder of the distance to the goal-line and a touchdown." Bezdek insisted: "Those two plays defeated Nebraska."[61]

Thereafter it was a hopeless battle for Nebraska. When the Cornhuskers offense stalled at its own 28-yard line on their ensuing possession, Penn State increased its lead with another touchdown, this time a 4-yard plunge by Killinger. The hardened quarterback's score through the center of the Nebraska line stretched Penn State's lead to 20–0. The game ended moments later.

In all, Killinger dropped back to pass 30 times during the game. He completed eight of 15 attempts, while scrambling for yardage on the remaining passing plays. Thinking back on the victory, Bezdek said, "about half the number of plays [against Nebraska]" were forward passes, "and spectators declared it to be the greatest game that they witnessed."[62] Killinger left his mark on every end of the field. Penn State amassed 385 total yards. Killinger threw for 178 yards, an unprecedented feat for 1920, while he and his teammates rushed for 207 yards. He picked up 42 yards on 13 punt returns in addition to punting ten times for a 39-yard average.[63]

• • •

Indeed, the victory over Nebraska created a distraction among the faithful at State College. Sportswriters immediately began suggesting that a postseason showdown between Penn State and Notre Dame be arranged to decide the nation's top team. "If Notre Dame and Penn State could be brought together, a national football championship would not be mythical," proclaimed United Press sportswriter Henry Farrell.[64] The talk around the country crept into Bezdek's locker room at Penn State. And the impact was detrimental to his team.

Penn State followed the Nebraska victory by almost sinking its season against Lehigh College. Lehigh was hardly a slouch. Earlier in the fall, it had defeated Rutgers, 9–0, and tied West Virginia, 7–7. Lehigh and Penn State shared lopsided victories over two common opponents, Lebanon Valley and Muhlenberg.

During the November 13 game, big plays—usually runs by Hinkey Haines and forward passes from Killinger to Haines or George Brown—were often negated by penalties, or spoiled by subsequent turnovers or tackles for loss. With Charlie Way preserved on the sideline for much of the contest because of his ailing hip, Killinger was Mr. Do-it-all. He received punts and

Penn State's 7-0-2 football team in 1920. Killinger is sitting in the front row, seventh from the left. Beside him, sixth from the left, is Henry "Hinkey" Haines. Coach Bezdek is back row, first on the left, in his Pittsburgh Pirates uniform. Standing beside him is assistant coach Dick Harlow (Penn State University Libraries).

kicks and operated as Penn State's punter. On defense, he intercepted a pass and on several occasions read run so quickly that he stormed through the line from his safety position to tackle Lehigh ball carriers in the backfield. Penn State dominated everything except the score and found itself down, 7-0, deep into the fourth quarter.

Killinger accepted responsibility for the deficit. In denial of the media's coverage of his performance, he said, "I played my poorest game against Lehigh and was directly responsible for allowing Lehigh to complete an easy pass over my head for their TD." Killinger conceded that his team's week of preparation for Lehigh "was horrible." No one on the team took Lehigh seriously, he said. "Bezdek was after us constantly," he acknowledged, "and his theme song that week was that Lehigh would beat us easily and he was nearly correct." Lehigh's quarterback was George Rote, a graduate of Harrisburg Central High School and hometown adversary of Killinger in football and baseball. "We had played baseball that summer together on Hinky [sic] Haines's Red Lion team," Killinger recollected. "He told me how he had scored the winning TD in their game with a good Lafayette team by running a bootleg fake buck around his right end to score." When Lehigh had third down on Penn State's 20-yard line, Rote ran the same bootleg play. Killinger, who was readily waiting in anticipation for the play, ran up from his safety position to tackle Rote, who at the last moment before being tackled lofted a pass over Killinger for a touchdown. "Rote lobbed a pass over my head to the right end who had run ten yards in back of me and I completely ignored him," said an outwitted Killinger.[65]

In the fourth quarter, Way was sent into the game as the clock ticked close to the end of regulation. It was then that Penn State opened a volley of forward passes. Killinger hit Haines on three consecutive short passes over the line for nine yards, 12 yards, and seven yards. Then Killinger called a trick play. He stacked the backfield, including himself, on the right side of the center. He positioned Haines deepest, directly behind the center. On the snap, Killinger darted left into the flat as a decoy, hoping to take out a man in the Lehigh secondary. The right end streaked down the field while the fullback and halfback ran off-tackle on the heels of one another, circling the linebackers. Haines, with his big league baseball talent, took the direct snap and ran toward the line of scrimmage before pulling up short. His options were to throw a deep ball to his end, Brown, or a mid-range pass to the halfback, Way, who divided his route between the fullback's pattern and the end's fade route. Haines saw Brown open down the field and shot him a pass for 29 yards. Killinger handed off to Way for a 7-yard gain to Lehigh's 15-yard line. Way was given the ball once more, taking it the distance for the touchdown. The Penn State contingent held its breath as they watch Dick Rauch execute the goal after touchdown to tie the game.

On a late drive, Lehigh was close enough to attempt a winning field goal, which barely missed. In a bizarre transition allowed according to the rules in 1920, the kicking team could recover a missed kick. Author of *Penn State Football Letter*, Ridge Riley described the sequence: "as the ball bounced around in the end zone, a Lehigh player was in position to recover for a touchdown. Instead, a local fan ran onto the field, picked up the ball, and helpfully tossed it to the referee."[66] The game ended, 7–7.

"I really went out of my way to avoid a confrontation with Bezdek after the game," Killinger admitted. "I had lost my concentration and it cost us a win as we were easily the better team."[67]

The stalemate against Lehigh did not terminate the discussion of setting up a title match against Notre Dame. But for that to happen, Penn State had to get by its final opponent. On tap for Thanksgiving Day was the annual showdown against Pop Warner's University of Pittsburgh 11, which still featured the fine running of All-American halfback Tom Davies. The drubbing that Penn State laid on Pitt the previous fall was surely on the minds of the folks in the Steel City. Both teams entered the game undefeated and with one tie. The showdown offered itself as the Eastern football championship game.[68]

By the time the contest with Pitt began, Bezdek's men were exhausted and ailing from a week spent practicing in eight inches of snow, rain and sleet combined with chilling wind and freezing temperatures.[69] Penn State was thought to be the better ball club, with Way now healthy enough to start and Killinger and Haines playing as well as anyone in the country at their positions. The defenses were both strong, but Penn State seemingly had the dominant line. Although Pitt had one of the nation's most elusive and powerful halfbacks in Tom Davies, Penn State had more overall speed.

Unfortunately, for the second time in three years, the clash was marred by rain and mud. "Forbes Field was a quagmire," recalled Killinger."[70] The conditions did not stop a boisterous crowd of 35,000 from watched the Keystone foes slug it out in six inches of mud, which negated the speed of both teams and, arguably, the speed and power of Penn State's line. Pitt received the ball first. The home team made no yards on its opening drive. Killinger then fielded a punt from Davies but was stopped dead his tracks, stuck in the mud, at the 35-yard line. He flung a forward pass to Haines for a short gain. On second down, he called a successful double pass to Haines, which placed the ball on Pitt's 35-yard line. There the drive stalled, and Killinger punted over the goal line. Rival stars Killinger and Davies were each guilty of frequent fumbles caused by the wet ball. The game carried on in this fashion for four quarters. At game's end, both teams had punted 12 times, and total yardage was virtually equal, 198 yards for Pitt and 182 yards for Penn State.[71] The result was a dispiriting 0–0 tie—the scoreless effort marked the first time in Bezdek's three seasons at Penn State that his team was held without a point.

With the season now at its end, Penn State found itself a somewhat disappointing 7–0–2, again in limbo for the Eastern football crown. The brooding began among the sportswriters, who weighed strength of schedule, game performances against common foes, total points scored verse total points given up, home game performances measured up against road performances, which teams were playing its best ball at the end of the season, and what would happen in hypothetical matchups. What was for certain was that no game would be scheduled against Notre Dame, which was unanimously given the intercollegiate Western football championship. In the East, sportswriter George Curry ranked Penn State fourth behind Princeton (6–0–2), Harvard (8–0–1), and Pittsburgh (6–0–2).[72] Just like that, two ties kept Penn State from a repeat Eastern championship.

Some of the pain about losing out on a championship lessened in December when Killinger was named one of 15 quarterbacks nationwide to the Charles Evans National Honor Roll. In addition, he was selected to Pop Warner's "All-Star Eleven," a team composed of the best 11 players made up by the University of Pittsburgh's 1920 opponents. The anointment was a big deal, especially considering that teammate Charlie Way was picked by Walter Camp as a first-team All American halfback and Hinkey Haines was placed on Camp's third-team All American roster. Linemen Clarence Beck and Red Griffiths, along with end George Brown, received honorable mention consideration on some All-Eastern teams.[73]

The season gave Killinger much to think about. Although a senior academically, he had played just three years of football and therefore possessed one more year of eligibility if he chose to delay his graduation and return in the fall. On paper, Penn State's 1921 team would to be depleted with

Glenn Killinger with his dog "Bobby" about 1928 (Jessica Killinger).

the graduation of seven starters, including half the line and backfield stars Way and Haines. Even Killinger admitted that expectations for the next team were reasonably low. He said, "I did not think that our prospects were too bright for the 1921 season after losing two All-Americans from our backfield by graduation." Fortunately for Killinger, he had time to think. The upcoming basketball season would serve as a distraction and, by the way, was touted as Killinger's best sport.

Part Four: Fourth Quarter

10

Class of 1921

The blaze of the best year of Glenn Killinger's collegiate career ignited in the Armory, an 80 by 120-feet space already badly damaged by the Student Army Training Corps in 1918, when it was utilized as an assembly room and storage facility. The building itself was always unsanitary. The men's showers were located in one corner of the basement, while no such accommodation was provided for women. Despite the building's defects, it was a place Killinger always considered his sanctuary. He would visit its hardwood floor as often as possible until it was torn down in 1964.

The Armory, with its triangular exterior, rubble stonewalls, brick chimney, and picturesque tower, was long used for weekend events. More distinctly, perhaps, it was used as the college's home basketball venue. Here, at the Armory, Glenn Killinger clinched his athletic celebrity.

With Killinger's help during his junior season, Penn State's basketball team entered the winter of 1920–1921 with high expectations. When a team finishes 12–1, as Penn State did the previous year, people crave more of the same. The Nittany Lions were returning all five starters, and in Killinger, who was unanimously selected captain by his teammates, at point guard, and Hinkey Haines at the shooting guard position, Penn State boasted the best backcourt combination in the country. "Basketball is probably Killinger's best sport," said the *Harrisburg Telegraph*, "and although he has won his varsity letter at baseball and football also, he really prefers the indoor game."[1]

The Nittany Lions opened at the Armory against Juniata on December 16. With several hundred fans seated on the floor and a hundred more standing in the mezzanine balcony, the student body witnessed a convincing 45–13 victory. Killinger dropped six points. Haines added four. Their defensive effort was more impressive, holding the visitors to single digits before three starters were pulled from the game.[2]

With Killinger leading the way in scoring and defending, Penn State routed its next six opponents: Dickinson, 48–19; Washington and Jefferson, 53–20; West Virginia, 52–14; Susquehanna, 47–13; Lebanon Valley, 51–12; and

Carnegie Tech, 62–17. He scored 72 points in the first seven games, including a 20-point effort against Carnegie Tech.

Penn State's first real test came against Pittsburgh on February 4 at a jam-packed Motor Square Garden filled with 4,000 enthusiastic fans accompanied by the Pitt marching band. Penn State jumped to an early 7–0 advantage before Pitt's forwards helped tighten the score. When Pitt took a 32–30 lead in the second half, Killinger "came through with another basket again tying the count," reported the *Pittsburgh Daily Post*. Pitt was held without a field goal in the final minutes while Killinger hit another basket and helped break the game open for Penn State, and the game ended 38–33.[3] The 33 points ended up being the largest point total scored on Penn State all year.

On the next night, Penn State improved to 9–0 with a 26–23 squeaker over Washington and Jefferson. The road trip proved exhausting as the Nittany Lions lost their first contest, 29–23, to Virginia Tech as Killinger was held to four points.[4]

Penn State rebounded with blowout victories over Pittsburgh, 50–28, Buffalo, 43–16, and Swarthmore, 34–11. The Pittsburgh press said, "Killinger and Haines were mainly responsible" for the pounding handed to the Panthers. Killinger's 12 points was the game's highest output.[5] Against Swarthmore, he scored ten points. It was on the defensive side where Killinger and his teammates shined most against Swarthmore. Penn State allowed just two field goals all game, both made by Swarthmore's center.

Perhaps looking ahead to the season finale against the nation's best team—the Pennsylvania Quakers—Penn State was upset by the worst team in the Ivy League, Yale, 23–20, on March 8. Due in part to Killinger's team-leading three field goals in the first half, Penn State led 14–12 at halftime. In the second half, however, Killinger was held scoreless and Hinkey Haines had trouble guarding Yale's Harry Alderman, who nailed seven field goals from the top of the key and converted five free throws that eventually determined the game. "Nobody could have stopped those shots," Killinger said in defense of his friend. Near the end of the game, Haines was injured and taken out. More bad luck struck Penn State when center Bill Wolfe, who tried to play through pneumonia, eventually was substituted out and rushed to New Haven Hospital after the game.[6]

In the locker room after the game, Coach "Dutch" Hermann, a person Killinger always considered "one of the greatest [coaches]," while admitting, "I've been around a lot of good ones," scolded the team for their performance. "He told us we were the lousiest team he had ever coached," Killinger recounted. "I went berserk at his remarks." Killinger ripped off his uniform, rolled it up, and threw it at Hermann's head. It was the "first and only time" he ever displayed that level of anger toward a coach, he confessed. "I was crying like a baby because his criticisms were so completely unethical and out of order." Killinger glared at the team manager, Malcolm Myers, and insisted that he get him a train ticket back to State College. He was adamant that he was not going to accompany the team to Philadelphia, where they were scheduled to play Penn in two days. "Hinky [sic] and the other players finally calmed me and I agreed to stay that night with the team."[7]

The peace was restored between Killinger and Hermann in a matter of hours. And the loss to Yale lit a fire for the March 10 showdown with the 18-1 and No. 1-ranked Pennsylvania Quakers. Penn State needed to play inspired basketball without its center, Bill Wolfe, who was also the team's foul shooter (this era of basketball allowed one man to shoot all the foul shots for the team). Meanwhile, Killinger was assigned to guard Lou Martin, the top scorer in the Ivy League.

"We played like a bunch of maniacs," Killinger proudly testified of his team's effort. The fans who piled into Weightman Hall saw five ties during the contest. Killinger was held scoreless in regulation, but his contribution on the defensive end helped his team rally from a 12-10 halftime deficit. "I held Lou Martin to one goal and [he] missed a hard lay-up shot," that could have won the game for Penn, he recalled. "It was a dog-eat-dog game" which was tied 19-19 at the end of regulation. In the extra period, Killinger was called on by his coach, with whom he almost got into fisticuffs 48 hours earlier, to shoot a pair of foul shots. He was successful with each attempt, which turned out to be the difference in Penn State's 21-19 upset victory in overtime. Upon the final whistle, the

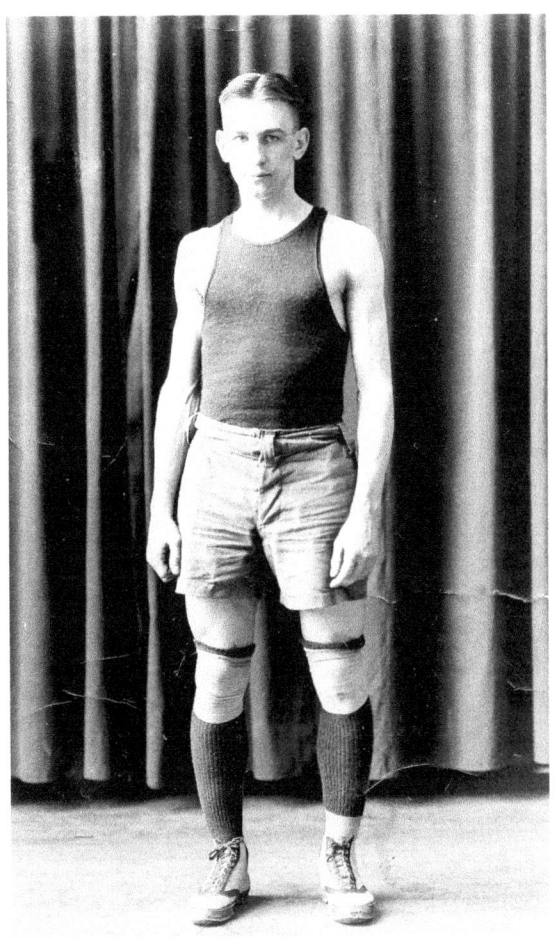

Killinger was captain of the basketball team in 1921. This is an image of him during his senior year (Jessica Killinger).

Penn State contingent swarmed the court and carried Killinger off on their shoulders.[8]

Killinger's superlative performance felt like another Harold Lamb moment. It must have been some experience for the heralded senior. In his last college basketball game, Killinger helped his team defeat the two-time sportswriters' national champion and the nation's No. 1-ranked team; and he did it in overtime by nailing the game-winning foul shots.[9] To be carried off the floor by his peers certainly cemented the moment among the most dramatic in Killinger's lifetime. Basketball was not an incredibly popular sport. The media posted box scores inconsistently after each game. The sportswriters refrained from naming mythical champions of the East or West, or even the nation for that matter. The writers were not even keen on naming All-American teams like they did for football. If more attention had been paid to college basketball during the golden age, writers would have argued that Killinger—one of the nation's top defensive players who also scored 126 points for an average of eight points a game—was among the best all-around guards in the East Coast, if not the country. Those accolades certainly would have helped bolster him among the best to play in the shadow of Mount Nittany. Penn State finished the season 14–2, among the nation's best in total points—643—and among the best in fewest points allowed—318. The 1920–1921 season ranked "among the greatest in the history of the Blue and White institution," declared the nationally syndicated *Washington Post*. "Capt. Killinger and his mates can well be proud."[10]

Killinger could be incredibly proud. In the three seasons he earned varsity letters, his basketball teams finished with an astonishing overall record of 37 wins against five losses.

• • •

On March 15, 1921, Glenn Killinger wrapped up his senior basketball season, grabbed his cap and glove, and set out for his final adventure as a baseball player at Penn State. It would be a season in which he would establish himself as a remarkable talent in intercollegiate baseball circles, becoming as much of an attraction to spectators as he had been during the football and basketball seasons.

In this final year, he clung tight to his Penn State family: outfielders Hinkey Haines, Horace "Rip" Koehler, and Joe Lightner (his tie to Harrisburg), pitchers Clyde Mellinger, Myles Thomas, and John Robert Hunter, and fellow infielders Nelson "Red" Korb, Walter "Kid" Mearkle, and Bob Ullery.

In one year under Hugo Bezdek as manager, good hitting and lots of scoring had characterized the baseball team. Yet the 167 runs scored in 1920 wasn't enough. By the end of his senior year, Killinger's team drove in 192 runs and not only defeated several of the best teams that the East and South had to offer, but annihilated many of those teams by double-digit margins. The 1921 Penn State baseball team featured two starters who batted over .400 and four others at .350 or better. The team's three best pitchers from the previous season returned to the rotation. The team's star, Hinkey Haines, was voted captain. Previously a left fielder, Bezdek moved him to center field where, the coach said, "his speed will prove to be more of an asset."[11] In addition to Haines in the outfield, Bezdek had inherited a brilliant infield. Led by Killinger and celebrated as the "Million Dollar Infield," each had potential to make the big leagues.

One year earlier, Killinger missed the team's opening road trip through the South to accompany his meteorology class on a graded field trip. This year, he was again forced to join his class on a mining inspection expedition in Pittsburgh lest he fail the course.[12] Killinger was forced to miss six games played in Maryland, Washington, D.C., and Virginia. Even without Killinger, the Nittany Lions won all six games by defeating Navy twice, 8–6 and 4–1; Virginia, 14–2; Virginia Military Institute, 8–4; Washington and Lee, 18–9; and Georgetown, 7–0.

Killinger's first game was a 7–0 victory over Gettysburg on April 11. Hitting second in the batting order, he singled, doubled, and tripled. He also stole a base. A friendly wager was made between Killinger and Haines during the game—who would be the first to steal home? Haines tried it in the eighth inning against Gettysburg, but was thrown out.[13] After a 7–1 victory over Delaware on April 15, Killinger tried stealing home on April 23 against Lebanon Valley. In the sixth inning, up 2–0, Killinger's single was followed by a Haines drive to the outfield. With Killinger now on third and Haines on first, the friends attempted a double steal, but Killinger was tagged out at the plate. Haines was driven in later in the inning. Penn State won, 3–0.[14]

Penn State blasted Carnegie Tech, 18–0, and won a squeaker against Bethany College, 4–3, to extend its record to 12–0 halfway through the season. Dating back to 1920, Penn State had now won 23 consecutive games. The milestone was impressive, but it wasn't until Penn State's Eastern jaunt that featured contests against Princeton, New York University, and Yale that the sportswriters started to cover the win streak.

On May 12, Penn State pulled out a 6–5 victory in ten innings over Princeton. Host Princeton scored runs in the first, fifth and seventh innings, with Penn State pushing over two runs in the fourth and one in the eighth. In the ninth inning, both teams had runners on second and third, but neither scored. With one down in the top of the tenth, Kid Mearkle, Killinger, Haines, and Joe Lightner all singled, netting three runs. In the bottom of the tenth inning, Princeton scored two runs before the final out was recorded.[15]

Penn State pulled out another one-run victory over New York University

Penn State's "Million Dollar Infield" in 1921. This infield was a big reason the baseball team set a record of 31 consecutive victories. Left to right: Glenn Killinger, Nelson "Red" Korb, Walter "Kid" Mearkle, and Bob Ullery (Penn State University Libraries).

on May 12, 4–3. One day later, the men from Mount Nittany handed a beating to Yale, 9–3. Killinger hit a single and a double, and was robbed of a home run in the fifth inning when the score was 3–1. Yale tied the game at three-all in the sixth inning. However, a six-run ninth inning broke the game open.[16] Penn State's win streak on the season reached 15. Its streak overall was at 26 and counting.

By now, interest in the streak was at fever pitch. The number of writers who started to cover Penn State grew exponentially up and down the coast. The Nittany Lions defeated a plucky Lehigh team, 5–4, to make it 27 straight. On May 17, the Pittsburgh nine, guided by the ubiquitous Tom Davies, visited Glenn Killinger territory and was handed an embarrassing 15–2 defeat.

The victory over Pitt officially gave Penn State the consecutive wins record. "By this victory," the *Harrisburg Evening News* wrote, Penn State "set the record in college circles for this year at least, and it is believed to have set a new record for consecutive wins in college baseball, for it was the twenty-eighth straight game won by Hugo Bezdek's aggregation."[17]

After the unbeaten Nittany Lions methodically took care of Pittsburgh, a significant blow was rendered to the team. Officials from the University of Pittsburgh brought to light the fact that Penn State's captain, Hinkey Haines, had played a few professional baseball games in the Virginia League under the name of "Hinkie" in 1918. "I played league ball for a very short time during the summer of 1918 without knowing that it was against the eligibility code," Haines testified. "As soon as I learned that my eligibility to participate in college athletics was jeopardized, [I] stopped. This was before I entered Penn State and the authorities here knew nothing about the matter, as I have told no one." To avoid damaging "the college that I love," Haines abruptly left the team.

In the modern era of sports, the National Collegiate Athletic Association would have likely removed all 36 wins during the two years that Haines played baseball at Penn State in addition to reversing the 14 football and 26 basketball victories he shared. Surely, the NCAA would have imposed additional postseason sanctions and fines, and Coach Bezdek would likely have been suspended. Nevertheless, the NCAA dished out no punishments in 1921. It could not. The NCAA had no power to legislate or enforce rules until after World War II. Haines dismissed himself from the team immediately. Within two weeks after the scandal broke, Haines passed on a contract with the New York Giants to sign with the emerging American League power New York Yankees. He spent much of the summer playing in 71 games for the Yankees' Class-A team, the Hartford Senators of the Eastern League.[18] Occasionally, he returned home to play for his hometown's twilight team and with Killinger in the Allison Hill League. He even flirted with Lebanon Valley College after the institution offered him the director of athletics position in June. Instead, he signed a contract to become an assistant football coach at Gettysburg College in the fall 1921.

Penn State moved quickly to avert the attention toward anything but the Hinkey Haines scandal. The team voted three-year starting second baseman "Kid" Mearkle captain and began preparing for a doubleheader scheduled against the University of Detroit. In the team's first games without Haines, the *Pittsburgh Post Gazette* wrote: "The whole Penn State infield played sensationally."[19] Penn State dropped Detroit, 8–2 in the first outing and 4–3 in the second.

The streak-watch continued as Penn State handed Pittsburgh its first home loss of the season in extra innings on May 25. Pitt led, 2–1, entering the ninth inning, when Penn State tied the contest. In the top of the tenth, Killinger hit a shot to deep left field. The ball bounced off the fence, driving in two runners. One batter later, Killinger scored. The host team was held scoreless in the bottom of the tenth, allowing Penn State to clinch the game, 5–2. In addition to the two-run triple that he hit in the extra inning, Killinger hit a double and played solidly at third base. His counterpart, Tom Davies,

Pitt's shortstop, recorded two hits but never reached home plate.[20] Penn State's win streak stretched to 20 on the season and 31 overall.

• • •

A break in the schedule after the Pittsburgh victory allowed Killinger time to visit his family in Harrisburg during the final week of May. Accompanying him on the trip home was Hinkey Haines. The two college stars joined Killinger's older brother Earl in a game with the Rosewood Athletic Club on the evening of May 27. Killinger used the evening to tune up for his game against the Pennsylvania Quakers, while Haines prepped himself for his audition with the Yankees' farm team. Haines turned in an impressive performance at the plate, connecting safely on three hits in as many at-bats, and was able to score on each occasion. Killinger's outing was unimpressive, having gone hitless.[21]

Two nights later, Killinger was with his Penn State team in a major showdown against the University of Pennsylvania on Franklin Field. The game was tied, 2–2, through eight innings when Penn scored two runs and held on in the ninth for the victory.[22] After winning 31 consecutive games, Penn State's streak ended there in Philadelphia.

"That defeat was hard to take," Killinger wrote in his memoir. Penn's second baseman, Danny McNichol, who also started at guard for the Quakers' basketball team, approached Killinger after the game. He remembers McNichol saying "that their victory evened the score for the one game they lost to us in basketball."[23]

The loss seemingly put out the fuse that fueled Penn State's record-breaking engine. Penn State downed Bucknell on consecutive days, winning 6–5 and 14–6. But on the final road trip west to finish out the season, Penn State lost both games in a two-game series against Pittsburgh. In the first game, an extra-inning affair, Killinger hit three singles and scored three times, including an amazing steal of home. He assisted on five outs, but the team gave up five runs in the tenth inning and lost, 12–8. The 12 runs was the most any team scored against Penn State all season. In game two, a 10–7 setback, Killinger recorded a hit and scored a run. The star of the series was Pittsburgh's Tom Davies, who went 3-for-5 and 4-for-5, including a home run, a triple, and three doubles.[24]

Penn State's season ended quietly with a record of 23–3. Killinger had his best year, batting .371 in 19 games. He recorded 28 hits. Included in his total were two home runs, three triples and four doubles. He scored 25 runs. In the field, Killy committed just six errors in 74 chances, making 24 putouts and 44 assists.[25]

After three years of baseball at Penn State, Killinger shared 50 wins and nine losses with his teammates. If championships were granted during the era, he likely would have been part of two, arguably three, national titles. The numbers, combined with Coach Bezdek's connections, made him a top prospect for a dozen major league ball clubs, including the New York Yankees and Detroit Tigers.

The close of the 1921 school term brought an end to a memorable three-year run by one of the most successful groups to set foot on the athletic fields at Penn State. Glenn Killinger found among his football, basketball, and baseball teammates at Penn State a wealth of friendships such as he would ever know again. There can be no doubt that the Class of 1921 shared a deep affection for their school and an emotional bond brought together by sports and war.

While considered the Class of '21, Killinger graduated from Penn State on January 31, 1922, after his ninth semester. This is his senior portrait (Penn State University Libraries).

Further, as was already clear, they had endured a broken college experience during the Great War: semesters cut short, a campus turned into a military outpost, curriculum taken over by the War Department. It was a time when Americans in abundance were asked to make courageous decisions of sacrifice as never before. Some went overseas and saw first-hand the horrors of mechanized warfare, while others remained home to work in defense industries and train as captains in the Army, with the belief that their day in combat would soon arrive.

Members of the Class of 1921 would never forget the period. Nor would Glenn Killinger. Nor would they ever again enjoy such a time together. In June 1921, Killinger said goodbye to his friends. He would choose to return to Penn State for one more fall to play his final semester of football and to make up his final eight credits that he failed to attain earlier in his college career.[26]

11

A Crafty Field General

Surprisingly, the football world again turned its eyes towards State College in 1921. To the surprise of nobody, Glenn Killinger, who filled out and looked like a major college football player, was projected to be QB-1 on the first day of team practice. In previous years, Killinger was a scrawny but fast and modestly determined backfield player. As he reached his 23rd birthday, still a smidgen on the thin side, he entered his final year with lean yet awkwardly bowed legs, a broad back, and ripped arms. Clocked by Coach Bezdek at 10.2 in the 100-yard dash while in his uniform, he carried himself with rigidity and confidence.

After losing seven two-year starters, including All-American Charlie Way, the entire team was built around Killinger's 5'10", 165-pound frame. Although not selected captain—that duty was bestowed on fullback George Snell—he had already won over his teammates. As one correspondent for the *Harrisburg Telegraph* wrote before the start of the season, Killinger was "the all-around star" of the team.[1]

Killinger struggled early in football camp with his annual hay fever symptoms. "I reported with red and swollen eyes that constantly watered," said Killinger. The effects of the affliction were so dreadful that it took all of his willpower to make it through the first two days of practice. Then things got worse for the veteran quarterback.

On the third day of camp, Killinger separated his shoulder during the team's first inter-squad scrimmage. It was September 4, and the first game of the season was scheduled to kick off in 20 days. The injury forced Killinger on the sideline for three weeks. "The injury, coupled with the pollen fever attack, prompted me to return home and I seriously considered giving up football," he said with remorse. "I was greatly discouraged about the entire football situation."[2] His health, plus the departure of his close friends Charlie Way and Hinkey Haines to graduation, in addition to the recent news that the team's captain and star fullback George Snell was lost for the season because of a throat infection was, for a moment, too much for the four-year veteran to deal with.

According to Bezdek, his quarterback's injury and mental state were hardly a concern. "The bump was not serious," Bezdek told reporters when asked why Killinger wasn't participating in practice. Since the team was shy on quarterbacks, he said, there was no point taking "chances on losing the services of the Harrisburg lad."[3]

Coach Bezdek had already complicated matters for Penn State in the off-season by lining up, as he said, "one of the hardest [schedules] ever arranged for a blue and white eleven," including games at home against North Carolina State and Lehigh, and contests with Harvard, Georgia Tech, Navy, and Pittsburgh on foreign gridirons.[4] But now with Killinger out, and the previous year's scrub team quarterback, Tommy Ritner, splitting time with junior Michael Palm, the fate of the season was in question.

Bezdek found Killinger an osteopath from Bellefonte to treat his shoulder five days a week. After evening training table, the coach and his scion would walk to their respective abodes together: "Bezdek kept needling me, saying that Mike Palm would take my quarterback job away from me," said Killinger, who found his customary genial attitude after the hay fever symptoms subsided. "Little did I realize that he was very anxious to have me get healthy in a hurry." Each day at practice, Bezdek ran Killinger through non-contact quarterback drills. But once the inter-squad scrimmaging began, Killinger was forced to run 20 laps around the field. "One day at practice I was feeling very miserable after running my laps. Bezdek was sitting along a pile of dismantled wooden bleachers. As I came abreast of Bezdek, I said sarcastically, 'Is that enough laps?' Bezdek replied, 'No, wise guy, five more laps.' Never again did I make any wise cracks to Bezdek."[5]

After three weeks, a joyous Killinger was cleared to play by trainer Bill Martin and the Bellefonte osteopath Bezdek provided for his rehabilitation. But in spite of being dressed in full gear and running through daily drills with what Killinger described as an "eager-beaver attitude," Bezdek kept him out of the contact scrimmages. "I ran my usual 20 laps with a greater enthusiasm, making sure Bezdek observed my antics," the signal caller recounted. There was "Still no response."[6] Later in the week, when Killinger told his roommate at the Alpha Chi Sigma house, Bill Sieg, he was not starting in the opening game, "Bill broke down and cried like a baby," he noted.

Many were surprised to see Killinger with his helmet on, dressed in his number-2 jersey but standing on the sideline at the beginning of the season opener on September 24. It was a 53–0 drubbing handed to Lebanon Valley College, hardly a formidable opponent. The strength of Penn State's offense was its powerful backfield, comprised of Ruel "Pete" Redinger, Joe Lightner and Frank Hess, which averaged 175 pounds. Reserve fullback E. H. Cornwall, weighing over 180 pounds, was the heaviest backfield candidate. The Nittany Lions also featured sophomore marvel Harry "Light Horse" Wilson, future two-time All-American and the younger brother of former team captain Lloyd Wilson, as a reserve halfback.[7]

Inexperience, however, was costly for Penn State in the opening quarter, especially with Tommy Ritner, who had beaten out Michael Palm, at quarterback. The Nittany Lions played "over-anxious and as result were given numerous penalties." Penn State held a 7–0 lead entering the second quarter when, as the Dutchmen were forced to punt the ball away, Killinger replaced Ritner and quickly ran for a touchdown. Killinger recalled, "Bezdek was obviously disgruntled with the team and substituted me to return the [Lebanon Valley] punt." Killinger caught the ball on the run at the 15-yard line, sprinted up the middle for 15 yards, then cut to the right. He tiptoed down the sideline for the touchdown.[8] Killinger scored once more on a 20-yard off-tackle run in the second half.

The following morning, the *Pittsburgh Daily Post* wrote, "A strange feature of the game was that the second team sent in by Coach Bezdek looked better than the first." This was "largely due to the sensational running back of punts by Killinger," the newspaper added, who "showed flashes of greatness while piloting the second team and seemed to be recovered from the injury secured during practice."[9]

Killinger started the following week in a surprisingly close 24–0 victory over Gettysburg. Penn State played without Joe Lightner, its bruising halfback, who sprained his shoulder in the previous contest. Penn State scored within two minutes of the opening kickoff when a Gettysburg punt was blocked and recovered. On Penn State's first play from scrimmage, Killinger handed off-tackle to sophomore E. H. Cornwall, who skirted 20 yards for a touchdown. Killinger also scored on a plunge through the middle in the fourth quarter.[10] The press learned after the game that Bezdek had told Gettysburg's coach Bill Wood that his team would not throw any passes and would run plays only to the strong side of the line.[11]

Of great interest to fans before and during the game was the presence of Hinkey Haines, who worked as the backfield coach at Gettysburg. "Hinkey Haines may mean nothing more than a Czecho-Slovak dispatch to the average country newspaper but to the real football and baseball fan-well in the words of the poet, 'Hinkey' is some pumpkin," heralded the *Gettysburg Times* before the game, "It was he who with Charley [*sic*] Way and Killinger … gave Penn State its greatest backfield."[12]

Seven days later, Killinger was back to full form as quarterback, safety and punter against Penn State's "first real test," the *Twin-City Daily Sentinel* alleged, the "scrappy" North Carolina State Wolfpack.[13] Killinger "scintillated all afternoon," reported the *Harrisburg Telegraph*.[14] The most spectacular play of the game was Killinger's 70-yard punt return along the right sideline for a touchdown in the third quarter. On a subsequent possession, Killinger had

11. A Crafty Field General

The 1921, 8-0-2 Penn State Nittany Lions. Killinger is back row, second from the left. Killinger never lost a game he started at quarterback (Penn State University Libraries).

a 54-yard touchdown called back. According to an old Bezdek custom, he explained, when a touchdown was called back for a penalty, the coach demanded that same play would be run again. "We ran the same play," he recalled, "and I scored the TD," a 59-yard jaunt through the center of the line. For the second consecutive year, Penn State held the team from Raleigh scoreless, winning 35-0.[15]

Penn State's third straight shutout was overshadowed by a development coming out of Pittsburgh. For the first time in the history of college football, play-by-play of a game was commercially broadcasted over the radio. The so-called "Backyard Brawl," an annual contest played between the University of Pittsburgh and West Virginia University, aired on Westinghouse's KDKA. Not even a year old, KDKA wasted little time before it began broadcasting boxing matches and major league baseball games. Hugo Bezdek lobbied to no avail to get the Pittsburgh-based station to transmit Penn State games. In fact, in what is considered the first collegiate broadcast by the station, KDKA had aired Bezdek's address to the Pittsburgh Chapter of the Penn State Alumni Association on April 9, 1921.

This was a revolutionary innovation. Radio's ability to reach large numbers of people simultaneously could irrefutably help promote his football team, Bezdek thought. In particular, it could help give exposure to his quarterback, for whom he had been petitioning Walter Camp hard for consideration to the Camp All-American team. When he failed to get a commitment from Westinghouse even to broadcast the future Thanksgiving Day game against Pittsburgh, Bezdek reached out to an old rival for another means of exposure. Talks began in mid-October between Bezdek and Enoch Bagshaw, first-year head coach of the University of Washington Sun Dodgers, to arrange an extra game after each team finished its regular season schedule. No commitments were made as of yet, but the prospect that Penn State could play a season finale in the state of Washington excited a lot of people. The coastal matchup would go a long way for placing Penn State in contention for a national title in the opinion of the sportswriters as well as make a case for Killinger as the top quarterback in the land. And quite possibly the game could be broadcasted on Penn State's newly minted radio station, operating under the call name 8XE, which had obtained an experimental license from the U.S. Department of Commerce earlier that year.[16] As exciting as the prospect of playing a game 2,500 miles from campus was, Penn State had to get through its challenging schedule first.

Killinger at Penn State football practice in 1921. He was made captain of the team after George Snell suffered a season-ending illness (Jessica Killinger).

A few days before Penn State's next game against Lehigh in State College, Bezdek pulled his starting backfield from practice and replaced them with the second string. Lehigh was without a loss, had just defeated Rutgers, 7–0, and had yet to give up a point in the young season. On Bezdek's mind additionally was Penn State's languid effort against Lehigh the previous season that had ended in a tie and likely ruined its chances to be crowned best team in the East. So he sent a message to Killinger and his teammates that if they failed to play with precision in the early stages of the intrastate contest, he wouldn't hesitate to insert a different backfield tandem into the game.

The skull session helped. On the afternoon of October 15—homecoming at Penn State—the unbeaten Nittany Lions methodically took care of Lehigh in front of 10,000 spectators. Penn State scored in the first minute of play when left end Stan McCollum picked up a Lehigh fumble and raced 36 yards for a touchdown. They scored again in the second quarter after a series of off-tackle runs saw Pete Redinger skirt off the right end for a touchdown. Joe Lightner and Killinger added touchdowns in the fourth quarter, and the game ended 28–7.[17]

By now, everyone in the East was talking about Penn State's potential as a legitimate contender. Work began immediately to prepare for undefeated Harvard, whose defense had given up just seven points through their first five games. "The Pennsylvanians are fast rounding into a powerful machine, one of the strangest Hugo Bezdek ever turned out," wrote sportswriter William Abbott, adding "Penn State elevens always play hard and smart football."[18] History, nonetheless, was against the Nittany Lions. Harvard and Penn State had met just three times previously. Harvard led the series, 2–0–1.

Bezdek adopted the slogan "On to Harvard!" in the week leading up to the game. Citing previous success against major Ivy League opponents, such as the University of Pennsylvania in 1919 and 1920 and Dartmouth in 1920, Bezdek said, "all other thoughts [other than on Harvard] are relegated to the background until after the contest with the Crimson."[19]

Like many footballers, Glenn Killinger was superstitious. All season long he took the same route to and from the practice field each evening. He got in and out of bed on the same side every night and morning. And on game days, he wore his stockings turned inside out.[20] As illogical as those behaviors sound, and despite the ribbing that came from his teammates, he paid extra attention to those habits in the lead-up to the Harvard contest.

On to Harvard the team went. After an overnight train ride on sleepers departing from Tyrone, Pennsylvania, the Nittany Lions arrived in Boston as slight underdogs. "Harvard supporters are given odds of 10 to 8 that their team will win," the *Harrisburg Telegraph* reported.[21]

The pivotal East Coast matchup featured contrasting styles in quarterbacks. Like Killinger, Harvard's Charley Buell was a candidate to be an All-American selection. The Ivy Leaguer's method of play differed greatly from Killinger's run and gun style. Writing for the *New York Herald*, Grantland Rice described Buell's traditional approach as more suited to make him the best field general in the East. Buell selected the plays and was a fine punter. He seldom received the snap and did little running or passing. "Harvard's system is to use the quarterback as a field general almost exclusively," said the *Oregon Daily Journal*. "No quarterback can be tackled, hammered and constantly battered, and have the brain function properly. Harvard depends on the quarterback for strategy."[22] Killinger, meanwhile, touched the ball on nearly every play. In addition to sizing up the defense and calling plays accordingly, "Killinger passes the ball, punts, drop-kicks, and runs," said Robert "Tiny" Maxwell of the *Philadelphia Evening Public Ledger*. "He is an ideal combination man."[23] Killinger represented a new, ever more important quarterback just beginning to manifest itself in a kind of practical gridiron impulse. Killinger was very much a man of his time: he punted, passed, kicked, ran, and barked out signals better than any of his childhood heroes ever had. If Penn State could pull off the upset, sportswriters believed, Killinger would become the trendsetter for a new age of quarterback play.

During pregame preparations, Bezdek's assistant Dick Harlow reported that every visiting team had fumbled the ball over to Harvard on the first play of the game. Bezdek looked at Killinger and said, "Killy, you are an old veteran, you carry the ball off-tackle on the first play. You won't fumble!" The game began when Killinger returned the opening kickoff to the 30-yard line. Then, just as his coach requested, he called his own number for an off-tackle run to the right. Just as he drove through a small hole at "full speed ahead," he met a Harvard linebacker head-on. "I went about five yards back and the ball flew five yards forward with Harvard recovering the fumble," Killinger wrote in his memoir. He refrained from making eye contact with his coach "for the remainder of the half."[24] Harvard's possession ended in a missed field goal. On their next possession, however, Harvard proceeded to score off of a series of line plunges and buck sweeps. Minutes later, the Crimson scored once more to lead by 14 points.

The Nittany Lions re-entered the game in the second quarter after Killinger shook off nerves to pilot his team 70 yards on 17 plays for a touchdown. Acting as captain for the injured George Snell, Killinger called close formations that positioned all four backfield players up close to the line of scrimmage. Before the snap, he quickly signaled shifts to the right or left, then "uncorked a series of plays that completely bewildered Harvard," said the *Pittsburgh Post Gazette*. The plays that Killinger called embodied a mix of line plunges, double passes to receivers streaking down the field, and short, delayed passes directly behind the linebackers. Inside the 5-yard line, the determined quarterback called his own number by showing a forward pass, but as he rolled to his right, he tucked the ball away and plunged over the goal line for Penn State's first score.[25] Harvard led 14–7 at halftime, but Penn State had the momentum.

Bezdek's first words to Killinger since the fumble on the opening play came as the team jogged off the field at the half. "I saw Bezdek walking towards me," Killinger said. "I angled away from him but he kept coming and finally I was trapped." The impassioned coach said only one thing: "Killy, you are an old veteran, you won't fumble." Bezdek did not say another word to his quarterback. "We were a sober and angry team between halves," recalled Killinger, who did most of the talking. He openly criticized himself for fumbling, which he said led to his team's early 14-point deficit. Years later, he could still remember the feeling of his team regrouping in the locker room: "I knew we were ready to play a tough second half and I could hardly wait."[26]

Penn State had taken its beating in the first half. Rags Madera, the team's big left tackle who was also an intercollegiate heavyweight boxing champion, suffered a career-ending broken leg on the opening kickoff.[27] Starting fullback Frank Hess and halfback Pete Redinger were also knocked out of the game. As expected, Killinger put the team on his back in the second half. He and reserve halfback Harry "Light Horse" Wilson are credited with carrying the ball on 90 percent of Penn State's running plays.

After forcing a Harvard punt in the third quarter, Penn State's first drive of the second half began in the shadow of its own goal posts at the 6-yard line. With the help of sophomore sensation Wilson, Killinger guided his team 94 yards for a game-tying touchdown and extra point. Using his earlier tactics, Killinger drove the ball to the 33-yard line. "The Crimson found it difficult to find the man with the ball," the *Harrisburg Evening News* noted. "Killinger, the Penn State quarterback, kept his plays covered up and had Harvard at sea guessing to whom he would pass the ball or whether he would run with it himself."[28] Near midfield, Killinger called a misdirection play, giving the ball to Wilson, who broke clean to the Harvard 8-yard line. The halfback, Joe Lightner, scored three plays later to tie the game, 14–14.

There was a play during the drive when Wilson was slow to get off the ground. Killinger approached him and said, "Come on, Harry, give the referee the ball." Wilson had been kicked in the mouth and lost a tooth. His nerve was exposed. "Killy didn't have much sympathy," Wilson recalled. The young halfback remembers Killinger saying, "What can we do about that?" Later that night, as the team boarded a train at the Boston station, the referee spotted Wilson and handed him his tooth.[29]

After two punt exchanges, Penn State had the ball at its own 15-yard line in the fourth quarter. Killinger ran for a gain of 40 yards and completed two passes to McCullom, reaching the Harvard 15-yard line. After two losses for five yards on first and second downs, Penn State faced third down and 15 yards to go. Killinger threw a forward pass directly over the middle of the defense, where Lightner circled out of the backfield and took the ball to the 8-yard line. On fourth and short, most people present thought Killinger would call his own number; instead, he audibled a play for Lightner, who broke through the defense and scored a touchdown. Penn State obtained its first lead, 21–14, and was on the brink of pulling off the biggest upset of the season.

On the ensuing possession, in conditions so dark that sportswriter Will B. Johnstone said, "one could see flashes of cigarets [sic] in the darkened stands," Harvard's Charles Buell threw a rare pass, letting loose a long heave down the right sideline where end Little "Winnie" Churchill, a remarkable running back so nearsighted he was normally useless in the pass game, had gotten behind Killinger to make a running catch about five yards from the Penn State goal.[30] Churchill carried Killinger over the goal line for the score. The extra point by Buell was good.

In the pitch-blackness that had enveloped all of Cambridge, Penn State mounted one final attack to score. Starting the drive at the 13-yard line, Killinger completed a 22-yard pass to Lightner. After another first down, a roar from the crowd went up as Killinger faked a pass and ran toward the right sideline, then reversed field, galloped across the field to the left and was brought down at Harvard's 15-yard line. There was time for one play, but Killinger was sacked for a loss when he dropped back to heave a final pass. The game ended, 21–21.

In the dark evening air, Killinger told reporters crowded around him that he "would have opened up his aerial attack but for the fact that darkness made it decidedly too big a risk with a tie assured." Since both teams were wearing dark uniforms—Harvard wore dark crimson jerseys with black helmets while Penn State had on Navy blue jerseys and black helmets—he said, "it was too dark to distinguish readily between friend and foe at some little distance away."[31]

Sportswriters covering the 1921 team considered the tie with Harvard a triumph for Penn State, and many hinted that stars were born that weekend. A day after the game, the *Pittsburgh Daily Post* reported that Penn State had a new dynamic duo in its backfield in Killinger and Joe Lightner. Both hailing from Harrisburg, and both having played together on Penn State's record-breaking 1921 baseball team, Killinger and Lightner were now among the best backfield tandems in the country. "The pair scored every one of the 21 points the visitors rolled up [against Harvard]," wrote the *Daily Post*.[32] At this point in the season, Lightner's five touchdowns and nine extra points—for a total of 39 points—ranked sixth in the nation in scoring. Lightner's milestone was doubly impressive considering he missed two of Penn State's five games. Killinger's five touchdowns placed him 12th in the country.

The hoopla before the next game against Southern powerhouse Georgia Tech was unprecedented for Penn State. The contest, played at the Polo Grounds in upper Manhattan (located in present-day Harlem), was blessed with the presence of two World War I heroes, General John J. Pershing of the American Expeditionary Force and Ferdinand Foch, Marshal of the French Army during the Great War.[33]

Originally called the Georgia Institute of Technology, the Yellow Jackets gained notoriety as one of the country's top football teams under the tutelage of John W. Heisman. During the wartime adventure of 1917, Georgia Tech split the first International News Service national championship with Pittsburgh.

Sports columnist Hal Reynolds of the *Atlanta Constitution* coined a nickname for Heisman's 1917 squad, the Golden Tornado. The Georgia Tech student body fancied the new moniker and adopted it as their catchy mascot for the next 12 years.[34]

After 16 seasons and 104 wins, Heisman moved on to the University of Pennsylvania after the 1919 season.[35] With Heisman's assistant, Bill Alexander, as their new coach, the Golden Tornado still dominated the Southern Intercollegiate Athletic Association, having won the conference title in 1920 (and later in 1921 and 1922). Georgia Tech had just come off a 48–14 trouncing handed to Rutgers, whose coach said after the game, "The Georgia Tech backfield in the game against my team did things that brought me to my feet applauding instinctively an exhibition of football that I rarely have seen equaled on any field by any team."[36] Although its schedule was not as strong as Penn State's, the Golden Tornado had given up only 14 points all season—all to Rutgers—and won by margins of 42–0 over Wake Forest, 70–0 over Davidson, 69–0 over Furman, and 41–0 over Oglethorpe. The sportswriters questioned whether Penn State had the defensive power to stop four-time All-Southern quarterback David "Red" Barron, who was also the South's 60-yard indoor sprint champion, four-year starter and wrecking-ball, All-American fullback Julian "Judy" Harlan, and the mighty Georgia Tech offense.

In truth, Georgia Tech's and Penn State's styles resembled one another. Assistant coach Dick Harlow, who scouted Georgia Tech in Atlanta the previous week, said "their team was easily the equal of our team and possibly better if we did not play up to our ability."[37] They each possessed a diverse attack that included line plunges, misdirection buck sweeps off tackle, perimeter runs, and what the *New York Tribune* called "a liberal mixture of forward passing."[38]

Sportswriter William Abbott said before the game that Killinger could be the difference maker. Abbott claimed, "Killinger at quarterback is the keystone of the team's offense. He is a veteran, a crafty general, who can run and throw with equal skill."[39]

At its pep rally the day before the game, the captains of Georgia Tech sang a few lines of a song they composed about the game. "We are on the way to the Polo Grounds to smash the Yanks from the opening down. We are big and tough enough, we are the fighting engineers from Georgia Tech." The ditty, Killinger wrote, "really aroused our anger and made us a more determined football team."[40] Meanwhile, at Penn State's pep rally, held at an undetermined location in New York City, Killinger was told by his coach to make a speech to the crowd. Penn State fans had nothing to worry about, he told listeners. "Our forefathers stopped the Rebels at Gettysburg," and Penn State "would stop them at Polo Grounds!" That remark incited the crowd, who embarked on an impromptu parade downtown.[41]

Time spent inside the exalted Polo Grounds ballpark before the game could have obstructed the players' focus, as Penn State dressed in the New York Giants' locker room. "I could hardly believe that my idolized Giant baseball heroes had dressed in this same room," Killinger said with reverence, adding, "I pictured John McGraw, Christy Mathewson and all the other N.Y. Giants of national fame gathered in this room." As Penn State took the field for warm-ups, Killinger admitted, "I was further awed when I saw the high capacity crowd of some 33,000 spectors [sic]. The grass on the outfield was cut short like a golf green and was fast and a pleasure to run on. The weather was perfect and our team was sky-high and ready to go."[42]

Near the end of pregame activities, the referee called Killinger, who was again acting as team captain in place of the sickly George Snell, to the center of the field, where he met Georgia Tech's captain, Judy Harlan, who towered over the much shorter and gaunt Nittany Lion quarterback. There were two dozen New York photographers taking pictures as the two shook hands while the referee tossed a silver dollar in the air for the coin-flip, which was won by the Southern contingent.

What happened next was history for the men from Mount Nittany. Led by Killinger, who turned in his most brilliant performance of his career, Penn State pulled off a 28–7 upset win over one of Georgia Tech's strongest teams ever.

Georgia Tech scored first in the opening quarter when the "Red" Barron picked up 60 yards on a wide toss and Harlan followed with a buck sweep off tackle that found the end zone. Penn State found itself trailing for the third consecutive week. The moment, though, was fleeting.

Killinger fielded the ensuing kickoff at the 15-yard line, weaved through the defenders and raced down the right side of the field, all the way for a touchdown. He recalled with pride, "I put my chin on my chest and really sprinted about 50 yards for the TD. I heard footsteps thundering behind me and I dove over the Ga. Tech goal line."[43] At a cocktail party in New York years later, Killinger was approached by future Baseball Hall of Fame infielder Frank Frisch, who told him "he had a seat on the 50 yard line at the Ga. Tech game. When I ran for the TD, he ran the last 50 yards in the aisle. When he returned to his seat he discovered that he had torn ... his pants by catching his pants in the folding seat."[44]

Killinger's score became the talk of the country. One witness said "our voices left us with Killinger's remarkable run." The renowned sports editor of the *New York Tribune*, Grantland Rice, described the play: "Georgia Tech made six first downs against nothing for Penn State, but on the next kick-off the ball settled lightly into the arms of Killinger and the 'Red Deer' was on his way through the golden autumn afternoon with the entire Tech team in pursuit." Rice said onlookers were "lucky" to witness a kickoff returned for

Killinger (right) with Georgia Tech captain Judy Harlan before the Penn State–Georgia Tech showdown at the Polo Grounds on October 29, 1921 (author's collection).

a touchdown in "one of the big games." He added, "Only a great back of the Killinger type is qualified to make such a play, and as he bounded into the open beyond midfield the entire stand arose to pay him tribute."45

Walter K. Ross, an impartial spectator who traveled from Washington, D.C., to attend the game, wrote to his father in Harrisburg, "Killinger's fine run had robbed the Georgians of their courage and resourcefulness."46 Penn State went on to score three more unanswered touchdowns, including a 12-yard, off-tackle run to paydirt by Killinger, to win by an impressive margin. The difference could have been worse, but Georgia Tech prevented Penn State from scoring on two additional occasions inside the 10-yard line. Ross continued, "The forward passes, some of which were executed superbly, added greatly to the brilliant work of State's quarterback, and should cause Walter Camp to place him on his All-American eleven without further consideration. Harrisburg may well be proud of Killinger, as the college undoubtedly is."

Calling Penn State a "Wonder Squad," Southern sportswriter Cliff Wheatley asked, "What hit us?" He wrote, "Penn State had everything. There is nothing that I can think desirable in a football team that these Nittany Lions don't possess ... strength ... power in the backfield, good punting, fine generalship, a bewildering pass system, and a general attack that is as varied as it is effective."[47]

The *Atlanta Constitution*, Georgia Tech's hometown newspaper, praised Killinger's performance.

> Penn State's aerial system would be a complete failure without the services of an accurate tosser, but Killinger [sic] tops off his incomparable broken-field running and kicking with unnerving accuracy in throwing, making him one of the few football players in the country at this time around whom a triple threat could be built. When he starts calling signals from any formation, a team is likely to start centering their eyes on him, and another runner is given a mighty good chance to gain some ground.[48]

In addition to his two touchdowns, Killinger accounted for 200 punt and kickoff return yards. He added another 100 yards either running the ball or passing to his receivers. Wheatley said, "he is simply not capable of being brought down by a single tackler." He added after the game, "it is doubtful if he can be left off any of the all-American selections."[49]

In the locker room after the game, Georgia Tech's coach, Bill Alexander, congratulated Killinger. Alexander said the Nittany Lion quarterback played "the best game he had ever seen a quarterback play in his many years at Ga. Tech." Bezdek then called Killinger to his dressing room, where he was talking with what Killinger described as, "a very distinguished looking gentleman who was neatly dressed and had a small mustache." It was Walter Camp, the foremost authority on college football. Standing there in his signature trench coat and bowler fedora, Camp congratulated Killinger on winning the game. Killinger wrote nostalgically in later years, Camp "especially mentioned that I had demonstrated remarkable ability in open-field running with the ball."[50]

A few days later, the *New Castle News* called Killinger: "concentrated T.N.T." "How many quarterbacks," the newspaper queried, "could possibly be much better than this lad is hard to figure." The *Philadelphia Evening Public Ledger* followed up the comment by saying, "Killinger is one of the best quarterbacks in football today. He's a 'bad man' in the broken field, he runs well from scrimmage formation and is a good field general."[51]

With a lot of media attention on Glenn Killinger after the victory, people started to notice that Penn State had not lost in 20 consecutive games. It was the longest active streak in college football, dating back to the 1919 season, when Penn State last lost to Dartmouth in week three of Killinger's non-letter year.

Seven days after the trouncing of the Golden Tornado, Penn State started slowly, but ultimately took care of business in a snowstorm by defeating Carnegie Tech of Pittsburgh (present-day Carnegie Mellon), 28–7. For the fourth straight week, Penn State found itself losing by seven early after a hook-and-ladder play yielded a 55-yard touchdown for Carnegie Tech. In the second quarter, Killinger intercepted a Tech pass deep in Penn State's territory and, moments later, scored his team's first touchdown to tie the game, 7–7. He later fumbled on Tech's 10-yard line, which kept the game tied at halftime. After Killinger's 45-yard kick return to open the second half, he threw a 40-yard pass to Harry Wilson. Then Joe Lightner took the ball over the goal line for the lead. Wilson added two more scores in the second half to give Penn State a comfortable margin of victory.[52]

On November 12, with the odds stacked against them, Penn State had their chance to shock the sports world once again as it matched up against the Naval Academy in a game the *Washington Times* said "will largely determine the final rating for both teams."[53] Under the coaching of Bob Folwell, Navy presented itself as another opponent that entered the game undefeated and without having given up a point. In fact, Coach Harlow, who returned from scouting the Midshipmen's game against Princeton, a 13–0 drubbing in which Navy did not yield a first down, reported to the team that Navy was definitely the best team on their schedule. During his chalk talks all week, Bezdek hammered away at the fact that Navy was bigger and better. "Bezdek needled us and told us that Navy was too tough for us and would run us off the field," recalled Killinger, who knew what his coach was trying to do, but it "still got my temper so high that I was about ready to explode."[54]

In the locker room before the game, Bezdek made one final speech in front of the 24 players who traveled to Philadelphia's Franklin Field, the neutral site chosen for the game to accommodate the demand of a growing fan base. "He began his talk by describing the Navy team and their strengths and weaknesses," Killinger illustrated. "He kept repeating how tough they were and he doubted our ability to stay on the same field with Navy." He said with fury, "The longer Bezdek talked the more angry I became. Finally, I exploded." Bill Martin, the team's manager, was standing near the exit with the game ball in his hands. "I jumped up and yelled, 'Come on, fellas!' I brushed Bezdek aside and nearly flattened him. I grabbed the football and rushed to the exit door with the entire squad following close behind. We sprinted out to the playing field yelling like a bunch of lunatics."[55]

The scoring began in the first quarter when Navy, featuring a split formation that Penn State had not seen all season, recovered an onside kick to start the game and marched 45 yards to score their first, and only, touchdown of the game. It was the fifth consecutive week Penn State fell behind to begin a game. Killinger trudged his team down the field with misdirection runs on the ensuing possession. He scored from 22 yards out around the left end, which, incidentally, was the first score of the season against the Midshipmen. The Penn State contingent, however, had to watch nervously for the next quarter after Lightner missed the extra point and the Nittany Lions trailed 7–6. Killinger remembered: "When Lightner and I were try[ing] for the goal, Navy gave us a lot of remarks about little boys and how they would run us off the field." The trash talking was of a "vulgar character" that Killinger described as "unprintable." One for never backing down, he admitted, "I was not bashful and made some ungentlemanly remarks about their ancestors and the Naval Academy."[56]

As confident as ever, and in a steady drizzle, Killinger led his team to another score before the end of the first half. Starting from the Penn State 12-yard line, Killinger broke a run off tackle to Navy's 43-yard line. After two Wilson runs mounted a first down, Killinger flung a forward pass to Lightner to the 25-yard line. Seven running plays later, Lightner went over top of the Navy defense for the go-ahead score. Penn State led 13–7 at half time.[57]

Killinger made another play for the ages early in the third quarter to foil Navy's second half scoring threat. Navy's offense had relative success mixing forward passes with line plunges in the first half. Its game plan was to continue the same diet of runs and passes in the second half. Early in the third quarter, with the ball at its own 23-yard line, Navy plunged through center for four yards. On second and six, Navy called a play-action pass that nearly burned the Nittany Lions for a score. Coach Bezdek fondly remembered the incident:

> We were playing a regular box defense to stop their passes, with Lightner and Knabb close behind the line and Harry Wilson and Killinger farther back. 'Killie' had to watch for a quick kick, run, or most anything unexpected, for he was our safety man.... The Navy called a pass play and Harry Wilson, then but a sophomore, was sucked in toward the center. The man he was to cover was off to the side ready to take an easy pass for a touchdown. Killinger diagnosed the play like a flash, saw Wilson's plight and the open Navy man. Tearing at full speed across the field, he made a flying leap into the air, snatched the pass almost out of the arms of the waiting Middie end, and undoubtedly saved a touchdown by his alertness.[58]

Penn State threatened the Navy defense on several occasions in the second half. Killinger's 54-yard touchdown run on a trick play was negated by an offside penalty. Another scoring opportunity was halted when Killinger's long pass to Ross "Squeaks" Hufford was dropped at the 5-yard line. Then the drizzle hardened to a downpour in the final period, which hindered the footing of players on both squads. The condition of the field played a large part in the second-half stalemate.[59] When the game ended, Bezdek praised Killinger for his interception that "saved the game for us."[60]

The milestone victory over Navy was hailed as one of the most extraordinary feats in the annals of Penn State football. Glenn Killinger's performance dispelled any last lingering doubt as to his talents as a field general and as a pure athlete. "There was no defense in the country that could have stopped him," Grantland Rice wrote in *Leslie's Weekly*, "as the strong Navy defense soon found out." Navy was deemed infallible, having shut out every opponent before and after the showdown with Penn State. "Up field and down field," Rice wrote in the *New York Tribune*, "the Blue and White marched steadily, surely and relentlessly."[61] This would not have been but for Killinger's unrivaled speed. "He is as fast as a grayhound [sic] and as hard to pull down as a rhinoceros," said Rice. "He starts at top speed and once under way can slip through an opening that is less than a span in width. He is one of those fast, elusive, hard running backs who is first hard to catch and then hard to stop even with a clean, hard tackle."[62]

The *Pittsburgh Gazette Times* echoed Rice's remarks about Killinger's performance. In the *Times'* postgame analysis, Penn State's quarterback was made out to be the game's "dominating figure." It wrote, "His open field running, generalship and defense on forward pass plays were factors that raised him into the class of all-American players."[63]

There seemed to be some great significance in that, as Killinger's steady field generalship was every reason why the Nittany Lions had extended its no-loss streak to 22 games.

• • •

Penn State played a lot of big games in its history, including several in the 1921 season. Perhaps no game was more built up by the media than the much-awaited Thanksgiving Day intrastate clash against the University of Pittsburgh.

Glenn Killinger had a distinct history playing against Pitt. In 1918, his S.A.T.C. team lost, 28-6. During his non-letter season in 1919, although he stood on the sideline in uniform, he watched his team win over Pitt, 20-0. The two foes battled to a scoreless tie on a mud-covered field in 1920. Additionally, Glenn Killinger and Tom Davies, Pitt's three-time All-American halfback who was considered by the *Pittsburgh Gazette Times's* sports editor Harry Keck as "one of the greatest and most popular players that ever wore the Blue and Gold," would meet face-to-face one last time.[64] The fabled individual rivalry between the two multi-sport athletes that dated back to 1918 would come to an end on Thanksgiving Day 1921.

The game was marketed as a Killinger-Davies showdown more than it was for Bezdek and Pop Warner—the two future Hall of Fame coaches. The athletic department at Pittsburgh reported it sold out all 32,000 seats at Forbes Field, although Karl Davis, graduate manager of athletics at the university, said it could have sold 75,000 tickets if that many seats were available. The capacity crowd, said Harry Keck, "will be privileged to look at the greatest quarterback in the East and probably in the country in the person of Glenn Killinger."[65]

Despite a persistent drizzle, the city of Pittsburgh was crawling with people the day before the game. A large parade proceeded from Oakland to the downtown section.

Killinger is shown kicking the ball during practice in 1921 (Jessica Killinger).

"Beat State" signs were hung up all over the city. More than 500 students and the band arrived from State College on the New York–Chicago express. The fans engaged in the usual pregame trash talk. The bookmakers were favoring Penn State over the Panthers, offering bettors ten-to-six odds. And yet, in more than one way dark clouds hung atop the city the evening before the game.

The Penn State factions grew nervous 24 hours before kickoff when the *Pittsburgh Gazette Times* ran an article suggesting that Killinger was involved in a professionalism scandal similar to the one that took down Hinkey Haines the previous spring. The newspaper claimed that Pitt's athletic department was going to protest Killinger's eligibility, suggesting he was paid to play professional baseball and basketball. Details about the allegations were murky. The *Gazette Times* report did not give specifics. The accusations may have originated from Killinger's ball-playing days with the Klein Chocolate Company semiprofessional baseball team in the summer of 1919. Later, in a postseason interview with one of his hometown's reporters, Killinger insisted that neither the Klein brothers nor any of the various summer twilight teams he played for during his summers of high school and college ever paid him. The *Harrisburg Evening News* defended him. The newspaper did not give specifics about Killinger's relationship with the Klein brothers. Instead, it reported only on a transient moment when Killinger played in the Allison Hill League. It said, "During the two seasons with which he played with the Rosewood club in the Hill league here he passed up many opportunities to earn ready change with semi-professional organizations of other places, and in many of the games in which he participated here he performed without remuneration."[66] Although believable, Killinger had lied to the local newspaper. He did get paid to play semiprofessional baseball; if he didn't get as much as money for travel expenses from the Klein Chocolate team in 1919, he revealed in his unpublished and incomplete memoir, written in 1987, that he was paid $85 a game, eight games total (played only on Sundays), by Wilkes-Barre of the Lycoming League during the summer before his senior football season.[67]

There was a subsequent problem that surfaced just before the trip to Pittsburgh. Two recent articles in the *Harrisburg Evening News* and the *Scranton Republican* may have stirred the detractors. In late October, both newspapers reported that Killinger committed to play professional basketball for the Coatesville Coates of the Eastern Basketball League. The element that the pundits failed to acknowledge was that Killinger had not yet signed a contract with Coatesville. He was scheduled to sign the contract after the new year, on January 1.

In a quick retraction that put the rumors to rest, Pittsburgh's athletic department wrote a letter to the *Gazette Times* affirming that they did not plan on protesting the allegations against Killinger. Graduate manager Karl Davis said, "The story is absolutely without foundation."[68] Since it was Pitt that reported on Hinkey Haines' professionalism violation the previous spring, Penn State did have just concern over the rumors.

Frankly, Killinger was lucky.

• • •

Any accusation involving Glenn Killinger was forgotten on the afternoon of November 24 when a capacity crowd turned out for the game that was played on a cold, cloudy, windy, and wet day.

From the outset, it became clear that both teams were going to have trouble moving the football, as the game was virtually a replica of the waterlogged 1920 contest when the two teams slugged it out on a surface of mud and puddles. "[F]rightful weather conditions," said Princeton head coach Bill Roper, marred the day. "I have never seen a field in worse shape."[69]

The result was a 0–0 tie for the second successive year. Sportswriters were forgiving to the Nittany Lions, who were not dropped from consideration in the Eastern rankings. Walter Camp called the game "a joke." He ranted, "It was a great pity that the Penn State–Pittsburgh game was played, as last year, in a sea of mud. The game promised to be one of the best of the year."[70]

The conditions made for an anticlimactic finish to the rivalry between Killinger and Tom Davies, although the play-by-play of the game makes it appear that they were the only two athletes on the field during the contest: either Killinger punting to Davies, or vice versa. "The battle between Davies, the Pitt captain and star, and Killinger, the State quarterback and acting captain, was about an even thing," said the *Gazette Times's* Harry Keck. The Steel City sports reporter gave a slight edge to Killinger. "Killy was slightly steadier on his feet than Tom, and his sure handling of punts was remarkable," wrote Keck, adding, "He caught the slippery ball on the dead run, high or low, scooped up bounders and made pickups, and never was guilty of a slip." Killinger also impressed with his kicking. Keck said, "He got greater distance to his kicks on average than Tommy, and he placed some of them in great style." Keck granted a slight advantage to Davies for yardage on the ground. He said, "[Davies] advanced 23 yards and lost only one from scrimmage. Killinger gained eighteen yards and lost three."[71]

Most of Penn State's offensive attack was limited by the conditions. The slippery and muddy ball made it nearly impossible for Killinger to pass with accuracy. Without traction on the surface, Penn State's backs and ends couldn't get open. The conditions, wrote the Penn State beat writer for the *Harrisburg Evening News*, "choked all the glitter and whirl and glory of a great football battle, and reduced it to a mere clutch and batter and spatter in the mud and wide, shallow pools of water."

Penn State had one opportunity to score in the second quarter when a Killinger punt that went over Davies's head was picked up and fumbled by a Pitt player. Penn State regained possession at the Pitt 18-yard line. On the next play, Penn State's sophomore halfback, Harry Wilson, unfortunately fumbled, giving possession back to Pitt. The ball was in Pitt territory most of the game, but the Nittany Lions couldn't score. Penn State was never in danger of being scored on.

• • •

Immediately following the game with Pitt, the Nittany Lions left muddy Pittsburgh for a post-season contest against the University of Washington Sun Dodgers in Seattle for the 16th East-West Classic. The post-season game pitting the two coastal teams against one another was actually a commonality by 1921 as colleges believed national exposure would "increase their drawing power." Historian Benjamin Rader writes, "all major college teams [in the 1920s] attempted to schedule at least one big intersectional game per season."[72] Penn State already had plenty of those, but a trip to the West Coast would bring a new level of attention to the remote college situated within the mountains of Central Pennsylvania.

Adding to the hype surrounding the road trip, Penn State's licensed radio station announced it would broadcast the game to the student body. This would not be the first commercial radio broadcast of a college football game. That honor belonged to the Backyard Brawl played between West Virginia and the University of Pittsburgh and aired on KDKA Radio in Pittsburgh with Harold W. Arlin providing the commentary. And it would not be the first non-commercial radio broadcast of college football: the October 9, 1920, clash between Texas A&M and Southern Methodist in Dallas owned that crown. Instead, Penn State's low-budgeted and student-run broadcast that would soon be known as WPSC could only reach the students on campus.

The game was actually scheduled at the midpoint of the season after Penn State emerged as a top contender in the East. The University of Washington had, in many regards, according to sports historian Daniel James Brown, the most successful football program of any team along the Pacific coastal states. Largely due to the leadership of two famed coaches, Gil Dobie and Enoch Bagshaw, Washington had racked up 63 consecutive victories without a defeat between 1907 and 1917. During that stretch, the Sun Dodgers amassed a record 1,930 points to its opponents' 118. It must be noted that Hugo Bezdek, as coach at the University of Oregon for five years, was twice among the victims that fell prey to the Sun Dodgers. In 1921, however, the team from Seattle limped into the season finale. After winning its first three games against non-major college teams, Washington entered its contest against Penn State with a record of 3–3–1, including a humiliating 72–3 loss to its Pacific Coast rival, California.

Regardless of its record at that point in the season, Washington possessed several undeniable advantages over its upcoming foe. For one, the game was to be played on Washington's home turf. The playing surface, made of sand and sawdust, was particularly abnormal for the nomads from Pennsylvania. Moreover, Penn State was asked to travel a long distance and across three time zones. These facts would no doubt leave the visitors in a state of lethargy. Last, a vigorous hatred of Eastern colleges might carry the Sun Dodgers to victory. Brown expounds upon the cultural attributes that structure the coastal rivalry. Those in the East embodied attributes in stark contrast to their Western counterparts. Brown said Westerners seemed "self-made, rough hued, wild, native, brawny, [and] simple."[73] Those in the East appeared "a bit superior," well-bred, sophisticated, moneyed, well-read, and refined. Eastern snobbery habitually prevailed in the national press. Newspapers like the *New York Times* and *Pittsburgh Post Gazette* outright ignored teams on the West Coast. And during the few occasions when an East Coast school was defeated by a West Coast foe, media biases prevailed in the form of tailored stories around what the Eastern team did uncharacteristically wrong, as opposed to crediting what the Western team did right. The 1921 East-West Classic between Penn State and Washington was once again inked by the media as a clash between Eastern privilege on the one hand and western incivility on the other.

Although most observers saw Penn State as the true champion of the East, Bezdek, a Westerner, considered the game a chance to showcase his football program in front of a Pacific audience, hoping that a good showing would bolster consideration for a national title. Most people in this part of the country still confused Penn State with the University of Pennsylvania. A special telegraph to the *Gazette Times* in Pittsburgh said, "In spite of the great record made by the football team, there is still a rather hazy idea in the minds of most football followers as to just where Penn State hails from."[74]

Penn State's team, composed of 23 players, traveled alone on a Pennsylvania Railroad train pulling ten Pullman cars complete with a formal dining car with tables for four and waiters wearing white jackets serving fine food. The train had a club smoker, although Bezdek and his training staff enforced a policy restricting his players from the habit. Killinger and his teammates behaved like eager college kids, as courteous porters, not much older than they were, provided free pillows and service with a smile. It was especially amusing to see childlike excitement befall the football stars as they monopolized the women's toilet facilities and loitered in the club car. Upon reaching Bezdek's hometown of Chicago, the team boarded a Northern Pacific Railway train destined for St. Paul, Minnesota, where the coaches allotted a few hours for the boys to explore.[75] At other terminal stops along the "Route of the Great Big Baked Potato," a slogan used by Northern Pacific to promote the railway's historical connection to the oversized potato crops grown in the Yakima Valley of Washington state, the team's trainer, Bill Martin, forced the players off the train for conditioning and sprints. Killinger remembered it as the time of his life: "Every time the train stopped at the numerous water tanks to take on cool water, we went outside with a few footballs and limbered-up by passing and kicking practice in our regular garb and jogged through signals."[76]

The Keystone travelers most enjoyed the train's layover at the Flathead Indian Reservation in Montana, where they entertained the Salish and Kootenai tribesmen with football drills. With celebrity appeal, Killinger and his teammates showed the onlookers, who crowded around them, how to throw and punt a football. They even demonstrated how to tackle. Killinger said,

"They stood around with mouths agape and were truly amazed at our maneuvers." He expressed that the footballers shared the tribesmen's admiration for cultural novelty. "I believe we got a bigger thrill at watching the Indians in their native dress draped in colorful blankets and some with feathers stuck in their block western hats."[77]

Bezdek's plan was to arrive a week early, on Monday, November 28, to give his players enough time to get accustomed to the "climate, air currents, and the like," the coach said to reporters. There were four inches of snow on the ground at the beginning of the week. The weather had a clear impact on the team's focus and energy. On Wednesday, November 30, the team had a lackadaisical showing at practice. Bezdek's short fuse ignited as he kicked all of the first-team players off the field except for Killinger and Harry Wilson. "Killy, you are next," Bezdek indignantly chided to his quarterback, who retorted, "I didn't come 3000 miles to lose my job." The next day, all of the starters were back in the lineup.

In addition to the lousy conditions, the Nittany Lions would be without fullback George Snell and halfback Joe Lightner. Snell, who had been plagued by injuries and a throat illness since late September, traveled west with the squad but was still not cleared to play.[78] And in practice two days before the game, Lightner, a certain all-star selection, suffered an ankle injury, knocking him out of the lineup. The absence of Lightner bestowed all of the kicking duties to Killinger, who was already the team's punter. The injury now meant that Killinger was forced to handle kickoffs, field goals, and extra points.[79]

The absence of Lightner and Snell from the backfield hardly mattered in the game's lopsided outcome, although their presence could have increased the margin of victory. The added responsibilities only allowed "Glenn the Great," as Matt Zabitka of the *Wilmington News-Journal* called him, to close out his college career by masterminding Penn State to a brilliant 21–7 win over Washington in front of 35,000 fans on December 3.[80]

The first score came in the opening quarter when a torrent of Killinger runs and forward passes to Stan McCollum brought the ball to Washington's 8-yard line. Arthur Knabb then went through the line for the touchdown. Killinger kicked the extra point. A few moments later, after Killinger fair-caught a Washington punt, Penn State went on a 75-yard drive capped by a Killinger-to-McCullom forward pass for a touchdown in the second quarter. Inspiration for that drive spilled out from an altercation between Killinger and a Washington player moments after his fair catch. He recalled:

> Their left tackle was a rough and tough player, according to his own thoughts. They had to punt and their punter kicked a very high punt. I called for a fair catch with half their team waiting for me to catch the punt and run. I knew I had no chance to gain yardage and made the only sensible decision. Their left tackle was crowding me

and he called me several unprintable names for playing it safe. I told him that I was running the first four plays over his position and we would see how tough he was.[81]

Killinger returned to the huddle before the ensuing play and told his teammates what just happened: "I wanted our blockers to concentrate on him and everybody that could hit him legally, to do so." After four running plays off tackle, Killinger boasted, "they carried him off the field." Killinger recalled their captain apologizing for the lack of sportsmanship. He said, "Their left tackle caused trouble in practically every game."[82]

The Nittany Lions scored their third touchdown in the third quarter. The *Gazette Times* described the drive: "Killinger fought his way through on play after play, amazing the stands by his superb running."[83] Penn State had possession near Washington's goal line when Killinger called Redinger's number, and he swept around the left end for the third unanswered score. Killinger kicked his third extra point, putting Penn State up, 21–0. Washington's touchdown came in the fourth quarter after a Penn State fumble.

Penn State's offensive statistics were spectacular. Behind the generalship of Killinger, the Nittany Lions gained 530 yards from scrimmage against 90 for Washington; recorded 32 first downs to five for Washington; and completed 11-of-14 pass attempts—an aspect of the game that Washington was not yet accustomed to. In what was believed in 1921 to be an intercollegiate record, Killinger's offense ran off 114 plays from scrimmage while Washington attempted just 14. "Killinger [is] one of the best quarter-backs ever seen on a [West] coast gridiron," reported the Penn State beat writer for the *Harrisburg Telegraph*, who added with distinction, "Killinger's equal is not in the Pacific Conference."[84]

After the game, Killinger and many of his teammates took a celebratory dive into icy Lake Washington. Unlike his celebrated game performance, that decision is recorded in the Penn State annals as one of Killinger's worst calls of the season.

• • •

The Nittany Lions finished the 1921 season with a record of 8–0–2, ranked by all of the leading sportswriters, including the *New York Times*', as the best team in the East. "Considering the schedule Penn State has waded through and the fact that the men of the Nittany Mountain stand undefeated, it seems only proper that Hugo Bezdek's protégés should be ranked as the champions," said *Times* sports columnist Ray McCarthy.[85]

The two authorities on national rankings, Lawrence Perry and Walter Camp, ranked Penn State third in the country behind Notre Dame and Iowa.[86] However, sports columnist Robert "Tiny" Maxwell rated the Nittany Lions as the country's best team. He wrote in the *Philadelphia Daily Ledger*,

Penn State ended a transcontinental season in Seattle, Saturday, winning from the University of Washington 21-7. This victory gives State a clear title to any championship it wishes to claim, for the best teams in the East, South, and Far West have either been defeated or tied. State also traveled more than any other team and faced a harder schedule. Taking all in all, Penn State met all comers, dodged no opponent, went through a stiff schedule and has yet to lose a game. A record like that is worthy of recognition and we believe the Nittany Nomads are entitled to all championship honors that are lying around loose.[87]

Indeed, the performance throughout the 1921 season was magnificent. The Nittany Lions had given Georgia Tech and Navy their only losses of the season. They went on the road and tied Ivy League powerhouse Harvard, and were just yards away from winning before the final whistle blew. Still, some sportswriters asked how could Penn State be ranked ahead of some of the Midwestern teams after tying Pittsburgh, which had three losses? Granted, Pitt's losses were to 10-0-1 Washington and Jefferson, 7-1 Nebraska, whose only setback was to Notre Dame, and 9-0 Lafayette, which flaunted wins over Rutgers and the University of Pennsylvania, and ranked fourth in Eastern polls and fifth in the country when the national rankings were released. The answer apparently was that football in the East was much better than the West in 1921. Notre Dame played a rigorous schedule, even though they lost one game, to Iowa, 10-7, in week three of the season. The Irish finished much stronger with impressive wins over Army, Rutgers, Nebraska and Michigan State. There was also Big Ten champion Iowa, which touted Frederick "Duke" Slater, the school's first great African American, who lettered four years as a tackle, and Aubrey Devine, the Iowa City "wonder man" who was perhaps the only quarterback in the country whose performance during the season measured up to Glenn Killinger's.[88] The flaw for Iowa was its weak schedule. After its victory over Notre Dame on October 8, none of Iowa's five remaining opponents had a winning record.

At season's end, Penn State's record-breaking streak of games without a loss had extended to 24 games. (The streak would eventually stretch to 30 games before a loss to Navy in the post–Killinger era on November 3, 1922.) Glenn Killinger was likely the reason. In his four seasons, 1918 to 1921, Killinger compiled a 23-3-5 record. He started 19 of 31 games. He played in 23 of those contests at either halfback or quarterback. Of the 19 games he started, 15 were at quarterback. Penn State never lost a game that Glenn Killinger piloted from the quarterback position. The Nittany Lions, with Killinger as a starter at either position, amassed a record of 13-1-5. Perhaps, the biggest accomplishment during his four years was the honor of winning two East Coast titles in 1919 and 1921, and being given one national title by a Philadelphia sports authority. The thought of coming close to a third championship in 1920 but for two games ending in ties makes for a troubling reality of life in sports.

Asked many years later to explain how valuable Killinger was for his teams at Penn State, Hugo Bezdek said, "As a quarterback I would put Glenn up against any player I ever coached, ever seen or ever heard of in my many years in football. Glenn was a smart player, always thinking and alert to choose the right play for any situation. Not only would Glenn tell his fellow players what to do but he could and would do it himself."[89]

12

All-American Hero

Glenn Killinger generally enjoyed train travel, which was the best method of traveling to away games. The excursions to Pittsburgh for the annual Thanksgiving Day game were especially important for bonding the team together. Penn State's exceedingly tough travel schedule in 1921 had included trips to Cambridge to play Harvard, Philadelphia to play Navy, New York City to oppose Georgia Tech, the Steel City to face Pittsburgh, and, obviously, Seattle. The Nittany Lions covered a distance of 8,500 miles during the season, a feat matched by no one until Notre Dame's 10,500 miles of travel in 1924. *Philadelphia Public Ledger* sports columnist Robert "Tiny" Maxwell gave Bezdek's boys the nickname "Nittany Nomads." One editorial in the *Pittsburgh Gazette Times* called them the "Nittany Tourists."[1]

Bezdek and his assistant, Dick Harlow, arranged sightseeing stops in Salt Lake City and Denver, but not before spending a night in Portland, where the alumni of his former team, the University of Oregon, honored Bezdek.[2] The team enjoyed salmon steak in Portland and a Western steak dinner at the famous Manhattan Restaurant in Denver. But in the down time on the train, Killinger had plenty of one-on-ones with his coach.

On this particular trip, the six-day journey home from Seattle did much to strengthen the bond between Killinger and Bezdek. The coach's scion had a plethora of options in front of him. He was already sought-after by several major league baseball teams, he was now brooding about signing a contract with professional basketball's Coatesville Coates, and he wished to try his hand in coaching. All of these options, and Killinger had yet to graduate from Penn State. Along the way back to Pennsylvania, Killinger needed Bezdek's advice.

Talk of Killinger's selection to a multitude of All-East and All-American teams was already underway before the Penn State football team arrived back on campus. During the Golden Age, sports columnists from various newspapers would select their own All-American teams. In addition, more than 250 coaches would come together to make their selections of who they thought formed the best 11 in the country. Killinger was selected first team in every poll—nine total. The most prestigious honor was to be named to Walter Camp's list.

After playing and coaching at Yale in the last three decades of the 19th century, Walter Camp became the foremost authority on intercollegiate football. He was the Navy Department's athletic commissioner in 1917 and 1918 when he helped devise an organized sports program to help servicemen become more physically fit. It was Camp who offered up Hugo Bezdek's name as a leading candidate for the Student Army Training Corps. Camp was the originator of the All-American idea. He first selected an All-American team in 1889. Ever since that inaugural squad, Camp's selections, though not always agreed to by the majority of sports followers, were considered official.[3]

Shortly after the game with Washington, Killinger was named to Walter Camp's All-American first team at the position of halfback. The quarterback position was given to Aubrey Devine of Iowa. Devine and Killinger were spitting images at quarterback and multisport luminaries on their respective campuses (Devine became a nine-time letterman at Iowa in football, basketball, and track and field.[4]) Camp said, Devine's "play has been a model of consistency throughout the season on a team which has gone undefeated." He commended Devine's ability "to interfere and take hard knocks without exhaustion or injury." As for Killinger, Camp said that although he played quarterback at Penn State, he "played virtually the halfback position." Camp said Killinger possessed, "the most peculiar elusiveness of any back on the field this year, and that, too, when apparently about to be stopped."[5]

Glenn Killinger became Penn State's fourth football player selected to Camp's All-American first team, following on the heels of center William "Mother" Dunn in 1906; and two of Killinger's former teammates, end Bob Higgins and halfback Charlie Way, in 1919 and 1920, respectively. The first to tell Killinger the news was former University of Pennsylvania tackle Lou Little, a 1919 All-American selection. Little was, at the moment, trying to recruit Killinger to play for the Canton Bulldogs of the professional football league. Proud, but naturally coy, Killinger told his hometown newspaper: "[It's] Very nice to get an All-American place, but a good bit of it was luck." He wrote many years later, "I was completely amazed and my joy knew no bounds."[6]

The entire experience was humbling, in fact, considering that Killinger's career started on the cold and hard, sometimes snow-covered field at Harrisburg's Island Park with his brother Earl, learning the ins and outs of football. Nobody forgot that young Killinger was cut from the varsity team in high school every year except his senior year. Even then, he started only one game, which was a losing effort that found him back on the bench by halftime.

Killinger's career of gridiron feats was something to marvel upon. John

Heisman, former coach of the University of Pennsylvania who witnessed Killinger's abilities directly in a 28–7 setback to Penn State in 1920, would publish "Heisman's Hundred in the Hall of Fame" with William Randolph Hearst's King Features Incorporated in 1928. In "Heisman's Hundred in the Hall of Fame," Heisman rated Killinger among the top college football players ever to play the game. Heisman's approbation was directed at Killinger's unrivaled football speed. The coach claimed, "On cinder tracks many men can go pretty fast in track suits but put a heavy football uniform on them and cumbersome shoes with cleats on their feet and they don't look too much for speed. But Killinger fairly flew in any kind of togs." The fact that Killinger was, as Heisman put it, "a self-made athlete," was an unrivaled feat. It's a "point worth dwelling on more than the number of long runs he made," said Heisman, adding, "and he made a lot of them."[7] Killinger must have had an idea that the legendary coach had honored him. "Heisman's Hundred" was reprinted in newspapers throughout the country. If so, in classic Killinger style, he never related the accolade to anyone.

Attention was drawn back to Killinger decades later. In 1931, 12 Hall of Fame coaches including Pop Warner, then at Stanford, Gil Dobie of Cornell, Princeton's Bill Roper, and Hugo Bezdek met to create a list of the best college football players of all time. The coaches awarded five points for first-place votes, four for second, three for third, two for fourth, and one for fifth. Being on the committee allowed Bezdek to have some influence on the voters. In the end, Killinger tied for 17th, behind players like Jim Thorpe, the easy selection for football's greatest star, George Gipp and Harold "Red" Grange.[8]

The Walter Camp All-American honor was a wonderful tribute to the Harrisburg lad, who lined up a busy month before his graduation from Penn State. The college granted its students an extended vacation before they had to return to take final exams after the New Year. Killinger had until January 3 to return for finals. His graduation was scheduled for January 31, 1922.

In a way that few would understand, Killinger spent nearly every waking moment of that break playing sports for profit. He was not the first collegian yet to graduate before capitalizing financially upon his fame; nor would he be the last. In truth, he had to. Killinger was in debt to family friends who helped pay some of the costs so that he could attend Penn State.[9]

With help from Hugo Bezdek, Killinger announced his willingness to play professional football as soon as a team would have him. Professional football operated in an obscure manner under the auspices of the American Professional Football Association (the initial name of the National Football League, founded in 1920). Players of the APFA (NFL) weren't always committed to one team and often played for up to three teams during the course of a season. Killinger was in need of money, so he wasted no time shopping for a professional contract.

In early December, Killinger signed a one-game contract with Leo Conway, manger of the Philadelphia Quakers, to play in a game against the Canton Bulldogs. The game was played on Saturday, December 18, in Philadelphia. His mentor, Hugo Bezdek, watched from the sideline during the game. He had good reason. A considerable number of his former players were suited up that day. Canton's roster included four of Bezdek's former captains at Penn State: tight end Bob Higgins, center Larry Conover, and halfbacks Charlie Way and Harry Robb. Meanwhile, Killinger and his good friend Hinkey Haines were assigned to play the halfback positions in the Quakers lineup. There were other college star players who, like Killinger, had just finished their senior seasons, including Lafayette's wonder-boy quarterback, Johnny Scott, for Philadelphia and Notre Dame's sensational guard, Hartley Anderson, who played for Canton.[10] Two weeks prior, Canton had edged out a 14–9 victory over Philadelphia, but the additions to the Quakers' roster greatly improved the team's talent.

Glenn Killinger dazzled in his professional debut in front of 12,000 fans at Phillies Park. The *Harrisburg Telegraph* called his performance for the Quakers "sensational." Killinger threw a touchdown pass to Hinkey Haines and was responsible for three other scores after breaking several long runs deep into Canton territory. The Quakers won, 34–0.[11]

The APFA season was already near its end, and a former three-sport star at the University of Illinois and ensign in the U.S. Navy during World War I, George Halas, coached the Chicago Staleys, who had already claimed the championship of the APFA in this pre-playoff era (the title was confirmed in January 1922 by the association's executive committee). However, the addition of Killinger and Haines to the Philadelphia Quakers had sportswriters reconsidering who the best professional football team was at the end of the season. Sports columnist Jinx Tucker of the *Waco News-Tribune* argued, "the recently organized Philadelphia Quaker team appears much stronger on paper and in Hinkey Haines and 'Kill Em' Killinger, Penn State heroes, the Quakers have an attack hard to beat." Tucker drew a comparison: "The Staleys were able to defeat Canton only 10 to 0, while the Quakers won from the same club 34–0."[12]

The bearer of the APFA's title was not important for Killinger. Making money drove his brief experience in professional football. Killinger's professional debut with Philadelphia had been played on a Saturday because Pennsylvania blue laws prohibited professional sports on Sundays. Knowing that other professional teams preferred to play games on Sundays, Killinger had earlier reached out to both the Canton Bulldogs and Washington Professionals, who were scheduled to play one another the following day, to see if one or both would sign him, and if so, what team would offer a better contract. That night, after helping Philadelphia maul Canton, Killinger announced he would wear a Bulldogs uniform on Sunday. So Killinger hopped a train from Philadelphia to Washington, D.C., to play games on back-to-back days with two different teams.[13]

The largest crowd of the season for the host—7,000 fans, which was nothing close to what Killinger had experienced during his college football season—arrived at American League Park to witness the game between Canton and Washington. "Probably half of the crowd turned out lured by the prospect of seeing Glenn Killinger," suggested Ray Helgesen of the *Washington Herald*. Killinger did not start, but when he was substituted into the game, three of the Bulldogs' backfield players represented Penn State—Robb, Way, and Killinger. The Bulldogs' captain was former Nittany Lion Bob Higgins. Canton won the game, 28–14. The analysis of Killinger's performance, however, "proved more or less of a disappointment," opined the *Herald*. His mediocre performance should have been expected, since he had just played his first professional football game less than 24 hours earlier. The *Herald* pontificated, "while brilliant in spots, [Killinger] was far from the form he flashed during the college season." Killinger was criticized for fumbling five times, though it should have been expected for never having practiced snaps with the center or the timing of Canton's plays with the backfield. The "Red Deer," the *Herald* called him (a Grantland Rice moniker), "lacked the drive and polish which marked it during the college season." Killinger was tasked with the kicking duties for the Bulldogs. His punts, reported the *Herald*, averaged almost 50 yards and "were always well placed and with distance he always managed to get sufficient height, so that his ends were generally waiting for the ball to fall into the receiver's arms."[14]

Though not as high-profile as when "Red" Grange joined the professional ranks with the Chicago Bears before his graduation from the University of Illinois in 1925, Killinger's two professional games on successive days created quite a stir within the sporting world. Team-jumping didn't cause the controversy—this was a common feature in professional football in 1921. Instead, like Grange four years later, many decried Killinger for not yet having graduated from college. "The fact that Killinger has turned to professional athletics so soon is not to his discredit," the *Harrisburg Telegraph* defended him. The hometown daily added, "when one is offered several hundred dollars for an hour's work, it is a temptation that is hard for any person to resist, particularly a lad who is working his way through school."[15]

The professional experience was rewarding for a reason other than earning a quick buck. When Killinger grabbed the newspaper on the morning of December 24, he was delighted to see an image of himself superimposed on the sports page alongside three-time Olympic gold medalist Ethelda Bleibtrey, U.S. Open champion Molla Mallory, PGA champion Jack "Jock" Hutchison, member of the 1920 Olympic rowing team Clyde King, Grand Prix champion

Johnny Duff, and baseball luminary George Herman "Babe" Ruth as the Associated Press's "Champions in Sport" for the 1921 calendar year.[16] The honor meant that he was selected the most valuable player in the game of football, both professionally and collegiately. It was an honor that left him speechless for the rest of his life.

While it was fun getting his feet wet playing professional football, Killinger's plan was to join the Coatesville Coates of professional basketball's Eastern League, which competed against teams from New York, Trenton, Camden, Wilkes-Barre, and Reading. Earlier in November, he had made arrangements with John Behney, coach of the Coates, to join the team on New Year's Day in a game against the barnstorming New York Celtics at Madison Square Garden. Yet when January 1 arrived, Killinger was not in a basketball uniform.

Instead, Hugo Bezdek, acting in his role as athletic director, offered Killinger a more secure job as head coach of Penn State's freshman basketball team. He accepted the position rather than play for Coatesville, which eventually earned a 6–14 record that season.[17]

Basketball practice at Penn State was to begin on January 3.

• • •

Glenn Killinger leaned hard on Bezdek immediately following his senior football season. Coaching sports was something he longed to do. Knowing this, in addition to hiring him to coach basketball at Penn State, Bezdek helped him get his first head-coaching job in football at a small but historic liberal arts college in Carlisle, Pennsylvania, called Dickinson College.

The lowly football program at Dickinson had floundered near the bottom of the football ranks in the years following the Great War. In the three football seasons since World War I, Dickinson had trouble scoring and had attained an overall record of ten wins, 12 losses, and three ties between 1919 and 1921. In December 1921, Forrest E. Craver resigned as head coach but agreed to stay on as the director of physical education and athletics to counsel the new hire, if asked to do so.[18]

The Dickinson Athletic Association was charged with finding a new coach. The college needed a celebrity coach, the kind people would get animated about. There were only two people in Pennsylvania that Dickinson's Athletic Association could think of who were looking to coach and who met that criteria: Glenn Killinger and Tom Davies. Hugo Bezdek sold his protégé pretty hard to the selection committee, knowing that Davies's coach, Pop Warner, had strong ties to the college town after serving as the football coach at the nearby Carlisle Indian School from 1899 to 1903, and again from 1907 to 1914. "Killinger plays the game scientifically," Bezdek told the committee, "he is a natural football player and has a good head to command men."[19]

Dickinson was not only one of the worst programs among the small colleges on the East Coast, but the sport was nearly terminated by the school's administration in 1916.[20] A change in leadership and a last-minute decision by the Athletic Advisory Committee to save the sport kept the program intact just before the United States entered the war. Then the 1917 team lost many of its players and coaches to the war, and one year later the college was converted into an S.A.T.C. institution with mediocre intercollegiate talent. By 1921, the team was not competitive and townsmen were losing interest in Dickinson football.

How could a competitor like Killinger tolerate as much imperfection as he would see at Dickinson? Glenn Killinger was an extroverted and a gregarious leader who overcame steep odds by working hard all of his life. Yet the question remained: a young man with a proven temper, could he remain poised enough to perform a job that required patience and tact? Killinger had been a leader at Penn State, having been elected captain of the basketball and football teams because of his ability to exert his influence on behalf of the team.

Then there was the proximity between Carlisle and Harrisburg, where the best football talent in Pennsylvania over the last ten years was produced. Just 20 miles separated the two communities. Killinger's ties to Central Pennsylvania would likely be a better fit to draw the best possible talent to Dickinson. The author of *History of Football at Dickinson College*, Wilbur "Goby" Gobrecht, who also coached at Dickinson from 1965 until 1979 and one season in 1984, claimed "'Killy' was to use his influence to get alumni support and material out of the Harrisburg area."[21] Recruitment methods at this stage of college sports history were rudimentary and simple, nothing compared to the ingenuity of college visits, letter writing, and level of courtship used for recruiting in the 21st century. Talented prospects in this critical era of football were sought out, not by the coach, but by alumni, team members and students. Sometimes elite colleges in the Northeast—namely the Ivy League schools—were able to recruit promising players from preparatory schools, but for smaller and less remarkable colleges, the big draw was the name of the coach.[22]

Then again, why would Killinger want the job? If he really desired, it is likely Bezdek would have placed him on his coaching staff at Penn State. Moreover, Killinger had not yet signed a contract with a major league baseball club, which was certainly going to happen after the New Year. At Dickinson, he would be inheriting one of the worst small college programs in the East, with no tradition and uncertain support from the college's administration. Actually, there was a bright side to coaching at Dickinson. If he chose to accept the position, Killinger, a 24-year-old, first-year head coach, would be the benefactor of modest expectations. If the team's record got no better, people would say that the players were awful and he would not be blamed. If the team improved, however, he would likely get the credit.

Negotiations between Killinger, via Hugo Bezdek, and the Dickinson Athletic Association began as early as Penn State's road trip to Seattle to play the University of Washington. On December 3, the *Harrisburg Evening News* broke the story that Dickinson had made Killinger an offer.[23] According to the *New York Tribune*, Killinger verbally accepted the job on December 29 under the terms that the college would not penalize him if the major league baseball team that he would eventually sign with had a season that runs beyond the start of the football season.[24] Killinger stated that he would sign the contract in February 1922, after his graduation from Penn State.

Upon signing the contract with Dickinson College, Killinger would become the 11th player under Hugo Bezdek at Penn State to become a college football coach. Bob Higgins at West Virginia Wesleyan and Harry Robb at Catholic University, members of the one-loss 1919 team, were already working as head coaches. Eight others had become assistant coaches by 1922, including Ben Cubbage at Virginia Polytechnic Institute, Larry Conover at Clemson, Hinkey Haines at Gettysburg (though about to join Bezdek's staff at Penn State), Charlie Way at Dayton University in Ohio, Harold Hess at the University of Southern California, and Dick Rauch at Penn State (he later coached at Michigan).[25] Clarence Beck eventually signed on to assist Killinger at Dickinson in the fall. (Joe Lightner would ultimately become the head coach of Dickinson College after Killinger's departure.) Of that group, Bob Higgins returned to Penn State to replace Bezdek as the head coach in 1930.

These were all young 20-somethings taking on important coaching roles around the United States. It was more popular and financially advantageous to go into college coaching instead of pursuing a long career in professional football. Moreover, since colleges played games on Saturdays while most professional games were scheduled for Sundays, many young college coaches, like Killinger, could spend the week coaching only to moonlight as professionals on Sunday afternoons. Unlike baseball, where the major league offered more suitable contracts, longevity and fame, the pre- and early-NFL era of football lacked officialdom. Players were paid on a game-by-game basis, there was no playoff system, champions were selected by a vote of the American Professional Football Association's executive committee, and the media hardly paid any attention to the professional football ranks.

Killinger's quest to play professional football was based solely on earning a quick buck. His coaching career, as unmapped as it was in 1921 and 1922, was to become a livelihood. Killinger's career, of course, as a head football coach hinged on his success as a major league baseball player.

• • •

The owners of baseball's New York Yankees were Jacob "Jake" Ruppert, a former member of the United States House of Representatives from New York's 15th and 16th districts, who spoke with a heavy German accent and had made a fortune as the owner of several breweries along the East Coast, and Tillinghast Huston, a Spanish-American War veteran. The New York Yankees had been a cellar-dweller in the American League for years when Ruppert and Huston bought the franchise in 1915 for $480,000. Their first dynasty-creating move as co-owners was to poach the young, pipe-smoking Miller Huggins from the St. Louis Cardinals to manage the Yankees. This was done following the 1917 season. After the announcement that Huggins had accepted Ruppert and Huston's offer, the *East Liverpool Evening Review* said, "The bravest deed since war was declared [was] Miller Huggins signing to manage the Yanks."[26] Huggins proved to be a success, leading his team to a fourth-place finish in 1918, third in 1919 and 1920, and becoming winners of the franchise's first American League pennant and a World Series appearance in 1921. Huggins made an unprecedented number of personnel changes during that stretch, which included obtaining such players as George Herman "Babe" Ruth, Wally Schang, and Waite Hoyt from the Boston Red Sox.

Having come off a championship season and the prospect of playing beside popular American cultural icon Babe Ruth made the Yankees the clear frontrunner for Glenn Killinger, who was working closely with Hugo Bezdek to score a major league contract. Additionally, the chance to live and play baseball in Manhattan during the Jazz Age was a welcoming thought for the spirited twenty-four-year-old.

The 37-year-old Bezdek used his connections as the former manager of the Pittsburgh Pirates to attract contract offers for Killinger from seven major league franchises including the Detroit Tigers, Philadelphia Athletics, and New York Yankees. Bezdek told the management of each club, "He is one of the best infielders I have seen in years and will make good at second, third or shortstop. I believe he will make good in fast company."[27]

When it came time to pick a contract, Killinger seemingly allowed Bezdek to make the decision for him. "In closing with the [New York] Americans Killinger was governed wholly by the advice of Hugo Bezdek," reported the *Harrisburg Telegraph*. Bezdek believed New York was the quickest way to the majors. The reason is speculative, but manager Huggins was dealing with a controversy at third base that traced back to the 1921 season. John "Home Run" Baker, a future Hall of Famer, was once the starter at third, but when his wife died of scarlet fever and his daughters were stricken with the disease, he missed much of the season so that he could tend to his family. Huggins replaced Baker with Mike McNally as the Yankees reached the World Series. A quarrel among the three—Baker, McNally, and Huggins—persisted as spring training neared. Bezdek believed that the acquisition of Killinger might solve Huggins's problem; furthermore, the decision to go to the Yankees might give Killinger the best chance to contribute in his first year in the majors.

The Detroit Tigers, with star player Ty Cobb, to whom many sportswriters like Grantland Rice already compared Killinger, needed a shortstop. The comparison spoke volumes, as Cobb was on his way to breaking nearly every possible record in major league baseball; Rice called Cobb "one of the finest hitters I have ever seen."[28] The Tigers made "a particularly strenuous effort to obtain [Killinger]," reported the *Telegraph*. However, the contract that Bezdek was able to negotiate with Ruppert and Huston made all the difference in why Killinger chose the Yankees.[29] The contract gave Killinger a "fancy" salary that included a $5,000 signing bonus, $800 monthly, 50 percent of his selling price if he was released under optional agreement, and a clause that the New York club had to retain Killinger for one year regardless of how well he performed. One newspaper chided, "Hugo Bezdek who handled his affairs with the major league clubs naturally arranged a contract that protected the youngster."[30]

Yankees scout Paul "Krich" Krichell explained why Ruppert, Huston, and Huggins were so interested in Killinger. He suggested, "Killinger is every bit as promising now as Frankie Frisch was at a corresponding period of his sensational career." Frisch was a four-sport legend at Fordham University who signed with the New York Giants in 1919 and moved directly into the starting lineup without playing a moment in the minor leagues. "But do not quote me as predicting that Killie [sic] will break right into the Yankees batting order as Frisch broke in with the Giants," Krich added. "That sort of thing doesn't happen more than once in 10 or a dozen years." Killinger had the tough task of trying to outdo "Home Run" Baker and Mike McNally, "and that's a tough assignment to wish on any kid," professed Krich. "But you can never tell," he carried on, "Killinger is mightily fleet and has a great pair of hands and a wonderful arm and takes a fine clout at the ball."[31]

On December 19, Miller Huggins actually announced at a press conference with New York City reporters that Bezdek had informed him that Killinger was set to sign with the Yankees.[32] Killinger's commitment to the Yankees received national attention that reaped an excess of skepticism. The *New York Daily News* downplayed the news. "Some little excitement was shown in the announcement that the New York Yankees had prospects of signing Glenn Killinger," it declared on December 29. "Unless he's one out of a thousand, he would do the Yankees no good next year."[33]

In spite of the criticism, Bezdek was a terrific agent for Killinger. His reach extended well beyond that of his quarterback. As he was managing Killinger's professional ambitions, Bezdek worked hard for many of his other protégés, including Hinkey Haines, who was retained by the Yankees as an outfielder in 1922. Paul Krichell said, "Haines is a major league fielder right now." The question about his game was batting. "He was a fine, free hitter in college," where Haines batted .426 to lead the nation, Krich articulated, "but looked as though he was shoulder-bound the few times I saw him play with Hartford" of the Eastern League earlier that summer. He finished, "Hinkey is too good a fielder to be kept out of the majors by inability to hit big league pitching."[34]

Killinger's signed contract with the Yankees reached the front office on January 6, 1922. The legal agreement now offered him the chance to play professional baseball on the Polo Grounds, site of his legendary football game against Georgia Tech a few months earlier. His next move with the New York club was spring training in New Orleans, beginning in March.[35]

He still had a busy month of playing in exhibition football and basketball games in his hometown, a freshman basketball season to coach at State College, and a commencement ceremony to attend. Killinger's life was definitely moving forward in a way that very few had ever experienced.

• • •

The public in Harrisburg possessed a brazen sense of pride in its homegrown athletes during the winter of 1921. The indelible Glenn Killinger, the town's Walter Camp All-American, had much to do with that. On returning home for the holidays, Killinger found himself a celebrity since all the newspapers in Central Pennsylvania had carried stories about his recent college and professional achievements.

Proprietors of the West End Athletic Club prevailed upon Harrisburg's newest professional athlete to participate in a series of exhibition games of football and basketball between Christmas and New Year's. The games would support the West End Twilight League's charity drive benefiting the Commonwealth baseball club. The featured attraction was the multitude of college stars who were back in Harrisburg for the holidays. A best of three basketball series between the local college stars and an independent community team was arranged at the Chestnut Street Auditorium between December 24 and January 1. In addition, a football game between the Harrisburg All-Collegiates and the Williamsport All-Collegiates was planned for December 26. As it was, Killinger was the biggest draw at every event.[36]

The charity games offered a way for the community to honor Killinger— and for the hometown boy to capitalize on his fame. The recent news about his head coaching position at Dickinson College, the major league contract offers, and the Walter Camp All-American selection made Harrisburg relevant in the sports world. The *Harrisburg Evening News* called the first charity basketball game "Killinger Night at Chestnut Street." Headlines and editorials in the local newspapers about Killinger's recent feats, along with the presence of other local college stars, were printed to boost attendance for every holiday event. In addition, another unique draw to the basketball games, at least, was the matchup between the Killinger brothers, Glenn against his elder brother Earl. "Greek against Greek," the *Telegraph* called it.[37]

In the first basketball game, played Christmas Eve, the elder Killinger bested his younger brother when the local independent team stunned onlookers by defeating the college athletes, 26–24.

Two days later, Killinger laced up his spikes to play in the charity week's showcase event. At 2:15 in the afternoon on December 26, the best college football players from Harrisburg, most graduates of Harrisburg Technical High School, and the best college football players emanating from Williamsport High School clashed on the city's Island Park. Advance ticket sales at Shenk and Tittle Sporting Goods Store on Market Street were conducted under placards and newspaper announcements that said, "See Killinger, Harrisburg's All-American."[38] Killinger, wearing jersey number 3, a break from his traditional 2, played quarterback. He was joined by two of his former Penn State teammates: Clarence Beck at left tackle and Dick Rauch at right tackle. His childhood adversary, Carl Beck, Clarence's brother, was also a Harrisburg team member. One former Penn Stater, E. H. Cornwall, who played under a false name because he was still eligible to play intercollegiate football and was in the process of transferring to Colgate University, appeared on the Williamsport team.[39]

A large crowd of 5,000 people paying $1 per ticket packed into the lower field on Island Park to witness the Harrisburg All-Collegiates hand Williamsport's college men a 66–0 shellacking. Killinger rushed for over 100 yards and scored two touchdowns on runs of 25 yards and six yards. The other star of the game was Carl Beck, the former West Virginia halfback who had transferred to University of Vermont, who scored three touchdowns and displayed "mustang running," as one local newspaper reported.[40]

That same night, Killinger was back on the hardwood at Chestnut Street gymnasium for game two of the collegiate men series against the independent locals. Killinger and his teammates got their act together in the second game as they pulled off a decisive 35–18 victory, setting up game three on New Year's Day.

In the final contest Killinger scored six points, an unspectacular output that seemingly impressed everybody, in his team's 37–36, exhilarating victory to close out the week's charity sporting events.[41]

• • •

Because this was Glenn Killinger, there would be no rest before he headed off to training camp with the Yankees.

He returned to Penn State on January 3, 1922, to balance final exams with the freshman basketball season. His debut as a college coach was nearly flawless. After he reduced the roster down from 75 candidates who showed up on the first day of tryouts to nine regulars, Killinger's squad rolled through an eight-game schedule unbeaten.

The first two victories came on January 14 and January 20, a 33–16 win over Altoona High School and a 26–21 score over Bellefonte Academy. The *Harrisburg Telegraph* suggested, "Coach Killinger's first-year quintet looks like the best yearling combination to represent Penn State in years."[42] Then a break in the basketball schedule arrived as the semester came to an end.

During the following week, Killinger's degree work concluded with the submission of his undergraduate thesis on metallurgy, which was titled "Investigation of the Durability of a Solid Carburizing Material."[43] After finally completing his course work in the School of Mines, Killinger received his diploma from the Pennsylvania State College in a small ceremony held inside the Armory on Tuesday, January 31. Since he was delayed in his college work because of his enlistment in the Student Army Training Corps in 1918, he received a special military certificate from the college in addition to his diploma.[44] The ceremony was unusually attended to capacity by the student body that arrived merely to give Killinger a "rousing sendoff," reported the *New York Times*.[45] An unpredictable four and a half years of one accomplishment after another due to skill, auspicious timing, uncommon resiliency, and pure luck found Killinger with an impressive vitae that included membership in the social service campus society called Parmi Nous, the underclassmen athletic society called The Friars, and induction into the Lion's Paw, an exclusive senior service fraternity devoted to the moral and ethical upkeep of the college.

That night after the ceremony, Killinger's brothers in the Alpha

Killinger on the eve of his graduation from Penn State (Jessica Killinger).

Chi Sigma fraternity held a banquet tendered in his honor. A nine-time letterman at Penn State and already a two-sport professional, Killinger was given a silver loving cup in appreciation for the dignity that he brought to both Penn State and Alpha Chi Sigma.[46]

One day after his commencement, Killinger found himself back at freshman basketball practice. He was committed to seeing the team through to the end of the season. His yearlings played impeccably well, winning six more games while defeating the freshman teams from Pittsburgh twice, West Virginia twice, Kiski Area High School, and Bellefonte Academy for a second time. "Glenn Killinger's opening assignment as a college coach resulted most successfully this winter," expounded the *Harrisburg Telegraph*.[47]

On February 24, Killinger packed his bags and bid adieu to Penn State. He had one final brunch with his coach and mentor, Hugo Bezdek, before boarding a train to Harrisburg, where the Dickinson Club of Harrisburg was hosting a dinner in his honor at the Plaza Hotel. A group of students surrounded the Pullman to see him off and to wish him success at the Yankees' spring training camp.[48] While he was as optimistic about his future as ever before, the sendoff was an indication that he had left an indelible mark on the institution.

Epilogue
Post Game

In the summer of 1988, W. Glenn Killinger, then 89 years old, was often visited by his son, Bill, and two grandchildren, Mark and Jessica, at the Delaware retirement home where he was living with his wife, Wilda, after 65 years of marriage. The couple had moved into the Churchman Village Retirement Community in Newark in 1984 to be close to their grandkids.

Their life together in retirement was calming. There were no more scouting trips or long hours spent apart due to various coaching duties. Killinger could concentrate solely on his family. He had been good about it too. Occasionally friends and former players visited the Killingers. At times, he would be pulled away from his wife and taken on trips back to Penn State to watch practice or a game. Once, before the 1979 Sugar Bowl, Killinger was invited by coach Joe Paterno to watch a practice as the Nittany Lions prepared for the national championship game against the University of Alabama and its legendary coach Paul "Bear" Bryant, who was also an old friend. After practice, Killinger, 28 years Paterno's senior, said, "You're working these kids too hard." The reaction by the throng of people standing around Killinger and Paterno was comical. Did Glenn Killinger, the institution as a coach who was trained in the military style of Hugo Bezdek and had become a Hall of Famer in his own right as a coach, just tell Joe Paterno he was working his players too hard? One week later, Penn State played sluggishly and lost in heartbreaking fashion, 14–7. Maybe the old man was right.[1]

More than 60 years after Walter Camp selected Killinger as the best player in college football, he conceded those memories to the past. His focus was on family.

Starting in 1980, Killinger began suffering from progressive vision loss in both eyes. The frightening experience was caused by age-related macular degeneration. "It very slowly got worse," said his son, Bill. "My mother was blind [with macular] for 50 years, but you would have never known it."[2]

While taking a break from baseball practice at West Chester State Teachers' College, Killinger poses with his grandson, Mark, in the early spring, 1955 (Jessica Killinger).

Killinger, on the other hand, grew sick at a much faster pace and was taken to Christiana Hospital for treatment in July 1988. At his request, he soon returned to Churchman Village after responding poorly to treatment. Glenn Killinger died in his retirement home bed on July 25, 1988.

The Killinger family, although prepared for the loss, was devastated. Before his death, Killinger told his son that he did not want a funeral. "That's one thing my father told me," noted Bill. "He said, 'Whatever you do, when I pass away, don't have a service for me. I don't want anyone to know.' So we didn't do anything."[3]

"We could have had a parade in town with fire engines," stated Dick Yoder, one of Killinger's former quarterbacks who eventually became the Mayor of West Chester. "Killy was a great man. Can you imagine the number of people that would have come to his funeral?"[4]

There would in fact have been hundreds of people at Glenn Killinger's funeral. But true to his character, attention was not what he wanted. He had made his points; he had taught his lessons.

Yet, at the moment of death, for all of his admiring fans and loved ones, he was a young man standing in the batter's box at the New York Yankees' spring training, waiting for the first pitch; waiting still for a long and flourishing career in athletics, both as a resilient player and as a transformative coach.

• • •

On the morning of February 27, 1922, Glenn Killinger and Hinkey Haines met in Baltimore to catch a train that would take them the remainder of the way to the Yankees' training camp in New Orleans.[5] Once camp got underway, the "Penn State Twins," as everyone in the Yankees organization called them, had very different starts. Haines immediately impressed. Killinger, conversely, was disparaged from the start. Phil Schenck, the Yankees groundkeeper, failed to recognize Killinger when he arrived at the ballpark. "No, siree. You can't kid me that way," Schenck said to Yanks catcher Fred "Bootnose" Hofmann, who pointed out Killinger among the crowd of gathering ballplayers. "I saw Killinger play at the Polo Grounds, when he threw a whole Golden Tornado for a loss, and that little fellow ain't the same bird."[6]

"Yes, it is," replied Hofmann.

Schenck inquired, "Then who cut him in half?"

Killinger was slow to shake off nerves as he was tried out at second base, third base, and shortstop. He additionally showed poorly at the bat. "Glenn Killinger, college star of football fame, is failing to show a great amount of stickwork at the plate," several newspapers reported.[7]

When asked after his first day of spring training, Killinger responded to the sportswriters with a mea culpa about preferring football over baseball: "I like to play baseball and will try my best to succeed in this business, but I must admit that I can't get as much thrill out of baseball as football." He preferred studying football plays and the physical contact of the game. He admitted, "I guess I would rather play football than do most anything else." He was speaking the truth, but it came off flippantly. He dug a deeper hole: "If I find out after a year or so that I am not a big leaguer I will get into some other business."[8]

Killinger seemingly came into his own during the team's first intra-squad scrimmage on March 10. Before the game, manager Miller Huggins named Killinger and Haines rival captains of the two teams. Killinger selected Babe Ruth, "my favorite player," he conceded, with the first pick. Even with the Bambino on his team, it was Killinger who impressed everyone that day as he rose out of his slump by pasting a home run ten feet over the left field fence. "It was a rookie who made the longest drive of the day and the best clout of the season to date," reported the *Scranton Republican*.[9] Surprisingly,

The "Penn State Twins," Glenn Killinger (left) and Henry "Hinkey" Haines at the New York Yankees' spring training camp, March 1922 (Jessica Killinger).

that hit was not the highlight for the rookie that day. Killinger would later describe his experience. From his third base position, Killinger started a fast double play from third to second to first. Babe Ruth, who was at first base, yelled "loud enough to be heard almost to New York City," described Killinger, "'Hug [short for Miller Huggins] that kid is the best third baseman in camp.'"[10]

The *New York Times* responded to the performance by reporting, "Killinger appears to be getting over his anxiousness, and to-day showed a great improvement."[11]

The early performance was good enough to get Killinger into the starting lineup in three spring training games against New Orleans. In his first game, on March 11, Killinger had one hit in one official at-bat. On March 21, he went 0-for-1 with three put outs.[12] In the third contest, played on March 23, he again went 0-for-1 and failed to make a play in the field.

Killinger made it to the March 24 cut before getting optioned to the Yankees' farm team in Jersey City. Management told Killinger it would be to his advantage to play in the minor league, where he could gain more playing experience, rather than sit in the Yankees' dugout all season.[13]

The Jersey City Skeeters finished the 1922 season with 81 wins and 81 losses, and in fourth place of the International League. Killinger was a consistent player at second base most of the season, but saw some time at shortstop and center field. He finished the summer batting .275 with five home runs before he left Jersey City early to assume his football coaching duties at Dickinson College.[14]

• • •

Glenn Killinger's 31-year college football head coaching career began at Doubling Gap near Carlisle, Pennsylvania, on September 6, 1922. He instructed all 25 players on his roster at Dickinson College, plus his friend and new assistant coach Clarence Beck, to report for eight days of training camp in the mountains of Central Pennsylvania before the official opening of the college season. In addition to regular drill work, Killinger forced his team to go on long hikes and undergo "considerable mountain climbing," described in the *Harrisburg Telegraph*. After his signature preseason camp, Killinger arranged for the Gators of the University of Florida to practice against his team as the latter journeyed north to play Harvard.[15] The experiences helped him breeze into the season with confidence, even telling friends that "he hopes to bring as much fame to this conservative old English town as Pop Warner did with the famous Carlisle Indians."[16]

Dickinson started the season on fire by winning its first four games, including a 27-7 victory over Swarthmore College that the *Philadelphia Daily News* called "the weekend's greatest football upset." The game was played on Island Park in Killinger's hometown of Harrisburg. His ability to lead Dickinson out of the cellar to a 4-0 start won him considerable media attention. The *Harrisburg Evening News* editorialized, "with his football instinct and developed grid brain, aided by his knowledge gained while starring at Penn State, has shown that when it comes to strategy or a little use of the old gray matter, he is a Marshal Foch himself."[17] The praise by the local daily compared Killinger to the World War I field general Ferdinand Foch. It was evidence that in the postwar era the country was seeking fresh heroes from within the sports world. The association to the French military commander credited with taking down the Germans at the First and Second Battles of the Marne was a boon to Killinger's coaching acumen. Unfortunately, Dickinson lost the next game to Gettysburg College, 23-6. As the game was locked in a fourth quarter stalemate, 0–0, Killinger's team became demoralized when Gettysburg executed the "hidden ball" trick play for a touchdown. Dickinson collapsed thereafter, allowing Gettysburg to run away with the victory.

Rumor had it that Killinger was to received a purse of $1,000 from the college's athletic committee if Dickinson defeated its greatest rival.[18] Instead, Dickinsonians ailing from the loss chose to blow the whistle on an apparent violation of Dickinson College policy. Killinger had been moonlighting as a professional football player on Sundays for the Baltimore Pros, an independent team with games scheduled against professional clubs from Ohio, Delaware, Maryland, and Pennsylvania. Included on the schedule were the Oorang Indians, a team that featured Killinger's childhood hero, Jim Thorpe, as player-coach. Killinger was an exceptional halfback and safety for Baltimore. In a game against the Wilmington Chesbrooks, he scored four touchdowns and kicked two extra points in his team's 39–0 victory. His name began headlining newspaper columns to help market the profession. This infuriated the Dickinson College contingent, including the president, James Henry Morgan, and many in the community, who considered Killinger's decision to play football on Sundays a debauchery. On October 16, 1922, an alumnus, F. Y. Jaggers, wrote to college President Morgan, "It was with no little chagrin that I read in the *Balt. Sun* of last Monday that Glen [sic] Killinger Dickinson's coach leads Semi Pros to victory on the gridiron on Sunday afternoon. Perhaps it is not possible to control a coach's actions on the Sabbath but I do think the good old name of Dickinson should not be dragged in the mire."[19]

Morgan responded, "I agree with you entirely … and have made arrangements whereby the thing to which you objected will no longer exist."[20] When reproached by Morgan, Killinger chose to ignore the president's directive. He was back on the field against the Washington Pros on Sunday, October 22, a game in which he made the headlines again after he intercepted a pass and returned it 55 yards for a touchdown in his team's losing effort, a 7–6 defeat.

The entire ordeal with Dickinson College frustrated Killinger. At football practice a few days after the loss to Gettysburg, he told the players in the locker room that he would resign his coaching duties at the conclusion of the season.[21]

Dickinson finished the season with six wins and two defeats. It was the college's best football season in the postwar era. Rumors started swirling about where Killinger would end up coaching. Reports ranged from Columbia University to Wesleyan College, and the University of Oregon to the University of Alabama.[22] Dickinson's president was happy to see Killinger go, and he made no reservations about voicing his distaste for the young coach. When asked by Fred Hixson, the president of Allegheny College, who was considering making Killinger an offer to be their next football coach, for a recommendation, Morgan said, "he is altogether disloyal to the college administration, considers us back members because we will not throw everything into the athletic grist.... He is not profane, I think, but is so overbearing and brutal in his attitude toward his men that I am informed on good authority that his men are practically in revolt, certainly they are not playing for him."[23]

By the end of the fall, the ultimate triumph of his Carlisle experience was meeting his future wife. Wilda Evelyn Holtzworth of Gettysburg was a radiant, headstrong young woman who graduated from Drexel Institute in 1921 with a degree in Dietetics and who loved sports. Wilda had a bubbly personality; her college friends, who called her "Bill," said she possessed "the spirit of deepest loyalty."[24] The two met at Carlisle Hospital, where Wilda had worked as a dietitian since June 1922. Killinger was there visiting one of his injured players and instantly fell for her.

Their fling quickly developed into an engagement. Killinger and Wilda were married on August 25, 1923, in the presence of family and a few invited guests at St. James' Lutheran Church in Gettysburg.[25] The two honeymooned in Atlantic City. For Killinger, who spent his life committed to sports, Wilda's unconditional love produced only a slight change in his sports-is-life behavior.

Killinger's passion for Wilda was deep, but he was also, in a way, still

Killinger with his wife, Wilda, on their wedding day, August 25, 1923. From left to right: Earl Killinger, Glenn, Wilda, and Ira Stone (Jessica Killinger).

self-absorbed in his coaching obligations and professional pursuits. The newlyweds left Carlisle for a home at 504 Pugh Street in State College. Killinger's former coach, Hugo Bezdek, had offered him coaching jobs in basketball, baseball, and, if his reappearance with the Yankees failed to work out, football.[26] Between winter 1923 and spring 1926, Killinger spent two seasons as the head coach of Penn State's freshman basketball team (1924–1925), three seasons as the head coach of the varsity baseball team (1924–1926), and two years assisting Bezdek on the football team (1923–1924).

He spent his summers during that period playing on various minor league ball clubs. In 1923, the New York Yankees sent Killinger to play for Atlanta of the Southern Association, where he appeared in 105 games as the Crackers' second baseman. He batted .268 with 95 hits and five home runs.[27] At the conclusion of the season, he requested that the Yankees place him on the voluntarily retirement list so he could devote his time to coaching at Penn State, where his duties were expanding. In 1924, Killinger worked as Bezdek's assistant Athletic Director and was named backfield and specialist positions coach and scouting director for the football team.

The coaching timetable at Penn State enabled Killinger to play minor league baseball in the New York–Pennsylvania League (NYPEN) during his summers. On July 2, 1924, the midpoint of the season, he signed a player-coach contract with the Harrisburg Senators. Before season's end, he set a NYPEN record for scoring 13 runs in ten games.[28] When he left the Senators on September 12 to report to football camp at Penn State, Killinger ranked third in the NYPEN with a batting average of .347.[29]

The following summer, Killinger signed to play second base for the Williamsport Grays, where he batted .315. The Grays lost to York in a best of five series for the NYPEN pennant.[30]

In May 1926, Killinger found himself unemployed after the Penn State Athletic Committee informed him that his contract as assistant athletic director was not going to be renewed. He and Wilda returned to Harrisburg and moved into a home at 17 North Nineteenth Street. Later that same month, Killinger was offered a player-manager contract with the Shamokin Indians of the NYPEN. He accepted the contract and appeared in 76 games at second base, batted .290, and had a fielding percentage of .952 for the Indians before suffering a compound fracture of his right wrist. In the eighth inning of the second game of a doubleheader between Shamokin and Elmira played on July 24, Killinger attacked umpire Hanson Horsey by punching him three times after he ran onto the field to dispute a call at home plate.[31] Killinger was suspended by the league commissioner for the remainder of the season.

In September 1926, Killinger, with his good friend Hinkey Haines, obtained a contract to play football for the New York Giants, which was entering its second season in the National Football League. (The NFL in 1926 featured 22 teams. It was the largest number of teams in the league until exceeded in 1970.) He shined "brilliantly," reported the *Mount Carmel Daily News*, in the season-opening 19–0 victory over the Hartford Blues. "Killinger was one of the stars of the game, making numerous long runs, sharp line plunges and on one occasion carried the ball over the line for a six-pointer." The newspaper added, "He is counted upon to scintillate for the Giants thruout [sic] the season, thus resuming his place in the football sun."[32] His durability in the professional ranks was regretfully exposed shortly after that initial game. Although it seemed as if Killinger was due for a breakout season with the Giants, his time in the NFL was short-lived. Before the next game against the Providence Steam Rollers—a game the Giants won 7–6—the Giants' front office announced that he had re-fractured his right wrist in the Hartford game.[33] Two weeks later, the Giants released Killinger from his contract, citing that "because of a distressing fracture to his arm that he received in baseball last season and which prevented him from playing his usual game."[34]

In the first week of November, Killinger received a fortuitous offer from the Philadelphia Quakers, the team he once played a game for in 1921. The Quakers were one of nine teams competing in the NFL's rival association: the American Football League.[35] In his first game with the Quakers on November 6, he intercepted a pass, completed several forward passes, and caught a 55-yard touchdown pass. His team defeated Rock Island (Illinois), 24–0. His former Penn State teammate, Charlie Way, joined him in the Quakers backfield and scored two touchdowns.[36] Then Killinger fractured his right arm for a third time one week later in Philadelphia's 3–0 loss to the Chicago Bears (formerly the Chicago Staleys). It was his final appearance in a football uniform.[37] Unfortunately for Killinger, the Quakers went on to win the American Football League football championship by defeating Red Grange's New York Football Yankees, 13–6.[38] He could only read about it from his home in Harrisburg. (The AFL dissolved with the conclusion of the 1926 season.)

The failed venture in professional football put Killinger in a state of depression. With the book closed on his playing career, he returned to his hometown to manage the family hardware store while playing in a handball league at the Harrisburg Y.M.C.A. He additionally played in a basketball showcase against Jim Thorpe's World-Famous traveling LaRue Indians at the Chestnut Street Auditorium. Neither Thorpe or Killinger scored in the game, but the *Harrisburg Evening News* reported, "Killinger played an excellent game on the defense" in spite of his team's 41–33 setback to Thorpe's "all-star Indian basketball team."[39]

His luck change near the end of the winter when he accepted two contracts. On February 12, Killinger, then 28 years old, was announced as the new football coach at Rensselaer Polytechnic Institute in Troy, New York.

That summer before leaving for Troy, he played second base for the Harrisburg Senators. His return to the Senators garnered attention from the management of the St. Louis Browns, who considered offering Killinger a second chance at the majors. Killinger led the New York–Pennsylvania League in fielding with a .962 fielding percentage in 133 games. He recorded 333 putouts, 438 assists, 30 errors, and 31 double plays.[40] Unfortunately, the contract offer never came. Killinger received some pleasure in helping the Senators win the 1927 New York–Pennsylvania League pennant.

On September 9, the Killingers arrived at their new home in Troy, where Glenn was to begin a five-year career as head coach at Rensselaer (RPI). He arrived as a hero, still touted as the All-American who in 131 career varsity games played in three sports at Penn State, lost but 17 contests. Surprisingly, his record as boss of the Engineers was anything but brilliant. His five teams (1927–1931) at RPI attained a cumulative 14–24–3 record. The poor record is misleading; his total wins and losses can easily be accepted as the reason for his eventual departure. As a matter of fact, the lack of production on the football field had little to do with his dismissal from RPI in 1931. When the time came to either retain or release their football coach, the president of the institute chose to terminate all part-time contracts due to Depression-era budget cuts. Killinger accordingly lost his job. His split with the technical school was much more of an amiable experience than his departure from Dickinson College almost ten years earlier. Harry Van Velsor, RPI's athletic director, called Killinger "likeable" and "a credit to the coaching profession."[41]

At any rate, Killinger's life in Troy was erratic. He could never offer any explanation for why he refused to invest more of his attention into the lives of the boys on campus. He spent only the falls there during his tenure. He would returned to Harrisburg each winter, where he played professional basketball for the Harrisburg Velveteers during the winter of 1927–1928. He signed on as the Harrisburg Senators' player-manager in the spring of 1928. As manager of the Senators later that summer, he arranged a game against Babe Ruth, Lou Gehrig and the New York Yankees on Island Park. Ruth went 3-for-5, including a home run and two stolen bases, but the Senators were able to tie the Yankees, 6–6. Killinger went 2-for-4, stole two bases, and scored a run. The Senators repeated as champions of the New York–Pennsylvania League later that summer.

In 1929, Killinger returned to the Williamsport Grays as player-manager. By season's end, he batted .318 as the Grays finished in second place for the NYPEN pennant. He remained with the Grays for two more years. In 1930, Killinger helped Williamsport set the NYPEN record for double plays, tallying 182—Killinger took part in 134 of them. He also batted .344 with 181 hits, nine home runs, 33 doubles, 111 runs, 64 RBI, 20 stolen bases, and a slugging percentage of .526. In 1931, he batted .272 with six home runs.

His final year in minor league baseball was 1932, when he signed on to play for and manage the Allentown Buffaloes of the Eastern League, which had a higher classification in the minor leagues than the New York–Pennsylvania League. However, the Eastern League disbanded in mid-July. Not surprisingly, Killinger was recruited back to Williamsport as player-manager. He finished the season batting .196, with just 35 hits in the 55 games he played for the Grays. Upon his retirement from the minor leagues, Killinger's lifetime batting average was .292.[42]

• • •

The highlight for Killinger during that period was the birth of his namesake. On December 11, 1927, Glenn and Wilda gave birth to their only child, a boy that they named William Glenn Killinger, Jr., whom they called "Billy." The birth announcement in the *Harrisburg Telegraph* pronounced, "New Ball Player! Killinger Will Hand Out Cigars."[43] The headline and accompanying article completely ignored Wilda's role in the birth of the child, thus reflecting the patriarchal nature of American sporting culture of the '20s.

Ever cognizant of the kind of benevolent father he had, Killinger assumed a larger role than the family's prize breadwinner. He unconditionally loved his son. With a military bent, he sternly parented. Yet one thing was certain: he was an embracing and loving father who spent every available moment with Billy. When it came to parenting norms, he appeared to be ahead of his era. In *American Fatherhood* (2016), Lawrence A. Samuel provides an illustration of the evolving role of the American father during the 20th century. Citing psychologist Joseph Peck, Samuel writes of 19th and early 20th century fathers as "godlike figures" whose job it was to serve as the "moral compass of the family" by modeling spirituality and the importance of obtaining a quality education. When Billy reached his adolescent years, Killinger became his son's "model of masculinity." Fatherhood changed during and after World War II, Samuel argues, when "men held onto their moral and financial responsibilities but took on the greater purpose of serving as models of masculinity," including gender roles characterized by a "more traditional and conservative cultural climate." It became atypical in the 1940s and 1950s for fathers to embrace female characteristics resembling that of loving nurturer or domestic caretaker while parenting. This was reason enough, Samuel claims, "for men to impart a maximum amount of masculinity to family life."[44]

It was within this cultural climate that Killinger molded his son into a sports-crazed scion of the Killinger clan. They were together on the golf course and on scouting trips, and even during his many years coaching, he gave Billy full access to visit practice, stand on the sideline or sit in the dugout. "The coach rarely makes a trip without Billy," reported the *West Chester Daily*

Local News in 1936, "He has traveled all over the East, South and Middle West. Some of the trips are with the teams; others?—Oh, just the Killingers taking a jaunt to see some sporting event, and maybe do a little scouting." Billy spent so much time with his father in the sports environment that he was labeled by the *Daily Local News* as a "Sports Library" at age eight. "Billy's a very important member of the Killinger board of strategy. His Dad's the skipper; Billy's the clipper. He clips all the papers and keeps a rather complete reference department."[45]

While Killinger was once a mediocre academic in his own right, Billy was generally a run-of-the-mill student as well. Nevertheless, the patriarch insisted on extraordinary marks from his son. Once, as a ninth-grader at West Chester Junior High School, Billy brought home a C in English. "My father is sneaky," the Killinger scion recalled. "I said, Cs aren't bad, it's passing." Unhappy with the boy, "he went to my basketball coach and had me suspended from the team.... He said, '[when] You get Bs you can play basketball. No Cs!'"[46] Billy's weak academic record was not the product of carelessness. Rather, it may have been nurtured. Killinger once wrote to Lt. Richard Nye, one of his former West Chester football players, in 1945 that while Billy was excelling at basketball and baseball at The Hill School in Pottstown, Pennsylvania, he was "doing as well as a Killinger can do academically."[47] The two undistinguished students eventually grew to enjoy reading Louis L'Amour's Western novels.

Killinger always had a tight bond with Billy, who was as busy an athlete as his father had been at similar ages. (Billy would go on to become an All-American third baseman at Lafayette College and play two years for several St. Louis Cardinals minor league teams, two years for Chicago White Sox's farm teams, and one year with the Detroit Tigers' farm teams). There was always a hint of rivalry between father and son, but Killinger did not waive his resume in his son's face. Billy was not made to live in a shrine of his father's accomplishments. The newspapers did a fine enough job reminding him who his father was. "Every time I did something that was good," Billy explained in 2015, "the paper would say, 'the son of Glenn did this.' It drove me crazy." The father-son rivalry did not discourage the loving support from Billy, who admitted to seeing 609 football and baseball games that his father either played or coached in.[48]

Billy would meet his wife, Karol Marie, while playing ball for the Omaha Cardinals in 1952. They married on November 25, 1953. The newlyweds gave Glenn and Wilda their first grandchild, Mark William, on September 28, 1954. Almost three years later, on March 30, 1957, a second grandchild, Jessica, came along. The two grandchildren were the only people on earth who could pull Killinger's attention away from sports.

• • •

Killinger with his son, Billy, in 1936 (Jessica Killinger).

There was a scary moment in 1931 when Killinger was forced by school officials to resign his post as the head football coach at Rensselaer in order to give the position to a full-time member of the Physical Education Department. The moment of his departure marked the end of the second year of the Great Depression, and RPI, like many other colleges and universities, were cutting budgets. Rensselaer wanted to fill all coaching positions with their full-time employees.

Killinger was exhausted after years of overtaxing himself for coaching and professional playing jobs. In July 1932, he enrolled in the Teachers' College of Columbia University to attain a Master's degree in Physical Education.[49] The program lasted one year, and in April 1933, Columbia's College Placement Office notified Killinger that there was a physical education opening at

Moravian College in Bethlehem, Pennsylvania. Killinger had already turned down coaching jobs at Albright College and an offer to return to Dickinson College. The position at Moravian was offering longevity: the job was to make him the Director of Health and Physical Education, in addition to the head football and basketball coaching positions.

Killinger completed the necessary 34 credits needed to graduate from Columbia with a master's degree, which was conferred on June 6, 1933. He started at Moravian in September. The *West Chester Daily Local News* named his football team, which finished the season 8–1, "one of the best small college teams in the country."[50] In addition to the exceedingly successful football season, Killinger created an impressive college curriculum. Wesley P. Cushman, a staff member at Moravian, said, "[Killinger's] greatest contribution was ... the development of a sound program with required courses in health and physical education and an intramural sports program."[51]

Killinger's year at Moravian had won him attention from other colleges in Pennsylvania. In March 1934, he would make a decision that decades later etched his name within the pantheon of great college coaches. He was approached by Howard A. Wescott, the head football coach at West Chester State Teachers' College in Chester County, to see if he would be interested in replacing him as boss of the football team.[52] The contract also included jobs as director of the Health and Physical Education Department, head basketball coach, and head baseball coach. Killinger accepted the offer.

For those who have heard of W. Glenn Killinger, it is likely that they know more about his tenure as the football and baseball coach at West Chester than his feats as an athlete at Penn State. (His tenure at West Chester is worthy of a book of its own). In 23 seasons as the football coach of West Chester, his teams attained 147 wins, 41 losses, and 12 ties. Killinger's teams won five Pennsylvania State Athletic Conference championships, one mythical sportswriters' conference title, and played in four bowl games—the Burley Bowl and Cigar Bowl in 1947, the Burley Bowl again in 1948, and the Pretzel Bowl in 1952. He was always a rock as coach. But he let his guard down at halftime of West Chester's final game in 1958 when, against Baldwin-Wallace, the No. 1-ranked small college team in the country, he let his players see tears well up in his eyes and said, "You are the greatest team I have ever coached."[53] After West Chester's 69–12 trouncing of Baldwin-Wallace, his players carried him off the field. That 1958 team finished second for the Lambert Cup, beaten out by the University of Buffalo for the small college East Coast Championship. Even though many in the sports world felt West Chester was robbed of a national title, Killinger got to experience one final Harold Lamb moment as his players carried him off the field as their hero and into the locker room.

He led West Chester one more season and ended his coaching career as the head coach of the Small College All-Stars against the Big College

All-Stars in the January 2, 1960, All-American Bowl in Tucson, Arizona. When he retired from coaching football at age 62 after the 1959 season, he proudly said, "I wish to thank everybody at West Chester who has made the job of Head Coach of Football a very pleasant experience. No football coach has ever received more wonderful cooperation."[54] There were rumors that he was leaving to manage the Philadelphia Phillies' minor league team in Johnson City, Tennessee, but he remained at West Chester to coach baseball and concentrate on his administrative job as Dean of Men for 11 more years.[55]

Killinger's baseball teams at West Chester were always among the best small college ball clubs in the country. In 32 years as manager of the Rams, just five of his teams finished with losing records—four of which came before World War II. He claimed two Pennsylvania State Athletic Conference titles, 335 wins, 161 defeats, and six ties on the West Chester baseball diamond before his retirement in 1970.[56]

Early in his career at West Chester, Killinger was named Dean of Men. He remained in the position until his retirement. His duties included the responsibility to approve adequate off-campus housing for male residents, supervision over the use of automobiles on campus, and, most importantly, command over the behavior of the male students. His policies were strict, and Killinger carried a short leash. Dick Yoder, one of his former football players, recalled, "We weren't allowed to keep our cars on campus. If he'd catch ya, he'd throw you out." The students tried to find a parking garage in town, but he knew what was going on. "He'd go around checking. It was almost every night. He rode around in his car—uptown, down the streets, and he'd see a car with a certain license plate, he'd have a flashlight and he'd check."[57]

Glenn Killinger was made Dean of Men at West Chester State Teachers' College in Chester County, Pennsylvania. He served in that role between 1936 and 1970 (Jessica Killinger).

In 1936, Glenn, Wilda

and Bill moved into Wayne Residential Hall, where an apartment was constructed for the family. "What I remember most about Wayne Hall," recalled Bill, who was still very young when they moved into the dormitory, "was my dad going into his office to write his book." In 1938, Killinger wrote *Football*, an instructional book for football novices and experts alike published by The Ronald Press Company that was released as part of William L. Hughes's sports series called "The Book of Major Sports." The students, though, remember life under the same roof as Killinger much differently. Bob Warner, a baseball player for Killinger, amusingly recalled, "Once I was coming up the steps, I had just taken a shower. I was pulling my shirt on, buttoning it up. He was standing at the top of the steps. He grabbed me and put me up against the wall and put his nose in my eye. And told me, didn't I realize that his wife lived here and that he never wanted to see me unless I was completely dressed."[58] While Warner and his friends often got away with the typical antics, there was always one eye looking out for the deterring old man. One such occasion occurred in 1957, when three anonymous students tied a hawser rope to the chassis of his black 1955 Roadmaster Buick parked in back of Wayne Hall, next to the fence surrounding the campus' tennis courts. After trying to pull out of his parking spot, he let a sortie of profanities fly once he realized why his tires were spinning and the fence had nearly collapsed on top of his car.[59]

Killinger's tenure at West Chester was split in half by World War II. On December 11, 1941, three days after America's declaration of war on Japan, Killinger assumed the role of Chief Air Raid Warden and fire protection officer on campus. On March 19, 1942, he obtained a leave of absence from West Chester after he accepted a commission as a lieutenant in the United States Naval Reserves. At 10:00 a.m. on March 23, he reported for active duty at the United States Naval Academy in Annapolis, Maryland, where he underwent a 30-day indoctrination V-5 Instructors Course. He was taught how to administer and organize various athletic programs for the different branches of the United States Navy.[60] On April 18, he was told to report to the Naval Aviation Selection Board in Philadelphia, where he was given orders to recruit cadets into the Navy's V-5 pilot program. One of the recruiting stops was a visit to Penn State on April 29.

While Killinger underwent training in the early months of 1942, the Navy Department worked to create a program designed to prepare Naval cadets to become fighter pilots with competence enough to maneuver modern war machines. Captain Arthur W. Radford, head of Naval Aviation Training for the Navy's Bureau of Aeronautics, a position created after Pearl Harbor, suggested after thorough observations that pilots who were not in good physical condition could not stand the pace that the Navy set in its flight training. Captain Radford accordingly set out to conceive a rigorous athletic program, one inspired by World War I S.A.T.C. training, but built to condition fliers to handle modern equipment and survive the pressure of fighting against a modern enemy. We are trying "to develop in the embryo pilots that all important spirit—the will to win," Radford told reporters at a 1942 press conference, "Pre-Flight training started with the purpose of making Uncle Sam's Navy fliers the roughest, toughest and smartest in the world."[61] Several colleges and universities throughout the country were vetted before being selected to host these V-5 Pre-Flight training programs. Four schools, one for each region of the country, were initially chosen: the University of Iowa, St. Mary's College in California, the University of Georgia, and the University of North Carolina in Chapel Hill.

Lieutenant Commander Thomas Hamilton, a former football player and coach at the Naval Academy, was given charge of creating an extensive physical fitness program for the rookie pilots. Hamilton aspired to toughen up the program's cadets, most of whom, he knew, were going to arrive with privileged backgrounds. "Our pilots to be inducted into the Naval Service in general come from a soft, luxurious, loose-thinking, lazy, peacetime life," Hamilton claimed. He believed that intense competitive training would foster a realistic view of combat, plus give America's pilots an edge over the already seasoned German and Japanese fighters.

Much like the Student Army Training Corps program during the final three months of World War I, the physical training endured by the cadets at the Pre-Flight Schools was designed to incorporate competitive sports into the daily routine of all cadets.[62] Each cadet participated in athletic training that increased their strength and physical fitness, as well as competitive sports that drove their will to win. The sports used in training included swimming, boxing, wrestling, basketball, football, soccer, gym and tumbling, and track. If a sport was not viewed as useful to the physical conditioning or mental development of a cadet, it was not used. In Hamilton's own words, competitive sports at Pre-Flight Schools aspired "to give the Navy the best pilots possible; put learning in his head, muscles on his bones, steel in his soul, and fire in his heart."[63]

Sportswriters considered football the most useful sport to train pre-flight cadets. In a 1943 poll of Eastern journalists conducted by the Public Relations Office of the North Carolina Pre-Flight School, football was unanimously voted as the top sport for physical training. All of the sports listed, which, in addition to football, included track and field, baseball, and basketball, were considered useful because they nurtured "physical endurance, agility, coordination, poise, confidence, and fighting spirit."[64] Grantland Rice, still one of the foremost sportswriters in the country, buoyed the football claim in 1943: "football ... is probably the best game to develop quick thinking under pressure."[65] Football prepared cadets not only for increased physical fitness and fighting spirit, but also for when a pilot needed to make a quick decision in combat.

The importance of football as training by the Pre-Flight Schools was not lost on the Navy men themselves either. On a visit with Pre-Flight cadets at Chapel Hill, heavyweight boxing champion Lieutenant Jack Dempsey eagerly gave his view on sports as a method of training. "Competitive athletics make men though, instills a fighting spirit, builds morale we need in our fighting forces," the Golden Age's boxing champion said, "Give 'em football, boxing, and other body contact sports to make 'em rough."[66]

Yet not every cadet at the Pre-Flight Schools grew up playing competitive sports. Most had little or no sports background. This meant that most of the cadets who arrived at Pre-Flight Schools lacked the traits of courage, toughness and decisiveness that characteristically are fostered by athletic competition. The U.S. Department of Navy believed that sports at its Pre-Flight Schools were to develop that dogged spirit.

Glenn Killinger's metallurgical engineering degree made him valuable to the Navy's war preparedness effort. On May 28, 1942, he was assigned to the North Carolina Pre-Flight School at Chapel Hill with duties to work as the Athletic Construction Officer responsible for overseeing the erection of new wartime barracks, dining halls, playing fields, and a bowling alley.[67] In addition, he was given the job as head baseball coach of the Pre-Flight School's baseball team: the Cloudbusters. He was an obvious choice for those positions, having become one of the successful dual-sport coaches in the college ranks and carrying with him a degree in engineering. His annual allowance was $2,640.[68] Killinger and his family accordingly moved into a house at 411 McCauley Street in Chapel Hill.

The Pre-Flight School must have been analogous to Killinger's experience as an undersized S.A.T.C. private and athlete at Penn State during the First World War. During that era, 24 years earlier under the tutelage of Hugo Bezdek, Killinger was prepared for war while playing sports that called for physical toughness in addition to great stamina and mental power. Football especially, with its savagery and rigid rules that compelled players to remain on the field as they played through injuries, helped to enrich his win-at-all-cost attitude.

To be eligible to coach a sport at the Pre-Flight School, faculty members had to possess a record of athletic participation and coaching, be between the ages of 21 and 50, exemplify "clean living," and possess a "rugged manhood."[69] America's best coaches arrived in Chapel Hill, including Oliver Owen Kessing, football coach at the Naval Academy; James Crowley, one of Notre Dame's "four horsemen" and head football coach at Fordham; Harvey Harmon, head football coach at Rutgers; and Don George, the former World Wrestling Champion.

Among the cadets at Chapel Hill that Killinger worked with were several major league baseball all-stars, including Ted Williams, Johnny Pesky, Johnny Sain, and Joe Coleman. Future Presidents of the United States George Herbert Walker Bush and Gerald Ford were stationed at Chapel Hill for short periods. And in 1944, the pre-flight cadets were visited by World War I "ace" Eddie Rickenbacker, who had recently survived 24 days on a life raft when his plane was forced down in the Pacific Ocean.[70]

To Killinger, sports on the home front during World War II were more than inconsequential games. In 1942, he used the baseball diamond at Chapel Hill to train the brightest young men in the country to make sacrifices for their country. Killinger's team ended up winning 14 of 19 games.[71]

Many months after the baseball season ended, he was reassigned to active duty with the Atlantic Fleet on December 28. He was stationed at Quonset Point Naval Air Station in Rhode Island, where he was to supervise the physical training of all aircraft pilots onboard the carrier *U.S.S. Essex*.[72]

Lieutenant Glenn Killinger at the North Carolina Pre-Flight School in 1944, before his promotion to Lieutenant Commander (Jessica Killinger).

The commission on the *Essex* was brief—eight months total—as Killinger found himself back at the North Carolina Pre-Flight School within a year's time. An announcement was made in July 1943 that Killinger was to be reattached to Chapel Hill and assigned to work as an assistant football coach under former Baylor boss Frank Kimbrough.[73]

The Cloudbuster football team ended the 1943 season with a substandard record of 2-4-1. The team was recognized not for its success on the field, but for its spirit. In an article titled "Serving Its Purpose," the school's weekly newspaper *The Cloudbuster* reminded the cadets, "spirit on the battlefield and football field go hand in hand."[74] It is regrettable to say that the 1943 football season was the Pre-Flight School's worst. They won against North Carolina State and Camp Davis (NC), but lost to wartime powerhouses Duke University, Georgia Pre-Flight, Wake Forest, and the Naval Academy. They tied with Camp Lejeune.

In February 1944, the *Cloudbuster* announced that Killinger was promoted to the position of head football coach, and he retained his position as manager of the Pre-Flight baseball team.[75] Coach Killinger led his baseball club to a 10–2 record and the Ration League pennant that spring.

As for the gridiron that fall, it was a very difficult task for anyone to manage a complicated sport like football, especially when players came and went as cadet reassignments were issued out frequently. On top of that, it was extremely difficult to squeeze two-hour football practices into days filled with military drills and aviation courses while sharing facilities with civilian students on campus. No one had a clue how good Killinger's gridiron Cloudbusters were going to be in 1944. Not even the school's newspaper could report a few days before the start of the season on the team's prospects. The weekly wrote, "Little is known [of] the quality, and no information will be available before the latter part of August."[76] Suddenly, quality players and coaches arrived in droves. A month before the season began, Killinger obtained a top-rate second-in-command when former Vanderbilt assistant coach Paul "Bear" Bryant arrived at the Pre-Flight School after 15 months spent on sea duty in the Atlantic. Then, just days before camp, ex-professional Ray Bray of the Chicago Bears, All-American halfback and basketball guard from Northwestern Otto Graham, and the East's leading touchdown maker from Holy Cross, Stan Koslowski, were transferred to Chapel Hill.[77]

Killinger developed something special that fall. He switched from the single-wing offense to the t-formation at Chapel Hill. He moved Graham to quarterback in the new system and had Koslowski at fullback. With "Bear" Bryant coaching the line, the team was called "the finest to wear Cloudbuster colors."[78] That was a bold prediction since several of the nation's best football teams were on the schedule. So how good did Killinger's team become? That season, the Cloudbusters ranked as high as #2 in the Coaches' Poll. He took his ragtag group of players into Durham and defeated Duke, 13–6.[79] He led his team into Annapolis and upset the highest-ranked team in the country, the Naval Academy, 21–14. The Cloudbusters remained undefeated until November 5, when they lost 49–20 to unbeaten Bainbridge Navy, a team riding a 21-game winning streak and loaded with ex-professional stars and youth sensation Charlie "Choo Choo" Justice.[80] The Cloudbusters lost one more game before the season ended, resulting in a 6–2–1 overall record. Killinger's unit rated among the top third in the country.

Killinger (second from the left) was manager of the North Carolina Naval Pre-Flight Cloudbusters baseball team in 1942 and 1944 (Jessica Killinger).

For his leadership and assiduous work for the Navy Department, Killinger had been promoted to the rank of Lieutenant Commander earlier that spring.[81]

On February 9, 1945, Killinger was detached to work as athletic director and Military Training Officer at the Naval Air Station in Deland, Florida. His replacement as football coach was "Bear" Bryant, who never got to coach a game as the boss at the North Carolina Pre-Flight School. Germany surrendered in May. The Japanese submission followed a few months later. The school was decommissioned just weeks after the Japanese surrender.[82]

After the war, Killinger and Bryant both applied for the University of Maryland's vacant head coaching position. Bryant, who received the endorsement of Washington Redskins owner George Preston Marshall, won the job. Killinger was gracious in defeat and subsequently returned to West Chester on October 3, 1945.[83] The two gregarious coaches remained friends throughout Bryant's legendary career at the University of Alabama, at times notifying one another about potential recruits for their respective teams. When Bryant

THE UNITED STATES NAVY PRE-FLIGHT SCHOOL
CHAPEL HILL, NORTH CAROLINA

"CLOUDBUSTER" FOOTBALL AWARD

FOR THE SEASON OF 1944

This is to Certify that **Lt. Comdr. W.G. Killinger - Head Coach** was a member of the Cloudbuster Football Team for the 1944 season. The team met and defeated NAVY, DUKE, CHERRY POINT MARINES, GEORGIA PRE-FLIGHT, N.A.S. JACKSONVILLE, and achieved an outstanding rating among all College and Service Teams of the nation.

This award is made by the Cloudbuster Athletic Association in recognition of his participation in the varsity football program and of his personal exemplification of the high spirit of athletic competition and fair play in NAVAL AVIATION TRAINING.

The certificate given Killinger at the end of the 1944 college football season. Killinger's signature is accompanied by Paul "Bear" Bryant, Glenn Presnell, and John Roning (Jessica Killinger).

wrote his memoir in 1974, *Bear: The Hard Life and Good Times of Alabama's Coach Bryant*, Killinger was among the people credited for helping the Hall of Famer become a national title-winning coach.

• • •

In reality, Killinger's return to West Chester after World War II was just the beginning of his Hall of Fame coaching career. He could have chosen a different life, but he loved the town of West Chester, and he appreciated how the people on campus treated him and his family.

He was greeted with delight by the West Chester faculty upon his return in September 1945. At this time, the students were new and had heard little about Killinger before his arrival. In addition to his coaching duties, Killinger assumed jobs as faculty director of the Veteran's Emergency Housing Units and the Veterans Club. As the coach of two sports, he held a distinct bond with many of his students and athletes who had served in either World War II or the Korean War during the remainder of the '40s and '50s.

Coach Killinger in 1949 showing the stiff-arm technique to West Chester backs Joe Carlozo and Joe DaLonzo (Jessica Killinger).

In 1951, on the 30th anniversary of his Walter Camp All-American year, Gettysburg College gave him an honorary doctor of science degree in Physical Education.[84] "My dad was always so proud of that honor," said Bill Killinger. The prefix stuck, as many of his football and baseball players at West Chester thereafter called him "Doctor Killinger" instead of "Coach Killinger."

Although frightened most of the time by his presence, the students at West Chester were always enamored with him. The 1958 college yearbook, *The Serpentine*, was dedicated to him. It read: "In every age capable leaders are needed to guide and to inspire youth. West Chester is fortunate to have as a member of its professional staff Dr. W. Glenn Killinger.... He represents that great combination of strength in mind and in body which opens doors to education and to success." Ten years later, the W. Glenn Killinger Men's Residence Hall was dedicated in his honor. As of 2018, Killinger Hall is the oldest building remaining on West Chester's campus.

The tributes continued to come. In October 1963, Killinger was inducted alongside Chuck Bednarik into the Pennsylvania Sports Hall of Fame's first class.[85]

In January 1970, the American Association of College Baseball Coaches inducted Killinger into the Coaches' Hall of Fame. He was honored at a banquet in Washington, D.C., with a plaque that had been placed in the Coaches' Baseball Hall of Fame when it was once located at Western Michigan University in Kalamazoo.[86]

Then, on February 21, 1971, after finishing as a finalist many times before, and 50 years after his record-breaking senior year at State College, Killinger finally made it into the College Football Hall of Fame for his accomplishments as the quarterback at Penn State. The banquet's keynote speaker was California Governor Ronald Reagan.[87]

In 1979, several alumni established the Killinger Hall of Fame at West Chester University and the W. Glenn Killinger Football Scholarship Foundation. The fact that the foundation exists carries a surfeit of irony. In his day, Killinger was always opposed to scholarships. He paid for his own education at Penn State. Scholarships didn't exist at West Chester when he paced the sideline. Everything that he accomplished as a player and coach was done through his own unremitting determination.

Killinger with his wife, Wilda, at the Killinger Foundation Football Hall of Fame and Scholarship Foundation dinner in 1979 (Jessica Killinger).

"I believe that not many persons have lived a happier or more exciting life," Killinger said to his son, Bill, a few months before passing away on July 25, 1988.[88] Word of his death spread quickly throughout the country after he died, as an incalculable number of Killinger-Men lived coast to coast. The honors already bestowed were all that Killinger could bear. He asked his son to have his body cremated and the ashes buried in Evergreen Cemetery in Gettysburg, Pennsylvania.

His wife Wilda lived until March 31, 2001. She died at the age of 99, just 16 days shy of her 100th birthday. Her ashes are buried next to Glenn's at Evergreen.

In contrast to the somberness of his grave, the effect does not feel that lonely. There is a sensation of that Glenn-Killinger-self-assurance that permeates his burial site and makes one think of his resilience to overcome uncontrollable circumstances. Even though he is long dead, his presence is so strong that one feels as if he will reach out beyond the grave to scold us for not being willing to put forth every ounce of our potential to a certain task. At one of the annual gatherings of former Killinger-Men—a group of football and baseball players who once played for Killinger and now meet twice a year to talk about the good-old-days at West Chester—John Ford, a left-handed pitcher in 1959, warned, "This book better be good, because if it's not, the old man will jump out of his grave and let you know about it."[89]

Chapter Notes

Preface

1. Michael Oriard, *Reading Football: How the Popular Press Created an American Spectacle* (Chapel Hill: University of North Carolina Press, 1993), 30–36; Julie Des Jardins, *Walter Camp: Football and the Modern Man*. (New York: Oxford University Press, 2015), 2–4.
2. Theodore Roosevelt to Walter Camp, March 11, 1895; Scott A. McQuilkin, and Ronald A. Smith. "The Rise and Fall of the Flying Wedge: Football's Most Controversial Play," *Journal of Sports History*, Vol. 20, No. 1 (Spring 1993), 59.
3. Ridge Riley, *The Road to Number One: A Personal Chronicle of Penn State Football* (Garden City, NY: Doubleday, 1977), 180.
4. Steven W. Pope. *Patriotic Games: Sporting Traditions in the American Imagination, 1876–1926* (New York: Oxford University Press, 1997), 149.
5. "Penn State Squad Shattered by War," *New York Tribune*, September 23, 1917, 20.
6. Michael Bohn, *Heroes and Ballyhoo: How the Golden Age of the 1920s Transformed American Sports* (Lincoln, NE: Potomac Books, 2009), 1–12.
7. Gladys L. Knight. *Pop Culture Places: An Encyclopedia of Places in American Popular Culture*, 3 vols. (Santa Barbara, CA: ABC-CLIO, 2014), 700.
8. Benjamin G. Rader, *American Sports: From the Age of Folk Games to the Age of Televised Sports*. New York: Prentice Hall, 1999), 183.
9. Bohn, *Heroes and Ballyhoo*, 13.
10. *Penn State Alumni News* 8, no. 2, October, 1921, 20; "Penn State Crowd Will Miss Supper to Read Foot Ball," December 3, 1921, Intercollegiate Athletics, Hugo Bezdek Scrapbooks, 1920–21, M/04.29, Box 1," PSULSC; Edwin Sparks, *President's Report to the Board of Trustees*, January 22, 1919, Board of Trustees Supporting Papers, Group 6, AR 04.04, Box 17, PSULSC; "Tune in Your Radio and Get State College News," *Penn State Alumni News* 9, no. 3, November 1922, 10; Kathleen M. O'Toole, *Intercollegiate Football and Educational Radio: Three Case Studies of the Commercialization of Sports Broadcasting in the 1920s and 1930s* (Dissertation, The Pennsylvania State University, August 2010), 200–203.
11. *Evening News*, August 1, 1924; John Heisman, "Heisman's Hundred in the Hall of Football Fame," *Marion Star*, October 27, 1928, 1.
12. "Great Quarterback Crop Developed in 1921 Grid Season," *Arizona Republican*, December 3, 1921, 10; *Philadelphia Evening Public Ledger*, November 14, 1921; Grantland Rice, "Big Guns of the Gridiron: Men and Teams Whose Work Has Featured the Football Season Just Closed," *Leslie's Weekly* 133, 1921, 797–798, 826.
13. James Mennell, "The Service Football Program of World War I: Its Impact on the Popularity of the Game," *Journal of Sport History* 16, no. 3 (Winter 1989), 248–260; David M. Kennedy, *Over Here: The First World War and American Society*. (New York: Oxford University Press, 1980), 109.

Chapter 1

1. William Glenn Killinger Jr., Personal interview with the author, Glen Mills, PA. January 17, 2015.
2. Ibid.
3. John J. Furlow, Telephone interview with the author, Selbyville, DE, May 18, 2015.
4. Robert "Gump" May, Personal interview with the author, Hershey, PA, January 3, 2015.
5. William Glenn Killinger Jr., Personal interview with the author, Glen Mills, PA, April 4, 2015.

6. Rick Barras, "Advice Shaped Grid Star's Life," Newspaper and date unknown, found in John Furlow, *West Chester Football: An Ongoing Tradition in Ram Pride*. (Kennett Square, PA: KNA Press, 1983), 8–9.
7. Richard B. "Dick" Yoder, Personal interview with the author, Gap, PA, March 22, 2015.
8. Lulu Frances Black, *Annals of Harrisburg, Comprising Memoirs, Incidents, and Statistics from the Period of Its First Settlement*. (New York: Evangelical Publishing, 1906), 428–432.
9. Luther Reily Kelker, *History of Dauphin County, Pennsylvania, Volume 3*. (Philadelphia: Lewis Publishing, 1907), 170–171.
10. City of Harrisburg. *Harrisburg, PA, Business Directory and Map of the City*. (Albany, NY: Joseph Rippey, 1887), 35–37.
11. Luther Reily Kelker. *History of Dauphin County, Pennsylvania, Volume 3* (Chicago, IL: Lewis Publishing Co., 1907), 171.
12. "Father of City's NY-P League Team Manager is Dead," *Harrisburg Telegraph*, October 20, 1928, 1, 15.
13. Charles W. Henry Jr., *William Glenn Killinger: Athlete and Coach: A thesis in Physical Education* (The Pennsylvania State University, Department of Physical Education, September 1966), 7–8; Year: *1900*; Census Place: *Harrisburg Ward 9, Dauphin, Pennsylvania*; Roll: *1403*; Page: *15A*; Enumeration District: *0078*; FHL microfilm: *1241403*
14. Henry, *William Glenn Killinger*, 8.
15. W. Glenn Killinger, *A Penn State Walk-On* (Unpublished memoir, Wilmington, DE, 1986), 2.
16. Maris Harvey Taylor (1876–1982) had became a nationally known member of the Republican Party by the 1930s. He is celebrated in Harrisburg as superintendent of parks and public property, one of his first positions held as a public figure. He was one of the frontrunners of the beautification movement in Harrisburg. He helped in the creation of the Sunken Gardens within Riverfront Park. Taylor was a leading figure in the development of Wildwood Park, including the operation of its zoo between 1929 and 1950. He died less than a month from his 106th birthday.
17. "Little Fir Trees Whisper Secret: Miss Elizabeth Killinger is to Marry Earl Lyter Kunkle," *Harrisburg Telegraph*, June 11, 1918, 6; "Home with Parents," *Harrisburg Telegraph*, November 7, 1918, 6; "Track Athletes Practice Daily," *Harrisburg Telegraph*, April 14, 1917, 14; "Former State Track Star to Coach Central High," *Harrisburg Telegraph*, March 3, 1917, 11; "Central Faculty Elects New Coach," *Harrisburg Telegraph*, March 3, 1917, 11–14; *Harrisburg* Telegraph, June 11, 1918, 6.
18. The Pennsylvania State University, *La Vie* (State College: Penn State University Press, 1916), 318.
19. Henry, *William Glenn Killinger*, 7; "Widow Inherits Killinger Estate," *Harrisburg Telegraph*, October 25, 1928, 1.
20. Henry, *William Glenn Killinger*, 8.
21. Henry, *William Glenn Killinger*, 8–10.
22. Oscar Handlin, *The Uprooted: The Epic Story of the Great Migrations that Made the American People* (Boston: Little, Brown & Co., 1951), 223.
23. William Glenn Killinger, Jr., Personal interview with the author, Glen Mills, Pennsylvania, January 10, 2015.
24. Killinger, *A Penn State Walk-On*, 2.
25. Henry, *William Glenn Killinger*, 9–10.
26. Harrisburg School Board of Directors. *Annual Report of the Public Schools of Harrisburg, PA, With Manual For the Year Ending the First Monday in June, 1906* (Harrisburg, PA: The Telegraph Printing Co., 1907), 250–256.
27. Harrisburg Technical School. *The Tech Tatler*, Harrisburg, PA, 1916; *Harrisburg Telegraph*, September 17, 1918, 10; "Fixed Rules for System Contest," *Harrisburg Telegraph*, December 10, 1915, 18.

Chapter 2

1. Ronald A. Smith, *Sports and Freedom: The Rise of Big-Time College Athletics*. New York: Oxford University Press, 1988. ix–xi, 23–24.
2. Killinger, *A Penn State Walk-On*, 1–2.
3. Benjamin G. Rader, "The Quest for Subcommunities and the Rise of American Sport," *American Quarterly* 29, no. 4 (Autumn, 1977): 357; Oscar Handlin. *The Uprooted: The Epic Story of the Great Migrations that Made the American People* (Boston and Toronto: Atlantic Monthly Press Book, Little, Brown & Co., 1951, 1973), 224.
4. *Ibid.*, 361; Richard Sorrel, "Sports and Franco-Americans in Woonsocket, 1870–1930," *Rhode Island History* 31 (Fall 1972), 112.
5. "M'Creath Again Tennis Champ," *Harrisburg Daily Independent*, August 11, 1913, 9; "Local Tennis Stars Hold Championships," *Harrisburg Telegraph*, August 11, 1913, 9.
6. Smith, *Sports and Freedom* 83–86.
7. Des Jardins, *Walter Camp*, 2–4; Julie Des Jardins, "Man-making, Not Man-breaking: How We Expect Boys to Prove Their Manhood on the Football Field," *Salon Media Group, Inc.*, November 8, 2015. Visited on January 7, 2016. https://www.salon.com/2015/11/08/man_making_not_man_breaking_how_we_expect_boys_to_prove_their_manhood_on_the_football_field/.

8. Grantland Rice, *The Tumult and the Shouting: "My Life in Sport"* (New York: A. S. Barnes, 1954), 219.
9. Rader, *American Sports*, 89.
10. Smith, *Sports and Freedom*, 84.
11. Rader, *American Sports*, 90.
12. *Ibid.*, 91.
13. John S. Watterson, "The Gridiron Crisis of 1905: Was It Really a Crisis?" *Journal of Sports History*, Vol. 27, No. 2 (Summer 2000), 292.; John S. Watterson, "The Football Crisis of 1909–1910: The Response of the Eastern 'Big Three,'" *Journal of Sports History*, Vol. 8, No. 1 (Spring 1981), 35; Watterson, John S. *College Football: History, Spectacle, Controversy* (Baltimore: Johns Hopkins University Press, 2000), 69, 411.
14. "Earl D. Wilson Partly Paralyzed from Injury in Football Game," *New York Tribune*, October 18, 1909, 3.
15. "The Football Deaths," *Burlington Free Press*, November 8, 1909, 3; "Strikes His Head and Dies," *Democrat and Chronicle*, November 2, 1909, 19.
16. Watterson, "The Gridiron Crisis of 1905: Was It Really a Crisis?" 295; "Virginia Halfback, Archer Christian, Fatally Injured," *Washington Sunday Star*, November 14, 1909, 1; "Football Perils Arouse the Public," *Washington Herald*, November 17, 1909, 1, 8.
17. Watterson, "The Gridiron Crisis of 1905: Was It Really a Crisis?" 294; "Fifteen Deaths Gridiron Toll," *Harrisburg Telegraph*, December 1, 1915, 12.
18. Watterson, "The Gridiron Crisis of 1905: Was It Really a Crisis?" 297.
19. *Ibid.*, 295; John S. Watterson, "The Football Crisis of 1909–1910: The Response of the Eastern 'Big Three,'" *Journal of Sports History* 8, no. 1 (Spring 1981), 37–38; "College Authorities Express Their Views" and "Strikes His Head and Dies," *Salt Lake City Deseret Evening News*, November 1, 1909, 20.
20. "The Twelfth Player in Every Football Game," Library of Congress, Illustration from the New York World; John McCutcheon, *Chicago Tribune* (Chicago, IL), "The Educational Influence of College Football," October 21, 1905; Watterson, "The Gridiron Crisis of 1905: Was It Really a Crisis?" 296; "Flying and Diving Tackles and Onside Kicks Dangerous," *Rochester Democrat and Chronicle*, November 2, 1909, 19; Scott A. McQuilkin, and Ronald A. Smith, "The Rise and Fall of the Flying Wedge, 57–64.
21. Rader, *American Sports*. 184–185; George Ashworth, *A History of the Development of the Rules of American Collegiate Football*. (Unpublished Manuscript: Indiana State Teachers College, Pennsylvania, 1948), 20–27, 36.

22. John M. Heisman, and Mark Schlabach, *Heisman: The Man Behind the Trophy* (New York: Simon & Schuster, 2012), 34.
23. Chris Willis, *Old Leather: An Oral History of Early Pro Football in Ohio, 1920–1935* (Lanham, MD: Scarecrow Press, Inc. 2005), xii.
24. W. Glenn Killinger, *Football* (New York: A. S. Barnes, 1938), 10–11.
25. George Ashworth. *A History of the Development of the Rules of American Collegiate Football* (Unpublished Manuscript, Indiana State Teachers College, Indiana, PA, 1948), 20–27, 36–43.
26. *Ibid.*, 22–23.
27. Willis, *Old Leather*, xiii.
28. S. W. Pope, *Patriotic Games: Sporting Traditions in the American Imagination: 1876–1926* (New York: Oxford University Press, 1997), 60.
29. *Harrisburg Patriot-News*, January 11, 1917.
30. *Harrisburg Telegraph*, February 11, 1916, 20; "Tech Plays Academy Today," *Harrisburg Telegraph*, April 27, 1916, 10; "Tech to Meet Academy in Second Championship Game," *Harrisburg Telegraph*, May 2, 1916, 10.
31. Geoffrey C. Ward, *Unforgivable Blackness: The Rise and Fall of Jack Johnson* (New York: Knopf Doubleday, 2010), 18.
32. Rader, *American Sports*, 152–54.
33. *Ibid.*, 89.
34. *Ibid.*, 40–41.
35. *Ibid.*, 42.
36. Killinger, *A Penn State Walk-On*, 12.
37. Rader, *American Sports*, 35.
38. "Grant First Permit for Boxing Show at Orpheum," *Harrisburg Telegraph*, February 18, 1916, 16.
39. "Boxing Tonight," *Harrisburg Telegraph*, February 25, 1916, 22; "Boxing, Chestnut Street Auditorium," *Harrisburg Telegraph*, February 24, 1917, 20; "Boxing Season Gets Late Start," *Harrisburg Telegraph*, January 11, 1917, 15.
40. "Winter Sports Continue to Show Strenuous Times in Harrisburg," *Harrisburg Telegraph*, January 11, 1917, 15.

Chapter 3

1. Killinger, *A Penn State Walk-On*, 2.
2. *Harrisburg Patriot*, November 22, 1912.
3. "Local star athlete honored by foremost gridiron critic," *Harrisburg Evening News*, December 20, 1921, 11.
4. Killinger, *A Penn State Walk-On*, 2; "Indian Victory Over Villanova," *Harrisburg Daily Independent*, October 3, 1912, 10.
5. "Thorpe is Army's Nemesis," *Richmond Times Dispatch*, November 10, 1912, 7; "Thorpe

of Carlisle, Leads Field in All Lines of Sports," *El Paso Herald*, November 21, 1912, 28; "Jim Thorpe the Ideal White Hope," *Grand Forks Evening Times*, November 30, 1912.

6. Shorty Miller (1890–1966) was a 5' 5" quarterback who attended Harrisburg Tech, class of 1909, and The Pennsylvania State College, class of 1913. He was a four-year letterman who quarterbacked Penn State to 8–0 records in both 1911 and 1912. He was selected by Walter Camp as a third-team All American in 1912. He also earned three varsity letters as an outfielder and captain on Penn State's baseball team. He played professional football with the Massillon Tigers. In 1974, he was inducted into the National Football Foundation College Football Hall of Fame; Killinger, *A Penn State Walk-On*, unmarked page.

7. "Tech Jrs. Win Championship," *Harrisburg Patriot*, November 28, 1913, 11.

8. "Glenn Killinger Was Successful Athlete Despite Big Handicap," *Harrisburg Telegraph*, January 12, 1922, 17.

9. In January 1922, the *Harrisburg Telegraph* ran an editorial praising Glenn Killinger for his accomplishments despite the difficult road in sports. The article's anonymous author said that he interviewed a good friend of Killinger's who traveled almost every year with Ira Stone to Penn State games. "Glenn Killinger Was Successful Athlete Despite Big Handicap," *Harrisburg Telegraph*, January 12, 1922, 17.

10. *Ibid*.

11. "Football Teams Work Hard; Tech Squad Out Yesterday," *Harrisburg Telegraph*, September 15, 1914, 8.

12. *Harrisburg Star Independent*, October 07, 1914, 9; *Harrisburg Telegraph*, October 07, 1914, 8; *Harrisburg Star Independent*, October 14, 1914, 5; *Harrisburg Star Independent*, October 17, 1914, 12; *Harrisburg Star Independent*, October 22, 1914, 8; *Harrisburg Star Independent*, October 12, 1914, 9.

13. *Harrisburg Star Independent*, October 12, 1914. 9.

14. *Harrisburg Star Independent*, October 20, 1914, 8; *Harrisburg Telegraph*, October 27, 1914, 9; *Harrisburg Star Independent*, November 9, 1914, 5; *Harrisburg Star Independent*, November 23, 1914, 5; *Harrisburg Star Independent*, November 27, 1914.

15. In 1895, the foul shot as we know it today—a free shot 15 feet from the basket— was implemented into the basketball rulebook by James Naismith. Until 1924, a coach would designate one player to shoot the team's free shots. Coaches understandably selected the team's most consistent shooter, someone who specialized in making free-throws. *Harrisburg Star Independent*, March 20, 1915, 9; *Harrisburg Star Independent*, February 27, 1915, 12; *Harrisburg Star Independent*, January 16, 1915, 12; *Harrisburg Star Independent*, March 25, 1915, 8.

16. *Harrisburg Telegraph*, February 8, 1915, 9.

17. "Comparison in Ages and Weights of Players on Central and Tech Teams," *Harrisburg Telegraph*, November 24, 1915, 12.

18. *Harrisburg Telegraph*, May 22, 1915, 5.

19. "Coach for Tech High May be Lehigh Star," *Harrisburg Telegraph*, September 10, 1915, 12.

20. "Comparison in Ages and Weights of Players on Central and Tech Teams," *Harrisburg Telegraph*, November 24, 1915, 12.

21. Harrisburg Technical High School, *Tech Tatler* (Yearbook, 1916); "Tech Wins Game with Substitutes," *Harrisburg Telegraph*, November 22, 1915, 12; "Tech Loses out at Lancaster," *Harrisburg Telegraph*, November 15, 1915, 11; "Steelton High Slams Tech Team," *Harrisburg Telegraph*, November 8, 1915, 11; "Three Winners is Today's Dope, *Harrisburg Telegraph*, October 30, 1915, 15; "Greensburg Students to Travel in Auto Truck," *Harrisburg Telegraph*, October 28, 1915, 13.

22. "Tech Loses Out at Lancaster," *Harrisburg Telegraph*, November 15, 1915, 11.

23. Smith, *Sports and Freedom*, 79–83.

24. *Ibid*., 81; *Chicago Tribune*, November 29, 1894, 13.

25. "Pick Central to Win Classic Game," *Harrisburg Telegraph*, November 23, 1915, 12.

26. "Pick Central to Win Classic Game," *Harrisburg Telegraph*, November 23, 1915, 1, 12; "Central High Humbles Tech with Record Score," *Harrisburg Telegraph*, November 26, 1915, 19.

27. Historian Benjamin G. Rader writes about annual "Big Game" rivalries in his book *American Sports: From the Age of Folk Games to the Age of Televised Sports*. See Chapter 6. He writes mostly about college rivalries that entailed winning or losing a traditional trophy: Stanford and California play for the Axe, Minnesota and Michigan play for the Little Brown Jug, and Purdue and Indiana compete fro the Old Oaken Bucket.

28. "Gifts for Tech Football Stars," *Harrisburg Telegraph*, December 23, 1915, 11.

29. Riley, *The Road to Number One*, 180.

30. "Sauerkraut Renamed Into Patriotic Dish," *Harrisburg Telegraph*, April 9, 1918, 2; "Ohio Citizens Compel Germans to Kiss the Flag," *Harrisburg Telegraph*, April 2, 1918, 2; "High School Pupils Are Dropping German Tongue," *Harrisburg Telegraph*, April 11, 1918, 1.

31. William Glenn Killinger, Jr., Personal interview with the author, Glen Mills, PA, January 17, 2015.

32. "Many Interesting Facts About the

World's Greatest Motion Picture, Coming to the Orpheum," *Harrisburg Telegraph*, February 10, 1916, 14.

33. Robert Bennett Bean's brain study was immediately rebuked by his former teacher and mentor, Dr. Franklin P. Mall of Johns Hopkins University, who found no difference in the weight, size or brain power of white and black brains. Mall also criticized Bean for not using a blind sample of brains in his study. Dick Lehr, *The Birth of a Nation: How a Legendary Filmmaker and A Crusading Editor Reignited America's Civil War* (New York: Public Affairs, 2014), 128–129.

34. *New York American*, February 28, 1915, 9, in Slide, *Griffith Interviews*, 20; Lehr, *The Birth of a Nation*, 133.

35. *Ibid.*, 291.

36. "The Ku Klux Klan Menace A Blow at Law and Order," *Harrisburg Courier*, September 18, 1921, 8.

37. "'Movie' Color Line in Superior Court," *Harrisburg Telegraph*, March 10, 1915, 1.

38. "Tech High Loses Game; York Shows Great Form," *Harrisburg Telegraph*, December 11, 1915, 14; "Records by Tech Tossers Best in Local School History," *Harrisburg Telegraph*, January 31, 1916, 11.

39. See John Christgau's *The Origins of the Jump Shot: Eight Men Who Shook the World of Basketball* (Lincoln: University of Nebraska Press, 1999) for clarification on the origins of the jump shot; "Tech is Winner over Lancaster," *Harrisburg Telegraph*, January 8, 1916, 6; *Harrisburg Telegraph*, March 19, 1918, 11.

40. "Tech Tossers to Play Lewistown," *Harrisburg Telegraph*, March 30, 1916, 10; "Steelton High Tossers Win in Final Game with Tech; Locals Still in Cellar," *Harrisburg Telegraph*, April 1, 1916, 12; "Interscholastic Season Ends with this Week's Schedule," *Harrisburg Telegraph*, March 27, 1916, 11.

41. *Harrisburg Telegraph*. February 11, 1916, 20; Henry, *William Glenn Killinger*, 21.

42. Henry, *William Glenn Killinger*, 14.

43. "Tech Plays Academy To-Day," *Harrisburg Telegraph*, April 27, 1916, 10; "Tech to Meet Academy in Second Championship Game," *Harrisburg Telegraph*, May 2, 1916, 10.

44. "Dr. Fager Names Tech Honor Men," *Harrisburg Telegraph*, June 1, 1916, 1–2.

45. "Accepts New Position," *Harrisburg Telegraph*, September 20, 1918, 8.

46. Killinger, *A Penn State Walk-On*, 2–3; Henry, *William Glenn Killinger*, 14.

47. "Rosewood Team Lands Hill Flag," *Harrisburg Telegraph*, August 25, 1916, 11.

48. "Amateurs Play All-Star Team," *Harrisburg Telegraph*, September 14, 1916, 10.

49. Henry, *William Glenn Killinger*, 14–15; *Harrisburg Patriot*, June 2, 1916, July 25, 1916, August 25, 1916, September 14, 1916.

50. "Rosewood After Games," *Harrisburg Telegraph*, November 17, 1916, 19; *Harrisburg Telegraph*, December 30, 1916, 8.

51. *Harrisburg Patriot*, March 23, 1917; *Harrisburg Telegraph*, February 29, 1916, 9.

52. "Rosewood Falls to Motive Power," *Harrisburg Telegraph*, April 23, 1917, 10.

53. "Liberty Loan Will Pass Four Million Mark," *Harrisburg Telegraph*, June 11, 1917, 1.

54. "Home Garden Move Well Under Way," *Harrisburg Telegraph*, April 10, 1917, 2.

55. "Hoover to Enlist Women to Save Nation's Food," *Harrisburg Telegraph*, May 28, 1917, 11; "Enroll Women to Save Food," *Harrisburg Telegraph*, June 26, 1917, 4; "Housewives are asked to save supply of food," *Harrisburg Telegraph*, June 27, 1917, 1.; "Not Hamburger Any More, Harrisburgers Instead," *Harrisburg Telegraph*, April 9, 1917, 1.

56. "Wilson's Message is Prepared for Study in Schools," *Wilkes-Barre Evening News*, June 12, 1917, 8; "U.S. Will Publish War Booklets on Country's Position," *Wilkes-Barre Evening News*, June 20, 1917, A3; "U.S Book on War Shows Germany to Be Aggressor," *Pittsburgh Daily Post*, June 25, 1917, 1.; Frederic J. Haskin, "The Four-Minute Men," *Pittsburgh Gazette Times*, September 7, 1917, 4.

57. Alan Axelrod, *Selling the Great War: The Making of American Propaganda* (New York: Palgrave MacMillan, 2009), 114–116.

58. "15,000 to March in Harrisburg's Greatest Parade," *Harrisburg Telegraph*, April 12, 1917, 1–7; "Thousands of Patriots Will Display Loyalty," *Harrisburg Telegraph*, April 21, 1917, 1–2; "Fervid Profession of Patriotism," *Harrisburg Telegraph*, April 23, 1917, 1–12.

59. Henry, *William Glenn Killinger*, 15–16.

Chapter 4

1. Killinger, *A Penn State Walk-On*, 5.

2. *Ibid.*, 5; Henry, *William Glenn Killinger*, 17; "Local Mills Have Enormous Capacity for War Materials," *Harrisburg Telegraph*, August 12, 1915, 1.

3. "Walter Camp Puts Killinger At Half Upon All-American; Three Pennsylvanians on It," *Harrisburg Evening News*, December 20, 1921, 1.

4. "Ties Up Game in Hill League," *Harrisburg Telegraph*, June 23, 1917, 11.

5. "West End A. A. Has Close Call," *Harrisburg Telegraph*, August 27, 1917, 9.

6. Erwin W. Runkle. *The Pennsylvania State College 1853–1932: Interpretation and Record* (University Park: Nittany Valley Society, 2013),

79; "Nittany Lions to Close Big Season in Far West," *Pittsburgh Gazette Times*, November 20, 1921, 27.

7. "Freshmen Enrollment at Penn State Nearly 700," *Pittsburgh Gazette Times*, September 17, 1917, 8; Penn State University Budget Office, "Historical Fall Headcount Enrollment Since 1859," University Park: Penn State University, 2016. Accessed on February 8, 2016, http://www.budget.psu.edu/factbook/student dynamic/HistoricalComparisonOfEnrollment. aspx?YearCode=2015&FBPlusIndc=N.

8. W. Glenn Killinger to Dick Nye, Deland, FL, May 22, 1945; "Walter Camp Puts Killinger At Half Upon All-American; Three Pennsylvanians on It," *Harrisburg Evening News*, December 20, 1921, 1.

9. Student Record Card of W. Glenn Killinger, the Pennsylvania State University, University Park, PA; Henry, *William Glenn Killinger*, 135.

10. Student Record Card of W. Glenn Killinger, the Pennsylvania State University, University Park, PA; Henry, *William Glenn Killinger*, 17–18.

11. Henry, *William Glenn Killinger*, 18.

12. Killinger, *A Penn State Walk-On*, 3.

13. "Dick Harlow Succeeds Hollenback at State," *Harrisburg Star-Independent*, January 21, 1915, 8.

14. "Coach Harlow Building Strong 11 at Penn State," *Portland East Oregonian*, October 27, 1916, 8.

15. "Many Penn State Gridders Have Enlisted for Service," *Pittsburgh Gazette Times*, September 2, 1917, 19; The Pennsylvania State University, *La Vie*, 1919 (University Park, State College, PA, 1919), 324–330. "Penn State Squad Shattered by War," *New York Tribune*, September 23, 1917, 20; "Penn State Gridiron Star Enlists," *Washington Evening Star*, September 18, 1917, 15; "Penn State Eleven Is Rounded Into Shape," *New York Tribune*, September 30, 1917, 2.

16. "Colleges Favor Continuing Football in Spite of War," *Fort Wayne Sentinel*, August 15, 1917, 10; "Easter Colleges Football 'Slackers,'" *Lincoln Star*, August 16, 1917, 8.

17. "Sports to Harden Men for Warfare in Trenches," *Oneonta Star*, May 28, 1917, 3; James Mennell. "The Service Football Program of World War I: Its Impact on the Popularity of the Game," University of Illinois Press, *Journal of Sports History*, Vol. 16, No. 3 (Winter, 1989). 248–260; Pope, *Patriotic Games*, 145–45.

18. *New York Evening World* (New York, NY). "Look After Play Hours of Soldiers and Sailors," August 15, 1917, 8.

19. Grantland Rice, "Pittsburgh, Safely in the Cellar, Breaks Into Songfest to Cover Up the Woes of a Disastrous Season," *Philadelphia Evening Public Ledger*, September 1, 1917, 13.

20. "Inter-Games for Naval Stations," *New York Tribune*, October 23, 1917, 15; "Walter Camp Appoints Men to Boom Sports in Navy," *Brooklyn Daily Eagle*, October 24, 1917, 3.

21. "Famous Names Given to War Camps," *Prescott Weekly Journal-Miner*, August 1, 1917, 4; "Sport Coaches Selected," (Rochester, NY) *Democrat and Chronicle*, September 29, 1917, 21; "At Navy Yard," *Tacoma Times*, November 6, 1917, 6.

22. "Benefit Game Won by Pitt," *Pittsburgh Press*, December 2, 1917, 1; "Benefit Game is Won by Penn State," *Pittsburgh Press*, September 30, 1917, 23; "Football Team for Ambulance Camp," *Allentown Leader*, September 20, 1917, 3; "State Defeats Ambulance Team," *Pittsburgh Sunday Post*, September 20, 1917, 18.

23. Pope, *Patriotic Games*, 147.

24. Knights to Raise Big War Fund," *Poughkeepsie Eagle-News*, July 13, 1917, 6; Sol Metzer, "Amateur Sport Will Come Into Its Own After War Is Over," *Minneapolis Star Tribune*, August 26, 1917, 21.

25. Pope, *Patriotic Games*, 148.

26. "Boxing is a Big Aid to Bayonet Fighting," *Atlanta Constitution*, September 15, 1918, 3.

27. Pope, *Patriotic Games*, 148–50.

28. Walter Camp, "Football Will Be Popular in Service Camp," *Indianapolis Star*, October 13, 1917, 12.

29. *Ibid.*; Walter Camp, "Camp Predicts Much Football This Fall," *Pittsburgh Post Gazette Times*, October 14, 1917, 4.

30. Walter Camp, "Football Will Be Popular in Service Camp," *Indianapolis Star*, October 13, 1917, 12.

31. "Hamilton Boys Win Honor Parade," *Hamilton Evening Journal*, October 13, 1917, 2.

32. Editor of *Outlook* magazine quoted in Pope, *Patriotic Games*, 149.

33. James Mennell. "The Service Football Program of World War I: Its Impact on the Popularity of the Game," University of Illinois Press, *Journal of Sports History*, Vol. 16, No. 3 (Winter, 1989), 248¬–260.

34. "Camp says West Point Is Leader in the East," *Pittsburgh Gazette Times*, October 21, 1917, 5; John S. Watterson, "The Football Crisis of 1909–1910: The Response of the Eastern 'Big Three,'" *Journal of Sports History* 8, no. 1 (Spring 1981), 33–34.

35. David M. Nelson, *The Anatomy of a Game: Football, the Rules, and the Men Who Made the Game* (Wilmington: University of Delaware Press, 1994), 160–171.

36. Pope, *Patriotic Games*, 149.

37. Walter Camp, "Football Will Be Popular

in Service Camp," *Indianapolis Star*, October 13, 1917, 12.
38. Killinger, *A Penn State Walk-On*, 5.
39. Ibid.
40. Ibid.; "Penn State Players Begin Scrimmage Play," *New York Tribune*, September 22, 1917, 15; Pennsylvania State University, *La Vie*, 1918 (University Park, State College, PA, 1918), 371.
41. Killinger, *A Penn State Walk-On*, 5.
42. The Pennsylvania State University, *La Vie*, 1919 (University Park, State College, PA, 1919), 329.
43. Ibid., 358–359; Henry, *William Glenn Killinger*, 19.

Chapter 5

1. Annette D'Agostino Lloyd, *Harold Lloyd: Magic in a Pair of Horn-Rimmed Glasses and Other Turning Points in the Life and Career of a Comedy Legend* (Albany, GA: Bear Manor Media, 2009), 199–203.
2. Donald W. McCaffrey, *Three Classic Silent Screen Comedies Starring Harold Lloyd* (Madison, NJ: Fairleigh Dickinson University Press, 1976), 64.
3. Lloyd, 198–99.
4. Stephen Winer, "The Freshman: Speedy Saves the Day! A Harold Lamb Adventure!" *The Criterion Collection*, March 25, 2014. Accessed on October 7, 2016. https://www.criterion.com/current/posts/3112-the-freshman-speedy-saves-the-day-a-harold-lamb-adventure.
5. Rader, *American Sports*, 93.
6. *The Freshman*, DVD, directed by Fred C. Newmeyer and Sam Taylor (1925; Pathe Exchange, 1925); "Lloyd Makes his Bow as 'The Freshman," *Brooklyn Daily Eagle*, September 20, 1925, 71; "Harold Lloyd and Hazel Keener at Garden Today in Latest Gloom Chaser," *Davenport Democrat and Leader*, September 20, 1925, 20.
7. *The Freshman*, DVD; "Lloyd Makes his Bow as 'The Freshman,'" *Brooklyn Daily Eagle*, September 20, 1925, 71; "Harold Lloyd and Hazel Keener at Garden Today in Latest Gloom Chaser," *Davenport Democrat and Leader*, September 20, 1925, 20.
8. McCaffrey, *Three Classic Silent Screen Comedies Starring Harold Lloyd*, 57–59.
9. Killinger, *A Penn State Walk-On*, 5.
10. Ibid., 6–7.
11. Pennsylvania State University, *La Vie*, 1919 (University Park, State College, PA, 1919), 362; "Freshman Five wins Final Games," *Penn State Collegian*, March 20, 1918, 1.
12. Killinger, *A Penn State Walk-On*, 7.
13. The Pennsylvania State University, *La Vie, 1919* (University Park, State College, PA, 1919), 326–329; "Statistics of Penn State Varsity Football Squad," *Pittsburgh Post Gazette Sun*, October 5, 1919, 1.
14. Henry, *William Glenn Killinger*, 20.
15. "1,513 Penn State Men in Active Military Service," *Pittsburgh Gazette Times*, November 10, 1918; "State College Has 1,435 in Service; Five Killed," *Harrisburg Telegraph*, August 12, 1918, 9.
16. "Penn State Track Season Short One," *Washington Herald*, January 25, 1918, 10; "State's Colleges Hurt by Enlistment of Students," *Harrisburg Telegraph*, January 26, 1918; The Pennsylvania State University, *La Vie, 1920* (University Park, State College, PA, 1920), 276.
17. Henry, *William Glenn Killinger*, 20–21; The Pennsylvania State University, *La Vie, 1920* (University Park, State College, PA, 1920), 276;
18. "Penn State Plays Season in Single Day," *Philadelphia Evening Public Ledger*, April 25, 1918, 14; "State's Season Comes and Goes Victoriously," *Pittsburgh Daily Post*, April 25, 1918, 10.
19. Henry, *William Glenn Killinger*, 17.
20. "Hill League Opens Season," *Harrisburg Telegraph*, May 6, 1918, 9.
21. "Hill Teams in Lively Fray," *Harrisburg Telegraph*, May 8, 1918, 11.
22. "Mayor Keister A Baseball Fan," *Harrisburg Telegraph*, May 13, 1918, 1.
23. "Hill League Averages Up-to-date Showing Batting and Hitting Records," *Harrisburg Telegraph*, July 10, 1918, 9.
24. "'Soldier' Kent Helps Rosewood," *Harrisburg Telegraph*, July 19, 1918, 15; "No Champion Yet in Hill League," *Harrisburg Telegraph*, July 27, 1918, 11.
25. "In Heroic Pitching Bout Between John Jones and Earl Waltz Rosewood Wins the Allison Hill League Flag and City Title," *Harrisburg Telegraph*, August 7, 1918, 11; "Great Crowd at Hill Game," *Harrisburg Telegraph*, August 2, 1918, 15.
26. "In Heroic Pitching Bout Between John Jones and Earl Waltz Rosewood Wins the Allison Hill League Flag and City Title," *Harrisburg Telegraph*, August 7, 1918, 11.
27. "Tributes Paid to 1954 Rams Last Evening," *Pittston Gazette*, December 10, 1954, 1.
28. Killinger, *A Penn State Walk-On*, unmarked page.
29. "College Men Form New Army Division," *Washington Herald*, July 12, 1918, 1; "College Men and the War," *Logan Republican*, August 10, 1918, 1.
30. Benjamin F. Shearer, "An Experiment in Military and Civilian Education: The Students' Army Training Corps at the University of Illinois," *Journal of the Illinois State Historical So-*

ciety (1908–1984), 72, no. 3 (August 1979): 218; United States War Department, *Students' Army Training Corps Regulations, 1918* (Washington, Govt. print. Off., 1918), 5–6.
31. Shearer, 213–215; American Association for the Advancement of Science, "The Students' Army Training Corps," *Science*, New Series 48, no. 1238 (September 20, 1918): 288.
32. *Ibid.*
33. Shearer, 220; Norman MaClaren Trenholme, *Syllabus of The Background and Issues of the World War* (Columbia, MO: Missouri Book Co., 1918), 30–34.
34. Shearer, 223.
35. *Ibid.*, 220; War Department, Committee on Education and Special Training. "Students Army Training Corps Special Regulations," (Date unknown), 1–7; Penn State During World Wars Collection (1109), Penn State University Archives, Special Collections Library. Pennsylvania State University; United States War Department, *Students' Army Training Corps Regulations, 1918* (Washington, Govt. print. off., 1918), 14–15.
36. Pennsylvania State College. *Penn State in the World War*. Alumni Association of the Pennsylvania State College (State College, PA: Alumni Association of The Pennsylvania State College, 1921), 496.
37. "Ask Young Men to Join College Camps," *Logan Republican*, August 13, 1918, 1; "Students' Training Corps Part of National Army," *New York Evening World*, July 25, 1918, 2; "Status of the S.A.T.C. Boys," *Harrisburg Telegraph*, December 21, 1918, 1.
38. Kennedy, *Over Here*, 54–58; Norman MaClaren Trenholme, *Syllabus of The Background and Issues of the World War* (Columbia, MO: The Missouri Book Co., 1918), 33–35.
39. "Ohio Colleges and Students' Army Training Corps," *Democratic Banner* (Mount Vernon, OH), August 27, 1918, 5.
40. "Americans Brave Fire Worse Than Hell in Battle," *Harrisburg Telegraph*, August 22, 1918, 3; "Penn State Sends Many Athletes to 'Big Game,'" *New York Tribune*, January 6, 1918, 4.
41. Pennsylvania State University, *La Vie, 1919* (University Park, PA, 1919), 8–9.
42. Frank Aydelotte. *Final Report of the War Issues Course of the Students' Army Training Corps* (Washington DC: U.S. War Department, Committee on Education and Special Training, May 1919), 7.
43. Shearer, 216; "Army Officer to Train Cadets at Penn State," *Harrisburg Evening News*, September 17, 1917, 3.
44. Pennsylvania State College. *Penn State in the World War* (State College, PA: Alumni Association of the Pennsylvania State College, 1921), 505–515; Pennsylvania State University, *La Vie, 1920* (University Park, PA, 1920), 336–340; "Pennsylvania Men in Colleges," *Harrisburg Telegraph*, December 13, 1918, 12; "Bezdek to be Czar of Sports at Penn State," *Harrisburg Telegraph*, August 30, 1918, 15.
45. Mennell, "The Service Football Program of World War I: Its Impact on the Popularity of the Game," 248–260; Harrisburg "War Conditions Will Not Hinder Football Cards," *Evening News*, July 16, 1918, 7.
46. "Walter Camp Shows Rotarians How to Train," *New York Tribune*, September 27, 1918, 9; "National Move for Physical Regeneration," *Asheboro Courier*, July 18, 1918, 7.
47. Pope, *Patriotic Games*, 147–50.
48. "Athletics at Cornell Suspended During War," *Pittsburgh Post Gazette*, September 22, 1918, 18.
49. "War Brings Relief to Columbia Freshmen," *New York Tribune*, June 2, 1918, 9; "Mountaineers to Play Nebraska Next Season," *Washington Times*, August 12, 1918, 12.
50. "May Waive Freshman Rule," *New York Tribune*, September 26, 1918, 13.
51. James Carl Nelson, *Five Lieutenants: The Heartbreaking Story of Five Harvard Men Who Led America to Victory in World War I* (New York: St. Martin's Press, 2012), 9; *Penn State in the World War* (State College, PA: Alumni Association of the Pennsylvania State College, 1921), 25–28; "Penn State Coach Resigns," *Washington Evening Star*, August 5, 1918, 15; "State College Loses Its Coach, Richard Harlow," *Harrisburg Telegraph*, August 6, 1918, 11; "Harlow a Lieutenant," *Washington Times*, September 22, 1918, 18; "Bare Sporting Chance for U.S. In War Says Gen. Wood; City Asks Nation to Prepare," *Philadelphia Evening Public Ledger*, August 12, 1915, 3.

Chapter 6

1. David T. Zabecki, *Germany at War: 400 Years of Military History* (ABC-CLIO, 2014), 515–516.
2. "Grid Sport Assured at Penn State," *New Castle News*, August 26, 1918, 8; "State Gets Bezdek," *Washington Times*, August 27, 1918, 14.
3. "Charges Against Hugo Bezdek," *Chicago Tribune*, November 27, 1904, 2; "Of Course He Is An Amateur," *Minneapolis Journal*, April 11, 1905, 3.
4. John M. Heisman and Mark Schlabach. *Heisman: The Man Behind the Trophy* (New York: Howard Books, Simon & Schuster, 2012), 68.
5. "Trying Out Hugo Bezdek and a 'New Idea' in Baseball," *Ogden Standard*, October 6, 1917.

6. Hugo Bezdek's Career Reads Like Fiction," *New York Evening World*, October 29, 1921, 6.
7. Ridge Riley, "Hugo Bezdek: Martyr or Monster?" *Town and Gown*, September 1978, 46.
8. "Model Eleven," *Topeka State Journal*, December 18, 1905, 6.
9. "Bezdek to Play Ball," *Rock Island Argus*, March 26, 1906, 7.
10. "Bezdek to Coach at Oregon 'U,'" *Minneapolis Journal*, July 9, 1905, 8.
11. "Bezdek Chosen Coach At Oregon University," *Salt Lake Tribune*, July 22, 1906, 2.
12. Riley, "Hugo Bezdek," 46; "Hugo L. Bezdek Becomes New Head of Physical Training Department," *Oregon Journal*, September 19, 1916, 44.
13. Riley, "Hugo Bezdek," 47.
14. "The East vs. The West," *Los Angeles Record*, January 1, 1917; Bob Folwell, "Best Eleven Won—Matthews; Condition Told—Beckett," *Los Angeles Morning Tribune*, January 2, 1917; Joe Hendrickson and Maxwell Stiles Hendrickson, *The Tournament of Roses: A Pictorial History* (New York: Brooke House, 1971), 55.
15. *Seattle Star*, February 26, 1917, 9.
16. "Hugo Bezdek is Gloomy Over Oregon Prospects," *Tacoma Times*, October 13, 1917, 6; *El Paso Herald*, June 16, 1917, 15.
17. "Three Managers in Four Days," *Bismarck Tribune*, July 12, 1917, 6.
18. *Honolulu Star-Bulletin*, July 5, 1917, 8; *Washington Herald*, July 3, 1917, 10; *New York Tribune*, July 5, 1917, 11.
19. "Trying Out Hugo Bezdek and a 'New Idea' in Baseball," *Ogden Standard*, October 6, 1917.
20. "Pirates Prove Surprise," *Philadelphia Evening Star*, August 11, 1918, 2; "Bezdek Has Shown Results," *Beaver Herald*, August 22, 1918, 4.
21. "Athletics are Now Obligatory at Penn State," *New York Tribune*, October 13, 1918, 2; "Slam Mass Sports as Vote is Asked," *Washington Times*, October 12, 1918, 10.
22. "Bezdek to be Czar of Sports at Penn State," *Harrisburg Telegraph*, August 30, 1918, 15; "State Cards Big Sports Program for Saturday," *Pittsburgh Daily Post*, November 7, 1918, B1; "Make Sports Compulsory," *New York Times*, October 13, 1918, 31.
23. "Trying Out Hugo Bezdek and a 'New Idea' in Baseball," *Ogden Standard*, October 6, 1917.
24. Hugo Bezdek, "To The Members of the Committee of Board of Trustees on the Department of Physical Education," Mass Athletics File, Scott Etter Papers PSUA 280, Special Collections Library, The Pennsylvania State University, 1–15.
25. Ibid.
26. Ibid., 8–10.
27. Ibid., 9–10.
28. Killinger, *A Penn State Walk-On*, unmarked page.
29. "Hugo Bezdek Issues Call for Candidates," *Evening Public Ledger*, September 11, 1918, 16; "State Will Travel," *Washington Times*, September 17, 1918, 16.
30. "Three Men Out for Football At Penn State," *New York Tribune*, September 15, 1918, 19.
31. "United States World War I Draft Registration Cards, 1917–1918," index and images, *FamilySearch* (http://familysearch.org/ark:/61903/1:1:K6VF-D3M : accessed 17 May 2015), William Glenn Killinger, 1917–1918, citing Harrisburg City no. 2, Pennsylvania, United States, NARA microfilm publication M1509 (Washington D.C.: National Archives and Records Administration), FHL microfilm 1,893,233.
32. "Penn State Statistics," *Pittsburgh Daily Post Sun*, November 1918, 3.
33. Killinger mistakenly wrote in his unpublished memoir that he reported to football camp on September 12, 1918.
34. Killinger, *A Penn State Walk-On*, unmarked page.
35. Ibid.
36. "Way to be a New Captain," *New York Tribune*, September 27, 1918, 13.
37. Riley, "Hugo Bezdek," 47.
38. Ibid.
39. W. Glenn Killinger, *GW's PSU Playbook and Notes*, 1921 (Unpublished).
40. Rick Barras, "Advice Shaped Grid Star's Life," *Philadelphia Inquirer*, date unknown; Furlow, *West Chester Football*, 9.
41. Riley, "Hugo Bezdek," 48–49.
42. W. W. "Bill" Roper, "Bezdek System and Hugo Get Fitting Praise," *Pittsburgh Post Gazette*, November 13, 1921, 29.
43. Ibid.
44. "No Football at Muhlenberg," *Harrisburg Telegraph*, September 18, 1918, 11.
45. "Athletics are Now Obligatory at Penn State," *New York Tribune*, October 13, 1918, 2.
46. "Football Grows Brighter at Penn State," *New York Tribune*, September 29, 1918, 2.
47. "Penn State Will Use its Freshies," *Washington Times*, September 28, 1918, 12; "Bezdek Likely to Use Freshies At Penn State," *New York Tribune*, September 22, 1918, 3.
48. "Penn State Planning to Readjust Schedule," *New York Tribune*, October 2, 1918, 14.
49. "Penn State Loses Two Players in the Army," *New York Tribune*, October 14, 1918, 15; "'Star Chamber' Football Planned for Tarsus at

Middletown, Sunday," *Harrisburg Telegraph*, October 18, 1918, 9; "Penn State Loses Stars," *Washington Herald*, October 14, 1918, 8; "Bezdek Chooses Men," *New York Tribune*, October 19, 1918, 17.

50. "On the Football Field at Penn State College," *Pittsburgh Gazette Times*, October 13, 1918, 18.

51. E. B. Fink, Edwin O. Jordan and Dudley B. Reed, "Influenza in Three Chicago Groups," *The Journal of Infectious Diseases* 25, no. 1 (July 1919), 75.

52. "Spanish Influenza—What it is and How it Should be Treated," *Harrisburg Telegraph*, October 12, 1918, 5.

53. "Spanish Influenza Halts Athletic Plans," *Washington Times*, September 26, 1918, 13.

54. Christine M. Kreiser, "The Enemy Within: Influenza 1918," *American History* (December 2006): 23–26; Jeffery K. Taubenberger, "The Origins and Virulence of the 1918 'Spanish' Influenza Virus," *Proceedings of the American Philosophical Society* 150, no. 1 (March 2006): 90–91; John M. Heisman and Mark Schlabach, *Heisman*, 163-164.

55. "Spanish 'Flu' May Be Cause of Quarantines," *Washington Times*, September 26, 1918, 14; "Spanish Scourge Takes Hold Upon 29,002 in Army," *Harrisburg Telegraph*, September 26, 1918, 4; "Influenza Closes Public Places," *Harrisburg Telegraph*, October 3, 1918, 14; "Spanish Influenza puts ban on all football contests scheduled here today," *Harrisburg Telegraph*, October 5, 1918, 6; "Football Finds a New Enemy in Quarantine," *New York Tribune*, September 26, 1918, 13.

56. "Penn State Disappointed," *New York Sun*, October 20, 1918, 3; "To Be Played Later," *Pittsburgh Gazette Times*, October 29, 1918, 18.

57. Killinger, *A Penn State Walk-On*, unmarked page.

58. "Bezdek Will Stay as Coach at Penn State," *Harrisburg Courier*, November 17, 1918, 5; "Penn State Loses Bezdek," *Washington Evening Star*, October 28, 1918, 12; "Bezdek's Service Requisitioned by War Department," *New York Tribune*, October 28, 1918, 11; "Hugo Bezdek Must Assist Uncle Sam," *Washington Times*, October 28, 1918, 11; "Penn State System will be Employed by War Department," *Scranton Republican*, November 6, 1918, 10.

59. "H. Bezdek's Ability Has Been Recognized," *Oakland Tribune*, November 21, 1918, 10.

60. "W. G. Killinger, of Tech, Now a Star at Penn State," *Harrisburg Telegraph*, October 28, 1918, 9.

61. "Penn State Pleased by Work of Eleven," *New York Tribune*, November 4, 1918, 15.

62. The Pennsylvania State University, *La Vie, 1920* (University Park, State College, PA, 1920), 283–286; "Penn State is Tied," *New York Sun*, November 3, 1918, 3; Killinger, *A Penn State Walk-On*, 2.

63. "Motor to State College," *Harrisburg Telegraph*, November 9, 1918, 4; Pennsylvania State College, *La Vie*, 1920 (University Park, State College, PA, 1920), 333.

64. "Rutgers Overwhelms Penn State Eleven by 26 to 3," *New York Sun*, November 10, 1918, 3.

65. "Bezdek's Gridders Are Overwhelmed by Rutgers Eleven," *Pittsburgh Daily Post*, November 10, 1918, 19.

66. Fred T. Moore, "Fred T. Moore, District Business Manager, Third District, to College Presidents. Philadelphia, PA, November 12, 1918" (Penn State During World Wars Collection [1109], Penn State University Archives, Special Collections Library, Pennsylvania State University).

67. Simon Bronner, *Explaining Traditions: Folk Behavior in Modern Culture* (Lexington: University of Kentucky Press, 2011), 390–392.

68. Alan Dundes, "Traditional Male Combat: From Game to War," in *From Game to War and Other Psychoanalytic Essays on Folklore* (Lexington: University Press of Kentucky, 1997), 31–37.

69. Rice, *The Tumult and the Shouting*, 94–95.

70. "Walter Camp Compares Football With War," *Asbury Park Press*, November 5, 1917, 8.

71. Ibid.

72. Lehigh University. *Epitome: 1920* (Bethlehem, PA: Lehigh University, 1920), 340–343.

73. Killinger, *A Penn State Walk-On*, unmarked page.

74. "State Wins Hard Game From Lehigh Eleven 7–6," *Brown and White*, November 20, 1918, 1.

75. "Gee Whiz! Read How Native Sons Put Harrisburg on the Map Saturday," *Harrisburg Telegraph*, November 18, 1918, 11; Pennsylvania State College, *La Vie*, 1920 (University Park, State College, PA, 1920), 285–286.

76. College Football Data Warehouse: Pittsburgh All National Championships: Pittsburgh Total National Championships, accessed date January 22, 2016, https://www.sports-reference.com/cfb/.

77. Smith, *Sports and Freedom*, 78–79.

78. Rader, *American Sports*, 93–94.

79. Tim Panaccio, *Beast of the East: Penn State vs. Pitt: A Game-by-Game History of America's Greatest Football Rivalry* (West Point, NY: Leisure Press, 1982), 6.

80. "Yerger Runs State Squad," *Pittsburgh Daily Post*, November 23, 1918, 11.

81. "Bezdek Stages Final Hard Workout of Year," *Pittsburgh Daily Post*, November 27, 1918, 11.

82. "Contest With Great Lakes Eleven Abandoned after Many Futile Challenges," *Pittsburgh Post Gazette*, November 28, 1918, 1.
83. Notables to Honor Tom Davies Tonight," *Pittsburgh Post Gazette*, December 12, 1921, 7.
84. "Score is 28–6, Bezdek's Eleven Being First to Cross Goal Line," *Pittsburgh Daily Post*, November 29, 1918, 8.
85. "Penn State First Eleven to Cross Pitt's Goal Line," *New York Tribune*, November 29, 1918, 10; "Small Crowd Sees Panther Scored Against Early After Fumble in the First Period," *Pittsburgh Gazette Times*, November 29, 1918, 8; "Return of Injured Halfback Enhances Chance of Victory," *Pittsburgh Daily Post*, November 26, 1919, 13.
86. "Team Young and Green but is Full of Fight and Well Coached," *Pittsburgh Daily Post*, November 24, 1918, 19.
87. Rick Barras, "Advice Shaped Grid Star's Life," *Philadelphia Inquirer*, date unknown; Furlow, *West Chester Football*, 9; "Football Team Proves Surprise," *Penn State Collegian*, January 8, 1919, 1.

Chapter 7

1. U.S. Army, "Order of Battle of the United States Land Forces in the World War," Washington D.C.: The Center of Military History, United States Army, 1988, 566–558.
2. Henry W. Valentine, Second Lieutenant, Infantry, Company G. "William G. Killinger Enlistment Record," October 19, 1918; James Dayley, U.S. Army, Retired. "Honorable Discharge from the United States Army," December 18, 1918.
3. "Status of the S.A.T.C. Boys," *Harrisburg Telegraph*, December 21, 1918, 10; Killinger, *A Penn State Walk-On*, 2.
4. "Bezdek fears injury; gives shadow drill," *Pittsburgh Post Gazette*, November 25, 1919, 1.
5. Killinger, *A Penn State Walk-On*, unmarked page; Henry, *William Glenn Killinger*, 25.
6. "Football Letter Awards," *New York Times*, January 12, 1919.
7. "Basketball Coach is Shell Shocked," *Scranton Republican*, January 8, 1919, 12; Pennsylvania State College. *Penn State in the World War*. Alumni Association of the Pennsylvania State College (State College, PA, 1921), 120.
8. "Harlow is to Assist Hugo Bezdek at State," *Harrisburg Evening News*, January 8, 1919, 13.
9. *Pittsburgh Post Gazette*. September 15, 1919; "Bezdek Fears Injury; gives Shadow Drill: Killinger, 1918 Star, to Sub for Lightner in Contest with Pitt," *Pittsburgh Post Gazette*, November 25, 1919, 1; *Penn State Collegian*, February 5, 1919, March 19, 1919; "Penn State Here Tomorrow," *Lehigh Brown and White*, January 31, 1919, 1; "State Noses Out Lehigh Five," *Lehigh Brown and White*, February 1, 1919, 1.
10. Henry, *William Glenn Killinger*, 24.
11. Penn State University, *La Vie, 1921* (University Park, Penn State University, 1921), 347.
12. Ibid., 349.
13. "Penn Flyer Was Killed," *Indiana Gazette*, February 17, 1919; Pennsylvania State College. *Penn State in the World War*. Alumni Association of the Pennsylvania State College (State College, PA, 1921), 365.
14. "Marylanders Defeat Penn State by 7 to 1," *Washington Post*, April 19, 1919.
15. "C.U. Defeated by Penn State Nine," *Washington Post*, April 20, 1919; "Penn State is Beaten by C.U.," *Washington Post*, April 22, 1919.
16. Penn State University, *La Vie, 1921* (University Park, Penn State University, 1921), 347–350.
17. "Army Nine Badly Routed," *New York Times*, May 8, 1919.
18. Penn State University, *La Vie, 1921* (University Park, Penn State University, 1921), 349.
19. Ibid.; Penn State University, *La Vie, 1922* (University Park, Penn State University, 1922), 386–390; Penn State University, *La Vie, 1923* (University Park, Penn State University, 1923), 422–426.
20. "Map Showing Ramifications of the Bomb Plot," *New York Tribune*, May 1, 1919, 8.
21. Paul Avrich, *Sacco and Vanzetti: The Anarchist Background* (Princeton, NJ: Princeton University Press, 1991), 140–156.
22. "36 Were Marked As Victims By Bomb Conspirers," *New York Times*, May 1, 1919, 1.
23. Henry, *William Glenn Killinger*, Official Transcript Record, The Pennsylvania State college, Copy of W. Glenn Killinger's Student Record Card, lox. Cit. 26, 135.
24. Richard B. "Dick" Yoder, Personal interview with the author, Gap, Pennsylvania, March 22, 2015; Killinger, *A Penn State Walk-On*, 26.
25. "First Place in Reading's Grip," *Harrisburg Telegraph*, May 30, 1919, 17; "Levan is Leading Hill League List of Hard Hitters," *Harrisburg Evening News*, July 11, 1919, 20.
26. Rader, *American Sports*, 55.
27. Fran Strouse, Telephone interview with the author, June 19, 2015.
28. "Base Ball News," *Hershey Press*, June 12, 1919, 6; "Klein Team is Given Farewell," *Harrisburg Telegraph*, October 8, 1919, 16; "Boston Falls Before Klein," *Harrisburg Telegraph*, September 26, 1919, 21; "Red Sox Get 13 Bingles

and Defeat Klein Team," *Harrisburg Evening News*, September 27, 1919, 11; "Dodgers Fall Victims of Klein Chocolate," *Pittsburgh Post Gazette*, September 23, 1919, 19; "Red Sox Lose to Klein; Babe Ruth Fans Twice," *Pittsburgh Gazette Times*, September 26, 1919, 16.

29. "Big Day at Elizabethtown When the Klein Company Opens Athletic Field," *Harrisburg Telegraph*, May 31, 1919, 13.

30. "Klein Chocolate Lads Beat Altoona by Heavy Hitting," *Harrisburg Telegraph*, June 16, 1919, 13.

31. "Peanut Bars Win Two Games," *Harrisburg Telegraph*, July 14, 1919, 13.

32. Henry Beech Needham, "The College Athlete: How Commercialism Is Making Him a Professional," *McClure's Magazine*, June 1905, 260–261.

33. Ibid., 262–63.

34. "Lebanon Lost Both Games of July 4th Bill," *Lebanon Evening Report*, July 5, 1919, 5; "Klein Nine Will Have Busy Week," *Harrisburg Evening News*, July 14, 1919, 11; "Klein Nine Wins In Hill Contest," *Harrisburg Evening News*, July 9, 1919, 13.

35. "Change in Batting Leaders of West End League During Games Played Last Month," *Harrisburg Evening News*, August 4, 1919, 11.

Chapter 8

1. Sidney Sanes, "Watch Penn and State," *Pittsburgh Gazette Times*, September 8, 1919, 11.

2. "Conover Comes Back," *Washington Times*, January 25, 1919.

3. "Good Talent for State Next Year," *Scranton Republican*, January 4, 1919, 1; Louis A. Dougher, "Harry Robb Makes Good on Two Varsity Teams," *Washington Times*, September 11, 1919; "Harry Robb Gets Columbia Letter," *Pittsburgh Post Gazette*, January 27, 1919; "Penn State Holds First Grid Workouts," *Pittsburgh Daily Post*, September 5, 1919; "State Loses Leader," *Harrisburg Evening News*, September 25, 1918, 9.

4. *Pittsburgh Post Gazette*, September 26, 1919.

5. Ibid.

6. Lebanon Valley College, *Quittapahilla, 1919* (Annville, PA: Lebanon Valley College, 1919), 138, 180–196; Killinger, *A Penn State Walk-On*, unmarked page; Riley, *The Road to Number One*, 196.

7. Killinger, *A Penn State Walk-On*, unmarked page.

8. "State's Gridiron Puzzles Continue; Bezdek is Absent," *Pittsburgh Daily Post*, September 28, 1919.

9. "State's Squad Puts on Hard Practice Game," *Pittsburgh Daily Post*, September 21, 1919.

10. *Pittsburgh Daily Post*, September 15, 1919.

11. "The Scrubs Beat First Team by Air Route," *Pittsburgh Daily Post*, September 28, 1919.

12. Killinger, *A Penn State Walk-On*, unmarked page.

13. "State Students Greet Bezdek," *Pittsburgh Post Gazette*, September 30, 1919.

14. Killinger, *A Penn State Walk-On*, unmarked page.

15. Riley, *The Road to Number One*, 182.

16. In an article titled "Penn State Footballers Triumph 33-0" on October 5, 1919, the *Pittsburgh Post Gazette* wrongly reported that Buck Williams was substituted into the game for Henry Robb. Williams had a broken hand and accordingly did not dress for the game. He did not play in any game until November 8 against Lehigh. In previous articles, the *Post Gazette* mistook Killinger for Williams.

17. "Penn State Footballers Triumph 33-0," *Pittsburgh Post Gazette*, October 5, 1919; "State Eleven in Late Rush Storms Goal and Trounces Old Soldiers," *Pittsburgh Post Gazette*, October 5, 1919.

18. "Penn Staters Find Bucknell Hard to Upset," *Pittsburgh Post Gazette*, October 12, 1919.

19. "Hugo Bezdek's Eleven Is Held to 9-0 Score," *Pittsburgh Daily Post*, October 12, 1919.

20. "Dartmouth Takes Hard-Fought Game," *New York Times*, October 19, 1919, 8.

21. Riley, *The Road to Number One*, 182.

22. Killinger, *A Penn State Walk-On*, unmarked page; "Review of Grid Year Reveals Tangled Mass," *Indianapolis Star*, December 16, 1919, 8.

23. Killinger, *A Penn State Walk-On*, unmarked page.

24. "State Stars Run Big Scores on Ursinus," *Pittsburgh Post Gazette*, October 26, 1919; "Ullery Proves Big Find in Penn State Backfield," *Pittsburgh Post Gazette*, October 23, 1919.

25. "Penn State Star's Record Unique One," *Harrisburg Evening News*, October 30, 1919, 15.

26. "State Team in Philly for Penn Contest," *Harrisburg Evening News*, November 1, 1919, 11.

27. "Penn State Defeats Pennsylvania, 10 to 0," *Pittsburgh Gazette Times*, November 2, 1919, 2; "Penn State Team Outclasses Penn," *Washington Times*, November 2, 1919, 22.

28. Robert S. Lyons, *Any Given Sunday: A Life of Bert Bell* (Philadelphia: Temple University Press, 2010), 18.

29. "Lehigh Bows to Penn State," *Lehigh Brown and White*, November 11, 1919, 1–3;

"Local Stars Prominent in Penn State Victory Saturday," *Harrisburg Telegraph*, November 11, 1919; "Penn State Beats Lehigh Easily," *Decatur Herald*, November 9, 1919; "Ithacans Baffled by Aerial Stunts of Bezdek's Team," *Pittsburgh Daily Post*, November 16, 1919; "Penn State Buries Cornell's Eleven," *Brooklyn Daily Eagle*, November 16, 1919.
30. Killinger, *A Penn State Walk-On*, unmarked page; "State Team Gives Out Straight Dope," *New Castle Herald*, December 5, 1919; "Penn State is Pitt's Betters," *Harrisburg Telegraph*, November 28, 1919.
31. Riley, *The Road to Number One*, 185–186.
32. *Ibid.*, 182.
33. *Ibid.*, 187.
34. "Rank Penn State As East's Leading Team," *Altoona Tribune*, December 15, 1919, 10; "Penn State is Picked as Best," *New Castle Herald*, December 19, 1919, 18; "Wonderful Record Made by Penn State Eleven," *Penn State Collegian*, December 17, 1919. 1.
35. Killinger, *A Penn State Walk-On*, unmarked page.
36. "But Twelve Penn State Players Gee [sic] Letter," *Washington Times*, December 6, 1919; "Penn State Gives Football Insignia To Only 12 Players," *New York Tribune*, December 7, 1919.

Chapter 9

1. W. Glenn Killinger, *GW's PSU Playbook and Notes*, 1921 (Unpublished).
2. Doug McDonald, "Very, Killinger Recall Days When Dutch Played, Coached," *Centre Daily Times*, June 28, 1977, 27.
3. "Police Docket Clear; Prohibition Gets Credit," *Harrisburg Telegraph*, January 28, 1920; "Philadelphians Sell Booze-Flavored Cigars," *Altoona Tribune*, January 29, 1920, 1.
4. "Search for Thieves Who Stole 78 Lbs. Whisky," *Harrisburg Telegraph*, January 23, 1920, 4; "Discharge Policeman After Testimony Shows he Visited Speakeasies When on Duty," *New Castle Herald*, February 2, 1920, 1.
5. "Over the River," *Harrisburg Telegraph*, January 16, 1920.
6. "State College Takes Basketball Game," *Lehigh Brown and White*, March 16, 1920, 1.
7. W. Glenn Killinger, *GW's PSU Playbook and Notes*, 1921 (Unpublished).
8. "Basketball With State College," *Lehigh Brown and White*, March 12, 1920, 1.
9. Pennsylvania State University, *La Vie, 1921* (University Park: Penn State University, 1921), 360–362; "Mullan Stars in State Win Over Juniata," *Pittsburgh Daily Post*, December 20, 1919; "Penn State to Meet Dickinson Tonight,"

Altoona Tribune, January 17, 1920; "State Quintet Easily Defeats W&J, 43–25," *Pittsburgh Post Gazette*, January 25, 1920.
10. "Honor for Killinger; to Lead Penn State Team," *Harrisburg Telegraph*, March 24, 1920.
11. Pennsylvania State University, *La Vie, 1922* (University Park: Penn State University, 1922), 386–391.
12. "Penn State Coach Rounds Up Players," *New Castle News*, March 12, 1920.
13. Pennsylvania State University, *La Vie, 1922* (University Park: Penn State University, 1922), 386–391.
14. "Penn State in Front," *Washington Post*, April 15, 1920; "G. Killinger on Penn State Nine," *Harrisburg Evening News*, April 20, 1920, 15.
15. "Penn State Defeats Swarthmore Nine, 8–4," *Pittsburgh Gazette Times*. April 25, 1920; Penn State Beats Fordham in 9th," *New York Sun and Herald*, May 5, 1920, 13.
16. *Pittsburgh Post Gazette*, June 10, 1920.
17. W. J. Macbeth, "Hugo Bezdek Strong in Praise of Both Killinger and Haines," *New York Tribune*, December 29, 1921, 13.
18. *Ibid.*
19. Killinger, *A Penn State Walk-On*, unmarked page.
20. *Ibid.*, 26.
21. *Ibid.*, unmarked page.
22. *Ibid.*, unmarked page; "More Stars for D-P Circuit," *Harrisburg Telegraph*, May 22, 1920; "Rosewood Slams Reading Team," *Harrisburg Telegraph*, July 13, 1920, 19; "Rosewood Back in Hill Lead," *Harrisburg Telegraph*, July 21, 1920, 11.
23. "West End Evens Up in City Championship Series," *Harrisburg Telegraph*, August 27, 1920, 17; "Rosewood Team Work is Big Factor in Victory; Take Game From West End," *Harrisburg Telegraph*, August 28, 1920, 11; "Generalship is Factor in Rosewood's Victory over West End," *Harrisburg Telegraph*, September 1, 1920, 11; "Rosewood Wins Title in Series with West End; to Take on Port Royal," *Harrisburg Telegraph*, September 3, 1920, 21.
24. "Rosewood and West End Ready for First Tilt," *Harrisburg Evening News*, August 24, 1920, 11; "State's Grid Men Now Reporting," *Harrisburg Evening News*, September 2, 1920, 13.
25. Killinger, *A Penn State Walk-On*, unmarked page.
26. "35 Gridiron Men At Penn State," *Altoona Tribune*, September 3, 1920.
27. "No More Pie for Penn State Men," *Harrisburg Courier*, September 26, 1920, 2; "Five Men Hurt at Penn State," *Reading Times*, September 9, 1920.
28. "Penn is Ready for the Gridiron," *Reading Times*. September 4, 1920.

29. "Killinger is back in game," *Harrisburg Telegraph*, September 23, 1920; "Local Stars at Penn State," *Harrisburg Telegraph*, September 9, 1920.
30. "State Humbles Muhlenberg in Easy Fashion," *Pittsburgh Daily Post*, September 26, 1920, 18; "College Athletics," *Harrisburg Evening News*, June 3, 1921, 16.
31. "Bezdek Not Satisfied; Orders Till Harder Work," *Altoona Tribune*, September 27, 1920, 13.
32. "Penn State Improves," *New York Times*, October 1, 1920, 12; "Penn State Wins Game, Clarence Beck Stars," *Harrisburg Telegraph*, October 4, 1920, 11; "Gettysburg Game Shows State's Weak Position," *Altoona Tribune*, October 4, 1920, 12.
33. Henry, *William Glenn Killinger*, 28–30.
34. "Penn State-Dartmouth Battle Saturday; 'Tis Alumni Day," *Pittsburgh Daily Post*, October 3, 1920; "Home-Coming Day Big Event at State College," *Harrisburg Telegraph*, September 20, 1920, 4; Killinger, *A Penn State Walk-On*, unmarked page.
35. Rader, *American Sports*. 94–95; Oriard, *Reading Football*, See Chapter 2.
36. "State's Alumni to Turn Out," *Pittsburgh Daily Post*, May 2, 1908, 8.
37. "Penn State Expects to Humble Quakers," *Washington Times*, October 23, 1911, 1; "Pitt and Penn State Will Close Gridiron Season Next Thursday," *Pittsburgh Daily Post*, November 26, 1911, 19.
38. Pennsylvania State University, *La Vie, 1915* (University Park: Penn State University, 1915), 69; Thomas E. Range and Sean Patrick Smith, *The Penn State Blue Band: A Century of Pride and Precision* (University Park: Pennsylvania State Press, 1999), 232.
39. Jackie Esposito and Steven Herb, *The Nittany Lion: An Illustrated Tale.* (University Park: Penn State University Press, 1997), 75–78; The Pennsylvania State College, *La Vie, 1908* (University Park, Penn State University Press, 1908); The Pennsylvania State University, *La Vie, 1987* (University Park, Penn State University Press, 1987), inside cover; *La Vie, 1907*, 93; *La Vie, 1984*, 33; Murray R. Nelson, *American Sports: A History of Icons, Idols, and Ideas* (ABC-CLIO, 2013), 528; "State's Alumni to Turn Out," *Pittsburgh Daily Post*, May 2, 1908, 8; "Penn State Expects to Humble Quakers," *Washington Times*, October 23, 1911, 11; "Pitt and Penn State Will Close Gridiron Season Next Thursday," *Pittsburgh Daily Post*, November 26, 1911, 19; "State's Alumni to Turn Out," *Pittsburgh Daily Post*, May 2, 1908.
40. Pennsylvania lore suggests that the word "Nittany" originates from the earliest days of the universe, when, according to Jake Faddy, a Seneca tribesman and one of the last Native Americans to wander the Juniata Valley, a war erupted between Southern tribes and Northern tribes for possession of the region. Chun-Eh-Hoe, chief of a Northern tribe, and his warriors were driven into the vicinity of present-day State College. Chun-Eh-Hoe died, and his daughter Nita-Nee became the tribal leader. She led her army to victory over the Southern tribes. Princess Nita-Nee lived to be 100 years old. When she died, she was buried beneath a mound of cedar branches. On the night of her burial, a storm blanketed the valley. When the sky cleared, there was a great mountain in what was once a valley. The people called it Mount Nittany. Ever since Penn State was founded as the Farmer's High School in 1855, Mount Nittany has cast its shadow over campus activities. It was the school's symbolic image. In 1907, Harrison Dennington "Joe" Mason Jr., wrote: "Every college the world over of any consequence has a college emblem of some kind—all but the Pennsylvania State College…. Why not select for ours the king of beasts—the Lion!!'" In several accounts, most notably *The Nittany Lion*, coauthored by Jackie Esposito and Steven Herb, Joe Mason is generally credited with making the Nittany Lion Penn State's mascot. Mason was a freshman third baseman at Penn State when on April 20, 1904, he and his teammates were led around Princeton's campus before their afternoon game against the Tigers. The tour ended at the Ivy League school's Bengal tiger, where the guide promised a Penn State defeat. Mason, a capricious individual who would later write for the college's yearbook and become his class's historian, fired back, "Well, up at Penn State we have Mount Nittany right on our campus, where rules the Nittany Mountain Lion, who has never been beaten in a fair fight." Penn State's baseball team defeated Princeton 8 to 1 that afternoon. Years later, during Dick Hoffman's sophomore year at Penn State, he secured a role as the lion for the Penn State Players theatrical group in George Bernard Shaw's *Androcles and the Lion*. It is believed that his attire for *Androcles* became the original costume that he wore as the mascot. In an interview he gave 40 years after he graduated, Hoffman remembered a little about becoming the Nittany Lion. He recalled it was "after World War I ended…. When all those 20-plus-year old brutes came back from France and back to college, Well, I decided athletics were not particularly down my alley. They were big and tough, and that's why I went out for Penn State Players. It seemed like dramatics was a lot safer." (SOURCE: Jackie Esposito and Steven Herb,

The Nittany Lion: An Illustrated Tale. (University Park: Penn State University Press, 1997), 75–76.
 41. "Penn State is Victor Over Dartmouth, 14–7," *Harrisburg Evening Star*, October 10, 1920, 27; Killinger, *A Penn State Walk-On*, unmarked page.
 42. Riley, *The Road to Number One*, 194.
 43. "Killinger's Play Gives State Edge on Dartmouth, 17–7," *Pittsburgh Daily Post*, October 10, 1920, 18.
 44. Killinger, *A Penn State Walk-On*, unmarked page.
 45. *Ibid.*
 46. "Killinger and Way Star for Penn State," *Penn State Collegian*, October 12, 1920, 1, 5; "Forward Pass Wins for Penn Staters," *Washington Post*, October 10, 1920, 17; "Penn State Wins," *Washington Times*, October 10, 1920, 26; "Penn State Overcomes Dartmouth," *Boston Post*, October 10, 1920, 40; "Dartmouth Grid Team Defeated in 14–7 Triumph," *Pittsburgh Post Gazette*, October 10, 1920; "State Rejoices Over its Victory," *New Castle Herald*, October 12, 1920, 12.
 47. Killinger, *A Penn State Walk-On*, unmarked page.
 48. "Killinger's Play Gives State Edge on Dartmouth, 17–7," *Pittsburgh Daily Post*, October 10, 1920, 18.
 49. "'Pie' Way Helps State Pile Up Big Score on Carolina," *Pittsburgh Daily Post*, October 17, 1920, 18; "North Carolina Tech Put Up a Game Fight," *Pittsburgh Daily News*, October 17, 1920, 14; "Penn State Easy Winner," *New York Times*, October 17, 1920, 127.
 50. "State Rolls up 109 Points Upon Lebanon Valley," *Pittsburgh Post Gazette*, October 24, 1920, 24; "Penn State Wins, 109–7; Quarterback Badly Hurt," *New York Times*, October 24, 1920, 18; "Lebanon Valley Trounced by Penn State," *Lebanon Daily News*, October 25, 1920, 5.
 51. "Killinger Still Unable to Play," *Harrisburg Telegraph*, October 28, 1920, 15; "Killinger's Injuries Slight No Broken Bones as Yet," *Harrisburg Telegraph*, October 26, 1920, 13; "Bezdek Drives State for Quaker Eleven," *Washington Post*, October 26, 1920.
 52. "Killinger May Not Play," *Philadelphia Evening Public Ledger*, October 25, 1920, 14.
 53. "Easy for Penn State," *Harrisburg Evening Star*, October 31, 1920, 29; "Penn State Wins over Univ. of Penn," *Wichita Daily Eagle*, October 31, 1920, 14; "Local Stars Aid to Penn State," *Harrisburg Telegraph*, November 1, 1920, 13; "Haines Makes 100-Yard Run Through Whole Pennsy Team," *Brooklyn Daily Eagle*, October 31, 1920, 61.
 54. "Easy for Penn State," *Harrisburg Evening Star*, October 31, 1920, 29.
 55. Riley, *The Road to Number One*, 195.
 56. John W. Heisman, "Heisman's Hundred in the Hall of Football Fame," *Marion Star*, October 27, 1928, 1.
 57. "Cross-buck is Best Play on Gridiron—Killinger," *Ironwood Daily Globe*, November 24, 1923, 13.
 58. *Bismarck Tribune*. November 22, 1920, 8.
 59. "Penn State Has Two Stars Out," *Harrisburg Telegraph*, November 3, 1920, 13; "Joe Lightner Goes to Practice in Aeroplane," *Harrisburg Telegraph*, November 2, 1920, 13.
 60. "Bezdek Machine Victorious in Grinding Battle With Huskers," *Daily Nebraskan*, November 8, 1920, 1–4.
 61. Hugo Bezdek, "The Headiest Play I Ever Saw; The Best Player I Ever Coached," (date, source unknown).
 62. "Bezdek is Against Football Changes," *New York Times*, December 27, 1920, 15.
 63. "Huskers Beaten By Penn's Open Game," *Sunday World Herald* (Lead, South Dakota), November 7, 1920, 18–21.
 64. "Notre Dame Has Class, East Says," *Sandusky Star Journal*, November 1, 1920, 15.
 65. Killinger, *A Penn State Walk-On*, unmarked page.
 66. Ridge Riley. *The Road to Number One: A Personal Chronicle of Penn State Football* (New York, NY: Doubleday, 1977), 199.
 67. "Penn State Held to 7–7 Tie by Lehigh," *Pittsburgh Post Gazette*, November 14, 1920, 24; "How Coaching Strategy Developed Trick Plays That Scored Many Points," *New York Evening World*, December 10, 1920; "Brown and White Eleven Outplays Unbeaten State," *Lehigh Brown and White*, November 16, 1920, 1, 4; Killinger, *A Penn State Walk-On*, unmarked page.
 68. "State's Supremacy of East At Stake in Game with Pitt," *Pittsburgh Daily Post*, November 21, 1920, 5.
 69. Killinger, *A Penn State Walk-On*, 3; "Penn State Works in Snow Like Polar Bears," *Harrisburg Telegraph*, November 17, 1920.
 70. Killinger, *A Penn State Walk-On*, 3–4.
 71. "Neither Panthers Nor Lions Score," *Boston Post*, November 26, 1920, 22; "Penn State and Panthers Play at Pittsburgh," *Lincoln Evening Journal*, November 25, 1920, 1; "State and Pitt Fight It Out to 0–0 Draw," *Harrisburg Evening News*, November 26, 1920, 23.
 72. George Curry, "Tiger and Crimson Outrank Pittsburgh and Penn State," *Brooklyn Daily Eagle*, November 30, 1920, 22.
 73. "Western Players Mentioned on Outing's Football Honor Roll," *Wichita Daily Eagle*, January 1, 1921, 4; "Pittsburgh Picks All-Star Eleven," *Lafayette* (Easton, PA), December 7, 1920, 1.

Chapter 10

1. "Local Stars to Play Cage Game," *Harrisburg Telegraph*, November 30, 1920, 15.
2. "State Five Opens Up By Swamping Juniata," *Harrisburg Evening News*, December 16, 1920, 17.
3. "Last Minute Rush by Nittany Crew Overtakes Locals," *Pittsburgh Daily Post*, February 5, 1921, 9.
4. "Lions Lose to Virginians, 29–23, After Nine Wins," *Pittsburgh Daily Post*, February 13, 1921, 21.
5. "Penn State Again Defeats Panthers in Brilliant Game," *Pittsburgh Daily Post*, February 20, 1921, 20; "Penn State Winner Over Swarthmore," *Pittsburgh Daily Post*, March 6, 1921, 19.
6. "Yale Five Stages Rally and Defeats Penn State," *New York Tribune*, March 9, 1921, 14; Killinger, *A Penn State Walk-On*, 21; "Lose Yale Game," *Penn State Collegian*, March 11, 1921, 4.
7. Doug McDonald, "Very, Killinger Recall Days When Dutch Played, Coached," *Centre Daily Times*, June 28, 1977, 27.
8. "State Five Wins on Penn Floor 21–19," *New Castle Herald*, March 10, 1921, 9; "State Five Wins From Penn," *Harrisburg Evening News*, March 10, 1921, 17; Killinger, *A Penn State Walk-On*, 23.
9. The University of Pennsylvania was retroactively recognized as the national champion by the Helms Athletic Foundation in 1919–1920 and 1920–1921, and the Premo-Porretta Power Poll for the 1919–1920 season.
10. "Penn State Quint Closes Best Season," *Washington Post*, March 20, 1921, 26.
11. "Penn State Nine Leaves for South Tomorrow," *Pittsburgh Post Gazette*, March 26, 1921, 9.
12. "State Nine to Start South," *New Castle Herald*, March 22, 1921, 13; *Harrisburg Evening News*, March 22, 1921, 13.
13. "Killinger Leads Team in Penn State Game," *Harrisburg Telegraph*, April 12, 1921, 13.
14. "State Blanks Lebanon, 3–0," *Pittsburgh Daily Post*, April 24, 1921, 18.
15. "State Nine Wins Thirteenth Fray," *Harrisburg Evening News*, May 12, 1921, 14.
16. "Yale Banged By Penn State," *Boston Post*, May 14, 1921, 7.
17. "State Nines Have Won 27 Consecutive Contests," *Harrisburg Evening News*, May 18, 1921.
18. "Haines Appointed Coach at Gettysburg College," *Pittsburgh Post Gazette*, August 17, 1921, 9; "Haines Goes to Yanks," *Charlotte News*, May 18, 1921; "Hinkey Haines Resigns; Awaits Faculty Verdict," *Harrisburg Telegraph*, May 21, 1921, 15.
19. "Haines Quits But Penn State Beats Detroit, 8–2," *Pittsburgh Post Gazette*, May 21, 1921, 10.
20. Cliff J. Ryan, "Pitt Beaten by State 5 to 3, in Ten Innings," *Pittsburgh Post Gazette*, May 26, 1921, 12.
21. "Haines to Join Yanks in June; May Also Coach at Annville," *Harrisburg Evening News*, May 28, 1921, 11; *Harrisburg Evening News*, June 3, 1921; "'Hinkie' Haines to Play with Rosewood Team," *Harrisburg Telegraph*, May 27, 1921, 21.
22. "Penn State Defeated," *Scranton Republican*, May 30, 1921, 14.
23. Killinger, *A Penn State Walk-On*, 25.
24. "Pitt Beats State Nine in 10th Inning," *Pittsburgh Gazette Times*, June 14, 1921; "Panther Nine Defeats Penn State Again, 10–7," *Pittsburgh Gazette Times*, June 14, 1921, 7.
25. "Killinger Batted .371 for Penn State Team," *New York Tribune*, January 20, 1922, 15.
26. Killinger, *A Penn State Walk-On*, 53.

Chapter 11

1. "Penn State has Three Veterans," *Harrisburg Telegraph*, August 27, 1921, 13; John W. Heisman, "Heisman's Hundred in the Hall of Football Fame," *Marion Star*, October 27, 1928, 1.
2. Killinger, *A Penn State Walk-On*, 28.
3. "Penn State Has Wet Ball Test," *Harrisburg Telegraph*, September 6, 1921, 13.
4. "Coach Bezdek Has Real Job on Hand," *Scranton (PA) Republican*, September 7, 1921, 16; "Penn State Grid Card Heavy One," *Harrisburg Evening News*, December 23, 1920, 15.
5. Killinger, *A Penn State Walk-On*, 29.
6. *Ibid*.
7. "Big Fellows for Penn State," *Harrisburg Telegraph*, September 8, 1921, 14; "Killinger is Flashy Player," *Harrisburg Telegraph*, September 29, 1921, 17.
8. Killinger, *A Penn State Walk-On*, 30.
9. "Penn State Walks Away with Lebanon Valley Eleven, 53–0," *Pittsburgh Daily Post*, September 25, 1921, 19; "Lebanon Valley Meets Defeat at Penn State Game," *Lebanon Evening Report*, September 27, 1921, 5.
10. "Penn State Beats Gettysburg, 24–0; "Visitors Surprise," *Pittsburgh Daily Post*, October 2, 1921, 25; "Penn State Wins Over Gettysburg," *Pittsburgh Gazette Times*, October 2, 1921, 26; "Lightner, Penn State Injured Shoulder In Lebanon Val. Game," *Lebanon Daily News*, September 28, 1921, 5; Killinger, *A Penn State Walk-On*, 30.
11. Killinger, *A Penn State Walk-On*, 31.
12. "Football Squad Working Hard for Opening Game with Penn State," *Gettysburg Times*, September 24, 1921, 6.
13. "Carolina State vs. Penn State," *Twin-

City Daily Sentinel, October 6, 1921, 6; "Penn State to Get Real Test," *Harrisburg Courier*, October 2, 1921.

14. "Snell is Star for Penn State," *Harrisburg Telegraph*, October 11, 1921, 13.

15. Killinger, *A Penn State Walk-On*, 31; "Penn State Winner over N. Carolina in Brilliant Struggle," *Pittsburgh Daily Post*, October 9, 1921, 25; "Penn State Easy Victor," *Fort Wayne Sentinel*, October 9, 1921, 8.

16. "Tune in Your Radio and Get State College News," *Penn State Alumni News* 9, no. 3, November, 1922, 10; Gilbert Crossley, "History of 8XE," December 1, 1952. A 555.02, Box 1: Campus Radio, PSULSC; Kathleen O'Toole, *Intercollegiate Football and Educational Radio: Three Case Studies of the Commercialization of Sports Broadcasting in the 1920s and 1930s* (Dissertation, The Pennsylvania State University, August 2010).

17. "Penn State Beats Lehigh in Alumni Day Contest, 28–7," *Pittsburgh Daily Post*, October 16, 1921, 19.

18. "Strong Penn State Team May Surprise Harvard in Big Game," *New York Evening World*, October 18, 1921, 22; "History of State-Harvard Battles Told by 'Daniel,'" *Harrisburg Telegraph*, October 21, 1921, 21.

19. "'On to Harvard' is Slogan at Penn State," *Scranton Republican*, October 19, 1921, 16.

20. "Penn State Players Not Superstitious, But—," *Pittsburgh Post Gazette*, December 9, 1921, 9; "Killinger Goes to Bed So-So To Thwart Jinx," *Indianapolis Star*, January 2, 1922, 14.

21. "Glenn Killinger to Pilot State," *Harrisburg Telegraph*, October 21, 1921, 21.

22. "Quarterback as Field General or Runner, Question," *Oregon Daily Journal*, December 18, 1921, 26.

23. "Two Navy Blunders in Fourth Quarter Ruin Chance to Win," *Evening Public Ledger* (Philadelphia, PA), November 14, 1921.

24. Killinger, *A Penn State Walk-On*, 32.

25. "Crimson Host, Near Defeat, Spurts to Deadlock, 21 to 21," *Pittsburgh Post Gazette*, October 23, 1921.

26. Killinger, *A Penn State Walk-On*, 32.

27. "Bezdek Admits Tech May Pull Big Surprise," *Pittsburgh Gazette-Times*, October 30, 1921, 27; Killinger, *A Penn State Walk-On*, 32.

28. "Local Boys Star in State Battle," *Harrisburg Evening News*, October 24, 1921, 11.

29. Riley, *The Road to Number One*, 205.

30. Will B. Johnstone, "Freak Football Plays," *Lincoln Evening Journal*, November 5, 1929, 18.

31. "Georgia Tech and Penn State Both Rely on Offensive Game," *New York Tribune*, October 27, 1921, 13.

32. "Penn State Holds Harvard to Tie in Spectacular Game," *Pittsburgh Daily Post*, October 23, 1921, 18; "Lightner Sixth Among Scorers," *Harrisburg Evening News*, October 25, 1921, 17.

33. "Foch and Pershing to Witness Tech Penn State Game," *Atlanta Constitution*, October 27, 1921, 1.

34. "Yellow Jackets Run Wild Over Penn," *Atlanta Constitution*, October 7, 1917, 3, 6; John M. Heisman and Mark Schlabach, *Heisman*, 155–157.

35. Heisman, 146–185.

36. William Abbott, "Teams are Evenly Matched in North vs. South Battle," *New York Evening World*, October 28, 1921, 34.

37. Killinger, *A Penn State Walk-On*, 36.

38. "Georgia Tech and Penn State Both Rely on Offensive Game," *New York Tribune*, October 27, 1921, 13.

39. Abbott, 34.

40. Killinger, *A Penn State Walk-On*, 38.

41. Ibid.

42. Ibid., 39.

43. Ibid., 40.

44. Ibid., 41.

45. "Killinger is Penn State Star," *Harrisburg Telegraph*, November 2, 1921, 17.

46. Ibid.

47. "Golden Tornado is Defeated 28–7 by Wonder Squad," *Atlanta Constitution*, October 30, 1921, 3.

48. Ibid.

49. Ibid.

50. Killinger, *A Penn State Walk-On*, 42.

51. "All-American Season is In," *New Castle News* (New Castle, PA). November 2, 1921, 6; *Evening Public Ledger*, November 9, 1921, 21.

52. "'On To State,' Tech Slogan As Game Looms," *Pittsburgh Gazette Times*, October 30, 1921, 27; "Irresistable [sic] Offense of Nittany, Warriors Downs Carnegie Tech Team, 28–7," *Penn State Collegian*, November 8, 1921; "Tech-State Game in Detail," *Pittsburgh Gazette Times*, November 6, 1921, 23; "Nittany Lions Unruly After Plaid Threat; Battle in Snowstorm," *Pittsburgh Gazette Times*, November 6, 1921, 23; "Penn State Keeps Record of Victories Unbroken," *Fort Wayne Sentinel*, November 6, 1921, 11; Killinger, *A Penn State Walk-On*, 42.

53. "Nittany Lions and Navy Draw Throng," *Washington Times*, November 6, 1921, 48.

54. Killinger, *A Penn State Walk-On*, 44.

55. Ibid.

56. Ibid., 46.

57. "Middies' Line Crumbles Before Driving Offense," *Penn State Collegian*, November 15, 1921, 1, 5; "Penn State-Navy Clash in Detail," *Pittsburgh Gazette Times*, November 13, 1921, 25.

58. Hugo Bezdek, "The Headiest Play I Ever Saw; The Best Player I Ever Coached" (date, source unknown); "Penn State-Navy Clash in

Detail," *Pittsburgh Post Gazette*, November 13, 1921, 25.
59. "Superior Attack of Bezdek's Boys Sweep Middies Aside," *New York Tribune*, November 13, 1921, 21.
60. *Ibid.*
61. *Ibid.*
62. Grantland Rice, "Big Guns of the Gridiron: Men and Teams Whose Work Has Featured the Football Season Just Closed," *Leslie's Weekly 133* (1921): 797–798, 826.
63. "Lions are Outrushed at the Outset but Win by Sudden Comeback," *Pittsburgh Gazette Times*, November 13, 1921, 3.
64. "Notables to Honor Tom Davies Tonight," *Pittsburgh Gazette Times*, December 12, 1921, 7.
65. *Ibid.*
66. "Walter Camp Puts Killinger at Half Upon All-American; Three Pennsylvanians on It," *Harrisburg Evening News*, December 20, 1921, 27.
67. Killinger, *A Penn State Walk-On*, 49.
68. "'Killie' May Play in Coatesville," *Harrisburg Evening News*, October 25, 1921, 17; "Penn State Star Will Play with Coatesville," *Scranton Republican*, October 27, 1921, 16; "Nick Colonna to Play Fullback; Three Other Regulars Replaced," *Pittsburgh Gazette Times*, November 24, 1921, 25–26.
69. W. W. "Bill" Roper, "Panther Given Edge in Mud Battle With Lion by Princeton Coach; Pitt Plays Out String," *Pittsburgh Gazette Times*, November 25, 1921, 9–10.
70. Walter Camp, "Development Shown in 1921 Grid Game Greatest in Decade," *Great Falls Tribune*, November 27, 1921, 12.
71. Harry Keck, "Local Eleven Scores 'Moral Victory' in Muddy-Field Battle," *Pittsburgh Gazette Times*, November 25, 1921, 9.
72. Rader, *American Sports*, 183.
73. Daniel James Brown, *Boys in the Boat* (New York: Penguin Books, 2013), 213–220.
74. "Nittany Lions to Close Big Season in Far West," *Pittsburgh Gazette Times*, November 20, 1921, 27.
75. "State Students Turn Eyes to Winter Sports," *Pittsburgh Gazette Times*, November 27, 1921, 24; Bill Howes and Joe Welsh, *Travel by Pullman: A Century of Service* (St. Paul: MBI Publishing, 2004), 36–59; The Pullman Company, *Instructions to Porters, Attendants and Bus Boys* (Oklahoma City: The Pullman Company, August 1, 1952); The Pullman Company, *Instructions to Conductors* (Oklahoma City: The Pullman Company, August 1, 1952); National Railway Publication Company, *The Official Guide To Standard Time of the Railways and Steam Navigation Lines of the United States, Porto Rico, Canada, Mexico and Cuba, Also the Table of Railroads in Central America* (New York: National Railway Publication Co., 1922).
76. Killinger, *A Penn State Walk-On*, 49.
77. *Ibid.*, 50.
78. "Snell goes West with Penn State," *Reading Times*, November 29, 1921, 10.
79. The Pennsylvania State University, *La Vie, 1921*. (University Park: Penn State University Press, 1923), 418; "Lightner, State Halfback is Ill," *New Castle Herald*, November 19, 1921, 13; "Lightner Sprains Ankle And May Not Start Game," *Harrisburg Evening News*, December 3, 1921, 17.
80. "Killinger gives another view," *Wilmington* (DE) *News-Journal*, December 3, 1984, C-7; "Killinger, Nittany Lion's Fine Quarter, Stars in Great Win," *Philadelphia Inquirer*, December 4, 1921, B19.
81. Killinger, *A Penn State Walk-On*, 51–52.
82. *Ibid.*
83. "Penn State-Washington Detail," *Pittsburgh Gazette Times*, December 4, 1921.
84. "Killinger ends Career with High Grid Honors; Final Penn State Victory," *Harrisburg Telegraph*, December 5, 1921, 17; "Manager of Shamokin's Baseball Team has had Meteoric Rise to Fame," *Shamokin News-Dispatch*, March 25, 1926, 2.
85. Ray McCarthy, "Nittany Lions of Penn State Ranked First," *New York Times*, November 28, 1921, 10; Cullen Cain, "Football Critics in Tangled Skein Selecting Choice," *New York Daily News*, November 29, 1921, 28.
86. "Penn State Rated Best Team in East," *New York Times*, December 4, 1921, 129; Robert "Tiny" Maxwell, "'Tiny' Maxwell Picks Penn State for Title," *Washington Times*, December 1, 1925, 25; Lawrence Perry, "Distant Games Make Easier Ranking of Football," *Ogden Standard-Examiner*, December 9, 1921, 12.
87. "Penn State Team Was Best in East," *Penn State Collegian*, December 9, 1921, 1.
88. "Devine After Ninth Letter," *Decatur Herald*, December 19, 1921, 4.
89. *West Chester Daily Local News*, March 17, 1948; Henry, *William Glenn Killinger*, 42.

Chapter 12

1. "Penn State Football Team Known as Nittany Nomads," *Brooklyn Daily Eagle*, November 18, 1921, 26; "Nittany Lions to Close Big Season in Far West," *Pittsburgh Gazette Times*, November 20, 1921, 27; Rader, *American Sports*, 183.
2. "Hugo Bezdek to Be Honored by Alumni," *Oregon Daily Journal*, December 4, 1921, 22; "State Students Turn Eyes to Winter Sports," *Pittsburgh Gazette Times*, November 27, 1921, 24.
3. "The All-Americans," *Pittsburgh Gazette*

Times, December 11, 1921, 7; "Gridiron's Brightest Stars," *New York Daily News*, November 29, 1921, 28; Smith, *Sports and Freedom*, 84.
  4. "Devine After Ninth Letter," *Decatur Herald*, December 19, 1921, 4.
  5. "Walter Camp Puts Killinger at Half Upon All-American; Three Pennsylvanians on It," *Harrisburg Evening News*, December 20, 1921, 27.
  6. "A Line of Talk," *Harrisburg Telegraph*, December 21, 1921, 1; Killinger, *A Penn State Walk-On*, 55.
  7. John W. Heisman, "Heisman's Hundred in the Hall of Football Fame," *Marion Star*, October 27, 1928, 1; John M. Heisman and Mark Schlabach, *Heisman*, 209.
  8. Duncan, C. William. "Who Is Greatest Grid Star?" *Oakland Tribune*, December 27, 1931, 59.
  9. Henry, *William Glenn Killinger*, 39–43; "Walter Camp Puts Killinger at Half Upon All-American; Three Pennsylvanians on it," *Harrisburg Evening News*, December 20, 1921, 27.
  10. "'Killie' To Play in Pro Grid Tilt," *Harrisburg Evening News*, December 15, 1921, 23.
  11. "Union Quakers Down Bulldogs," *Washington Post*, December 18, 1921, 27; "Glenn Killinger Stars in Professional Game," *Harrisburg Telegraph*, December 19, 1921, 17; "Killinger Aids Quakers in Win Over Bulldogs," *Pittsburgh Post Gazette*, December 18, 1921, 22.
  12. Tucker, Jinx, "Yanks Get Best of Boston Deal," *Waco News-Tribune*, December 22, 1921, 11; Robert W. Peterson, *Pigskin: The Early Years of Pro Football* (New York: Oxford University Press, 1997), 94–97.
  13. "Glenn Killinger Certain to Play," *Washington Herald*, December 18, 1921, 12.
  14. Ray Helgesen, "Killinger is in Bulldogs' Line-up, But Disappoints," *Washington Herald*, December 19, 1921, 7.
  15. "Walter Camp Puts Killinger at Half Upon All-American; Three Pennsylvanians on it," *Harrisburg Evening News*, December 20, 1921, 27; Rader, *American Sports*, 149–150, 197–198.
  16. "Champions in Sport-1921," *El Paso Herald*, December 24, 1921, 15.
  17. "Potters Win From Coatesville A Close Game," *Reading Times*, March 14, 1922, 10; "Coates Jump to Fourth Place," *Wilkes-Barre Record*, March 7, 1922, 17; "Penn State Star Will Play with Coatesville," *Scranton Republican*, October 27, 1921, 16; "Killie May Play in Coatesville," *Harrisburg Evening News*, October 25, 1921, 17; "Killinger is Three Time Pro," *New Castle Herald*, December 24, 1921, 15.
  18. "Little Lines from Nearby," *Harrisburg Telegraph*, August 5, 1919, 2.
  19. "Glenn Killinger Elected Football Coach For 1922," *Dickinsonian*, January 7, 1922, 1–3.
  20. "Dickinson Will Not Drop Football Sport This Season," *Harrisburg Telegraph*, January 31, 1916, 11.
  21. Wilbur J. Gobrecht, *The History of Football at Dickinson College, 1885–1969* (Carlisle, PA: Dickinson College, 1971), 149.
  22. Rader, *American Sports*, 175.
  23. "Rumors Intimate Dickinson Has Made Offer to Killinger to Coach Football Next Year," *Harrisburg Evening News*, December 3, 1921, 17.
  24. "Killinger to Join Yank Training Camp in Texas," *Dickinsonian*, January 14, 1922, 2; "Glenn Killinger Elected Football Coach for 1922," *Dickinsonian*, January 7, 1922, 1–3; "Killinger to Coach Dickinson Eleven," *New York Tribune*, December 30, 1922, 14; "Killinger Signs Contract to Coach Dickinson Team," *Dickinsonian*, February 11, 1922, 1.
  25. *New York Evening World*, October 29, 1921, 6; "Teach Coaching At Penn State," *Harrisburg Courier*, June 18, 1922, 3.
  26. "Predict Big Things for Yank Leader," *The Evening News* (Harrisburg, PA), November 15, 1917, 6.
  27. "Yankees Land Killinger is New York Report; Local Star Has Big Offers," *Harrisburg Telegraph*, December 20, 1921, 21.
  28. Rice, *The Tumult and the Shouting*, 18.
  29. Henry, *William Glenn Killinger*, 44–45.
  30. "Killinger Short of Big League Demands," *Daily Courier* (Connellsville, PA), May 24, 1922, 6; Killinger Comes to Crackers Under Optional Agreement—Former Gridiron Star Played Last Year with Jersey City," *Atlanta Constitution*, December 27, 1922, 7; "College Stars High in Price," *Harrisburg Telegraph*, January 30, 1923, 13.
  31. "Killinger Signs to Play With New York American Team, Will Also Coach at Dickinson," *Harrisburg Courier*, January 8, 1922, 2.
  32. "Yanks Sign Killinger," *Kansas City Kansan*, December 20, 1921.
  33. "Select Glenn Killinger to Coach Dickinson; May Not Join Yankees," *Harrisburg Telegraph*, December 29, 1921, 19.
  34. "Killinger Signs to Play With New York American Team, Will Also Coach at Dickinson," *Harrisburg Courier*, January 8, 1922, 2.
  35. "Killinger A Yankee: Train in New Orleans," *Logansport Pharos-Tribune*, January 6, 1922, 10; "Killinger Signs Up With Yankees," *Harrisburg Evening News*, January 6, 1922, 22.
  36. "Local College Stars to Play Basketball During the Holidays," *Harrisburg Telegraph*, December 22, 1921, 9; "College Boys Here Make Big Game A Certainty; Glenn Killinger To Play," *Harrisburg Telegraph*, December 22, 1921; "Classy Games During Holidays," *Harrisburg Telegraph*, December 23, 1921, 17.

37. "College Boys Hand Surprise," *Harrisburg Telegraph*, December 27, 1921, 13.
38. "Football," *Harrisburg Courier*, December 25, 1921, 6; "Harrisburg Football Stars to Play Game Here on Christmas Monday," *Harrisburg Telegraph*, December 12, 1921.
39. "How College Boys Size Up," *Harrisburg Telegraph*, December 24, 1921, 19; "College Athletes are Ready For Grid Game; To Entertain Visitors," *Harrisburg Telegraph*, December 24, 1921, 19; "State Loses Four Members of Grid Squad," *New Castle Herald*, August 31, 1922, 11.
40. "Collegians in Pleasant Romp On Island Field," *Harrisburg Evening News*, December 27, 1921, 13; "Harrisburg College Stars Shut Out Williamsport in Christmas Grid Game," *Harrisburg Telegraph*, December 27, 1921, 13; "Gettysburg Player In Christmas Day Football Game," *Gettysburg Times*, December 27, 1921, 6.
41. "Collegians Break Even With Harrisburg Five," *Harrisburg Evening News*, December 27, 1921, 13; "College Stars Win Cage Series," *Harrisburg Telegraph*, January 2, 1922, 13; "College Boys in Final Game," *Harrisburg Telegraph*, December 31, 1921, 15; "Collegians in Pleasant Romp On Island Field," *Harrisburg Evening News*, December 27, 1921, 13.
42. "Killinger's Freshman Team Starts Season Saturday," *Harrisburg Telegraph*, January 13, 1922, 19; The Pennsylvania State College, *La Vie, 1923* (University Park, Penn State University Press, 1923), 455; "High Tossers Force Freshies To Fight To Utmost For Win," *Altoona Tribune*, January 16, 1922, 9.
43. William Glenn Killinger, "Investigation of the durability of a solid carburizing material," Publisher not identified, 1922.
44. "To Graduate 67 from Penn State," *Harrisburg Telegraph*, January 30, 1922, 13; "Glenn Killinger to Receive His Diploma," *Harrisburg Telegraph*, January 30, 1922, 13.
45. "Penn State to Honor Killinger At Mid-Year Commencement," *New York Times*, January 24, 1922, 12.
46. "Honor Killinger After Graduation Ceremonies," *Harrisburg Telegraph*, February 2, 1922, 17.
47. "Killinger is Good Coach," *Harrisburg Telegraph*, March 8, 1922, 13.
48. "Killinger Bids State Farewell," *New Castle Herald*, February 25, 1922, 9; "Killinger Will Attend Harrisburg Club Dinner," *Dickinsonian*, February 11, 1922, 2.

Epilogue

1. Richard B. "Dick" Yoder, Personal interview with the author, Gap, Pennsylvania, March 22, 2015.
2. William "Billy" Glenn Killinger Jr., Personal interview with the author, Glen Mills, PA, January 10, 2015.
3. *Ibid.*
4. Yoder interview.
5. "Killinger Bids State Farewell," *New Castle Herald*, February 25, 1922, 9; "Local Baseball Stars Off To Southern Camps; Giants Here Yesterday," *Harrisburg Telegraph*, February 27, 1922, 13.
6. "Glenn Killinger Seems to be Getting Smaller," *Charlotte Observer*, March 5, 1922, 19.
7. "Killinger Fails to Show Good Stickwork," *Port Arthur News*, March 18, 1922, 3.
8. "Yankee Rookie Likes Football Over Baseball," *Washington Times*, March 4, 1922, 11.
9. "Rookie Killinger Bats Ball Over Park Fence," *Scranton Republican*, March 11, 1922, 18.
10. Henry, *William Glenn Killinger*, 46.
11. "Huggins Assembles Staff of Pitchers," *New York Times*, March 14, 1922, 13.
12. *Altoona Tribune*, March 23, 1922, 10; "Penn Twins are Parted," *Sporting News*, March 30, 1922.
13. Henry, *William Glenn Killinger*, 47; *Penn State Collegian*, March 23, 1926.
14. Henry, *William Glenn Killinger*; "Wingo Gains Home-Run Lead," *Reading Times*, August 8, 1922.
15. "Alligator For Dickinson," *Altoona Tribune*, October 13, 1922, 12; "Dickinson to Practice with Florida," *New York Times*, September 22, 1922, 13.
16. "Killinger Takes Job as Dickinson Coach Today," *Harrisburg Telegraph*, September 5, 1922, 12.
17. "Gettysburg Prepares for Contest with Dickinson," *Harrisburg Evening News*, October 31, 1922, 15.
18. "Echoes of Game Are Heard Here," *Gettysburg Times*, November 14, 1922, 1–4.
19. F.Y. Jaggers to J. H. Morgan, October 15, 1922.
20. J.H. Morgan to F. Y. Jaggers, November 1, 1922.
21. "Killinger Will Quit Dickinson; May Go To State," *Harrisburg Evening News*, November 9, 1922, 17; "Bezdek Drives Penn State For Tech Game," *New Castle Herald*, November 8, 1922, 12; "Killinger Says He Won't Coach Here Next Season," *Dickinsonian*, November 11, 1922, 3.
22. "Scott Will Leave Crimson Tide at Close of Season," *Wilkes-Barre Sunday Independent* (Wilkes-Barre, PA), November 12, 1922; "Killinger May Coach At Columbia," *Charlotte News* (Charlotte, NC), November 26, 1922, 21; "Killinger May Coach At Columbia," *Charlotte News*, November 26, 1922, 21.
23. Fred W. Hixson, Letter to J. H. Morgan,

Meadville, PA, November 21, 1922; J. H. Morgan, Letter to Fred Hixson, Carlisle, PA, November 23, 1922; Fred W. Hixson, Letter to J. H. Morgan, Meadville, PA, November 24, 1922.
  24. Drexel University, *Lexerd, 1921* (Philadelphia, PA); William "Billy" Glenn Killinger Jr., Personal interview with the author, Glen Mills, PA, January 10, 2015.
  25. "Gettysburg Girl Bride of W. Glenn Killinger," *Harrisburg Telegraph*, August 25, 1923, 3; "Athlete to Wed Gettysburg Girl," *Harrisburg Telegraph*, August 21, 1923, 4; "Miss Wilda Holtzworth and W. Glenn Killinger to Wed at Gettysburg," *Lebanon Daily News*, August 22, 1923, 3; "Miss Wilda Holtzworth Weds Glenn Killinger, Noted Athlete," *Gettysburg Times*, August 25, 1923, 1.
  26. "Killinger Will Assist Bezdek; Probably Lost to Local Team," *Atlanta Constitution*, January 11, 1923, 9; "Killinger Named Assistant to Bez as State Mentor," *New Castle Herald*, January 11, 1923, 13.
  27. "Killinger to Accept Minor League Berth," *Washington Herald*, December 29, 1922, 16; "Killinger to Leave Yankees," *Wilkes-Barre Record*, February 28, 1924, 20; "Coaching Preferable to Diamond, Killinger Holds," *Harrisburg Evening News*, February 28, 1924, 20; Henry, *William Glenn Killinger*, 47–48.
  28. "Killinger Joins Boynton with Senators; Engaging White Roses Twice Today," *Harrisburg Evening News*, July 3, 1924, 11; *Scranton Republican*, September 30, 1924, 17.
  29. Henry, *William Glenn Killinger*, 48–49.
  30. "Teams in Readiness to Decide Ny-P Tie," *Harrisburg Telegraph*, September 16, 1925, 17.
  31. "Movement is Launched for Re-Instating of Killinger," *Shamokin News-Dispatch*, August 14, 1926, 1–2; "Glenn Killinger Breaks Arm in Fistic Encounter with Ump; Is Suspended," *Harrisburg Evening News*, July 26, 1926, 17; "Killinger is Sore," *Harrisburg Telegraph*, July 27, 1926, 7; "Shamokin to Put Up Fight for Killinger," *Mount Carmel Daily News*, August 17, 1926, 6; Henry, *William Glenn Killinger*, 45.
  32. "Glenn Killinger Shines Brilliant with N.Y. Giants" *Mount Carmel Daily News*, September 29, 1926, 7.
  33. "Glenn Killinger on Injured List," *Mount Carmel Daily News*, October 6, 1926, 7.
  34. "Arm Was Trouble with Killinger," *Mount Carmel Daily News*, October 29, 1926, 10.
  35. "Joins Quakers," *Harrisburg Telegraph*, November 3, 1926; "Killinger Now with Quakers," *Mount Carmel Daily News*, November 5, 1926, 9.
  36. "Killinger Stars in Pro Battle," *Harrisburg Telegraph*, November 8, 1926, 15.
  37. "Killinger Hurt Again," *Harrisburg Telegraph*, November 24, 1926, 19.

  38. "Quakes Win," *Bend Bulletin*, November 27, 1926; "New York Yankees Beaten by Quakers," *Modesto News-Herald*, November 28, 1926.
  39. "Thorpe's Team Defeats Local Passers, 41–33," *Harrisburg Evening News*, March 22, 1927, 17.
  40. "Second Chance?" *Oshkosh Daily Northwestern*, August 26, 1927, 18; *Harrisburg Patriot-News*, April 20, 1927.
  41. Harry A. Van Velsor, "Harry A. Van Velsor, to Whom it may concern" (File letter of recommendation), December 16, 1931, Troy, NY.
  42. Baseball-Reference.com. "Glenn Killinger," Accessed August 17, 2015. http://www.baseball-reference.com/minors/player.cgi?id=killin001w–; Henry, *William Glenn Killinger*, 60–70.
  43. "Son is Born to Killingers," *Gettysburg Times*, December 14, 1927; "New Ball Player! Killinger Will Hand Out Cigars," *Harrisburg Telegraph*, December 12, 1927, 1.
  44. Lawrence R. Samuel, *American Fatherhood: A Cultural History* (New York: Roman & Littlefield, 2016), 55–57.
  45. "'Little Killy' Big Fan," *West Chester Daily Local News* (date unknown).
  46. William "Billy" Glenn Killinger Jr., Personal interview with the author, Glen Mills, PA, April 4, 2015.
  47. Lt. Commander W. G. Killinger to Lt. Richard Nye. A. A. F., Deland, Florida. May 22, 1945.
  48. *Ibid*.
  49. Teachers College, Columbia University, New York, "Record Book of Mr. William Glenn Killinger," 1932–1933 (Killinger Family Files, Jessica Killinger, Wilmington, DE); W. H. Hitchler, "W. H. Hitchler to Dr. Jesse Williams" (File letter of recommendation), March 14, 1932, Dickinson School of Law, Carlisle, PA.
  50. *West Chester Daily Local News*, April 8, 1934; Henry, *William Glenn Killinger*, 67–68; Teachers College, Columbia University, New York, "Record Book of Mr. William Glenn Killinger," 1932–1933 (Killinger Family Files, Jessica Killinger, Wilmington, DE).
  51. Henry, *William Glenn Killinger*, 68–69.
  52. Henry, *William Glenn Killinger*, 69; "Glenn Killinger to Head Footballers," *Quad Angles*, July 18, 1934, 4.
  53. Richard B. "Dick" Yoder, Personal interview with the author, Gap, Pennsylvania, March 22, 2015; Furlow, *West Chester Football*, 11.
  54. Glenn Killinger to Dr. H. LaRue Frain, Acting President of West Chester State Teachers College, West Chester, PA. December 10, 1959.
  55. "Retired Football Coach May Manage

in Minors," *Bloomington* (IL) *Pantagraph*, December 24, 1959.

56. John McCool, "Killy retires," *Quad Angles*, May 12, 1970, 3; "Killenger [sic] to be honored by friends," *Quad Angles*, April 28, 1970, 7.

57. Richard B. "Dick" Yoder, Personal interview with the author, West Chester, PA, May 21, 2015.

58. Bob Warner, Personal interview with the author, West Chester, PA, May 21, 2015.

59. Anonymous, Personal interview with the author, West Chester, PA, May 21, 2015.

60. "Miller Takes Job at West Chester," *Harrisburg Evening News*, June 26, 1942; "Dean Killinger Leaves College For Navy Job," *Quad Angle*, March 20, 1941, 1; "Farewell, Dean Killinger!" *Quad Angle*, March 20, 1942, 2.

61. "School Observes First Anniversary Tomorrow," *Cloudbuster*, May 22, 1943, 1–4.

62. Fletcher Pratt, *The Navy Has Wings* (New York: Harper and Brothers, 1943), 23–26.

63. Memorandum, Lt. Commander Thomas J. Hamilton to Captain Arthur Radford, "History of the U.S. Navy Pre-Flight School Chapel Hill," n.d., North Carolina File, U.S. Department of the Navy, Navy Historical Center, Naval Archives, Washington, DC; "School observes First Anniversary Tomorrow," *Cloudbuster*, May 22, 1942, 6.

64. "Sports Poll Rates Football Tops for Physical Training," *Cloudbuster*, May 1, 1943, 1–4.

65. *Ibid.*

66. "Pre-Flight Training Here is Praised: Navy Leaders Visit Station to Inspect Local Program," *Cloudbuster*, September 18, 1942, 5.

67. Navy Department, Bureau of Naval Personnel, "Officer's Qualification Record Jacket, William Glenn Killinger, File No. 133062," April 10, 1945. Killinger Family Files, Jessica Killinger, Wilmington, DE.

68. W. Glenn Killinger, "Change in Status of Applicant for Dependent Benefits," Commonwealth of Pennsylvania, February 22, 1943.

69. Mary Layne Baker, *The Sky's the Limit: The University of North Carolina and the Chapel Hill Communities' Response to the Establishment of the U.S. Naval Pre-Flight School During World War II.* (Unpublished Manuscript, Chapel Hill, 1980), 36–40.

70. "Captain Rickenbacker to Speak Tuesday," *Cloudbuster*, May 6, 1944, 1.

71. William "Billy" Glenn Killinger Jr., Personal interview with the author, January 10 and 31, 2015, Glen Mills, Pennsylvania; "Cloud Buster Nine Closes Season With Hot Win Record," *Cloudbuster*, September 19, 1942; "Del Monte Selected For Fifth Navy Pre-Flight School," *Cloudbuster*, December 19, 1942.

72. Mrs. Earl L. Killinger, "Mrs. Earl L. Killinger to F. Steward Hartman," February 23, 1943, Harrisburg, PA; W. M. J. McClure, "W. M. J. McClure to Mrs. Killinger," February 17, 1943, Harrisburg, PA (Killinger Family File, Jessica Killinger, Wilmington, DE).

73. "Personnel Changes," *Cloudbuster*, July 31, 1943; Navy Department, Bureau of Naval Personnel, "Officer's Qualification Record Jacket, William Glenn Killinger, File No. 133062," April 10, 1945 (Killinger Family Files, Jessica Killinger, Wilmington, DE).

74. "Serving Its Purpose," *Cloudbuster*, October 2, 1943, 2; "Good Record Made by Grid Elevens Here," *Cloudbuster*, September 14, 1945, 4.

75. "Lieut. Killinger Named Head Football Coach," *Cloudbuster*, February 26, 1944; "Lieut. Killinger Will Coach 1944 Pre-Flight Nine," *Cloudbuster*, March 25, 1944; "Cloudbusters Will Play N.C. State on Easter Monday," *Cloudbuster*, April 8, 1944.

76. "Varsity Football Schedule is Announced," *Cloudbuster*, July 29, 1944.

77. "Football Prospects Good as Drills Start," *Cloudbuster*, August 19, 1944.

78. *Cloudbuster*, September 3, 1944.

79. "N.C. Pre-flight upsets Duke," *St. Petersburg Times*, October 8, 1944; "Ramblers Rated Top Eleven With Cloudbusters Second," *London Stars and Stripes*, October 12, 1944.

80. Wilbur D. Jones. *"Football! Navy! War!": How Military "Lend-Lease" Players Saved the College Game and Helped win World War II* (Jefferson, NC: McFarland, 2009), 11–12.

81. The Ration League was the wartime substitute for the Southern Conference. The Pre-Flight baseball team competed against the North Carolina Tar Heels' civilian team. "Four Man Staff To Have Charge of Cloudbusters," *Cloudbuster*, August 19, 1944; *Yackety Yack*, 1945, 237; "Varsity Football Schedule is Announced," *Cloudbuster*, July 29, 1944; "Killinger football head," *New York Times*, February 27, 1944.

82. Comdg. A. Laverents, "A Laverents, Comdg. To William G. Killinger," United States Naval Air Station, Deland, FL. September 28, 1945 (Killinger Family File, Jessica Killinger, Wilmington, DE); William "Billy" Glenn Killinger, Jr., Personal interview with the author, Glen Mills, PA, January 10, 2015; "Decommissioning of School will follow shortly," *Cloudbuster*, September 21, 1945; Report of Compliance With Orders. "Commanding Officer, U1 S. Nas. DeLand, Florida to Lt. Comdr. William G. Killinger, S(A) USNR," File No. 133062, February 10, 1945.

83. Paul Bryant and John Underwood, *Bear: The Hard Life and Good Times of Alabama's Coach Bryant* (Chicago: Triumph, 1975), 230–

245; William "Billy" Glenn Killinger Jr., Personal interview with the author, Glen Mills, PA, January 10, 2015; Corning, Captain, SC, USN, P.C. U.S. Navy Central Disbursing Office. "Claim of William Glenn Killinger, Lieut. Cdr. 133062 USNR (Killinger Family Files, Jessica Killinger, Wilmington, DE), October 8, 1945.

84. "Commencement Exercises at Gettysburg College to Open with Alumni Dinner Tonight," *Gettysburg Times*, June 1, 1951, 1.

85. "Bednarik, Killinger, Voted into Hall," *Reading Eagle*, October 28, 1963, 19.

86. "Killinger Enters Coaches Hall of Fame," *Delaware County Daily Times*, January 10, 1970, 16.

87. National Football Foundation, "1971 Hall of Fame Electees Announced; Induction Set in New York Dec. 7; Neely, Anderson, 8 Players Chosen," *Footballers,* March–April 1971; "Killinger Named To Hall of Fame," *Gettysburg Times*, February 22, 1971, 8; "Glenn Killinger, PSU Great, 'Hall' Finalist," *Hanover Evening News*, January 23, 1971.

88. Killinger, *A Penn State Walk-On*, 1.

89. John Ford, Personal interview with the author, West Chester, PA, May 21, 2015.

Bibliography

Census

Year: *1900*; Census Place: *Harrisburg Ward 9, Dauphin, Pennsylvania*; Roll: *1403*; Page: *15A*; Enumeration District: *0078*; FHL microfilm: *1241403*

Films

The Freshman. DVD. Directed by Fred C. Newmeyer and Sam Taylor. Buffalo, NY: Pathé Exchange, 1925.

Interviews

Bedell, Howard "Howie." Personal interview with the author. Pottstown, PA. February 11, 2017.
Campbell, Kenneth. Personal interview with the author. Hershey, PA. May 9, 2015.
Chalfant, Peg. Telephone interview with the author. June 18, 2015.
Chenger, Paul. Personal interview with the author. West Chester, PA. May 21, 2015.
Furlow, John J. Telephone interview with the author. Selbyville, DE. May 18, 2015.
Killinger, William Glenn, Jr. "Billy." Personal interviews with the author. Glen Mills, PA. January 10 and 24, 2015; April 4, 2015.
Leisey, Don. Personal interview with the author. West Chester, PA. May 21, 2015.
May, Robert "Gump." Personal interview with the author. Hershey, PA. January 3, 2015.
Strause, Fran. Telephone interview with the author. Elizabethtown, PA. June 19, 2015.
Warner, Bob. Personal interview with the author. West Chester, PA. May 21, 2015,
Yoder, Richard B. "Dick." Personal interview with the author. Gap, Pennsylvania. March 22, 2015.

Letters/Resumes/Personal Records

Bezdek, Hugo. Coach Hugo Bezdek to President Abbott L. Lowell, Harvard University, Cambridge, MA. May 4, 1926. (Hugo Bezdek scrapbooks and other materials, PSUA 105, Special Collections Library. Pennsylvania State University).
_____. Personal Record, The Pennsylvania State College, Director of the School of Physical Education and Athletics. January 20, 1930. (Hugo Bezdek scrapbooks and other materials, PSUA 105, Special Collections Library, The Pennsylvania State University).
_____. "To The Members of the Committee of Board of Trustees on the Department of Phys-

ical Education." Mass Athletics File, Scott Etter Papers, PSUA 280, Special Collections Library, The Pennsylvania State University.
Corning, Captain, SC, USN, P.C. U.S. Navy Central Disbursing Office. "Claim of William Glenn Killinger, Lieut. Cdr. 133062 USNR." (Killinger Family Files, Jessica Killinger, Wilmington, DE) October 8, 1945.
Dayley, James, Major U.S. Army, Retired. "Honorable Discharge from the United States Army." (Killinger Family Files, Jessica Killinger, Wilmington, DE) December 18, 1918.
DeWolf, Captain USNR M.M. "U.S. Naval Personnel Separation Center, U.S. Naval Air Station, Jacksonville, Florida." September 29, 1945 (Killinger Family Files, Jessica Killinger, Wilmington, DE).
Hamilton, Thomas J. Rear Admiral. *The Reminiscences of Rear Admiral Thomas J. Hamilton, U.S. Navy (Retired)*. U.S. Naval Institute, Annapolis, Maryland, 1983. (Killinger Family Files, Jessica Killinger, Wilmington, DE).
Herr, Donald D. Donald Herr to President Edwin Sparks, Pennsylvania State College, University Park, PA. May 19, 1917. Penn State During World Wars Collection (1109), Penn State University Archives, Special Collections Library, The Pennsylvania State University.
Hitchler, W. H. "W. H. Hitchler to Dr. Jesse Williams." (File letter of recommendation) March 14, 1932. Dickinson School of Law, Carlisle, PA.
Hixson, Fred W. "Fred Hixson to President James H. Morgan," Dickinson College, Meadville, PA, November 21, 1922 (Glenn Killinger File, Dickinson College, Carlisle, PA, 1922).
———. "Fred Hixson to President James H. Morgan," Dickinson College, Meadville, PA, November 24, 1922 (Glenn Killinger File, Dickinson College, Carlisle, PA, 1922).
Jaggers, F. Y. "F. Y. Jaggers to President James Henry Morgan," Dickinson College, Owing Mills, MD, October 15, 1922 (Glenn Killinger File, Dickinson College, Carlisle, PA, 1922).
Killinger, Mrs. Earl L. "Mariam Killinger to F. Steward Hartman." February 23, 1943. Harrisburg, PA (Killinger Family File, Jessica Killinger, Wilmington, DE).
Killinger, William Glenn. *A Penn State Walk On*. Unpublished memoir. Churchman Village, Wilmington, DE, 1986 (Killinger Family File, Jessica Killinger, Wilmington, DE).
———. "Change in Status of Applicant for Dependent Benefits." Commonwealth of Pennsylvania. February 22, 1943 (Killinger Family File, Jessica Killinger, Wilmington, DE).
———. "Glenn Killinger to Dr. H. LaRue Frain," Acting President of West Chester State Teachers College, West Chester, PA. December 10, 1959 (Killinger Family File, Jessica Killinger, Wilmington, DE).
———. "Lt. Commander Glenn Killinger to Lt. Richard Nye," Deland, Florida, May 22, 1945 (Killinger Family File, Jessica Killinger, Wilmington, DE).
———. "Investigation of the durability of a solid carburizing material." Pennsylvania State University, LIAS1878791, publisher not identified. 1922.
———. *PSU Playbook and Notes*, 1921. Unpublished (Killinger Family File, Jessica Killinger, Wilmington, DE).
Laverents, Comdg. A. "A. Laverents, Comdg. To William G. Killinger." United States Naval Air Station, Deland, FL. September 28, 1945 (Killinger Family File, Jessica Killinger, Wilmington, DE).
Lowell, Abbott. "Abbott L. Lowell to Hugo Bezdek." Hugo Bezdek Scrapbook and other materials, 1902–1928. PSUA 105. The Pennsylvania State College, University Park, PA. May 6, 1928.
McClure, W.M.J. "W. M. J. McClure to Mariam E. Killinger." February 17, 1943. Harrisburg, PA (Killinger Family File, Jessica Killinger, Wilmington, DE).
Morgan, James H. "James H. Morgan to F. Y. Jaggers." Carlisle, PA (Glenn Killinger File, Dickinson College, Carlisle, PA, 1922). November 1, 1922.
———. "James H. Morgan to Fred W. Hixson," President of Allegheny College, Carlisle, PA (Glenn Killinger File, Dickinson College, Carlisle, PA, 1922). November 23, 1922.
Moore, Fred T. "Fred T. Moore, District Business Manager, Third District, to College Pres-

idents." Philadelphia, PA, November 12, 1918. Penn State During World Wars Collection (1109), Penn State University Archives, Special Collections Library. Pennsylvania State University.

Navy Department, Bureau of Naval Personnel. "Officer's Qualification Record Jacket, William Glenn Killinger, File No. 133062." April 10, 1945 (Killinger Family Files, Jessica Killinger, Wilmington, DE).

Pennsylvania State College. "List of Men Enrolled in the Medical Reserve Corps at State College on Friday, June 1, 1917." Penn State During World Wars Collection (1109), Penn State University Archives, Special Collections Library. Pennsylvania State University.

Report of Compliance With Orders. "Commanding Officer, U1 S. Nas. DeLand, Florida to Lt. Comdr. William G. Killinger, S(A) USNR." File No. 133062, February 10, 1945.

Sparks, Edwin E. "President Edwin E. Sparks to Donald D. Herr," Rockefeller Building, Cleveland, OH. May 17, 1917. Penn State During World Wars Collection (1109), Penn State University Archives, Special Collections Library. Pennsylvania State University.

Teachers College, Columbia University, New York. "Record Book of Mr. William Glenn Killinger." 1932–1933 (Killinger Family Files, Jessica Killinger, Wilmington, DE).

United States Army, "Order of Battle of the United States Land Forces in the World War." Washington, D.C.: The Center of Military History, United States Army, 1988.

Valentine, Henry W, Second Lieutenant, Infantry, Company G. "William G. Killinger Enlistment Record." October 19, 1918 (Killinger Family Files, Jessica Killinger, Wilmington, DE).

Van Velsor, Harry A. "Harry A. Van Velsor to Jesse Williams." File letter of recommendation. December 16, 1931. Troy, NY (Killinger Family Files, Jessica Killinger, Wilmington, DE).

War Department, Committee on Education and Special Training. "Students Army Training Corps Special Regulations." (Date unknown), Penn State During World Wars Collection (1109), Penn State University Archives, Special Collections Library. Pennsylvania State University.

Manuscripts/Theses/Dissertations

Ashworth, George. *A History of the Development of the Rules of American Collegiate Football.* Unpublished Manuscript, Indiana State Teachers College, Indiana, PA, 1948.

Baker, Mary Layne. "The Sky's the Limit: The University of North Carolina and the Chapel Hill Communities' Response to the Establishment of the U.S. Naval Pre-Flight School During World War II." Master's thesis, University of North Carolina, 1980.

Gelfand, H. Michael. "'Tomorrow We Fly': A History of the United States Navy Pre-Flight School on the Campus of the University of Georgia, Athens, Georgia." Masters thesis, University of Georgia, 1994.

Henry, Charles W., Jr. "William Glenn Killinger: Athlete and Coach." Master's thesis, Pennsylvania State University, 1960.

O'Toole, Kathleen. "Intercollegiate Football and Educational Radio: Three Case Studies of the Commercialization of Sports Broadcasting in the 1920s and 1930s." PhD dissertation, Pennsylvania State University, August 2010.

Rominger, Donald William, Jr. "The Impact of the United States Government's Sports and Physical Training Policy on Organized Athletics During World War II." PhD dissertation, Oklahoma State University, May 1976.

Newspapers

Albuquerque Evening Herald
Altoona (PA) Tribune
Anniston (AL) Star
Atlanta Constitution

Beaver (OK) Herald
Bemidji (MN) Daily Pioneer
Berkeley (CA) Daily Gazette
Bisbee (AZ) Daily Review

Bismarck (ND) Daily Tribune
Bloomington (IL) Pantagraph
Brooklyn Daily Eagle
Brown and White (Lehigh College, Bethlehem, PA)
Burlington (NC) Daily Times-News
Carlisle (PA) Dickinsonian
Centre Daily Times (State College, PA)
Clearfield (PA) Progress
Cloudbuster (North Carolina Naval Pre-Flight School, Chapel Hill, NC)
Cumberland (MD) News
Daily Tar Heel (Chapel Hill, NC)
Daytona Beach (FL) Morning Journal
Decatur (IL) Herald
Delaware County Daily Times (Chester, PA)
El Paso (TX) Herald
Gettysburg (PA) Times
Hagerstown (MD) Daily Mail
Hanover (PA) Evening Sun
Harrisburg (PA) Evening News
Harrisburg (PA) Star-Independent
Harrisburg (PA) Sunday Courier
Harrisburg (PA) Telegraph
Hazleton (PA) Plain Speaker
Hazleton (PA) Standard Speaker
Honolulu Star-Bulletin
Indiana (PA) Gazette
Indianapolis Star
Lafayette (Lafayette College, Easton, PA)
Lebanon (PA) Daily News
Lebanon (PA) Semi-Weekly News
Lincoln Daily Nebraskan
Lititz (PA) Record
Lock Haven (PA) Express
Los Angeles Record
Milwaukee Journal
Monroe (LA) News-Star
Montana Standard (Butte, MT)
New Castle (PA) Herald
New London (CT) Day
New Philadelphia (OH) Daily Times
New York Daily News
New York Times
New York Tribune
Oakland (CA) Tribune
Ogden (UT) Standard
Oregon Daily Journal (Eugene, OR)
Penn State Collegiate (University Park, PA)
Philadelphia Evening Ledger
Philadelphia Inquirer
Pittsburgh Daily Post
Pittsburgh Gazette Times
Pittsburgh Press
Pittston (PA) Gazette
Pocono Record (Stroudsburg, PA)
Port Arthur (TX) News
Pottstown (PA) Mercury
Reading (PA) Eagle
Reading (PA) Times
Rensselaer Polytechnic (Rensselaer Polytechnic Institute, Troy, NY)
Rock Island (IL) Argus
St. Petersburg (FL) Evening Independent
St. Petersburg (FL) Times
San Bernardino (CA) County Sun
Sayre (PA) Evening Times
Scranton (PA) Republican
Seattle Star
Shamokin (PA) News-Dispatch
Shippensburg (PA) News-Chronicle
South Bend (IN) News Times
Spartanburg (SC) Herald
Sporting News (St. Louis, MO)
Stars and Stripes (District of Columbia)
Sweetwater (TX) Reporter
Tacoma (WA) Times
Troy (NY) Record
Troy (NY) Times Record
Tucson (AZ) Daily Citizen
Uniontown (PA) Evening Standard
Washington (DC) Evening Star
Washington (DC) Herald
Weirton (WV) Daily Times
West Chester (PA) Daily Local News
West Chester (PA) Quad Angles
Wilkes-Barre (PA) Record
Wilkes-Barre (PA) Sunday Independent
Wilmington (DE) News Journal
Wilmington (DE) Sunday Morning Star

Books and Articles

American Association for the Advancement of Science, "The Students' Army Training Corps," *Science*, New Series, 48, No. 1238 (September 20, 1918).

Axelrod, Alan. *Selling the Great War: The Making of American Propaganda*. (New York: Palgrave MacMillan, 2009).

Aydelotte, Frank. *Final Report of the War Issues Course of the Students' Army Training Corps.*

Washington, D.C., U.S. War Department, Committee on Education and Special Training, May 1919.
Barras, Rick. "Advice Shaped Grid Star's Life." Newspaper and date unknown, found in Furlow, John. *West Chester Football: An Ongoing Tradition in Ram Pride*. Kennett Square, PA: KNA Press, 1993.
Black, Lulu Frances (Morgan). *Annals of Harrisburg, Comprising Memoirs, Incidents, and Statistics from the Period of Its First Settlement*. Evangelical Publishing House, 1906.
Bohn, Michael. *Heroes and Ballyhoo: How the Golden Age of the 1920s Transformed American Sports*. Potomac Books, 2009.
Bronner, Simon. *Explaining Traditions: Folk Behavior in Modern Culture*. Lexington: University of Kentucky Press, 2011.
_____, ed. *Manly Traditions: The Folk Roots of American Masculinities*. Bloomington: Indiana University Press, 2005.
Brown, Daniel James. *Boys in the Boat*. New York: Penguin, 2013.
Bryant, Paul, and John Underwood. *Bear*. Chicago: Triumph Books.
Camp, Walter. *Walter Camp's Book of College Sports*. New York: The Century, 1901.
City of Harrisburg. *Harrisburg, PA., Business Directory and Map of the City*. Albany, NY: Joseph Rippey, Brandow & Speed, 1887.
Creel, George. "The Hopes of the Hyphenated." *The Century*, 91 (January 1916): 350–63.
Crossley, Gilbert. "History of 8XE," December 1, 1952. A 555.02, Box 1: Campus Radio, PSULSC.
Crosby, Alfred W. *America's Forgotten Pandemic: The Influenza of 1918*. Cambridge, UK: Cambridge University Press, 2003.
Des Jardins, Julie. *Walter Camp: Football and the Modern Man*. New York: Oxford University Press, 2015.
Douglas, Ann. *Terrible Honesty: Mongrel Manhattan in the 1920s*. New York: Farrar, Straus and Giroux, 1996.
DuBois, Charles C. "Molders of Men." *Town and Gown*, October 1993.
Dundes, Alan. 1978. "Into the Endzone for a Touchdown: A Psychoanalytic Consideration of American Football." *Western Folklore* 37, no. 2, Western States Folklore Society: 75–88.
_____. *From Game to War and Other Psychoanalytic Essays on Folklore*. Lexington: University Press of Kentucky, 1997. Available online at http://www.jstor.org/stable/j.ctt130hak1.
Fink, E. B., Edwin O. Jordan and Dudley B. Reed. "Influenza in Three Chicago Groups," *The Journal of Infectious Diseases* 25, no. 1 (July 1919): 74–95.
Furlow, John. *West Chester Football: An Ongoing Tradition in Ram Pride*. Kennett Square, PA: KNA Press, 1983.
Fussell, Paul. *The Great War and Modern Memory*. New York: Oxford University Press, 1975.
Gobrecht, Wilbur J. *The History of Football at Dickinson College, 1885–1969*. Carlisle, PA: Dickinson College Press, 1971.
Handlin, Oscar. *The Uprooted: The Epic Story of the Great Migrations that Made the American People*. Boston: Little, Brown, 1951.
Heisman, John M., and Mark Schlabach. *Heisman: The Man Behind the Trophy*. New York: Simon & Schuster, 2012.
Hendrickson, Joe, and Maxwell Stiles. *The Tournament of Roses: A Pictorial History*. Baltimore, MD: Brooke House, 1971.
Herget, James E. *American Football: How the Game Evolved*. Self Published, 2013.
Howes, Bill, and Joe Welsh. *Travel by Pullman: A Century of Service*. St. Paul: MBI, 2004.
Jones, Wilbur D. *"Football! Navy! War!": How Military "Lend-Lease" Players Saved the College Game and Helped Win World War II*. Jefferson, NC: McFarland, 2009.
Kelker, Luther Reily. *History of Dauphin County, Pennsylvania, Volume 3*. Chicago: Lewis, 1907.
Kennedy, David M. *Over Here: The First World War and American Society*. Oxford, UK: Oxford University Press, 2004.
Killinger, W. Glenn. *Football*. New York: A. S. Barnes, 1938.

Knight, Gladys L. *Pop Culture Places: An Encyclopedia of Places in American Popular Culture.* 3 vols. Santa Barbara, CA: ABC-CLIO, 2014.
Kreiser, Christine M. "The Enemy Within: Influenza 1918." *American History* 42, no. 5 (December 2006): 22–29.
Lehr, Dick. *The Birth of a Nation: How a Legendary Filmmaker and a Crusading Editor Reignited America's Civil War.* New York: Public Affairs, 2014.
Lloyd, Annette D'Agostino. *Harold Lloyd: Magic in a Pair of Horn-Rimmed Glasses and Other Turning Points in the Life and Career of a Comedy Legend.* Albany, GA: Bear Manor Media, 2009.
Lyons, Robert S. *Any Given Sunday: A Life of Bert Bell.* Philadelphia: Temple University Press, 2010.
McQuilkin, Scott A., and Ronald A. Smith. "The Rise and Fall of the Flying Wedge: Football's Most Controversial Play." *Journal of Sports History* 20, no. 1 (Spring 1993): 57–64.
Mennell, James. "The Service Football Program of World War I: Its Impact on the Popularity of the Game." *Journal of Sports History* 16, no. 3 (Winter, 1989): 248–260.
National Football Foundation. "1971 Hall of Fame Electees Announced; Induction Set in New York Dec. 7; Neely, Anderson, 8 Players Chosen." *Footballers,* March-April 1971.
_____. "Governor Regan's Magnificent Speech Highlights 1971 Hall of Fame Dinner." *Footballers,* December 1971-January 1972.
National Railway Publication Company. *The Official Guide Standard Time of the Railways and Steam Navigation Lines of the United States, Porto Rico, Canada, Mexico and Cuba Also the Table of Railroads in Central America.* New York: National Railway Publication, 1922.
Needham, Henry Beech, "The College Athlete: How Commercialism Is Making Him a Professional." *McClure's Magazine,* June 1905.
Nelson, David M. *The Anatomy of a Game: Football, the Rules, and the Men Who Made the Game.* Wilmington: University of Delaware Press, 1994.
Oriard, Michael. *Reading Football: How the Popular Press Created an American Spectacle.* Chapel Hill: University of North Carolina Press, 1993.
Panaccio, Tim. *Beast of the East: Penn State vs. Pitt: A Game-by-Game History of America's Greatest Football Rivalry.* West Point, NY: Leisure Press, 1982.
Pennsylvania State College. *Penn State in the World War.* State College, PA: Alumni Association of the Pennsylvania State College, 1921.
Peterson, Robert W. *Pigskin: The Early Years of Pro Football.* New York: Oxford University Press, 1997.
Poole, Gary Andrew. *The Galloping Ghost: Red Grange, An American Football Legend.* New York: Houghton Mifflin, 2008.
Pope, S.W. *Patriotic Games: Sporting Traditions in the American Imagination, 1876–1926.* New York: Oxford University Press, 1997.
Pratt, Fletcher. *The Navy Has Wings.* New York: Harper and Brothers, 1943.
Pullman Company. *Instructions to Conductors.* Oklahoma City: Pullman, 1952.
_____. *Instructions to Porters, Attendants and Bus Boys.* Oklahoma City: Pullman, 1952.
Rader, Benjamin G. *American Sports: From the Age of Folk Games to the Age of Televised Sports.* New York: Prentice Hall, 1999.
_____. "The Quest for Subcommunities and the Rise of American Sport." *American Quarterly,* 29, no. 4 (Autumn 1977).
Range, Thomas E., and Sean Patrick Smith. *The Penn State Blue Band: A Century of Pride and Precision.* University Park: Pennsylvania State University Press.
Rice, Grantland. *The Tumult and the Shouting: "My Life in Sport."* New York: A. S. Barnes, 1954.
Richards, J. Stuart. *Pennsylvania Voices of the Great War: Letters, Stories, and Oral Histories of World War I.* Jefferson, NC: McFarland, 2002.
Riley, Ridge. "Hugo Bezdek: Martyr or Monster?" *Town and Gown,* September 1978.
_____. *The Road to Number One: A Personal Chronicle of Penn State Football.* Garden City, NY: Doubleday, 1977.

Runkle, Erwin W.. *The Pennsylvania State College 1853–1932: Interpretation and Record*. University Park, PA: Nittany Valley Society, 2013.
Samuel, Lawrence R. *American Fatherhood: A Cultural History*. New York: Roman & Littlefield, 2016.
Sasso, Angela. "Froth Frowns at Prohibition." *Town and Gown,* July 1981.
Shearer, Benjamin F. "An Experiment in Military and Civilian Education: The Students' Army Training Corps at the University of Illinois," *Journal of the Illinois State Historical Society* 72, no. 3 (August 1979): 213–224.
Smith, Ronald A. "Intercollegiate Athletics/Football History at the Dawn of a New Century." *Journal of Sports History* 29, no. 2 (Summer 2002): 229–239.
_____. *Play-by-Play: Radio, Television, and the Big-Time College Sport*. Baltimore: Johns Hopkins University Press, 2003.
_____. *Sports and Freedom: The Rise of Big-Time College Athletics*. New York: Oxford University Press, 1988.
Taubenberger, Jeffery K., "The Origins and Virulence of the 1918 'Spanish' Influenza Virus," *Proceedings of the American Philosophical Society* 150, no. 1 (March, 2006).
Trenholme, Norman McLaren. *Syllabus of The Background and Issues of the World War*. Columbia, MO: The Missouri Book, 1918.
"Uplift Meetings Didn't Lift us Up Much." *Town and Gown,* December 1976.
United States War Department. *Students' Army Training Corps Regulations, 1918*, Washington, Government Printing Office, 1918.
Ward, Geoffrey C. *Unforgivable Blackness: The Rise and Fall of Jack Johnson*, New York: Knopf Doubleday, 2010.
Watterson, John S. *College Football: History, Spectacle, Controversy*. Baltimore: Johns Hopkins University Press, 2000.
_____. "The Football Crisis of 1909–1910: The Response of the Eastern 'Big Three.'" *Journal of Sports History* 8, no. 1 (Spring, 1981): 5–19.
_____. "The Gridiron Crisis of 1905: Was It Really a Crisis?" *Journal of Sports History* 27, no. 2 (Summer 2000): 291–298.
Wessell, Charles. "Gallery of Champions No 1: Hugo Bezdek, One of the Greatest Athletic Coaches of All-Time." *True Sport Picture Stories,* August 1944.
Willis, Chris. *Old Leather: An Oral History of Early Pro Football in Ohio, 1920–1935*. Lanham, MD: Scarecrow, 2005.
Winter, Jay. *Sites of Memory, Sites of Mourning: The Great War in European Cultural History*. Cambridge, UK: Cambridge University Press, 2014.
Winter, Jay, and Blain Baggett. *The Great War and the Shaping of the 20th Century*. New York: Penguin Studio, 1996.
Zabecki, David T. *Germany at War: 400 Years of Military History*. ABC-CLIO, 2014.

Yearbooks

Epitome. Lehigh University, 1918–1920.
La Vie. Penn State University, 1918–1928.
Lexerd. Drexel University, 1921.
Serpentine. West Chester University, 1934–1942, 1945–1971.
Tech Tatler, Harrisburg Technical High School, 1916.
Quittapahilla. Lebanon Valley College, 1920–1921.
Yackety Yack. University of North Carolina, 1942–1946.

Websites

Library of Congress. "Chronicling America: Historic American Newspapers." Visited September to December, 2015. http://chroniclingamerica.loc.gov.

Penn State University Budget Office. "Historical Fall Headcount Enrollment Since 1859." University Park: Penn State University, 2016. Accessed on February 8, 2016. http://www.budget.psu.edu/factbook/studentdynamic/HistoricalComparisonOfEnrollment.aspx?YearCode=2015&FBPlusIndc=N.

"United States World War I Draft Registration Cards, 1917–1918," index and images, *FamilySearch* (http://familysearch.org/ark:/61903/1:1:K6VF-D3M : accessed 17 May, 2015), William Glenn Killinger, 1917–1918; citing Harrisburg City no. 2, Pennsylvania, United States, NARA microfilm publication M1509 (Washington, D.C.: National Archives and Records Administration, n.d.); FHL microfilm 1,893,233.

Index

Abbott, William 169, 173
Alger, Horatio 69–70, 82; *see also* American Dream
All-American (Walter Camp) 5, 40, 42, 65, 84, 121–22, 152, 190–91, 199, 225
All-American Bowl (1960) 217
Allentown Buffaloes (Nypen) 213
Allison Hill 4, 18–23, 35–36, 41–52, 71, 75, 90, 116, 135, 161, 181; *see also* Rosewood Athletic Club
Alpha Chi Sigma 58, 60–61, 107–8, 165, 202
Amateurism 6, 8, 63, 118; *see also* professionalism
American Association of Baseball Coaches Hall of Fame 226
American Dream 70; *see also* Alger, Horatio
American League (baseball) 161, 197
American Professional Football Association 191, 196, 211
Amiens (Battle of) 82
Annapolis *see* Naval Academy
armistice 98, 107–9, 112, 121
Armory (Penn State) 70, 87, 111, 130–33, 155, 201
Army *see* West Point
Army Ambulance Corps (football team) 63, 65
Associated Press (United Press) 4, 128, 193–94
athletics 27–28; baseball 35; bowling 25, 29; boxing (Prizefighting) 6, 8, 36–39, 62–64, 80, 83, 87–88, 110, 167, 171, 219–20; football 29–35; gymnastics 63; ice hockey 19, 23, 28, 39, 62; rugby 29, 32, 34; swimming 8, 28, 50, 88; tennis 19, 23, 28–29, 40, 49–50, 87–88, 121, 218; wrestling 6, 8, 28–29, 62–63, 70–71, 73, 80, 87, 111, 219, 220
Atlanta Crackers 210

Bacharach Giants 117
Bainbridge Navy 222
Baker, John 197–98

Baker, Newton D. 62, 77
Ball, Ernest R. 25
Baltimore Professionals 208
Barron, David "Red" 173–74
Baublitz, Orville 112–13
Baylies, James 79
bayonet fighting 63–64
Bean, Robert Bennett 48, 233*n*33
Beaver Field 2, 8, 87, 94–96, 112, 124–25, 134–37
Beck, Carl 74, 116, 200
Beck, Clarence 63, 124, 243; 152, 196, 200, 207
Bedell, Howard W. "Howie" 1–3, 252
Bell, Bert 85
Bezdek, Hugo 4, 15, 82–85, 120–21, 133–98, 202–3, 210, 220, 229; Coach Harlow 122, 124, 126; coaching style 90–93; managing wartime football 94–108; as physical education director 86–88, 93; Pittsburgh Pirates 111–12, 122–24, 133, 150, 197; relationship with Killinger 107–8; rivalry with Pop Warner 99–104, 127–29, 151–52, 179–82
Birth of a Nation (film) 47–49
Bishop McDevitt High School 45
Boston Red Sox 117–18, 197
Brackenridge, Johnny "Jack" 117–19
Bray, Ray 222
Brickley, Charles 83
Bronner, Simon 99
Brown, George 100, 122, 143, 149, 152
Brunner, Bots 127
Bryant, Paul "Bear" 203, 222–24
Bucknell College 93–96, 113, 125–26, 162
Buell, Charley 169, 171–72
Byrne, Roy 31

Camp, Walter 1, 5, 7, 182, 186; All-Americans 40–42, 62–65, 80, 83–84, 121, 122, 144, 147, 152, 167, 176 190–91, 199, 203, 225; "Daily Dozen" 80; on masculinity 29–31, 144; on war and sports 66, 80, 100

Index

Camp Hancock 63, 94, 121
Canton Bulldogs (NFL) 190, 192–93
Carlisle Indian School 27, 38–39, 65, 102, 122, 194, 207
Carnegie Tech 73, 93, 113, 156, 159, 177
Catholic University 112, 133, 196
Central Pennsylvania Scholastic League 49
Chateau-Thierry 73
Chicago Bears (AFL) 193
Chicago Staleys (APFA, NFL) 192, 211
Christian, Archer 31
Churchman Village 14, 203–4
Cloudbusters, Pre Flight athletics 220–23
Coatesville Coates 181, 189, 194
Cobb, Ty 16, 27, 198
Coleman, Joe 221
Colgate University 129, 134, 200
Collier's 29
Columbia University 48, 81, 121, 208, 215–16
community sports 50–54, 74–76, 116–19, 135, 199–200; *see also* Rosewood Athletic Club
Conover, Larry 120–21, 125–27, 192, 196
Cooper, John Miller 49
Corbett, James 36
Cornell University 24, 32, 127–29, 191
Cornwall, E.H. 165–66, 200
Craver, Forest E. 194
Creel, George 54
Crowley, James 220
Crum, Henry 93–94
Cubbage, Ben 63, 196

Dartmouth College 61, 125–29, 137, 140–42, 169, 177
Davies, Tom 103–4, 128–29, 151–52, 160–62, 179–82, 194
declaration of war 52–55
Deland Naval Air Station 223
Delaware University 133, 159
Dempsey, Jack 120, 220
Des Jardins, Julie 29
Detar, Dave 71
Detroit Tigers 27, 163, 197, 198, 214
Devine, Aubrey 187, 190
Dickinson College 24, 132, 155, 194–96, 199, 202, 207–8, 212, 216
Dorais, Gus 65
dropkicking 34, 38, 41, 66, 90, 97, 101 104, 123, 142
Dundes, Alan 99
Dunkel, D. Forest 38, 41–42
Dunning, William A. 48

Eighteenth Amendment 131
Eisenhower, Dwight 39
USS *Essex* 221
Evergreen Cemetery 227

Fager, Charles 57–58
Farley, Gene 90

Farrell, Henry 149
Ferdinand, Francis 57
five-man weave 131
Flathead Indian Reservation 184–85
Fleming, Neil M. 96
Foch, Ferdinand 57, 82, 172, 207
Folwell, Bob 85, 177, 237
Football (book) 34; *see also* Killinger, Glenn
football rules and deaths 29–35, 65, 84; *see also* masculinity
Forbes Field 102–3, 127–28, 152, 180
Ford, Gerald 221
forward pass 31, 33–34, 40–41, 65–66, 79, 91, 97, 101, 128, 142–43, 147–52, 170–73, 176–79, 185, 211
Fosdick, Raymond 6, 62–64, 80
foul shot 157–58, 232n15
Four Horsemen 10, 220
Four Minute Men 54, 233
Franklin Field 8, 40, 127, 162, 177
The Freshman (film) 68–70, 101, 142; *see also* Lamb, Harold
freshman one-year residency rule 60–61, 73, 81, 104
The Friars 115
Frisch, Frankie 174, 198
Furlow, John 14

Gehrig, Lou 212
Gehring, Bill 93–94
Georgia Institute of Technology 102, 144, 165, 172–76, 189, 199, 245
Georgia Pre-Flight School 219, 222, 254
Gettysburg College 67, 92–93, 121–26, 137–38, 159, 161, 166, 173, 196, 207–9, 225
Gipp, George 1, 10, 191
Graham, Otto 222
Gramley, Eugene 112
Grange, Harold "Red" 1, 10, 191, 193, 211
Great Lakes Naval Station 63, 95, 110
Green, Fred "Red" 42–44
grenade tossing 63, 87
Griffith, D.W. 47–48
Griffiths, Red 143, 152

Haig, Douglas 82
Haines, Henry "Hinkey" 110, 113, 121–27, 130–36, 140–66, 180–81, 192–99, 205–10
Halas, George 192
Hamilton, Thomas 219
hand-to-hand combat 36, 63, 80
Harlan, Julian "Judy" 173–75
Harlem Hell Fighters 117
Harley, Dick 72–73
Harlow, Richard C. "Dick" 60–61, 66, 71–72, 80–82, 109–10, 120–28, 142, 150, 170, 173, 177, 189
Harper's Weekly 29
Harrisburg 16–18; Academy 35; All-Collegiates 199–200; Central High School

24, 41–42, 44–46; Chestnut Street Auditorium 37, 199–200, 211, 231; Orpheum Theater 37, 49; Technical High School 24–25, 29, 39–55, 57, 74, 200
Harrisburg Lincoln Giants 35
Harrisburg Pipe and Pipe Bending Works 58, 74, 116
Harrisburg Senators (NYPEN) 22, 35, 210, 212
Harrisburg Velveteers 212
Hartford Blues (NFL) 211
Harvard University 7, 31, 61, 80–81, 84, 129, 152, 169–72, 187, 189, 207
Heisman, John 10, 102, 144–46, 172–73, 191
Henry, Ralph 101
Hermann, Bill "Dutch" 61, 108–11, 120, 130–32, 156–57
Hess, William 123, 127, 136
Higgins, Bob 120–21, 125–28, 190–93, 196
Hoffman, Richard "Dick" 139
Holbrook, Pat 125
Hollenback, William M. 61, 234
homecoming (Penn State 1920) 137–140
Hoover, J. Edgar 114
Hoyt, Waite 197
Hufford, Ross "Squeak" 143, 148, 178
Huggins, Miller 197–98, 205–6
Hunter, John Robert 112, 130, 158
Huston, Tillinghast 197–98

Intercollegiate Rules Committee 31
Island Park (Harrisburg) 22, 35, 38, 50, 42–46, 102, 135, 190, 200, 207, 212
Ivy League 7, 30, 61, 81, 132, 144, 147, 156–57, 169, 187, 195

Jersey City Skeeters 207
John Harris High School 45
Johnson, Jack 36
Jones, John 75
Jordan, David Starr 32
jump shot 49
Juniata College 132, 155
Justice, Charlie "Choo Choo" 222

Keck, Harry 129, 179–82
Keep the boys in college! 7, 78–79
Kennedy, David 10, 78, 229, 236
Kessing, Oliver Owen 220
Killinger, Earl Wilson 6, 18–19, 21, 28, 37, 40–41, 50–52, 74–75, 107
Killinger, Elizabeth 19, 20, 230
Killinger, Florence 18–23, 36, 55, 97
Killinger, Jane Mumma 19, 52
Killinger, Jessica 11, 14, 44–45, 51, 53, 109, 140, 153, 157, 168, 180, 201, 203, 204, 206, 209, 214–15, 217, 221, 223–26
Killinger, John 17
Killinger, Karol Marie 214
Killinger, Mariam 253

Killinger, Marion 52
Killinger, Mark 14, 204
Killinger, Wilda 13–14, 203, 209–10, 213–14, 217, 226–27, 249
Killinger, William Glenn: baseball record 113, 159–62, 167; birth 16; buck sweep play 147; coaching at Dickinson 194–96, 199, 202, 207–8, 212, 216; coaching at Moravian College 216–17; coaching at Penn State 210–11; coaching at RPI 211–12, 215; coaching at West Chester 2, 3, 13–16, 29, 61, 76, 115, 137, 204, 213–18, 223–27, 230, 234, 237, 239, 246, 249, 250, 251; Dean of Men 2, 217; death 204, 227; family background 16–23; football record 113, 177–78, 187; grades 59–60, 115, 214; hay fever 38, 136, 164–65; high school basketball 49–50; high school football 39–55; honorary doctorate 225; injuries 51, 97, 103, 105, 109, 143–44, 147, 164–66; macular degeneration 13, 203–4; marriage to Wilda 209; player-manager (baseball) 210, 212–13; polo grounds performance 172–75; professional football 190–193, 210–11; professionalism scandal 118, 180–81; Tom Davies, rivalry 128–29, 151–52, 160–62, 179–82; Walter Camp All-American 187–93; with the Yankees 163, 197–202, 205–7, 210; see also Football (book); West Chester
Killinger, William Glenn "Billy," Jr. 213–15
Killinger, William H. "Billy" 17–18, 22–23, 50, 97
Killinger Hall 225–26
Killinger Hardware Store 6, 16, 18–21, 28, 50, 58, 79, 211
Kinley, David 77
Klein Chocolate Baseball, 116–19, 181
Klein, William and Frederick 16–19
Koehler, Horace "Rip" 158
Korb, Nelson "Red" 112–14, 158, 160
Koslowski, Stan 222
Ku Klux Klan 47–48
Kunkle, Earl 20

Lafayette College 71, 113,132, 150, 187, 192, 214
Lafayette High School, 71, 113, 132, 150, 187, 192, 214
Lamb, Harold 68–71, 101, 111, 142, 158, 216; see also The Freshman
Landis, Lefty 75
Lebanon Valley College 35, 113, 121–22, 132, 143, 149, 155, 159, 161, 165
Lehigh College 42, 93, 97–98, 100–1, 111, 127, 132–33, 149–51, 160, 165, 168–69
Lehr, Dick 48
Liberty Bonds 52, 54
Lightner, Joseph 112–13, 136–38, 141–42, 146–48, 158–59, 165–66, 169, 171–72, 177–78, 185, 196

Little, Lou 127, 190
Lloyd, Annette D'Agostino 68–69
Lloyd, Harold 68–70
Ludendorff, Erich von 82

Marshall, George Preston 223
Martin, Bill 66, 136, 165, 177, 184
masculinity 29, 36–37, 99–100; *see also* football rules and deaths
Mason, H.D. "Joe" 138, 242n40
massed athletics 10, 87–88; *see also* Student Army Training Corps
Massillon Tigers (Ohio) 42
Maxwell, Robert W. "Tiny" 9, 84, 129, 170, 186, 189
McCaffrey, Donald 70
McCullom, Stanley 171, 185
McCutcheon, John 32
McLaren, George 103–4
McMillan, George Ewing 110
McNally, Mike 197–98
Mearkle, Kid 158–61
Mellinger, Clyde 158
Mennell, James 10, 62, 65
Meuse-Argonne 109
military metaphors 99; *see also* Bronner, Simon
Miller, Eugene "Shorty" 39, 42, 50, 232n6
Mingle, David 112
Moravian College 216
Muhlenberg College 89, 92, 136–37, 149
Mullen, Bill 112, 130

Naismith, James 83, 232
National Collegiate Athletic Association (NCAA) 161
National Football League 191–92, 210
Naval Academy 4, 6–7, 31, 53, 61–64, 76, 97, 133, 159, 165, 172, 177–79, 187–92, 218–23
Needham, Henry Beach 118, 240
Negro Baseball Eastern Colored League 35
Nelson, David M. 65–66
New York Giants (MLB) 117, 121, 161, 174, 198
New York Giants (NFL) 113, 210–11
New York-Pennsylvania League (NYPEN) 22, 35, 117, 210–13
New York Yankees (MLB) 113, 161–63, 197–207, 210, 212
New York Yankees (NFL) 211
Nittany Lion (mascot) 138–40
North Carolina (Chapel Hill) Pre-Flight School 218–25
North Carolina State University 142, 165–66, 220, 222
Notre Dame 10, 65–66, 81, 129, 147, 149, 151–52, 186–89, 192, 220

Oklahoma Sooners 65
Oorang Indians 208
Osborne, Duke 97

Outings 29
Owen, Bennie 65

Palmer, A. Mitchell 114
Palmer Raids 114–16
Paterno, Joe 203
Patterson, John D. 50
Pearl Harbor 218
Pelham Bay Navy 98
Pennsylvania Sports Hall of Fame 225
Pennsylvania State College 59–60
Perry, Lawrence 186, 246
Pershing, John J. 172, 245
Pesky, Johnny 221
Philadelphia Athletics (MLB) 117–18, 197
Philadelphia Phillies (MLB) 2–3, 192, 217
Philadelphia Quakers (AFL) 192, 211, 249
Pittsburgh Pirates (MLB) 83, 85–86, 102, 111, 122, 124, 133, 150, 197
Plattsburgh Military Base 78, 81
Plessy v. Ferguson 35
Polo Grounds 6, 8, 147, 172–75, 199, 205
Pope, Steven W. 6, 35, 63
Princeton University 7, 44, 61–63, 80–81, 91, 96, 102, 134, 139, 146, 152, 159, 177, 182, 191
Princip, Gavrilo 57
professionalism 83, 116–19, 161, 180–81, 191–94; *see also* amateurism
Progressive Era 28, 30–32
prohibition 131–32
propaganda, 54, 57, 77–79
Pulitzer, Joseph 22, 32

Quonset Point Naval Air Station 221

race and ethnicity 46–48
Rader, Benjamin G. 8, 28, 30, 36–37, 69, 116, 138, 183, 232n27
radio 9, 15, 30, 167–68, 183
railroad (train travel) 117, 184, 189
Ralston, Jobyna 69
Ration League 222, 250n81
Rauch, Dick 66, 124, 142–43, 151, 196, 200
Raycroft, Joseph 62–64
Reagan, Ronald 226
Red Cross 64
Red Lion 122, 134–35
Red Scare 114–16
Rensselaer Polytechnic Institute 211–12, 215
Replogle, Nathaniel 130
Reservoir Park (Harrisburg) 19, 21, 23, 28, 35, 40
Rice, Grantland 9, 29, 62, 99–100, 169, 174, 179, 193, 198, 219
Rickard, Tex 36
Rickenbacker, Eddie 221
Ritner, Thomas 123, 165–66
Roaring Twenties 1, 11
Robb, Harry 120–28, 192–93, 196
Robertson, Jim 125, 141

Robeson, Paul 97-98
Rock Island (AFL) 211
Rockne, Knute 66, 147
Roosevelt, Theodore 5, 30, 144, 229
Roper, Bill 91, 182, 191
Rose Bowl 8, 85, 128
Rosewood Athletic Club 18, 35, 50-55, 58, 74-75, 116-17, 135, 162, 181; *see also* community sports; Hill, Allison
Ruppert, Jacob 197-98
Rutgers University 97-100, 147, 149, 168, 173, 187, 220
Ruth, Hermann "Babe" 11, 16, 39, 48, 50, 117, 194, 197, 205-6, 212

Sackett, Robert Lemuel 59
Sain, Johnny 221
St. Louis Browns (MLB) 212
St. Louis Cardinals (MLB) 197, 214
Sanes, Sidney 120
Schenck, Phil 205
Selective Service Act 80, 89
service sports 61-67, 80; *see also* Student Army Training Corps
Shamokin Indians (NYPEN) 210
Shelburne, John 141
Shenk and Tittle Sportings Good Store 200
Sheridan, J.B. 86
Simmons, William 47
Smith, Ronald A 27, 30, 44
Snell, George 93-94, 123, 136, 141, 143, 164, 168, 170, 174, 185
socioeconomic class and sports 27-36
Spanish American War 5, 7, 47, 197
Spanish Influenza 94-96
Sparks, Edwin E. 82, 87-88, 95
Spybuck, Roy 31
Stagg, Amos Alonzo 66, 83-84
Stiles, Maxwell 85
Stone, Ira 40
Student Army Training Corps 7, 9-11, 76-81, 86-88, 92-96, 98-107, 109, 121, 155, 190, 201, 219; *see also* massed athletics; service sports
Sullivan, John L. 36
Swarthmore College 132-33, 156, 207
Syracuse University 32, 129, 134

Taylor, Maris Harvey 19, 230*n*16
Thanksgiving Day football 44-47, 102-3, 128, 130, 151, 167, 179, 189
Thomas, Myles 112, 158
Thorpe, Jim 1, 10-11, 16, 27, 38-39, 61, 102, 173, 191, 208, 211
Traphoner, John 112

Unger, Frank 93, 100, 104
University of Arkansas 83-86, 108
University of California 69, 103, 134, 183, 196

University of Alabama 8, 203, 208, 223
University of Chicago 65, 83-85
University of Florida 207
University of Nebraska 28, 81, 138, 147-49, 187
University of North Carolina 32
University of Oregon 82-86, 108, 138, 169, 183, 189, 208
University of Pennsylvania 40, 96, 127-29, 132, 144, 146, 156-57, 162
University of Pittsburgh 93, 100-5, 127-29, 132-34, 138-39, 151-52, 156, 160-62, 165, 167, 179-84, 187, 189, 197, 202
University of Washington 9, 138, 144, 167-77, 184-90, 196
Ursinus College 97, 126-27, 129

Villa, Pancho 62
Villanova University 31, 38, 75

"War Aims" 78
War Department 6-11, 62, 73, 76-82, 86-89, 93, 95-97, 107, 109, 163
Warner, Glenn "Pop" 10, 65, 102-105, 120, 128, 151-52, 180, 191, 194, 207
Washington and Jefferson College 92-93, 132, 146, 155-56
Washington and Lee College 113, 159
Washington Professionals (APFA) 192-93, 208
Washington Redskins 223
Washington Senators 31, 35
Watterson, John S. 31-32
Way, Charlie 72, 88-90, 93, 97, 100, 120-28, 136, 140-52, 164, 190-92, 196, 211
Wayne Hall 218
Weightman Hall 157
Wescott, Howard A. 216
West Chester 2, 3, 13-16, 29, 61, 76, 115, 137, 204, 213-18, 223-27; *see also* Killinger, Glenn
West Point (Army) football 6, 31-32, 39, 61, 63, 65, 133, 187
West Virginia University 72, 75, 81, 113, 129, 132, 149, 155, 167, 183, 200
Wheatley, Cliff 176
Wheeling, George "Doc" 112-13
Whitney, Lawrence "Bud" 61
Wilder, Burt Green 32
Wilhelm, Kaiser 82
Willard, Jess 36
Williams, Ronald "Buck" 94, 96-97, 100, 104, 123, 136-37, 146-47, 240*n*16
Williams, Ted 221
Williamsport All-Collegiates 199-200
Williamsport Grays (NYPEN) 210, 212-13
Willis, Chris 34
Wilson, Earl 31
Wilson, Harry "Light Horse" 90, 165, 171, 177-78, 182, 185

Wilson, Lloyd L. 110, 130, 166
Wilson, Woodrow 54–55, 80, 98
Wingard, Edgar 95
Wissahickon Barracks 93, 96–97, 104
Wolfe, Bill 130, 156–57
Wolfe, Frank 111, 130

World War I (combat) 54–58, 73, 82
Wysocki, Vincent 101

Yale University 7, 42, 44, 61–62, 80–81, 102, 133–34, 138, 156–57, 159–60, 190
Yoder, Richard "Dick" 15, 115, 204, 217

www.ingramcontent.com/pod-product-compliance
Ingram Content Group UK Ltd.
Pitfield, Milton Keynes, MK11 3LW, UK
UKHW041931140426
5217IPUK00014B/419